INSIDE OUT
AND
OUTSIDE IN

INSIDE OUT
AND
OUTSIDE IN

Psychodynamic Clinical Theory and Practice in Contemporary Multicultural Contexts

Joan Berzoff, M.S.W., Ed.D.
Laura Melano Flanagan, M.S.W.
Patricia Hertz, M.S.W.

JASON ARONSON INC.
Northvale, New Jersey
London

First Softcover printing 2002

This book was set in 11 point Adobe Caslon by Alpha Graphics of Pittsfield, New Hampshire.

Copyright © 2002, 1996, by Jason Aronson Inc.

10 9

Library of Congress Cataloging-in-Publication Data

Berzoff, Joan.
   Inside out and outside in : psychodynamic clinical theory and practice in contemporary multicultural contexts / Joan Berzoff, Laura Melano Flanagan, Patricia Hertz.
      p. cm.

   Includes bibliographical references and index.
   ISBN 1-56821-777-3 (hardcover)
   ISBN 0-7657-0342-4 (softcover)
   1. Psychodynamic psychotherapy. 2. Personality development.
   3. Psychoanalytic interpretation. 4. Psychology, pathological.
   I. Flanagan, Laura Melano. II. Hertz, Patricia. III. Title.
   RC489.P72B47 1996
   616.89'14—dc20
                                                            95-47146

Printed in the United States of America on acid-free paper. For information and catalog write to Jason Aronson Inc., 230 Livingston Street, Northvale, NJ 07647-1726, or visit our website: http://www.aronson.com

To my sister, Barbara, whose friendship and love are well inside.

Joan Berzoff

To my beloved Smith students, who, for the past decade, have put up with me and the Martians. And to my patients, who have helped me grow and taught me well.

Laura Melano Flanagan

To my patients, who have taught me so much by sharing their life stories. To my students, who have challenged me to find the words to explain what I know and to learn more about what I don't know.

Patricia Hertz

Contents

Acknowledgments

This book has been long in the making. There are many people to acknowledge: those who have loved and supported me, those who have supported this project through arduous and sometimes painful times, and those who have made the work possible.

I can never sufficiently thank Lew Cohen, my husband, friend, editor, co-parent. He has been an endless source of knowledge, guidance, and wisdom. His love, his patience, and his balance throughout helped make this book possible. My sister, Barbara Shapiro, whose illness throughout this project had been so hard and so heroic, was a source of inspiration to me. Despite her death, her love and her humor are indelibly woven into these pages.

This book was begun when my second son, Jake, was 6 months old. I thank him for his unbounding affection and funny good cheer during all of his early years, although he saw far less of me, and I of him, than either of us would have wished. My elder son, Zeke, age 10, recently wondered aloud, " Why do you pressure yourself so to write this book, Mom?" Perhaps my own joy at now seeing him at work on *his* first book is part of the reason.

I have been blessed with friendships so dear that no words can ever acknowledge them. Jaine Darwin has given her love, her pen, her heart, and her undying loyalty to every chapter of my life and of this endeavor. Liz Bigwood has been a caring and ever present "sister" whose support and help have sustained me. Vivien Weiss and Adin Delacour have seen me through many moments of despair, and have provided a holding environment from which to draw strength. Kathryn Basham has given of herself; her wise counsel and humor have been invaluable. Bob and Cynthia Shilkret, Gerry and Steffi Schamess have been like family to me. Marge Bayes offered long-distance and long-standing support throughout. Ellen Kaufman has given support, faith, and finally her latent skills as a copy writer, aka gynecologist. Wendy Salkind, my oldest friend, has as always provided me continuity, and an abiding sense that from our roots, somehow, we could create good works.

I thank my mother, Myra Berzoff, who has also had the ability to support and encourage me throughout this and other creative endeavors, and my two nieces, Sarah and Kate Shapiro, who have also inspired me. I thank my sister Emily Entress for newfound strength. I thank my nephew, Zach Shapiro, my sisters-in-law, Toby Tider and Felice Grunberger, and my brother-in-law, David Noah Cohen. I want to acknowledge my grandmother-in-law, Hedy Gross; I have loved her joy at seeing all this unfold. I also want to acknowledge two people who are no longer with me but within me: Sydney Berzoff and Vera Cohen. Both of them would have delighted indeed to see this project complete.

There are many people and institutions to thank as well. I want to thank the Brown Foundation of the Clinical Research Institute of the Smith College School for Social Work for its funding support. Two deans of the school are to be thanked: Ann Hartman, who granted the sabbatical time to work on the book and who created a climate that valued scholarship and productivity, and Anita Lightburn, who also allowed me the needed leave time to finish it. I thank my colleagues and the staff of the Smith College School for Social Work who contributed their help when I was away and my students who offered so many insights and ideas.

Muriel Poulin, my administrative assistant, has been an incredible and tireless worker, who has lent her formidable organizational and technical skills, humor, and confidence to the book throughout. Without her, this truly would have been impossible. Gerry Schamess and I first developed the course that later became this book and I thank him for his generous ideas, scholarly approach, and mentorship in those years. I also want to thank Dorcas Bowles, who, although she ultimately could not be a writer for the book, shared her ideas and herself in its conception and development.

Joan Berzoff
Northampton, MA

Starting closest to home, I thank my wonderful sons, Michael and Brian, for their patience and forbearance during this lengthy process. They graciously endured my innumerable trips to Smith, my cranky moods when the words wouldn't come, and the piles of books and papers that eventually obscured our entire dining room table. Through it all they never ceased to have a truly lovely, infinitely supportive "go for it, Ma" attitude. I also learned invaluable lessons from the steadfast and courageous ways they pursued their own hopes and dreams. My mother, Maria Melano, has always been a great enabler of my teaching and writing both through her financial generosity, which bought me precious time, and by the example of her vibrant active life. At 84, she still travels alone by bus to audit classes at her alma mater, Barnard College.

To Judy Levin, I owe a debt of gratitude I cannot fully articulate in words. She read, she typed, she listened, she faxed, she edited brilliantly, and she was a major part of this process from beginning to end. Without her special insight into the material and her consistent, loving encouragement I would not have been able to persevere. Her unswerving belief in all of us made the book better. To my other dear friends, thank you for having the grace and the kindness to stop asking "Isn't that book done yet?"

At the Smith College School for Social Work I first thank Muriel Poulin, typist and coordinator extraordinaire. Since I don't type I could not have taken part in this project without relying on her formidable skills and competence. She was the best first reader an author could ever hope to have since she could always tell if the words and concepts worked on the page or not. I am forever indebted to Ann Hartman and Joan Laird for pushing, prodding, and coaxing me to expand my thinking about sociocultural concepts. That "stretch" has enriched both my teaching and my contributions to this book. My thanks also go to Michael Hayes, who was with us for a while as an author, is still with us as a teacher, and whose inspiration has endured. His ability to combine a sophisticated grasp of the fine points of psychodynamic theory with a loving gentle application of the theory to practice helped me retain the belief that this theory is indeed worth teaching.

Finally, and most importantly, my deepest gratitude goes to Joan Berzoff and Pat Hertz—colleagues, collaborators, dear friends. The path we walked to create this book has been joyful, arduous, exciting, frustrating, fun, and sometimes infuriating, but ultimately we walked it together.

Laura Melano Flanagan

I want to thank those who have been so close to me personally, who may not have read every draft of these chapters but without whom I could never have sustained the energy to complete this project. I want to begin by thanking members of my family, Meg, Marcia, Glenn, Bob, and my mother, Marilyn, whose love and support have made me what I am today and have helped give me the voice that is captured in some of these pages. I am grateful to Seth and Aaron, whose presence in my life has helped me keep perspective on what is truly important. I owe a heartfelt thank you to my wonderful group of friends (I wish I had the space to mention all of you!), who have been like family to me and always knew when to push for details about this project and when to help distract me from it.

On a professional note, I feel forever indebted to my colleagues at the "old" Revere Community Counseling Center, whose shared commitment, enthusiasm, and dedication to the clients brought forth what is most meaningful in clinical work. I want to thank Jon Slavin for his careful and constructive reading of my chapters, and for his unconditional faith in my professional development. I feel fortunate to have begun my teaching as part of a gifted team of colleagues at Smith College School for Social Work, whose ideas formed the basis for this book. Muriel Poulin somehow juggled the typing of the many versions of this book and miraculously made it come together into a coherent whole. I want to end with my gratitude to my students and clients, about whom and for whom these pages were written.

Patricia Hertz
Brookline, MA

Inside Out and Outside In

JOAN BERZOFF,
LAURA MELANO FLANAGAN,
AND PATRICIA HERTZ

Every human life is shaped by the interplay of forces that arise from within and without. This book is our attempt to introduce the psychodynamic theories of psychological development that help us understand the inner world and to enrich the usefulness of those theories by adding the biological and social aspects that they often lack. Psychodynamic theories do not purport to be all-inclusive. They look through a rather narrow lens deep into the inner psychological world. And yet to know a person more fully or do any kind of clinical work with her the lens has to include the biological and the social factors of their lives. This is why we so strongly believe in what is called the biopsychosocial approach to clinical work.

Each newborn arrives in this world with certain individual physical characteristics—green eyes or chocolate-colored skin or big feet or sweetly shaped ears. Even these seemingly "outside," objective concrete characteristics are deeply formative because they would be viewed and valued in vastly different ways in different cultures, thereby shaping the inner world right from the first moment of life outside the womb. And what of gender? Mary is a girl. John is a boy. The simple statements seem to describe objective facts, and yet they belie enormous complexity. Cultures, religions, social classes, even locales have different definitions of what it is to be a boy or to be a girl, as does each individual. When Freud (1925) said "biology is destiny," he meant that anatomical and biological differences shape goals, wishes, and personality traits. He was somewhat right but also very wrong. Gender is one of dozens of variables that will shape a life, but only one. The more correct statement would be "everything is destiny": every factor—biological, psychological, and social—makes its impact.

Every baby is born with innate, highly individual, indeed idiosyncratic inner characteristics, some of them biologically based. These traits—a quickness to anger, an easy smile, a way of being calm or fidgety, a lively curiosity, a tendency to melancholy—are not so easily visible, much harder to get to know, and ultimately always somewhat mysterious. Yet they too play a crucial, complex role in shaping the course of a person's life.

And the web grows. All babies with their own inner and outer characteristics are then born into an outer world with great specificities of its own: time, place, class, race, family, community, country, ethnic group, religion, political climate.

To be born a Caucasian middle-class girl of European descent in New York City in 1995 is to be born into a different world and a different life than a Caucasian middle-class girl of European descent born in New York City in 1940 or 1911. At a recent breakfast honoring young women in their twenties who had achieved rising-star status, the New York Women's Agenda organization also honored women in their eighties and nineties who had not been able to be stars in their field simply because of when they were born. Many of the older women were in tears, speaking about the pride, the envy, and loss they felt listening to the opportunities being made by and for the younger women today.

And these are only small examples of the variable of time. Every other variable is just as powerful. An African-American baby and a Korean-American baby and a Swedish-American baby born on the same day in the same hospital in Kansas City will each be strengthened or assaulted by very different outside forces.

Although we believe strongly in holding a balanced, comprehensive biopsychosocial view of assessment and treatment, valuing each of the components equally, not everyone agrees with this approach. There has always been vigorous debate about the relative importance of biological versus psychological versus social factors in development. We see this as a completely false and unnecessary dichotomy and try instead to teach the subtle and ever-changing interweaving of all the factors, the relative weight of which can change from moment to moment.

Because of serious problems in the cost and financing of mental health care in the United States today, an intense debate is going on about the relative importance of biological etiology and biological solutions. Under the pressure of these financial forces, the treatment of mental illness and psychological suffering is increasingly being dominated by shorter-term managed care, a heavier reliance on the use of medications, and brief, even single-session therapy. This in time exerts pressure on many clinicians to turn away from theories that try to describe and understand the forces in the mysterious internal world that govern human behavior. Many schools of social work, counseling programs, and psychiatric residencies have cut back or dropped their psychodynamic curricula. We believe that ultimately this results in a disservice to clients because a knowledge of psychodynamic forces can illuminate what is going on in any human interaction or communication, no matter how brief it is. If Prozac is prescribed for five people, it will have a different meaning for each, and the meaning (relief, insult, hope, failure, care) will have been shaped, at least partly, by psychodynamic forces. When two men on Social Security Disability were given carfare for clinic appointments, one accepted the money gratefully as a sign of concern and care, and the other felt belittled and ashamed. Again, the meaning of the benefit was radically different because of each man's internal and external life experience.

Ideological forces have also been at odds about whether to put the emphasis on the psychological or the social when looking at the causes and cures for mental illness and human suffering. Some lives are more cushioned from external challenges and oppressions than others. The artistry of clinical work comes from having a deep, wide-ranging knowledge of all forces inside or out as they shape and mold each client into a unique human being.

It must be noted that this bio-psycho-social balance is not an easy one to achieve and that we have not fully succeeded even in reaching our own goals. At first we hoped to fully integrate biological and social concepts throughout each chapter, combining them with a simple, introductory explanation of psychodynamic theories. This did not turn out to be possible, especially with regard to issues of race and gender. We have therefore included separate chapters addressing these factors—not to marginalize them, but rather to give them their due.

WHAT IS PSYCHODYNAMIC THEORY?

Since this book focuses predominantly on the psychodynamic part of the biopsychosocial matrix we need to explain what we mean by the word *psychodynamic*. The best place to begin is with simple dictionary definitions. Webster's New Twentieth Century Dictionary defines dynamic as "pertaining to energy or power in motion . . . the motive and controlling forces, physical and moral, of any kind; also, the study of such forces." *Psychodynamics* is defined by Webster as "the science of dealing with the laws of mental action" and by the *Random House Dictionary of the English Language* as the "systematic study of personality in terms of past and present experiences as related to motivation."

The many theories that fall under the term *psychodynamic*, then, all have to do with inner energies that motivate, dominate, and control people's behavior. These energies are based in past experiences and present reality. We use the term *psychodynamic* because it is broad enough to encompass any theory that deals with psychological forces that underlie most human behavior.

We also wish to distinguish the term *psychodynamic theory* from *psychoanalytic theory*, although this is by no means easy to do. The two terms are often mistaken for one another. Some clinicians use them interchangeably. Others insist they are vastly different. There is disagreement even among psychoanalysts as to what the term *psychoanalysis* encompasses—some reserving the term for the Freudian theory of unconscious conflicts about drives and desires, others including all theories that deal with anything in the unconscious.

There continues to be in psychoanalysis a sharp debate about its nature, purposes, and goals. Some, as Freud did, describe it as a branch of natural science and others, such as Lacan, as a form of hermeneutics in which personal narrative, not objective data, is the only thing of interest.

Richard Chessick (1993) in *A Dictionary for Psychotherapists* says the following about psychoanalysis:

> Psychoanalysis is in some ways very simple to define and in other ways very difficult. All psychoanalytic models have the same conceptual base, the dynamic unconscious, although they may differ in certain fundamental ways. All deal with transference and countertransference and use the method of free association. All view infantile and childhood experiences as crucial and stress preoedipal and oedipal factors to one degree or another. All in various ways and to varying degrees emphasize repetition, the role of the analyst, and the importance of interpretation. [p. 306]

Many of the theories presented in this book include these psychoanalytic concepts, and clinicians who use these theories in their practice often call themselves psychoanalysts. Yet we are not calling this a book on psychoanalysis because we are including dynamics that are not unconscious and also because we want to pay more attention to outside social and cultural forces. We view *psychodynamic* as a much broader, more inclusive term and *psychoanalytic* as having a more limited focus. To go back to the dictionary definition, psychodynamic applies to all forces at play in shaping the personality. In this book, we use it to mean *any forces*, internal or external, that have an impact on mental and emotional development.

Our hope is that this book will be useful and relevant for a wide range of mental health practitioners, including those who work in settings where transference issues or unconscious conflicts are not the main focus of treatment, either because of time constraints or the needs and goals of the clients. Psychodynamically informed treatment might focus absolutely appropriately on cultural struggles or issues of oppression, or on concrete and reality-based needs.

We believe that a knowledge of psychodynamic theory is not only useful but also invaluable, whether a clinician is treating someone in long-term psychotherapy or conducting diagnostic evaluations, whether one is making a hospital discharge plan or completing a housing application. Clinical knowledge grounded in psychodynamic theory is one of the most powerful ways we have to look inside someone's heart and mind. Without it, we are almost blind, limited to the surface, the concrete, the manifest.

Let us give two examples of why this is so. One of our authors taught in a post-master's program for advanced clinical social workers for over ten years. The students in the program had all received master's degrees in social work from fine schools, but schools that no longer taught psychodynamic theory. All of the students had been in practice for at least several years and many were still receiving supervision in their places of employment, which included hospitals, family service agencies, mental health clinics, addiction programs, prisons, and schools. The students were very knowledgeable and highly skilled in understanding and changing systems (including family systems), in helping clients get necessary services, and in empowering groups whose voices were not being heard. They were, in fact, expert at working from the "outside in." Yet they all applied for additional training citing a painful and frustrating dearth of knowledge about what was going on inside clients. They felt that they had never been taught to work from the "inside out" and that this lack greatly limited and hampered their clinical work.

In one particular case discussion, a student described trying to work with Michael, a 24-year-old Latino man who was living in a halfway house after psychiatric hospitalization. His history revealed severe and persistent abuse at the hands of his stepfather and abandonment by his mother, who fled from the home and left him with cousins when she herself was abused by the same man. Michael's main emotional problem was that he had divided himself into three parts, which he had named Good Michael, Bad Michael, and Middle Michael. Because of the fragmentation within him, members of the psychiatric team argued about his diagnosis. Some thought he was schizophrenic, others believed he suffered from multiple personality disorder, and still others saw him as having a borderline personality.

The post-master's student assigned to be Michael's clinician did excellent work helping Michael to adjust to life outside the hospital and get started in a sheltered workshop. But he was mystified about the meaning of the three different Michaels and uncomfortable when the patient referred to them. The student felt he had no vocabulary and no tools to understand the reason for the nature of the fragmentation, especially because Michael seemed at times to be very pleased to have these selves and other times to be in great pain because he was "so messed up."

A psychodynamically informed view of Michael's inner world ultimately allowed his therapist to enter into and understand Michael's separate selves. Michael spoke nervously about how his family held very strict Catholic views that he felt were almost impossible to reconcile with some of their own behavior and with the appeal of drugs and sexual activity so easily available in his neighborhood. At home he heard that giving in to the Devil would lead to an eternity in Hell, while on the streets his peers tried to lure him into drugs and sex. Early in his life Michael become overwhelmed by these confusing and conflicting forces that were both outside and inside himself, for he wanted to be good and close to God and his family, but he also wanted to experience the pleasure and power of the streets. Hence the creation of the three Michaels to reflect and embody these disparate, seemingly irreconcilable parts of himself. When the therapist truly understood Michael's need to divide his inner experiences into parts, and the risks of integrating them, Michael began to be able to weave the parts of himself together.

Another example was that of Martin, a 28-year-old black Haitian man, who came seeking mental health treatment because he could not stop worrying about what was to befall him next. His anguish had caused him to drop out of graduate school; he had lost his part-time job, and his marriage was in deep emotional trouble.

Martin, the son of a policeman, had grown up in a Caribbean Catholic culture with a father who expected his son to bring honor to the family. At age 20 Martin had emigrated to the United States to pursue an advanced degree, and was by all standards doing well. One evening he attended a party in a racially mixed part of the city that was rife with racism. The party became loud, the police were called. Martin, although quiet and soft spoken, was physically large and the officers who arrested him placed him overnight in jail. Fellow white prisoners assaulted him with racial epithets and doused him with buckets of urine. When released (with no charges) he was unable to function or concentrate. He lost considerable weight and could not stop dwelling on the humiliating experience. He berated himself and felt that somehow he deserved the punishment.

While the postgraduate student did an excellent job of connecting Martin to legal services and advocating on Martin's behalf educationally, she was bewildered about why Martin remained emotionally immobilized despite the resolution of his legal and educational concerns and his taking psychiatric medication. The student lacked the theoretical tools to understand that Martin had experienced the external racial assaults *internally*, and how the oppressive environment, which was once outside, was now inside, continuing to cause tremendous anxiety and self-reproach.

For Michael and for Martin, as perhaps for all clients, there is often no more profound experience than being heard, understood, and accepted. This requires that the clinician have empathy, the ability to project oneself into the experience of another. Empathy requires knowledge and skill. In this book we hope to tackle the first element of this formula, showing how knowledge about a client's inner life helps us enter into the client's whole experience. We hope to demonstrate how an understanding of internal psychological factors, as they are interwoven with external factors such as culture, gender, race, class, and biology, helps us understand the tapestry that becomes an individual self. It is from this perspective that we begin to learn how the outside comes to be inside a person, and, in turn, how the inner world shapes a person's outer reality.

WHO IS THIS BOOK FOR?

This book has been written for beginning clinicians who are about to make the long and challenging journey into clinical work. It is also written for those more experienced practitioners who may never have had a comprehensive understanding of psychodynamic theories and their uses in a multicultural world. It is for all students who want to understand how internal life is conceptualized within biological and social contexts, and for those practitioners and continuing students who want to learn to thoughtfully critique these theories. It is written for those practitioners who are challenged by the limits of managed care and who want to understand how what is inside and outside an individual comes to be metabolized as psychological strengths and disturbances. For many, we hope that it will serve as a useful review.

There are many psychological texts that discuss drive theory, ego psychology, object relations, self psychology, and interpersonal theory, and there are many texts about culture, race, and ethnicity. In this book, however, we combine a psychodynamic understanding of individuals with an understanding of how they function within their social contexts. To our knowledge this is one of the few attempts to look at the inside *and* outside concurrently, or at least with equal weight, which is difficult to accomplish because most psychodynamic theories are more heavily weighted toward the inner world. For years as teachers we would become defensive when those more interested in teaching about external realities and oppression would tell us that what we said about race, class, gender, and culture was always "just tacked on at the end." What we finally realized is that it sounds tacked on because it is. In fact, that is precisely the contribution we are trying to make. We are adding, completing, enriching, and, we hope, integrating knowledge from biology, sociology, anthropology, and folklore to psychodynamic theory. Starting with Freud, through Erikson to Greenberg and Mitchell in the present, theoreticians have been aware of and interested in the role of culture. However, to date no psychodynamic theory of development has been able to fully integrate issues of race, class, gender, and culture as it is being developed—hence the need to critique, add on, contextualize, and, we hope, enrich what is offered in the theories.

Similarly, there are many books that review the characteristics of different psychopathologies. *DSM-IV*, while demonstrating a greater awareness of cultural influence on diagnoses than previous editions, remains an atheoretical, descriptive text of objective criteria for mental illnesses. Some other texts offer an understanding of emotional disturbances by looking at them through a biological, cognitive, or psychodynamic lens alone, or by critiquing the current explanations of the etiologies of the disorders. We attempt once again to hold biological, psychological, and social lenses *concurrently* as we somewhat arbitrarily choose to look at several diagnostic entities. We try to resist the tendency toward polarization by exploring the contributions of psychodynamic, biological, and social factors in the development of emotional difficulties. Once again, while acknowledging that equal weight is not always given to each of these factors, our commitment is to demonstrate the relevance of both external and internal forces in shaping the lives of individuals and the mental disturbances that plague them.

A CRITICAL-THINKING STANCE

In this book we will study psychodynamic concepts and theories of psychopathology from the perspective of human behavior. Psychodynamic theories represent approximations of human experience, metaphors that have developed within particular cultures, during particular social times, and with particular social values. As such, we will state and restate our conviction that every theory is a social construction. By this we mean that all theories are of necessity a product of their time and place and culture. No thinker or writer or practitioner lives in a vacuum. Every theoretician is inevitably influenced by all the experiences of his or her life and therefore constructs theories out of the raw material of those experiences. What we have also noticed is that many theoreticians find it difficult to acknowledge that their ideas are socially constructed and culture bound. They often fall prey to the rather grandiose notion that their theories are universal and apply to all people at all times. We believe that no one theory or even any combination of theories can fully describe something as unique and complex as a human being. Even while using a comprehensive biopsychosocial approach, it is necessary for clinicians to recognize that all the theories in the world are not sufficient to explain everything about a person's feelings, strengths, or weaknesses. As Hamlet said to Horatio, "There are more things in heaven and earth, Horatio, than are dreamt of in your philosophy."

As we study each theory and pathology, we will ask of each theory: Who created this theory? What dominant ideologies does the theory represent? Who is not represented? What gender or racial biases are embedded in the theory of psychopathology? Does this theory apply to all people at all times?

Because many psychodynamic theories have been silent about issues of race and gender, while other theorists have openly devalued oppressed groups such as women or people of color, we will provide a gender and a racial critique of psychodynamic theories. Many students and their professors are tempted, when a theory is biased, to throw out the baby with the bathwater. We will be critical of some of the psychodynamic theories for their biases or omissions in terms of race or gender, for their devaluation of oppressed groups, and for who they include and exclude in the theory. But we will also see how some psychodynamic theories are invaluable in helping us understand how people experience oppression psychologically.

THEORY AND CULTURE

As we present psychodynamic theories and psychopathologies throughout this book, we want to remind the reader that definitions of health and pathology are always culture bound. In predominantly white Western cultures, for example, considerable value is placed on autonomy and individuation as the psychological developmental goal. Many Eastern, African, and Hispanic cultures, however, define health as the achievement of interdependence. This was brought home to us in the description of a normal psychological development class held in Iran in 1984 (Bateson, personal communication, 1985). Iranian psychology students were asked to observe two mother–child dyads: one American and the other Iranian. The American mother brought her toddler to class dressed in a pair of ragged jeans and dirty sneakers. Within minutes, the toddler was wandering among the students, eating candy they offered, straying far from the mother, who smiled as her daughter wandered from student to student. By contrast, the Iranian baby was extremely well groomed, her dress was formal, and she and her mother never left the elegant rug that her mother had so carefully set down. While the Iranian baby sat silently on her mother's lap, the students were asked to assess the psychological health of the dyads. Uniformly, the first mother–child pair was diagnosed by the Iranian students as highly pathological given the mother's "neglect" and the child's obvious "lack of attachment." The second pair was seen as normal and healthy because the child and mother were so tightly bound. Whereas in predominantly white Western cultures the baby is viewed as a dependent creature needing to begin the healthy journey toward independence and autonomy, in Iranian culture the baby is seen as already too separate and distinct, needing to be bound to the community. In this book, we will take the stance that normality is always in the eyes of the observer.

Consider another cautionary tale about the errors that can ensue when a well-intentioned clinician is unfamiliar with cultural traditions and so defines health in her terms.

Two years after receiving her M.S.W., the clinician was working in a large city hospital, assigned to the inpatient unit of the department of psychiatry. She had been working with the parents and young wife of a medical student who had become psychotic. The patient was suicidal and had been hospitalized on the very ward where he had been a promising and successful intern. The social worker had been seeing the parents together and the young wife alone for over six months.

Despite being medicated and having someone with him, the medical student committed suicide by throwing himself off the roof of the hospital. The task of notifying the family fell to the social worker. After spending some time with each shocked and grieved family member, the social worker was asked if she would pay a call to the parents' house the next evening, which she agreed to do.

Feeling quite shaken, she arrived promptly at 6 P.M. and observed the following: the door was propped open, the mirrors were covered with what looked like burlap, and several women were sitting on wooden crates. The women wore no makeup and their hair was uncombed; the men wore suits but their feet were in sneakers; the men also wore ties that looked ripped or cut up.

Despite coming from a bicultural, bilingual family and living in a multicultural city, the worker saw only strangeness and unfamiliarity and instantly "diagnosed" the entire family suffering from a simultaneous psychotic break. She remained frozen in the doorway while actually beginning to count the number of people in the room in order to tell 911 how many ambulances to send!

The mother of the dead medical student, however, was able to assess the clinician's predicament and very gently said, "No, it's not what you think. We have not all gone mad. We are sitting *shiva* and this is our way of mourning. Come in and let us explain it to you."

The importance of this vignette is that it illustrates how, in the clinician's own anxiety, she saw pathology in what was, in fact, cultural strength—the strength of a family to use their beliefs and rituals to engage in the process of grieving.

This book will attend to both the cultural relativity of our theories and our diagnoses and to the ways different racial, ethnic, and cultural groups have of coping with, and finding solutions to, what others may define as pathology.

An essential part of making a diagnosis and of ensuing clinical work is the capacity to identify strengths—of the individual, the family, the community, and the culture. No matter what degree of disturbance we encounter in our clients, there will also be in them sources of joy, ideals, flexibility, humor, ambition, and hope that give them strength, solace, and the potential for growth. These must be elicited, heard, respected, and understood with the same vigor with which we pursue the deficits, developmental arrests, and maladaptation that characterize their psychopathology.

HOW THIS BOOK IS ORGANIZED

First a word about language. We originally tried to write the book using the female pronoun *she* exclusively, in order to correct the centuries of books written only about *he*. Eventually this came to sound as stilted as any book written using only the male pronoun. We then tried "he or she" and "she or he" and even "s/he," but these combinations sounded forced and unnatural. What we finally settled on is our own idiosyncratic combination of *she*'s and *he*'s, which, after all, more accurately reflects the composition of the human race and the way people actually speak in real life.

In the first half of the book, the authors intend to examine and illuminate core concepts drawn from psychodynamic theories: drive theory, ego psychology, object relations, life cycle theory, interpersonal/relational theories, and self psychology. Each of these theories offers different lenses, many complementary and some contradictory, for understanding how the self develops in many contexts. We shall study these concepts historically and in terms of their applicability to clinical practice. We shall learn how each theory developed within its unique social context and is therefore a product of that milieu. We shall learn how each theory was revised by internal critiques within the theory itself and by external critiques outside of the theory, and how those critiques led to new theory development. We shall especially attend, in separate chapters, to the approach (or lack thereof) to race and gender in psychodynamic theories. In summary, the first half of the book examines different ways in which psychodynamic theories have conceptualized human problems from the inside out.

Because we think that psychodynamic concepts help us understand people in different social contexts, we have chosen to use cases drawn from our own practices in multicultural settings. Most books on psychodynamic theory illustrate their concepts using white and privileged middle-class clients who may be shielded from discrimination, poverty, homelessness, disabilities, discrimination based on sexual orientation, and severe and persistent mental illness. Our intent is to show how psychodynamic concepts are useful and apply to these populations. Hence we have chosen cases for their variations in race, class, gender, and sexual orientation.

In the second half of the book, we will use the theories and concepts discussed in the first half to understand four major psychopathologies. We will not be studying all of the diagnoses in the *DSM-IV*. Rather, we have chosen to study those diagnoses for which a knowledge of psychodynamic theories seems to be the best way to help the clinician into the internal world of the client. These four broad categories are the psychoses, personality disorders, depression, and anxiety.

Psychodynamic explanations alone do not account for all of human suffering. Social and biological influences will also be factored into the study of each of these disorders. As was true in the first half of the book, when we study the psychopathologies, we will continue to ask: How does the diagnosis reflect the dominant values and ideologies of the social times in which it developed? Who does it privilege? Who does it marginalize? What biases are inherent in the diagnosis? In addition, as we study each of these four major psychological conditions, we will attend not only to the experience of the client, but also to the experience of the helper. We will try to remember that not only are definitions of psychopathology socially constructed, but that beliefs about health are culture bound as well.

In this book we hope to convey some appreciation for the mysteries of another person's humanness. Respect for the mysteries inherent in clinical work can be particularly difficult when trying to learn a theory and its application. The developmental theories we will be studying are by nature causal and linear. They postulate that if certain experiences occur during certain stages of development, certain results are likely to occur. Sometimes they do, but often they do not, which must always be remembered to keep us honest, open, and alive to the sense of wonder with which human phenomena must be clinically approached.

There is a passage in Mary Gordon's *Men and Angels* (1985) that expresses how little can really be known about the relationship between a traumatic event in childhood and its effects on personality development. A mother, stunned after she has discovered the dead body of their babysitter who has committed suicide, holds her sleepy children in her arms. She thinks about the kinds of trauma that mothering sometimes inflicts and about how little we can know about its results. She muses:

And what could you say of it [mothering] that was true? She used to think it was of all loves the most innocent, but now she knew she had been wrong. There were mothers who loved their children in a way that cut the children's breath and stopped their hearts; there were mothers who, in a passion of love, took the children and pressed them to their bosoms and in the next moment threw the children scream-ing from them, covering them with blows. There were mothers for whom the sight of their children meant nothing; no love stirred, no part of their heart lifted. There were mothers who hated their chil-dren from the moment of their births; who hated the first touch of flesh on flesh and went on hating. There were mothers who loved their children but could not love them, for they bent to kiss the children's flesh and felt the flesh stop in their mouths and make them fear for their next breaths. *And children throve or starved, and no one knew why, or what killed or saved.* [p. 238, italics added]

It is crucial that when we learn developmental psychodynamic theo-ries, we are careful not to define the person's pathology by a specific defi-cit or trauma that occurred in one particular stage of development (e.g., there was a trauma when the client was 2 years old; therefore, he must have difficulties in separation and individuation and must be borderline). Instead, in every case, we need to know how the individual emotionally, constitutionally, and socially comes to be who she is and to explore the subtle, complex interplay between who the person is and what her envi-ronment provides. This is why a biopsychosocial approach to diagnosis offers the best chance for understanding a person in all her fullness.

This book then has many purposes. In it we hope to convey an appreciation for the value of psychodynamic theories as students try to learn how to enter into something as unique and complex as the inner life of another human being. We hope to show how a person takes in her environment and acts upon her environment based both upon her strengths and weaknesses, which she has developed from a complex web of experiences, relationships, innate abilities, biological endowments, and social conditions. We hope to articulate what motivates human behav-ior and some of the life experience and healing environments that pro-mote psychological growth. We want to stress the importance of social factors: culture, class, race, gender, and the physical surround on expe-riences of self and identity, and to emphasize how social work can pow-erfully contribute to or undermine optimal development. In addition, we hope that students will think critically about the theories they use and about the social and political contexts in which they always develop.

References

Chessick, R. (1993). *A Dictionary for Psychotherapists: Dynamic Concepts in Psychotherapy*. Northvale, NJ: Jason Aronson.

Freud, S. (1925). Some psychical consequences of the anatomical distinction between the sexes. *Standard Edition* 19.

Gordon, M. (1985). *Men and Angels*. New York: Random House.

2

Drive Theory

JOAN BERZOFF

We shall begin our study of psychodynamic theory with Freud's drive theory. Freud was among the first psychological theorists to posit that human beings are driven by powerful instinctual biological forces of which they are largely unaware. These forces of love or of hate, of sexuality and aggression, express themselves differently in each individual and ultimately shape how each individual functions and develops.

In his fifty-three-year career Freud developed a psychology of the mind in which he identified how the drives result in characteristic ways of being and living. He showed how the drives influence the development of symptoms and relationships with others.

In his evolving view of human behavior, Freud viewed humans as bestial in their natures (Mitchell 1988), fueled by forces, fantasies, longings, and passions beyond their control. He hypothesized that most psychological problems occur when the drives are opposed by other forces in the mind. Drive theory then became the first psychodynamic theory to posit that powerful forces, urges, and wishes exist within the mind and are perpetually in conflict with the self and society. His theory became the first psychological theory to organize those passions, into a systematic science of human behavior.

This chapter introduces some of Freud's core drive theory concepts that are still relevant to clinicians who are practicing today. We will begin our study of drive theory with Freud's first insights into the nature of psychological symptoms using the case of Anna O. We will study the methods he developed for "curing" people, and the absolute importance he placed on the therapeutic relationship for producing psychological change. As his career developed, Freud came to appreciate the importance of the therapist's self-knowledge for understanding the passions and yearnings that might exist in the client. In our study of drive theory, we will examine how Freud used his self-knowledge and his clinical mistakes to revise his theories when the clinical data did not fit. Freud developed many therapeutic methods such as the analysis of transference/resistance, free association, and the analysis of dreams as ways of gaining access into the psyches of his clients. We will study how Freud evolved a theory of drives that differ at each stage of childhood development, and how this psychosexual theory explains distinct kinds of character traits, relationships, and potential problems at different stages of development. Finally we will show how Freud came to think of psychopathology and of most of human suffering as arising from dynamic conflicts, within and between structures of the mind, which he would call his structural theory. Freud was always influenced by the belief that insight, self-awareness, and self-knowledge promote psychological development.

Although Freud used highly scientific and empirical language, his clinical theories were deeply grounded in the actual life experiences of his patients. In his clinical practice, he listened with what he came to call "evenly suspended attention," trying to be open to hearing what his clients said in ways that allowed the theory to evolve from the data. While Freud always grounded his theories in clinical data, the *inferences* he made about the data on women sometimes were contaminated by his limitations as a male.

INTELLECTUAL TRADITIONS

Freud was a physician and a scientist interested in the investigation of the psyche (the word *psyche* means the human soul in German). Many disciplines influenced his thinking. Because Freud was a neurologist, he conceptualized the mind in terms of neural excitations that were stored and needed to be discharged or tamed. Neurology also influenced his thinking that psychological functions occur in discrete or separate parts of the brain. From his neurological background, he envisioned each function of the mind as interdependent and acting upon the others. Physics also had a profound influence on Freud, leading him to view human behavior as a function of predetermined and predictable forces. Physics also contributed a hydraulic metaphor to Freud's thinking, that is, that there were finite amounts of energy in the mind that, if used in one place, were not available for other functions. Archaeology and geology also influenced him. He saw the mind as having a "prehistory" that needed to be "excavated" to be understood. Freud's scientific leanings were also leavened with a love of art, literature, religion, and philosophy, all of which contributed to his appreciation for the symbolic aspects of human behavior. Shakespeare influenced the romantic elements of Freud's thinking, especially about human tragedy and suffering. From Judaism emerged other strains: deep pessimism about the human condition, cultural prescriptions about the value of an individual life, and deep meaning assigned to the value of the nuclear family. Judaism also influenced the parts of Freud that were mystical and probed deeply into the inner workings of the soul.

SOCIOCULTURAL INFLUENCES

Throughout this book we will emphasize that each theory can be understood as a social construction emerging from the unique economic, cultural, religious, and political forces of the times in which it was developed. Thus to understand Freud's earliest psychoanalytic concepts, we have to look at how his culture informed his thinking, and how the social times in which he lived contributed to his worldview. Born in Freiberg, Moravia (now a part of the Czech Republic) in 1856 to a wool merchant, Freud moved with his family to Vienna when he was 4. At the height of the Victorian era, this city was considered to be the seat of licentiousness and sexuality in Europe. There was a façade of control and repression of sexuality within a largely Catholic culture. Yet men routinely went to prostitutes and women likewise had lovers. Women in Victorian Vienna were viewed either as sexual property among working classes, or as sexless objects with carefully prescribed social roles (Lerman 1986). In either case, women rarely were expected to fulfill their potential for whole human experience. Furthermore, the absence of means for birth control made the expression of sexuality in all social classes a dangerous enterprise. Freud thus grew up in a cultural context of sexual contradictions. It was within this social context that the concept of repressed sexuality, so central to Freud's thinking, emerged.

It is also important to note that Freud, as a Jew in Vienna, was the victim of rampant anti-Semitism, which marginalized him professionally and impeded his professional recognition. Many of his ideas remained outside mainstream medicine. Some of his views reflected his own experiences of oppression, so that by the end of this career, when he was forced to flee from Vienna in the face of Nazism, he came even more to believe that aggression was a central force not only in human development but in national development as well.

FREUD'S DISCOVERY OF A METHOD
FOR UNDERSTANDING HYSTERIA

Freud completed medical school in Vienna within three years and went on to study with Charcot, a Parisian neurologist who treated women suffering from hysteria. Charcot's female patients suffered many symptoms, including paralysis and blindness, for which there was no known organic cause. At that time it was thought that the symptoms these "madwomen" suffered had a particularly female etiology. Indeed the very word *hysteria* in Latin meant "uterus," and so it was common in those days to attribute a sexual etiology to certain kinds of madness. Charcot was experimenting with treating hysterical symptoms by such methods as hypnosis and the application of pressure to sensitive spots such as the ovaries. Freud studied hypnosis with him and began to suspect that hysteria was not solely a woman's disease and that hysterical symptoms were not simply fabrications of women's minds (Brill 1921). Freud made enormous intellectual leaps, however, when he went from hypnotizing women in Charcot's clinic in Salpêtrière to discovering key concepts in psychoanalysis that are still alive in our practices today. Let us then turn to one of the cases in which he discovered so many of these concepts.

Anna O.: The Case in which Freud Discovered Free Association, Symptoms as Disguised Wishes, Transference, Countertransference, Resistance, and Repression

In 1882, early in Freud's career, his colleague Josef Breuer consulted with him about a woman who came to be called "Anna O." This was a troubling case that had ended badly. Anna O. was a beautiful, intelligent, and willful 21-year-old woman whose symptoms included a nervous cough, anorexia, suicidal ideation, sleepwalking, rages at her governess, tics, squints, paralyses of her arms and neck, temporary blindness, an inability to speak in her native German, and episodes of changed consciousness. The patient was an intellectually gifted woman from an upper-middle-class Jewish family. Yet the choices available to young women in her day were to marry, become a governess, or tend to the sick. For such a creative and gifted young woman, these options were particularly oppressive.

When her father fell ill of pneumonia, she was charged with his care. After nursing him until his death, her symptoms became so overwhelming as to affect every aspect of her waking life. These symptoms continued for over two years. Anna O. also had a family history of psychological instability among her more distant relatives and had two siblings who died.

Breuer was a handsome middle-aged physician who began treating Anna's physical symptoms by hypnotizing her in the late afternoons at her bedside. He visited her three to four times a week and held her hand as she entered a hypnotic state. When he asked her about what may have caused a particular symptom, she would say whatever came to mind, without censorship. Often she would not recognize him, and would drift into trances, or following his visits, fall into deep sleep, or her "clouds." During these late afternoon meetings, she spoke easily (Freeman 1979).

It was Anna O. who named what was going on a "talking cure" and likened telling everything on her mind to "chimney sweeping." In fact, Breuer and Anna O. had developed a method that later became central to psychoanalysis, that of *free association*, in which access to hidden or forgotten feelings, memories, and wishes could be gained from saying without censorship whatever came to mind.

In the course of Breuer's work with Anna O., many ideas that gave rise to the field of psychoanalysis were developed. For example, Freud came to hypothesize that many of Anna O.'s fantasies contained sexual wishes and their prohibitions. They began to understand that if they could decode the symbolic texts of her dreams and fantasies, they might better understand how and why her illness developed.

Until his collaboration with Freud, however, Breuer still had no way of making sense of the many fantasies Anna O. produced. For example, he wrote:

> [In] July, 1880, while he was in the country, her father fell seriously ill of a sub-pleural abscess. Anna shared the duties of nursing him with her mother. She once woke up during the night in great anxiety about the patient, who was in a high fever. . . . Her mother had gone away for a short time and Anna was sitting at the bedside with her right arm over the back of the chair. She fell into a waking dream and saw a black snake coming towards the sick man from the wall to bite him. . . . (In reality, she had been recently frightened by *actual* snakes behind her house.) She tried to keep the snake off, but it was as though she was paralysed. Her right arm, over the back of the chair, had gone to sleep and had become anesthetic and paretic; when she looked at it the fingers turned into little snakes with death's heads. . . . When the snake vanished, in her terror she tried to pray. But language failed her: she could find no tongue in which to speak. . . . The whistle of the train that was bringing the doctor whom she expected broke the spell. [Freud and Breuer 1893, p. 39]

Imagine a woman reporting such a hallucination! Without a preexisting theoretical model, how would one give meaning to the symbol of the snake or to her experiences of paralysis and muteness?

Freud and Breuer began to hypothesize that this "waking dream" contained within it two states of consciousness. Today we might speculate that Anna O. wished her father's suffering to end and hence wished for his death. Perhaps Anna O. was angry at being left to care for her father and wished that snakes would kill him. Such aggressive wishes, especially at her own hands, however, would have conflicted with her role as caretaker and so would need to be kept out of consciousness. Perhaps, having nursed her father in the most intimate of circumstances, alone and at night, separated from her mother and deprived of any opportunities to be with men her own age, Anna O. felt sexual feelings toward her father. The snakes, which came out of her own hands, might have not only a biting and aggressive component, they might also rep-

resent forbidden sexual wishes she had for her father or perhaps mas-
turbatory impulses. Since these sexual feelings might have been unacceptable to her, they might have been out of her conscious awareness. It
is even possible, given the nature of her episodes—her difficulty swallowing, and her anorexia—that she might have been the victim of sexual
abuse and that the snakes might have represented memories of previous
sexual trauma. But all of these ideas were to follow later with the development of drive theory.

At this time in history what Anna O. *consciously* experienced was
paralysis and muteness. Freud would later hypothesize that in a con-
densed way, her physical symptoms expressed both her sexual and aggressive wishes as well as their prohibitions. Freud now began to think that
physical symptoms were internal psychological conflicts *converted* into
physical pathways. He later called these kinds of symptoms *conversion
hysteria,* and they are currently classified under the general rubric of
somatoform disorders.

As Anna O. and Breuer continued their work, many of her conversion symptoms began to have some association to previous trauma.
Her difficulty hearing seemed related to her father having asked her in
vain for some wine. Her squint appeared related to a time in which she
couldn't see her father because of the tears in her eyes. Her cough seemed
related to wishes to be elsewhere than with her dying father. Each symptom seemed to have some association with wishes or feelings that were
consciously unacceptable and had now been transformed into physical
states. As the associations were discovered, examined, and understood,
many of her symptoms abated.

Over time a deep relationship also developed between Anna O. and
her doctor. When he went on vacation, leaving another physician to look
in on her, she went into a deep depression, becoming paralyzed and mute
again. As she had been paralyzed under the weight of feelings toward
her father, some of her intense feelings now appeared to be occurring
within her current relationship with her physician. This experience of
bringing to the therapeutic relationship feelings, wishes, and assumptions from past relationships was the phenomenon we now refer to as
transference. Although neither Freud nor Breuer named it as such, transference refers to reexperiencing and reenacting in current relationships
earlier wishes, and feelings, and experiences from past relationships. This
takes place in all relationships but is a particularly useful tool for under-

standing the internal and *unconscious* aspects of clients' inner lives as they are lived out in the treatment process.

As episodes from the previous year in which she tended her sick father were repeated, remembered, and talked through, Anna O. seemed to improve, and Breuer attempted to terminate the treatment. To his great dismay, however, he was summoned to Anna O.'s bedside in the middle of the night to find her in the midst of a hysterical pregnancy. As she screamed and groaned in labor, she accused Breuer of being the father of the baby. Breuer was unaware of and certainly unprepared for the intensity of Anna's feelings toward him. Given that he had no theoretical model in which to conceptualize her sexual feelings for him, he hypnotized her a final time and is reported to have left for a second honeymoon, never to see her again (Jones 1953).

What Breuer could not know, and what Freud was to discover, was just how powerful, real, and urgent Anna O.'s sexual feelings were. These powerful feelings that had flourished during their regressive late afternoon sessions later came to be named *transference* feelings. Anna O.'s sexual and aggressive fantasies had been transferred to her current therapist and were experienced as if they were actually happening in their relationship. Because those feelings were not acknowledged, they became represented in her hysterical pregnancy. And because Breuer did not recognize his own feelings in himself, he said of his beautiful patient "The element of sexuality was astonishingly undeveloped in her" (Freud and Breuer 1893, p. 21). A therapist's own sexual and aggressive fantasies and feelings toward the client are called *countertransference reactions*. Breuer's unawareness of his countertransference probably resulted in his disavowed attraction to her.

Today we know that denying, avoiding, or repressing countertransference feelings interferes with the therapeutic process. In fact, the patient's growing conscious awareness of feelings for the therapist and the therapist's awareness of feelings for the patient provide some of the most useful data in clinical work. This process in which the client examines her own feelings, fantasies, and reactions to the therapist, and the therapist does the same toward the client, requires honesty, vigilance, and self-knowledge. When these intense feelings are recognized, Freud thought, they can be controlled. But when they are denied, resisted, or avoided, as Breuer did, they can negatively affect the course of treatment. Freud initially thought that transference should and could be avoided, but he would shortly discover, in the case of Dora, that transference was an unavoidable part of the talking cure. Even later he came to see transference not as an impediment, but as *the* major vehicle for psychoanalysis.

Anna O. did not do well immediately after her treatment with Breuer. She was hospitalized and even addicted to morphine for a time. But she later became a great feminist social worker, advocating on behalf of women who had been exploited—prostitutes, unmarried mothers, and young girls in the white slave trade. Perhaps her commitment to working with women oppressed by men had its roots in her unequal relationships with her brother and her father as well as with Breuer. We do know that she did not value psychoanalysis for her own clients and that she appeared never to have forgiven Breuer for "not knowing" (Freeman 1979).

Yet the irony is that because Breuer did not know, and because he dared explore an inner world that neither she nor he could understand, he unknowingly discovered the phenomena of transference and countertransference. Because he did not know, and because he dared to share his clinical errors with Freud, Freud was later able to use this case to illustrate core concepts still used in psychodynamic practice today.

THE BEGINNINGS OF CONFLICT THEORY

Let us now examine several of the concepts from this case that led Freud to develop his theory of the mind. First, the case of Anna O. led Freud to think that by free associating, by reliving the past, and by verbalizing repressed feelings, past trauma could be worked through and some symptoms could be relieved. Second, this case illustrated that traumatic experiences, when repressed, sought expression through physical symptoms. Freud would later show that by freely associating in the context of a trusting relationship, clients could gain access to powerful sexual and aggressive wishes. Freud also began to discover in his work with other hysterical women that their wishes and urges that sought release were always opposed by counterforces in the mind that resisted their coming into consciousness. This was the essence of his idea of a conflict theory, that unconscious sexual and aggressive wishes seek expression but are kept out of consciousness by other forces in the mind. Freud envisioned a censor in the mind that *resisted* unacceptable thoughts, feelings, and wishes. Later he identified the central mechanism for keeping unacceptable thoughts, urges, and feelings out of conscious awareness as *repression*. Repression is the defense that keeps out of consciousness that which is too painful, shameful, or dangerous to know or feel. The idea that there might be forces in the mind that keep unbearable feelings out of consciousness began to account for why hypnosis alone did not bring enduring symptom relief. To bring unconscious material to light was not enough. Clients needed help in overcoming their *resistances* and their *repression* in order to work through what was unconscious, dreaded, and feared. Psychological conflicts, Freud began to realize, were an inevitable part of psychic life.

In Freud's earliest cases, then, were the precursors to many critical concepts: *free association*, freely reporting whatever comes to mind; *resistance*, the forces that oppose the striving toward recovery (Freud 1912); *repression*, the unconscious mechanism that keeps unacceptable wishes and feelings out of consciousness; *symptom formation*, the nature of symptoms as symbolic, unconscious expressions of conflicts; *conversion*, the transformation of aggressive or sexual wishes into somatic pathways; *transference*, thoughts and feelings for a therapist that have their roots in earlier relationships; *countertransference*, thoughts and feelings in one's own earlier relationships; *symbolic content*, fantasies, hallucinations, and dreams contain symbols, which may condense many wishes and feelings; and *unconscious conflict*, unconscious wishes and fears that seek expression but meet with repression. Every one of these concepts is still a vital part of psychodynamic clinical work today.

THE EVOLUTION OF FREUD'S UNDERSTANDING OF PSYCHOPATHOLOGY

While Freud initially continued to hypnotize hysterical patients, he found that much of the same material was also accessible via free association in the analytic setting. In *Studies in Hysteria* (1895), he began to evolve a number of theories drawn from patterns in the hysterical women he treated. He noted that their symptoms such as dissociation, amnesia, and conversion disorders seemed related to *real* sexual traumatic events that they had experienced as children. Memories that could not be expressed emerged as symptoms. The cure for hysteria involved gaining access to unconscious memories through free association. The talking cure became a way to allow "strangulated affects," or feelings, to be discharged through speech. Cure involved *remembering the sexual trauma, making it conscious despite resistance, repeating it in the transference, and working it through* in the context of a therapeutic relationship.

However, between the publication of *Studies in Hysteria* in 1895 and its reception in 1905, Freud retracted his view that all hysterical women had suffered from *real* sexual trauma. Instead he began to view sexual seductions in childhood as wishes that were the products of his female patient's own desires. That a real event should so simply be disclaimed as a fantasied realization of a wish was problematic then, and remains a difficult part of the theory now. Indeed, discriminating memory from fantasy continues to be a raging debate in the trauma literature today (Loftus and Ketcham 1994). Freud's abandonment of the seduction theory, however, led to many decades in which the importance of real trauma has been minimized or denied (Masson 1984).

THE ANALYSIS OF DREAMS

Freud (1900) continued to investigate the internal lives of individuals by exploring their dreams. He noted that under the relaxation and regression of sleep, important sexual and aggressive wishes are expressed in disguise. What is remembered from dreams is called the *manifest content*, which contains symbolic representations of the drives. Like symptoms, but in a more normative way, dreams allow for the discharge of sexual and aggressive drives. The work of dream analysis, then, lies in making connections between the manifest content of a dream and *latent* or *symbolic content*, which includes unacceptable drives and feelings. Dreams provide access into some of the fragmentary, primitive, shameful, secret aspects of unconscious life. Freud believed that by following his patient's associations to dreams, he could decode their meanings.

Freud also continued to remain aware of a "censor" that keeps the forbidden meaning of dreams out of consciousness. During sleep, the censor relaxes, permitting the instinctual impulses of childhood to be expressed without regard to the concerns that operate in conscious life (Freud 1900).

THE ROLE OF SELF-KNOWLEDGE

As Freud refined his methods of free association through his own dream analysis and analyses of his patients' dreams, however, he was not satisfied to look at the passions of others only from the safe distance afforded the clinician toward the client. He undertook his own self-analysis. He began to identify within himself some of the passions and conflicts he was finding in his patients. He remembered, for example, his own shame as a boy at seeing his once powerful father humiliated by an anti-Semitic attack. He remembered his arousal at seeing his mother's naked body, and his guilt for having these feelings. What Freud uncovered in himself were his own repressed sexual feelings for his mother, wishes to be rid of his father, and fears of retribution or punishment for his incestuous wishes. Referring to *Oedipus Rex* by Sophocles, Freud conceptualized these themes as being *oedipal* in nature. From his own self-analysis, he began to develop a theory that there were universal themes of sexuality and aggression, as well as their prohibitions, at different levels of child development.

DRIVE THEORY: A MODEL · OF PSYCHOSEXUAL DEVELOPMENT

Over time Freud evolved a model for understanding how normal child development is shaped by the two powerful drives of sexuality (or libido) and aggression. He understood these drives to be biologically based phenomena that seek discharge or expression. There are many drives—hunger, sleep, and other biological regulatory functions. Freud postulated that the drives arise in the body, that they are unconscious, and that they become conscious as they seek expression. Toward the beginning of his career he emphasized sexuality as the major drive and an important factor in psychopathology. Later he introduced the importance of the aggressive drive.

Freud proposed that sexuality and aggression seek expression in the everyday lives of children. That children were sexual was a radical idea. That their sexual and aggressive drives evolve and become increasingly complex with their physical and psychological maturation was a substantive and creative leap. Freud's theory about the developmental course of the drives united embryological and developmental theories with Freud's neurological concepts of drives that seek discharge.

Freud's theory of *infantile sexuality* or of *psychosexual development*, as he called it, was epigenetic. It held that everything that grew had a predetermined ground plan. Developmental periods require that the individual meet and surmount critical tasks at the proper time and in the proper sequence. Development is hierarchical, invariant, and sequential. Each new piece of *psychosexual development* depends on the preceding stage. Within this paradigm, there are *regressions* (or returns) to earlier stages of functioning, and there can be *fixations* (getting stuck) at each stage of development, which may form the basis for pathological relationships or character traits in later life.

According to psychosexual drive theory, each phase of child development is shaped by an *erogenous* zone (a physical zone of sexual pleasure), a *drive*, an *object* (usually person) toward whom the drive is aimed, the *psychosexual issue* that the individual faces at that stage of development, the cluster of *character traits* that emerge at each juncture of childhood development, and the kinds of *symptoms* that might occur at each stage of development.

Freud now began to articulate a model of child development that viewed childhood as governed by internal sexual and aggressive urges, by physical maturation, by the passage of time, and by events in the real external world. Thus his psychosexual drive theory synthesized the concept of children's erogenous zones as being associated with the kinds of relationships and attachments, symptoms, character traits, and psychological preoccupations they face at each stage of development.

Freud divided childhood psychosexual development into five stages: infancy, toddlerhood, the phallic or oedipal stage, latency, and adolescence (the genital stage). Let us consider each of them individually. Before doing so, however, we want to issue a caveat. This theory about psychological stages often sounds vastly oversimplified—and it is. For example, descriptions of the oral stage make it sound as if the infant is simply one big mouth with no other interests and experiences. To focus on the fulfillment or frustration of oral needs, nothing else is described, which gives a very limited and distorted picture of that particular time in life. In reading about any particular stage, it is important to remember both that many other things are going on, and that what happens developmentally also depends on the individuality of the person and all the other factors influencing his or her life. Fred Pine (1990) offers the term *developmental moments* to replace the more rigid, monolithic idea of *developmental stages*. We find this concept useful because it is so much more fluid. The oral stage can then be understood as having many oral developmental moments and perhaps more oral moments than at any other time in life, but room is left to imagine the baby at that time as a many faceted, complex little person.

The Oral Stage

Freud proposed that at the oral stage (birth to 1½ years of age), babies experience pleasure and aggression primarily through their mouths, the first erogenous zone. Babies will stimulate themselves by sucking on a breast, fingers, or toys. Their needs, perceptions, and pleasurable and painful feelings are expressed principally through their mouths and tongues. Babies will scream to be fed; they will derive great pleasure from sucking and they will be satiated through their mouths. There are aggressive aspects to orality. Babies use their mouths to spit, to bite, or to chew. Some aggressive feelings can be pleasurable as well. Babies depend on relationships with their parents, their caregivers, or others, to regulate their tensions, and to soothe, feed, and comfort them. Freud thought that to the degree that babies can love, their love is invested in themselves. Other people are valued as the parts that serve the baby as need fulfillers or frustrators, as breasts or bottle carriers rather than as persons in their own right. The central psychosexual issue at this stage is to get basic needs met and to satisfy oral drives, both loving and aggressive. The healthy character traits that may emerge include the capacity for trust (Erikson 1950), self-reliance, and self-esteem. When oral issues are unresolvable, they show themselves in adult problems. Let us look for some of the oral themes that emerged with a therapy patient.

> William, a 31-year-old graduate student, came to treatment complaining of "glaring at people." He described a fantasy life populated by alligators. He imagined these vicious animals in a moat protecting him from the intrusions of others; anyone who tried to get close would be devoured.
>
> William had been an only child born to two middle-aged parents. He described his own mother as excessively dependent on his

grandmother who lived with them until her death when he was 8. His father was described as a rigid, removed, and distant military man. Neither parent was seen as reliably comforting. When William's grandmother died, he gained about forty pounds. He remembers that no one noticed. He grew up feeling chronically empty, hungry, and lonely.

When it came time to apply to colleges, William had his mother write his applications, including his autobiographical statement. She chose his college, and her choice reflected her own conservative values rather than William's values. Throughout college, his mother baked sugar cookies and sent them to him. He would reciprocate by sending her his laundry halfway across the country, believing that he could not do it for himself.

He described a worldview of relationships summed up by "I'll feed you if you feed me." True reciprocity was impossible, and his relationships were often marked by rage when he felt any deprivation. For example, when his landlord raised the rent, William threatened to pour boiling oil through the pipes. When a girlfriend became pregnant with his baby, he ended the relationship because her plan for an abortion was simply, as he saw it, an attempt to kill a part of him. At work he expected immediate rewards. When, during a blizzard, a computer program he had written could not be read immediately, he became irate and careened through the icy streets endangering himself and others. Often William would give presents but then would become disappointed by the lack of immediate payback and demand them back. Like the oral child who bites and rages when his need are unmet, William was not able to see relationships in any terms but his own.

Over the course of treatment, there emerged a gulf of loneliness and unfulfilled needs. Often he would bring a knapsack filled with bananas and milk and eat them in sessions as he recounted incidents of his emotional hunger. In fact, one of the more notable gains in treatment came when he was able to delay and anticipate his hunger, and discuss with me the ice cream cone he would like to have after the session. The ability to delay, and ultimately to feed himself, took many years. After four years of treatment, William was able to get the recipe for sugar cookies and actually bake them for himself. He stopped sending his laundry home, and he even entered into a work situation where he could be admired, while not having to work closely with people. His interpersonal relationships remained distant, but he was less driven by the intensity of his hunger, dependency, and rage.

William had serious difficulties tolerating his own oral needs: to be loved, to be satisfied, or to be appropriately gratified at the most basic level. Because his basic needs had been both overly gratified and not gratified enough, he could not see himself or others as whole. He had difficulty with empathy, with mutuality, and with love. In drive theory terms, William struggled with excessive and unneutralized oral drives—biting, hunger, oral greed coupled with a need for immediate gratification. This resulted in his prominent character traits of narcissism, dependency, envy, and rage.

The Anal Stage

By the second year of life (ages 1½ to 3) the capacity to walk and climb gives a toddler some degree of autonomy. Toddlers, however, are notable for their self-centeredness and limited capacity for reason. They do not see value in waiting to cross the street. They have not internalized a set of controls that prevent them from hanging from a light cord, putting a knife into an electric socket, kicking, biting, screaming, or lying down in a crowded airport or supermarket. Almost all of their behaviors seem aggressively intensified and directed toward testing the boundaries of what is acceptable and what is not. Toddlers must learn not only what is prohibited, but also how to internalize the prohibitions of others, thus making them their own. Their psychosexual tasks, then, are around the development of internal controls. This usually occurs first around toilet training. Ultimately toddlers must begin to manage their anal struggles over independence and autonomy by internalizing parental wishes and prohibitions. What motivates children at this stage to accommodate to social demands, Freud thought, was shame and the fear of loss of the parents' love.

The erogenous zone identified with the anal stage, is, as the name implies, the anus. Freud hypothesized that there was both erotic pleasure in, and heightened aggression over, the production of excrement. Two-year-old children, for example, show *anal eroticism* by delighting in, and expecting caregivers to equally applaud, the products of their bowels or bladders. They may show equal curiosity and delight in caregivers' toileting behaviors, following them to the bathroom, and discussing or insisting on inspecting their caregivers' excrement. Toddlers may show *anal aggression* in retaining, expelling, or even smearing their feces or urine. They may express these feelings through play with dump trucks, puddles, play dough, or finger paint.

Freud thought that both the loving and aggressive drives in the anal stage are aimed at trying to gain control first over their sphincter muscles, and then over the important objects (people) in their lives. Relationships at this stage involve two people, that is, they are *dyadic* in nature. The quality of their relationships is marked by struggles over self-control. Take, for example, Martin, whose account of himself when he was a child indicates that at age 5, he was still fixated at the anal stage.

His father was a naval officer, and Martin's favorite form of play was floating his toy boats in the bathtub and torpedoing them. Both parents had become frustrated with Martin because he consistently expelled his feces in his pants and not in the toilet. In desperation, they offered him twenty-five cents for every bowel movement he made in the toilet. Martin soon calculated that it was not in his best interest to become toilet trained, because to do so would mean that he would ultimately lose money. Instead he would use the toilet for three days to earn the money. But the only way to keep the money flowing was to lose control periodically, and this he would do at home or at the homes of his friends. One day, Martin's best friend's mother insisted that, at her house, he use the toilet. There she overheard him muttering to himself about Napoleon's battles. When he came out of the bathroom he informed her, "I'm Napoleon and Napoleon shits wherever he pleases!"

For Martin, toileting had become the battleground to control and dominate others. Not surprisingly, some of Martin's adult character traits were shaped by his early anal fixation. He had difficulty completing his master's thesis because he could only write "in spurts." He tended to have difficulty interpersonally, especially in control struggles with his advisors and in close relationships. Other anal character traits that Freud identified may include excessive cleanliness, hoarding, or frugality.

The Phallic Phase

By ages 3 to 5, children have entered an exciting world of fantasy, imagination, and budding romance. Suddenly their preoccupations are no longer around "poop" or "pee." Rather, they begin to have romantic feelings and sexual fantasies, often directed toward their parent or parent surrogate of the opposite sex. Children at this stage are just beginning to discover their own genitals. As pretend princes and princesses, kings and queens, husbands and wives, oedipal children become cognizant of sex roles and play out games of love and marriage on the playground and in the nursery school. One nursery school teacher reported that when she would instruct boys and girls to put their hands on their heads, on their toes, or the air, some little boy inevitably would call out, "Put your hands on your penis!" This preoccupation with genitals as the erogenous zone at the oedipal stage is natural and normative.

It is hard to imagine a 3- to 5-year-old as sexual or as having sexual feelings. But they often have erotic longings for an adult of the opposite sex. Often they play out their fantasies in which there is some sort of retribution from the parent or parent surrogate of the same sex. For example, a colleague described this conversation with her 4-year-old son, which took place in the bathtub:

> *Son*: I love you so much even my two arms can't show you enough.
> *Mother*: I love you so much my arms can't show it either.
> *Son* (said with a little discomfort): And Daddy too.
> *Mother*: And Daddy too.
> *Son*: You're so beautiful. I'd like to marry you. You know, Daddy could live down the street in a smaller house. In fact, you know, I've noticed lately that sometimes Daddy smells. Have you?
> *Mother*: You know, sweetie, as much as you love me, and I love you, you really can't marry me. I'm married to Daddy. But I bet that when you grow up, you'll marry someone even more beautiful than me.
> *Son* (now fondling his genitals): Do you really think I'll ever be bigger than him anyway?

Another mother described her son admiring her as she dressed to go out. He said, "You look lovely, my princess bride. May I suggest that you wear this (pointing to a necklace) to go out with me."

Indeed, in a wonderful poem by A. A. Milne (1927), a little boy is described at the height of oedipal longing:

James James
    Morrison Morrison
    Weatherby George Dupree.
    Took great
    Care of his Mother
    Though he was only three.
James James
    Said to his Mother,
"Mother," he said, said he,
"You must never go down to the end of the town if you don't
    go down with me." [p. 52]

A third mother remembered this event between her daughter and her husband. Four-year-old Lilly, who had been dressed for bed, suddenly began to take off her nightgown in a kind of strip tease before her father, saying, "Bosom Dance, Bosom Dance." ·

Her father responded, "Lilly, put your nightgown back on! What are you doing?"

Lilly replied, "Daddy, you know I've been thinking that a 3-year-old couldn't marry you but I bet a 4-year-old can!"

For the oedipal child, the penis or the vagina becomes the erogenous zone. According to drive theory, children experience their sexual desires directed toward the parent or parent substitute of the opposite sex; aggression is directed toward the same-sex parent. The oedipal child's world is not made up simply of dyadic relationships of the self and another, but includes *triadic* relationships. The oedipal child's world now requires reconciling sexual feelings and aggressive feelings that involve three people: the child, the mother, and the father, or parent substitute.

According to most societies, the child must not realize her own incestuous wishes for the opposite sex parent, and therefore these feelings need to be renounced and repressed. In addition, because the child also loves the parent or parent surrogate toward whom she feels competition and aggression, she begins to direct the aggression once felt for the same-sex parent against the self. Freud thought that children were motivated to give up their erotic feelings for their opposite-sex parent because they feared retribution coming from the same-sex parent. Often this is represented as some physical harm that may come to the child. He called this *castration anxiety* and saw it as a precursor to guilt. It is important to mention that castration threats to children were not uncommon in Freud's era. Castration anxiety later becomes an extremely important concept in Freud's understanding of guilt and the superego (see Chapter 3). While he viewed boys as fearing castration, he saw girls as feeling already castrated (see Chapter 10 for a fuller explication of Freud's views on women).

Freud hypothesized that children ultimately resolve their oedipal conflicts through developing a conscience. Through the process of *identifying* with the same-sex parent and by taking on the attributes, values, and ideals of that parent, a child's gender role identity is solidified. At the same time, by identifying with parental injunctions of right and wrong, a child at the oedipal stage develops an internalized set of moral principles. No longer motivated only by fears of loss of love, children at this stage are now motivated by guilt. *Guilt* is a feeling that emerges when internal moral prohibitions are violated.

With the development of a conscience, or what Freud called a *superego*, morality for the oedipal child now becomes an internal concern. No longer governed by external prohibitions only, the oedipal child now experiences the unpleasant feeling of guilt when she or he encounters sexual and aggressive longings that violate internal moral injunctions and social prohibitions.

Hence, the goal of the oedipal period is to establish, through identification, one's own gender role identity and to develop a conscience. Many kinds of neurotic disturbances derive from fixations at the oedipal stage. These include excessive competitiveness, emotionality, oversexualization, inhibition, and a sense of inadequacy or inferiority. While pathology may emerge as a result of a fixation at this stage, children's incestuous and aggressive wishes toward parents and parent surrogates are not, in and of themselves, pathological.

Brenner (1955) has written of oedipal feelings that "the single most important fact to bear [about the intensity of oedipal feelings] is the strength and force of the feelings of the people involved. This is the love of a real love affair. For many, it is the most intense of their entire lives. The intensity of deepest passion of love and hate, yearning and jealousy, fury and fear, rage within the child" (p. 106). Selma Fraiberg (1959) adds,

"Yet this is a dream which must end in renunciation and reconciliation" (p. 204).

Oedipal children are often drawn to fairy tales because these stories provide in fantasy both oedipal wishes and their resolutions. In the fairy tale "Jack and the Beanstalk," Jack is a young boy left alone to care for his widowed mother. Already this fact contains an oedipal boy's wish to have his mother exclusively. Jack trades in his mother's cow (Milky White—an oral image) for three beans. Jack brings the beans to his mother but she rejects these signs of his manhood, and throws the beans out the window. To Jack's phallic delight, up sprouts a large beanstalk, which he climbs three times (three being a symbol of triadic relationships) to do battle with a giant ogre (his rival and competitor who is bigger than he) so that he can support his mother. While Jack is sometimes saved by the ogre's wife, and regresses by hiding in her oven (womb), he is finally betrayed by her and must climb down the ogre's beanstalk. At the bottom, he looks up to see an image many oedipal boys experience when they view their own naked fathers—that of a giant man with a beanstalk (phallus) through his legs. Jack is terrified of being hurt, even devoured, by the giant who will punish him for trying to steal what is not his (the golden harp). And so Jack chops the beanstalk down with an axe, steals enough gold to provide for his mother, and marries a princess of his own.

"Jack and the Beanstalk" has a moral tale to tell to the oedipal child. Jack must come to terms with his wishes to have his mother exclusively, with his aggressive feelings toward a symbolic father, the giant, as well as with his fears that the giant will harm him. To deal with his forbidden sexual wishes toward his mother, he takes on the manly attributes of the giant (or father) and tries to kill him. Jack has expressed a universal oedipal fantasy of coveting what is not his. But by identifying with the giant's manly strengths, he ultimately gets rewarded by having a princess of his own.

Bettelheim (1983) has proposed that Freud's choice of the Oedipus myth as a guiding metaphor for psychoanalysis was not accidental. The myth of Oedipus is, in fact, the story of a boy who acts to kill his father due to a metaphorical blindness. He kills his father because he does not know himself.

The tragedy of Oedipus tells of a boy born to a king and queen who are warned that their son will murder his father. To avert that tragedy, they drive a spike through their son's foot and send him away to be killed. He is then adopted by the king and queen of Corinth, whom he believes are his real parents. When he consults an oracle, he is told that he will slay his father. To avoid that fate, he leaves Corinth, only to meet and murder a stranger on the road. Of course, that stranger is his true father. Oedipus, a seeming hero, then answers the riddle of the sphinx and is made king of Thebes, where he unknowingly marries his own mother. When a plague befalls his city, he tries to discover its source and in the process uncovers the truth, that by not knowing himself he has in fact murdered his father and married his mother. In his grief and despair, he blinds himself and his mother kills herself. Bettelheim (1983) writes:

> This is a crucial part of the myth: as soon as the unknown is made known—as soon as the secret of the father's murder and the incest with the mother are brought to light and the hero purges himself— the pernicious consequences of the Oedipal deeds disappear. The myth also warns that the longer one defends oneself against know- ing these secrets, the greater is the damage to oneself and to others. The psychoanalytic construct of the Oedipus complex contains this implicit warning too. Freud discovered both in his self analysis and in his work with patients that when one has the courage to face one's own unconscious patricidal and incestuous desires—which is tanta- mount to purging oneself of them—the evil consequences of these feelings subside. *Becoming aware of our unconscious feelings—which makes them no longer unconscious but part of our conscious mind—is the best protection against an Oedipal catastrophe.* [p. 15]

In trying to develop a corollary theory about the oedipal situation for girls, Freud's own self-analysis was not helpful. Indeed, both Freud and his female patients were embedded in a culture and a social milieu that devalued women. Within this culture (and his patients gave him plenty of evidence for his theory) he postulated that girls viewed their genitals as "inferior" and as evidence of having already been castrated. He believed girls are angry with their mothers for having given them an inferior organ, and that they envy boys. They turn to their fathers as heterosexual object choices because they want a baby as a compensation for their disappointment and anger with their mothers. Because girls see themselves as already castrated, and hence inferior, they normatively develop penis envy, and develop character traits of passivity, receptivity, narcissism, and masochism. His mistake was not in seeing penis envy but in minimizing its cultural sources. We will discuss the phallocentrism of this theory in our gender critique in Chapter 10. But Freud's articulation of different psychological development for girls and boys has provoked reactions from women that have lasted over three quarters of a century.

Latency

Freud thought of latency (6 to 11 years of age) as a time in which the sexual and aggressive drives are relatively quiescent. In latency, sexual and aggressive energy is no longer directed toward parents. The recently intense oedipal passions of romance, longing, and rivalry are transformed into behaviors that are calmer, more pliable, and directed toward peers (Noshpitz and King 1991).

As school-age children move out beyond the bounds of their nuclear families and into the world of school, their sexual and aggressive energies are now expressed as a drive to gain mastery of physical skills and cognitive learning. This is a time in which children are socialized into the culture's sex roles in which boys learn what the society values as masculine and girls learn what a feminine role means through identification with peers. In latency, one sees games, classrooms, and neighborhood configurations organized around same-sex segregation. These games often involve fantasies of superheroes, good guys, and bad guys. For boys, there can be endless delight in being Toxic Crusaders, Superman, or Power Rangers; for girls, April O'Neill, Wonder Woman, or Barbie may express identification with the culture's same sex ideals. What captivates the literary imaginations of latency-aged boys and girls are myths, legends, or mysteries such as *The Knights of the Round Table*, the Hardy Boys, or Nancy Drew. In all of these stories, themes of adventure and rescue can be found.

Peter Pan might be considered the quintessential latency-aged boy. Peter Pan lives with a tribe of lost boys in Never-Never Land, a world characterized by endless battles and chases made up of same-sex peers. In this story, Peter enlists Wendy and her two brothers to leave the real world and join him in his adventures involving pirates and Indians. But when Wendy expresses mildly romantic feelings for Peter, he is willing to lose her forever and even to forsake his tribe of lost boys, so that he can continue to live in a same-sex world of exploits and rescue. Sadly, Wendy returns to the real world of sexuality where she grows beyond the pleasures of latency and can never rejoin Peter. When Peter returns to find her, he discovers a world that has advanced developmentally beyond him.

In latency, aggression is freed from within the bounds of the nuclear family, and is expressed through competition with peers. Children at this age define their identities by virtue of their place among their peers—in spelling bees, team games, crafts, and sports. Loving and sexual feelings, once directed toward the opposite-sex parent, are often turned into idealizations of the same-sex parent or surrogate (teachers, coaches, etc.). Often latency-age boys and girls will insist that their fathers or mothers and coaches or counselors are the strongest, bravest, best in the world.

Because sexual and aggressive drives tend to be transformed into activity, the latency-age child is notable for exploring, skill building, learning, and socializing beyond the bounds of the nuclear family. This is a stage where children will collect rocks, stamps, baseball cards, bottle caps, dolls, models, and so forth. Freud considered these behaviors to all be in the service of controlling unconscious sexual and aggressive impulses. These sorting activities, he hypothesized, were purposeful behaviors to defend against unacceptable sexual and aggressive impulses.

Unlike the exhibitionistic phallic child, the latency-age child tends to be modest about his or her body. Now the child's body becomes a means for achieving in sports, for acquiring skills, and for developing muscles for games. When there are difficulties in body mastery, in learning, or in social interactions, there can be the potential for long-lasting character traits of inferiority, failure, and defeat. Freud also thought that some of the obsessive behaviors of this stage could lead to lifelong character traits marked by rigid thoughts and behaviors.

The Genital Stage (Adolescence)

Freud proposed that, in contrast to latency during which the sexual drives are quiescent, adolescence is a tumultuous stage of biological changes in which there is an upsurge of aggressive and sexual impulses. With rises of sex hormones and resultant physical maturation, boys and girls become keenly aware of their bodies and those of the opposite sex. Boys develop facial and pubic hair, their voices change, and they experience nocturnal emissions. Girls develop breasts and pubic hair and begin to menstruate. These physical changes affect cognition, emotion, and fantasy. In the cognitive realm, adolescents may be flooded with sexual and aggressive feelings that may interfere with learning. At the same time this affective flooding may enrich their curiosity and creativity. Adolescents tend to be highly emotional and often regress to earlier oedipal themes of grief, unrequited love, rage, longing, desire, and revenge. Given sudden hormonal changes, their mood swings are often intense, confusing, and overwhelming. Given the sexual transformations in their bodies, adolescents gravitate toward peers who can help them develop norms around sexuality. They voraciously seek out literature, movies, music, and other forms of popular culture that are sexually and aggressively explicit. For the adolescent, the world now becomes filled with sexually charged feelings about siblings, teachers, coaches, and peers. Whereas oedipal feelings and fantasies were repressed in latency, they are revived in adolescence. Since one of the goals of adolescence is to separate from the family of origin, sexual attraction to peers promotes disengagement from the adolescent's family. Adolescents also experience grandiosity and invulnerability in their thinking and judgment, believing that they have all the answers in contrast to their "over the hill" parents and teachers.

As the objects of their sexual drives shift, so too their aggression is redirected. Adolescents are known for their acting out and rebellious behaviors, their political and ethical stances that are in opposition to those of their parents, and their devaluation of authority in general. All of these expressions of their aggression, Freud suggested, are in the service of the goal of adolescence—that of separation from the family of origin.

Adolescence is also a time for the consolidation of a conscience and of aspirations and goals. Adolescents may go through an ascetic phase characterized by rigid morals and ideals. Their idealizations of idols, movie stars, rock figures, and even saints present them with opportunities to experiment with new values and new kinds of ideals.

Janna's parents called the community counseling center alarmed by the changes in their daughter's behavior. They reported that the school principal had suspended Janna that day for cutting class with her boyfriend and for smoking pot. Her parents lamented that their once responsible, sweet, cooperative girl had turned into a sullen, uncommunicative, and angry 15-year-old. Whereas she had once returned from school filled with stories to tell her family, she now spent most of her time at home on the phone with friends barricaded behind a closed bedroom door. She plastered her bedroom walls with posters of the rock group Metallica; she wore a nose ring, ripped jeans, and tattered shirts. She spent most of her spare time with her leather-clad boyfriend.

In the initial session, her father described how his daughter had been his "special girl," but how he refused to talk with her now while she was dating "that bum." Janna responded to the clinician's questions with shrugs, monosyllabic replies, and a gaze transfixed on a tree outside the office window. She noted that she just wanted "space . . . to live my own life and make my own decisions."

Janna's psychological goal was to separate from her family and to define her separate identity. Her sexual and aggressive acting out was her unconscious effort to deal with revived oedipal feelings. Freud would maintain that the way she expressed, modulated, and sublimated her aggressive and sexual drives would ultimately affect the course of her adult personality integration. Were she to remain fixated at this stage of adolescent development, some of the pathological character traits that might emerge include violations of social norms through acting-out behaviors, a lack of neutralized aggressive and libidinal drives, and a lack of age-appropriate identifications.

It must also be remembered that we now know that the task of each of these stages is not only biologically and psychologically determined, but also culturally and socially determined. Environmental influences may advance or assault personality development. While this will be more fully addressed in our discussion of Erikson's life-cycle theory and in our chapters on racial development and gender (Chapters 9 and 10), psychosexual theory did provide a way of viewing development as both biologically and psychologically determined.

TOPOGRAPHIC THEORY

Freud's archeological roots were never more obvious than in his first understanding of the mind as layered. Freud envisioned the mind as a map. In this map, conflict theory was implicit but underdeveloped. Given his interest in archeological and geological principles, he began to think of the mind as if it were in layers consisting of an unconscious, a pre-conscious, and a conscious. According to this model, the *unconscious mind* is governed by the *pleasure principle*. The unconscious is the unruly part of the mind not governed by the constraints of reality; it is the part of the mind in which wishing will make it so. It operates according to *primary process thinking*. This refers to the chaotic, disjointed world James Joyce so eloquently described in *Finnegans Wake*. It is a world of free association and fantasy, governed minimally by logic or reality.

The *preconscious mind* is that part of the mind that can be brought to attention but that is largely out of consciousness. Jokes and slips of the tongue are evidence of preconscious processes. The *conscious mind* is governed not by pleasure but by the *reality principle*. The conscious mind refers to the logical, orderly, rational, cognitive operations of everyday waking life. Within the conscious mind is the capacity for self-evaluation, for reason, for judgment, and for delay. The conscious mind uses a logical and sequential kind of thinking that Freud called *secondary process thinking*. Freud envisioned the conscious mind as striving to reduce excitation. He proposed that these parts of the mind try to achieve homeostasis whereby excitement is made neutral. These ideas became central to his understanding of hysteria.

STRUCTURAL THEORY: AN INTRODUCTION

By 1923, Freud began to observe that symptoms could not be explained solely as regressions or fixations of the drives at different stages of psychological development. Neither could symptoms be explained as expressing interactions between the three layers of the mind as his topographic theory had proposed. Rather, symptoms and related psychopathology seemed to occur both developmentally and as a result of conflicts between sexual or aggressive wishes, reality, and internal moral prohibitions. These internal, unconscious psychological conflicts seemed to result in problems of depression, anxiety, lowered self-esteem, and diminished psychological capacity to function freely. At the most extreme, conflicts between structures of the mind seemed to lead to breaks with reality. Freud began then to envision a theory of the mind in which psychopathology was related to conflicts between wishes, reality, and ideals, each represented by a different agency of the mind. Using this paradigm, he organized the mind into three agencies: the *id*, the *ego*, and the *superego*. These are not physical entities; they exist only metaphorically.

We have lost some of the passion and immediacy of Freud's writing in the process of translation from German to English, which has rendered it mechanistic and abstract. The very term *psychoanalysis* in German refers not to a medical science but to the investigation of the psyche or soul. While Freud spent a lifetime investigating the inner souls of individuals, we are left with abstract translations that make our most passionate urges and conflicts read as if they were foreign structures. Freud used the mythological character of Psyche as the symbol of having to enter a mysterious underworld to find oneself, because he believed that in exploring unconscious conflicts we come to know and ultimately control ourselves.

As we begin to study Freud's structural theory, let us also keep in mind that when American physicians appropriated psychoanalysis and excluded non-physicians from its practice, Freud's actual language and meaning became lost in the translation into a medical model (Bettelheim 1983). We are about to be introduced to a language of ids, egos, and superegos, words that do not capture the intensity of pleasure, love, anger, and ambition or the conflicts between darkest wishes and their prohibitions. So while Freud's writing in German captured the ambiguity of the human heart, American medicine has developed a highly technical language that often fails to capture the complex longings of the human soul.

FREUD'S THEORY OF THE MIND: REVISITED

Before pursuing a formal discussion of the structural theory as it explains unconscious conflict and symptom formation, let us review Freud's original theory of the mind. As Freud studied the interplay between unconscious desire and conscious prohibition as it was played out in the mental life of his patients, he developed the following explanatory paradigms:

1. a theory that all human thought and behavior is motivated by genetically determined, somatically rooted instinctual drives that achieve mental representation in the form of sexual and aggressive impulses;

2. a theory of unconscious influence that describes three strata of mental activity interconnected along a vertical continuum: a deep stratum composed of thoughts, feelings, and memories that are entirely unconscious; an intermediate ("preconscious") stratum composed of mental contents that are neither fully unconscious nor fully conscious; and a relatively small stratum in which all mental activity is logical, reality oriented, and consciously perceived (topographic theory);

3. a theory of psychosexual development emphasizing that, from the moment of birth, children pursue sexual and aggressive aims that evolve predictably through well-defined psychosexual stages;

4. a theory that explains psychopathology in terms of unconscious mental conflict between socially unacceptable impulses that reflect the "pleasure principle" (i.e., the search for gratification without concern for realistic constraints), and the efforts of a "censor" (repression), whose job it is to ensure that every conscious thought, feeling, and behavior is experienced and expressed in morally and socially acceptable terms.

These concepts focused attention on the essential role that unconscious mental processes play in both pathological and normal mental functioning. The first three formulations, in versions that are only slightly modified, inform psychodynamic thinking to this day. The fourth, having been substantially revised, provides a flexible and complex explanation of how mental conflict originates, and how it is resolved within the mind. Together, these four theories emphasize the causal relationship between early developmental experiences and the thoughts, feelings, and behaviors that characterize the mental life of adults. By his insistence on integrating past and present into a unified theory of mental functioning, Freud established a compelling agenda to which contemporary students of the mind must refer, whether they agree or disagree with his specific formulations.

While contemporary therapists tend to talk about developmentally early desires such as *wishes* or *passions*, Freud and his colleagues always used more forceful terms, especially in their early writings. They termed sexual and aggressive wishes as *drives*, *impulses*, or *instincts*, biologically based words that emphasize that the wishes actually motivate thought, feeling, and behavior. This view argues that we are often driven by psychological impulses that we do not understand and therefore cannot control through conscious thought. When viewed from this perspective, Freud's drive theory advanced the ideas that both sexual and aggressive impulses seek expression, but are in conflict with reality and with society. Drive theory led to his development of a theory of the mind as being in conflict with itself. Freud termed his theory a structural theory, which will be the object of our study in Chapter 3.

References

Bettelheim, B. (1983). *Freud and Man's Soul.* New York: Knopf.

Brenner, C. (1955). *An Elementary Textbook in Psychoanalysis.* New York: International Universities Press.

Breuer, J., and Freud, S. (1895). *Studies in Hysteria,* ed. A. A. Brill. Boston: Beacon, 1950.

Brill, A. A. (1921). *Fundamental Conceptions of Psychoanalysis.* New York: Harcourt-Brace.

Erikson, E. (1950). *Childhood and Society.* New York: Norton.

Fraiberg, S. (1959). *The Magic Years.* New York: Scribner.

Freeman, L. (1979). Immortal Anna O. *The New York Times Magazine,* November 11, pp. 30–38.

Freud, S. (1900). The interpretation of dreams. *Standard Edition* 4/5:1–626.

——— (1905a). Three essays in sexuality. *Standard Edition* 7:135–243.

——— (1905b). The aetiology of hysteria. *Standard Edition* 3:191–225.

——— (1908). Character and anal eroticism. *Standard Edition* 9:169–175.

——— (1911). Formulations on two principles of mental functioning. *Standard Edition* 12:213–227.

——— (1912). A note on the unconscious in psychoanalysis. *Standard Edition* 12:255–267.

——— (1914a). Remembering, repeating, and working through. *Standard Edition* 14:218–226.

——— (1914b). On the history of the psychoanalytic movement. *Standard Edition* 14:1–67.

——— (1915). Instincts and their vicissitudes. *Standard Edition* 14:117–140.

——— (1919). Some character types met with in psychoanalytic work. *Standard Edition* 14:311–333.

——— (1920). Beyond the pleasure principle. *Standard Edition* 18:7–64.

——— (1948). Some psychical consequences of the anatomical distinction between the sexes. In *Collected Papers,* vol. 5., ed. J. Riviere. London: Hogarth.

Freud, S., and Breuer, J. (1893). Psychical mechanisms of hysterical phenomena: preliminary communication. In Studies in Hysteria. *Standard Edition* 2:1–48.

Grimm, H. (1983). Peter Pan; Jack and the Beanstalk. In *The Complete Grimm's Fairy Tales*, pp. 1–212. New York: Pantheon, 1972.

Jones, E. (1953). *The Life and Work of Sigmund Freud*, vol. 1. New York: Basic Books.

Lerman, H. (1986). *A Note on Freud's Eye: From Psychoanalysis to the Psychology of Women*. New York: Springer.

Loftus, E., and Ketcham, K. (1994). *The Myth of Repressed Memory*. New York: St. Martins.

Masson, J. M. (1984). *The Assault on Truth*. New York: Farrar, Straus & Giroux.

Milne, A. A. (1927). *Now We are Six*. New York: Dutton.

—— (1925). *When We Were Very Young*. New York: Penguin.

Mitchell, S. (1988). Drive theory and the metaphor of the beast. In *Relational Concepts in Psychoanalysis*. Boston: Harvard University Press.

Noshpitz, J., and King, R. (1991). Latency. In *Pathways of Growth: Essentials of Child Psychiatry, Normal Development*, vol. 1, ed. J. Noshpitz and R. King. New York: Wiley.

Pine, F. (1990). *Drive, Ego, Object Self*. New York: Basic Books.

Rosenberg, M., and Muroff, M. (1984). *Anna O.: Fourteen Contemporary Reinterpretations*. New York: Free Press.

3

Structural Theory

GERALD SCHAMESS

This chapter presents an overview of structural theory as first articulated in Freud's "The Ego and the Id" (1923). In its original formulation, structural theory supplements and expands classical drive theory. It addresses a number of difficult theoretical and clinical issues that had been recognized during the first twenty-five years of psychoanalysis. The theory is called structural theory because it refers literally to structures—the three structures that Freud believed make up the human psyche: the id, ego, and superego. Structural theory presents us both with great contributions to the field and with problems. On the one hand, it is clear and lucid in its explanatory power. On the other hand, it is too concrete and rigid to explain anything as complex and fluid as the inner workings of a human being. The solid, architectural metaphor of the self as composed, indeed constructed, like a building out of three interrelated parts works well, but not fully.

This new theory affirms Freud's view that unconscious sexual and aggressive wishes motivate most, if not all, human behaviors. At the same time, however, it directs attention toward the central role the ego plays in organizing and synthesizing mental functioning. At its core, structural theory calls attention to the processes through which the ego regulates unconscious wishes that are morally and/or socially unacceptable. In their original form, such wishes are repugnant to the adult self and, in addition, violate the norms of ordinary social interaction. By emphasizing the ego's central role in organizing and balancing conflictual forces that arise within the mind, the structural hypothesis markedly expands the range of human behavior that can be explained by psychodynamic theory.

Over the course of the first twenty-five years of psychoanalytic practice, Freud began to recognize that his original ideas did not adequately explain his patients' psychological problems. The clinical data were particularly confounding in regard to two emotional states: depression and anxiety. Freud was keenly aware that, at best, these states are quite distressing, and, at worst, they disorganize mental functioning in extreme ways. Depression presented a serious theoretical problem because Freud's first theory of unconscious mental conflict did not provide a reasonable explanation of why aggression might be directed against the self. Since guilt and self-hatred are hallmarks of depressive illness, the lack of a viable explanation was quite disconcerting to patients and therapists alike. Anxiety was problematic because the early theoretical formulations suggested that it arose as a consequence of unsatisfied sexual desires. This formulation suggested that anxiety would disappear when clients uncovered the unconscious wishes they had previously repressed. While these ideas seemed reasonable from a theoretical perspective, it gradually became apparent that a significant number of clients became more, rather than less, anxious when they began to recognize their unconscious desires.

The theoretical and practical importance of these problems can best be illustrated by a case example (Hayes 1991):

> A therapist reported the treatment of a 9-year-old African-American girl, Shovanna, who suffered from episodic rages accompanied by the temporary loss of well-established psychological functions such as the capacity to speak. These difficulties had severely disrupted her life both at home and at school. Shovanna had seen her mother shoot and kill her father when she was 4 years old.

Prior to the killing she had regularly witnessed violent fights between her parents. During a play therapy session, she had her doll shoot an adult doll and then begin to drown a baby doll in a sink of water. As the play progressed, she panicked, screaming as if she were being killed. Quickly she became even more disorganized, perspiring profusely, wetting herself, and speaking incoherently. When the therapist realized what was happening he/she intervened to "save" the baby doll from "drowning."

An early drive theorist would explain Shovanna's disorganization in terms of unconscious wishes or memories breaking through the repression barrier into consciousness. This explanation would assume unconscious content related to either repressed aggressive wishes directed toward one or both of her parents or repressed memories of a traumatic event she had actually lived through. However, neither of these formulations explains why she turned her aggression against the baby doll after shooting the adult doll (it seems likely that, in fantasy play, the baby doll represented herself), or why she so quickly regressed to an almost infantile level of functioning, wetting herself and losing the capacity to speak coherently. Certainly, her anxiety did not decrease or disappear as she became aware of her aggressive wishes, nor were her depressive feelings ameliorated by her expression of anger (in the play situation) against the adult caregiver (doll).

Later in this chapter we will see that Freud's structural theory provides a more useful explanation of such dilemmas by postulating an unconscious conflict among the different "agencies" (id, ego, and superego) of the mind, with the ego mediating between the opposing forces. In Chapter 4 we will see that ego psychology suggests still another explanation by emphasizing the study of defense mechanisms and the importance of overall ego functioning. Although drive theory, structural theory, and ego psychology complement one another, each framework advances a somewhat different explanation for the same clinical problem. As we will see over the course of this book, the most useful explanations, from both the therapist's and the client's perspectives, are the ones that best take into account the client's level of emotional development, internal (psychological) organization, and capacity for object relations, as well as the social/economic and political contexts in which the client lives.

If we now return to the case vignette, we can probably agree that regardless of the theoretical perspective utilized to understand Shovanna's terror, "remembering" the wishes and/or events she had previously repressed initially made her worse. As her defenses crumbled, she was immediately overwhelmed by a combination of anxiety and terror. When she could no longer repress what had been unconscious, she became younger and younger in her emotional functioning in a desperate effort to reestablish her psychological equilibrium. By regressing to a more and more infantile level of functioning, Shovanna clearly communicated her need for a caring adult who would protect her against the memories, feelings, and wishes she had worked so hard and so long to "forget." Since her emotional response made it clear that she was incapable of managing the terrifying inner world she had thus far concealed both from herself and the world around her, the therapist acted quickly to support her ego by rescuing the baby doll, at which point Shovanna was able to pull herself together. We will discuss the concept of ego support in more detail in Chapter 4.

Freud addressed the theoretical problems related to depression, anxiety, and symptom formation in three major publications: "Mourning and Melancholia" (1917), "The Ego and the Id" (1923), and "Inhibitions, Symptoms and Anxiety" (1926). He was 61 when he published the first of these papers and 70 when he completed the third, quite an accomplishment for a man of his age. In these works he proposed a new and more complex model of the mind that has come to be known as structural theory. He also markedly revised his views about the nature of depression and anxiety, and about the roles these powerful emotions play in mental functioning.

TERMINOLOGY

Before discussing structural theory as it is currently conceptualized, it seems appropriate to revisit what we said in Chapter 2. In discussing how Freud's ideas were translated from German into English, Bettelheim (1982) contends that many of the original concepts were seriously distorted to make them seem more scientific, and therefore more acceptable to the American medical profession. He notes that in "naming" the structures of the mind which we now call the id and the ego the origin of the words id, ego, and superego were actually rooted in the everyday language of German children. "Das es," German for the id, referred to that which is irrational, uncontrolled. "Das ich," German for "I," actually referred to the self, to the idea of "me." Both the "id" and the "I" were imbued with feeling and meaning, which, when translated to the Latin, became cold, mechanistic, and technical.

> No word has greater and more intimate connotations than the pronoun "I." It is one of the most frequently used words in spoken language—and more important, it is the most personal word. To mistranslate *Ich* as "ego" is to transform it into jargon that no longer conveys the personal commitment we make when we say "I" or "me"—not to mention our subconscious memories of deep emotional experience we have when, in infancy, we learned to say "I." [Bettelheim 1983, p. 53]

Bettelheim goes on to explain that in choosing the term *superego* the translators rendered that concept more sterile also. The term Freud chose was *uber Ich* and again he used it as a noun. In English it would be the "Over I." In German *uber Ich* conveys the notion of mature conscience but also carries the feel of the tyrannical persecutory, immature inner forces that can be inappropriately self-blaming. Superego, not even being an English word, has no such resonance for us.

This commentary should be kept clearly in mind when studying structural theory. While the theory in its (mis)translated form has considerable explanatory power, Bettelheim is right in saying that the "scientific" language we currently use objectifies the intimate, emotionally powerful mental processes that define who we are as individuals, and what each of us shares with humanity at large. In the process, it distances therapists both from their own and their clients' inner lives. For these reasons, it is important to balance a thorough cognitive understanding of mental structure and organization with a keen appreciation for the personal meanings and the intensity of feeling that vitalize our inner lives. One way to stay as close as possible to Freud's original meaning is to remember the colloquial, childlike evocative words that he so purposely chose.

FREUD'S STRUCTURAL THEORY

Structural theory postulates that "recurring and enduring psychological phenomena are systematically represented and organized within the mind, and, that the nature of this organization can be usefully described" (Moore and Fine 1990, p. 120). Following from this principle, the theory proposes that all mental activity is organized around the interaction of three relatively stable and enduring structures or agencies of the mind: the id, the ego, and the superego. Each of these structures has a set of unique functions. Although the structures are interdependent, their aims and functions frequently conflict. As a result, their interaction within the mind generates considerable dynamic tension, or what is known as intrapsychic conflict. By studying their interaction, therapists have come to understand unconscious mental conflict, particularly as it leads to neurotic symptom formation (hysteria, phobias, compulsions, etc.). In addition, therapists have learned that the processes that synthesize inherently incompatible wishes and fears also lead to healthy adaptation, even among individuals who have been severely traumatized. Finally, structural theory has taught us to empathize with the unconscious struggles that our clients experience, even when the clients themselves know nothing more than that their symptoms make them feel utterly miserable.

Let us now turn to a fuller description of each of the three psychic agencies.

The Id

The id is described as the source and repository of sexual and aggressive impulses, the seat of all desire. It is the part of the mind that wants what it wants when it wants it. It is also the part of the mind that makes sure there is hell to pay if the gratifications it seeks are either delayed or denied. It is governed by the pleasure/unpleasure principle, the concept that the sole aim of all mental activity is to seek pleasure and avoid pain. It is not directly influenced by reality, morality, logic, or social convention. Classical drive theory assumes that its contents do not change after adolescent development has been completed. In spite of this formidable description, it is assumed theoretically that id impulses can be contained, rechanneled, or transformed as a result of ongoing interaction with the ego. Substantial evidence drawn from clinical practice supports that view.

The id is thought to be rooted in physiological processes that cannot be represented in the conscious mind. Accordingly, only derivative expressions of id aims and objectives reach conscious awareness. When derivatives become conscious they do so in the form of sexual and aggressive fantasies (and/or impulses to act), which allows dynamically oriented practitioners to make inferences about the influences the id is exerting on mental processes at given moments in time.

> A 44-year-old divorced woman who had been in treatment for six months told of a dream in which she had watched her highly respected and admired minister argue vehemently with his wife. At the height of the argument he turned to the client saying, "Let's go off together. I'm fed up with my wife and I'll be a lot happier with you than I ever was with her." The dream ended with the client and the minister going off happily together while his wife receded noisily into the background. Not surprisingly, the client felt considerable shame and guilt as she described the dream.
>
> Even though this dream comes close to conveying the underlying id wishes, it is derivative in that the "real" objects of the client's passion, competition, and disdain are still disguised. As treatment progressed, she revealed that her mother had been seriously ill when she was an adolescent, and that she had spent a great deal of time trying to care for her alcoholic father. She imagined that she would be able to convince him to stop drinking, and remembers thinking, when she was 13 or 14, that she could have been a much better wife to him than her mother ever was. Over time the underlying oedipal dynamics became quite clear, as did the fact that the minister and his wife were stand-ins for her father and mother.

Freud's (1940) formal definition states that the id "contains everything that is inherited, that is present at birth, that is laid down in the constitution—above all therefore, the instincts which originate from the somatic organization and which find a first psychical expression here (in the id)" (p. 145). Earlier, Freud (1933) had described the id as "the dark inaccessible part of our personality. . . . We approach the id with analogies: we call it a chaos, a cauldron full of seething excitation"

(p. 73). Since Freud never modified his view of the id, it is worth emphasizing that the concept of the id, over and above its usefulness as a theoretical paradigm, reflects a philosophical view of basic human nature—no exceptions and no apologies, at least not from Freud.

The Superego

The superego is conceived of as a relatively enduring organization of moral beliefs and prohibitions within the mind. Although psychodynamic practitioners tend to think of it as conscience (in the adult sense of the term), it also represents developmentally early, punitive, and persecutory tendencies. In essence it tells us how we ought to think and act, and how we may not think or act. It "sets up and maintains an intricate system of ideas, values, prohibitions and commands. . . . [It] observes and evaluates the self. . . . [It] compares [the self] with the ideal. . . . [It] either criticizes, reproaches and punishes, or [conversely] praises and rewards" (Moore and Fine 1990, p. 189).

While the superego can represent morality and civilized behavior, it can be as demanding and unreasonable as the id is in the pursuit of pleasure and vengeance. Depending on how and when moral expectations and prohibitions are internalized, the superego may or may not demonstrate an appreciation of moral complexity. In early childhood, it tends to be harsh, rigid, and punitive, often reflecting the principle that an eye for an eye and a tooth for a tooth is the only possible form of justice. If development progresses reasonably well, persecutory fantasies diminish and the superego gradually becomes more flexible, more reasonable in its expectations, and better able to appreciate realistic constraints on moral behavior. As this occurs the punishments it demands become less harsh, and within broad limits it becomes more tolerant of moral ambiguity. A 10-year-old may believe that it is "never, ever, ever okay to tell even the teeniest lie," while an adult may realize that it is sometimes appropriate or even necessary to tell a fib to protect or spare someone.

In performing its functions the superego may diminish or enhance self-esteem, often in extreme ways. In the psychodynamic literature it is frequently described as an internal authority or judge that functions below the level of conscious awareness. Typically, individuals do not recognize the ongoing mental processes of self-evaluation that so acutely affect how they feel about themselves. However, derivatives of these processes regularly become conscious in the form of fluctuations in self-esteem. When, as frequently happens, these fluctuations occur without apparent cause, individuals experience good or bad feelings about themselves that seem unrelated to anything happening in their day-to-day experience. Similarly, individuals may punish or endanger themselves in serious ways, without any conscious awareness that they are doing so.

> A 37-year-old divorced man entered treatment because of depression and the feeling that he could never develop a positive relationship with a woman. He had grown up in a very religious family with an abusive, alcoholic father and a resigned, long-suffering mother. His mother never acknowledged her husband's drinking or his abusive behavior. Although the client expressed a great deal of anger toward both his mother and his former wife, he maintained the view that he had been mostly, if not entirely, responsible for the breakup of his marriage and for the problems in his subsequent relationships with women. Well into the second year of treatment, he acknowledged, with enormous shame and guilt, that he had been sexually involved with prostitutes during his senior year in college. Although he had renounced his family's religious beliefs many years previously, he still felt strongly that his "unclean" sexual activities in college made him unfit to be with a "decent" woman.
>
> In the course of discussing these feelings and memories, he acknowledged for the first time that some of his recent sexual encounters with women had bordered on sexual harassment. It occurred to him that such encounters not only confirmed his view that no decent woman would want him, but also endangered his career. It was only then he realized that if he had been sued and/or fired from his job, he would have finally succeeded in punishing himself as he thought he deserved to be punished ("ruined forever"), for his "sinful" sexuality. It had never occurred to him that the behavior that for so many years had kept him at the edge of ruin might be related to guilt, shame, or a need to punish himself. Since sexual harassment is a problem rooted in social inequality as well as individual psychology, the psychodynamic examination of this client's behavior, while accurate for him, does not constitute a gen-

eral explanation for harassing behavior, nor does understanding these dynamics in any way excuse it.

Freud first proposed the concept of the superego in his 1923 monograph, "The Ego and the Id." In that work he attempted to solve a number of theoretical problems related to guilt, self-hatred, and the workings of an internal conscience. As stated in Chapter 2, he thought the superego came into existence through identification with the parent of the same sex during the resolution of the Oedipus complex. He also thought that, once the superego had been established, its contents remained relatively constant throughout life. In the psychoanalytic literature, identification is viewed both as an ego defense and as a process that contributes to intrapsychic *structuralization*—the creation and maintenance of psychic structure. In this second meaning, identification involves taking in selected aspects of a beloved person and incorporating those aspects as functional parts of the self, without conscious awareness of their origin.

Contemporary theorists think that the contents of the superego change throughout the life cycle. In addition, they view the *ego ideal* as a functional part of the superego. In structural theory the ego ideal plays a significant role because it is thought to contain representations of the attributes we value most in the people we love. It thus functions as the repository of our most cherished ideals, strongly influencing how we wish to lead our lives and whom we want most to emulate.

The Ego

Structural theory starts by postulating that, within the mind, the aims of the id and the superego are diametrically opposed. If structural theory is to work as a general explanation of personality organization, it must then postulate the existence of a third structure. This third structure is needed to mediate the conflicts generated by the two structures that oppose each other. Without a third structure, the mind would be constantly divided against itself, and it would be impossible to conceive of coherent functioning personality or of cohesive individual identity.

Structural theory, then, postulates the existence of the ego. If we think about the theory as a model of the mind in conflict, we recognize that the ego functions as a kind of internal gyroscope. Its most important task is to maintain psychological cohesion and stability in the face of the powerful, conflictual forces that arise when id, superego, and/or external reality clash, that is, when people experience a combination of wishes, moral demands, social expectations, and fears that are inherently incompatible.

Technically speaking, the ego is described in terms of a relatively stable group of functions that organize, synthesize, and integrate mental processes. In the early formulations (Freud 1923), its central role involved mediating between the conflicting demands of the id, the superego, and external (social) reality. Contemporary theorists have markedly expanded its functions to include (1) perceiving the physical and psychological needs of the self as well as the qualities and attitudes of the environment; (2) evaluating, coordinating, and integrating perceptions of the self and external reality, so internal demands can be adjusted to better correspond with external requirements; (3) finding ways of achieving optimal gratification of the sexual and aggressive wishes that are compatible with moral constraints and social norms; (4) repressing or rechanneling those wishes that offend or defy social norms; and (5) preserving a reasonable level of self-esteem by maintaining good relations with the superego. To accomplish these tasks, the ego must be as sensitively attuned to the demands of the physical world and social reality as it is to the demands of the id and the superego. Note that the first four ego functions listed above place as much emphasis on the ego's relationship with external reality as they do on its relationship with the other structures of the mind.

Over the course of psychosexual development, the ego develops a characteristic defensive organization that protects the self from what it perceives as internal and external danger. Different defense mechanisms operate below the level of conscious awareness and are brought into play automatically, whenever the ego begins to experience feelings of anxiety. Anxiety, as Freud reconceptualized it in 1926, is engendered when the different psychic structures come into conflict either with each other or with external reality. Generally speaking, defense mechanisms assist the ego in its efforts to resolve mental conflict. When a specific conflict cannot be resolved, the defense mechanisms work to encapsulate the conflict and reduce its effect on overall mental functioning. We will describe the defense mechanisms and their effect on functioning in some detail in Chapter 4.

COMMON MISINTERPRETATIONS

The concept of enduring mental structures can be quite misleading since it is easily misinterpreted. The first common misinterpretation is based on the idea that the id, ego, and superego are physiological entities located in specific areas of the brain. This idea leads practitioners to talk about the composition, contents, and functions of the various mental structures as if they were organ systems that can be isolated, mapped, and manipulated. The second misconception proceeds on the assumption that the structures of the mind are homunculi (imaginary, diminutive people) who live inside the brain where they perform specific tasks and fight with one another when their aims or functions conflict. When this way of thinking predominates, as it often does, even among knowledgeable clinicians, discussions of intrapsychic conflict take on the quality of battlefield dramas in which opposing armies attempt to defeat or dominate each other (e.g., a powerful id that overwhelms a poorly defended ego and a weak superego in the pursuit of sexual gratification).

In considering this problem, it is important to recognize that Freud and his colleagues deliberately used metaphors to convey complicated ideas about mental functioning that did not lend themselves to ordinary methods of exposition. For example, structural theory draws on architectural and/or anatomical metaphors. Conflict theory evokes images of warfare, while topographical theory (see Chapter 2) is rooted in the concepts and methods originally developed for the study of archeology and embryology.

In spite of their usefulness, metaphorical explanations are also problematic. They lack precision and they mean different things to different people. As a result, they are interpreted in a variety of idiosyncratic ways. For that reason if for no other, it is essential to remember that when we talk about structures of the mind, we are describing very complex mental processes in an evocative rather than a precise way. At its most useful, the structural metaphor encourages us to think in terms of mental functions that cluster together more or less consistently, and that therefore lend themselves to conceptualization as coherent agencies of the mind. In using the concept metaphorically, we are encouraged to imagine how our own and our clients' mental lives might be organized. Such acts of imagination make it possible to temporarily enter the minds of our clients, and are thus beneficial both to therapists and clients. That is, they are beneficial as long as the therapist remembers that structures of the mind are metaphors not metropolises or organ systems.

The following case example demonstrates how structural theory may be used to explain unconscious mental conflict and neurotic symptom formation. It describes how the ego reduces conflict within the mind by creating symptoms that are both pathological and, within the context of an individual's life history, adaptive. This paradox is intrinsic to the theory and is intentional. Freud believed that neurosis is the price humans beings pay for civilization.

A caveat is in order. Freudian theory, especially structural theory, can sometimes sound like a parody of itself. With its metaphors of pipes and dams and eruptions it easily lends itself to ridicule and has been the butt, as it were, of many jokes. It is attributed to Freud that even he said a cigar is sometimes just a cigar. Yet a cigar is sometimes a symbol for the penis and an explosion for an orgasm. In the following case it just so happens that structural theory was the most useful tool to illuminate and alleviate the client's suffering.

Mr. Johannson, a 57-year-old married Caucasian man of Scandinavian descent, requested treatment for compulsive symptoms and obsessive thoughts that interfered with his normal functioning and caused him considerable mental distress. He worked alone on the night shift as a technician in a hydroelectric generating plant, a responsible, well-paying job that he had held for almost twenty years. His final task was to turn off fifteen valves that controlled the passage of water through the turbines that generated electricity. He was supposed to complete this task at 1 A.M., the time of day when electricity demand was at its lowest point and his work shift ended.

In describing himself, Mr. Johannson recognized that he had always been a very "careful" person and a conscientious employee. In the past years it had taken him approximately half an hour to shut off and check the valves. That was twice the time it took the technician who relieved him on his days off. However, it was important to him that he do his work "correctly," so he was willing to take the extra time.

For six months prior to his request for treatment, he had been spending more and more time turning off the valves. The night before his first therapeutic appointment, it had taken him almost three hours to shut down the generating station. As a result he got home well after 4 A.M. In addition to his concerns about the extra time spent on the job and about getting home to his wife so late, Mr. J. said that he was consumed with anxiety about making a mistake. He felt that if he made an error in shutting down the plant, he would cause a massive flood that would injure people and destroy property. "Rationally" he knew this could not happen. Nonetheless, the prospect made him so anxious that he would return to the beginning of the sequence twenty or thirty times a night to make certain that he had not left a valve open. For example, he said, no sooner had he closed valve six, than he began to worry about whether he had fully closed valve two. This made no sense to him because even if he did leave a valve open, the only consequence would be that water would continue flowing through the turbines, drawing down the reservoir and perhaps, reducing the amount of water available to produce electricity the next day. In fact, one of the weekend technicians had done just that and had received a mild reprimand from the supervisor.

This compulsive symptom was making Mr. J. miserable. He complained that it interfered with his relationships with his wife and grown children, as well as with the daytime activities he enjoyed. However, he felt he had absolutely no control over the symptom, and that in fact the symptom was controlling him. He had begun to dread going to work, a feeling that was extremely distressing to him since he had always enjoyed his work.

Over the first three months of treatment Mr. J. explored how his symptom had affected relations with other family members. He remembered that the compulsion had begun at about the time he found he could not maintain an erection when attempting sexual intercourse with his wife. This had happened on two or three occasions, for the first time in his life. He had no idea of why he might have experienced this difficulty and was extremely upset by it. He had consulted his family physician who assured him that occasional impotence was not unusual for a man of his age, and that there was no reason for him to be concerned. He had not been reassured by the physician's advice.

As he continued to talk about his feelings, he realized that in fact, he had been avoiding sexual relations with his wife because he feared being impotent again. He also recognized that his compulsion at work reduced the opportunities for sexual relations with his wife, who in the past had waited up for him until he returned from work, but could not wait for him until 4:00 or 4:30 A.M. She worked during the day and needed a reasonable amount of uninterrupted sleep, a need Mr. J. accepted without question or complaint.

As treatment progressed he gradually recalled that his impotence had first occurred at a time when he and his wife were having a serious disagreement about how much financial support to offer a son who had lost his job. It was unusual for Mr. and Mrs. J. to have serious disagreements, but in this instance he felt his wife was being too indulgent. At one point he found himself secretly wondering whether his wife preferred his son to him, a thought he was quite ashamed of. In spite of his angry and jealous feeling, he had decided to "give in" to his wife's wishes because he remembered how stern and ungiving he felt his own father had been when he was growing up.

In discussing these feelings and memories, he recognized how hurt, angry, and upset he had been, both about his wife's attitude and his son's "inability to take care of himself." When the therapist suggested that these feelings might have contributed to his impotence, he expressed considerable interest in the idea. He decided to discuss his feelings with his wife and promptly did so. She had been unaware of how strongly he felt and was quite concerned about his hurt feelings. Over the next six months, his compulsion gradually disappeared and his relationship with his wife improved markedly. His fears about being impotent diminished, and he was able to resume a mutually satisfying sexual relationship with his wife.

As this case suggests, it would be possible to explain Mr. J.'s compulsion by applying Freud's first theory, that is, that his frustrated sexual impulses had been transformed into anxiety and symptomatic behavior. Yet the clinical material in its fullness required a more complex explanation. Using structural theory, Mr. J. and his therapist came to understand that the initial incidents of impotence stemmed directly from a conscious attempt on Mr. J.'s part to control his angry feelings (aggressive impulses) toward his wife and son. While this attempt was overtly successful, it had serious consequences at the level of unconscious mental functioning. The first consequence appears to have been his impotence, which was accompanied by guilt and a profound loss of self-esteem, as his superego "reproached" him for being so angry with his wife and son. Concurrently, his sexual desires were frustrated as a result of his impotence, and to make matters worse, his self-esteem (ego ideal) was injured when he was unable to live up to his own standard of masculinity. His ego, faced with a serious disruption of intrapsychic equilibrium, an upsurge of libidinal and aggressive impulses, and a significant loss of self-esteem, automatically instituted defensive measures. We will discuss the specific defenses he employed in Chapter 4. Suffice it to say at this point that the ego's work so far (note the anthropomorphism) kept Mr. Johannson's aggressive feelings toward his wife and son outside the realm of conscious awareness and prevented him from acting on them. However, the ego had not addressed the sexual frustration and loss of self-esteem that accompanied his impotence. His inability to maintain an erection threatened Mr. J.'s ideal image of himself (ego ideal), and interfered with the id's demand for genital orgasm. In attempting to provide the id with some measure of substitute gratification, the ego offered a compromise that involved regression to an earlier stage of psychosexual development. In doing so it temporarily diverted the id from its original aim (genital orgasm). With sadness and relief, Mr. J. realized that his wish for sexual intercourse was replaced by fantasies of phallic exhibitionism (see Chapter Two). These fantasies were expressed symbolically through his fear of opening a giant pipe and causing a destructive flood. At this point in the process of symptom formation, the ego was attempting to work cooperatively with the id to provide the best form of gratification that could be achieved within the context of superego and reality constraints.

As the foregoing analysis indicates, the process of symptom formation involves both effort and creativity on the ego's part. Often a symptom is a "compromise formation," combining, in symbolic form (so that different elements will not enter conscious awareness), a forbidden impulse, a threatened punishment, and a solution that attempts to reconcile the conflicting forces. Even when, as in Mr. Johannson's case, the solution is pathological and creates a great deal of psychological misery, it constitutes the best compromise the ego can devise at a particular moment in time given the client's idiosyncratic psychosexual history and the environmental context in which he functions. When symptoms successfully perform the function the ego intends, they encapsulate a troublesome intrapsychic conflict without unduly disrupting overall psychic functioning. For example, a mild handwashing compulsion will, for some people, stabilize unconscious conflict over forbidden sexual or aggressive impulses, without seriously interfering with the individual's day-to-day activities or relationships.

In Mr. J.'s case however, the symptom did not perform this function effectively, as evidenced by his increasing level of anxiety and the fact that, night by night, it was taking him longer to complete the ritual the ego had devised to deal with the conflict. Treatment was thus necessary to help Mr. J. deal more adaptively with this conflict. The case discussion illustrates the usefulness of structural theory in studying and understanding complex mental processes, especially those that lead to symptom formation.

OVERVIEW AND EVALUATION

In creating structural theory, Freud viewed the mind as an arena in which inherently incompatible forces contend with each other for primacy. He viewed the ego as a crucible in which wishes, fears, moral demands, and social expectations are synthesized. The structural hypothesis is thus a theory that explains how the mind is organized and how its different parts interact with one another. It is also a philosophical treatise that proposes a thought-provoking, but not entirely satisfactory, view of the relationship between individuals and the societies in which they live.

Structural theory, like drive theory before it, made a significant contribution to understanding human suffering as a result of intrapsychic conflict. It utilized and expanded drive theory, but gave more primacy to the role of the ego over the id, and eventually laid the groundwork for psychology of the ego. Let us now turn to the development of ego psychology to understand more fully the role the ego plays in maintaining healthy and adaptive functioning.

References

Bettelheim, B. (1983). *Freud and Man's Soul*. New York: Knopf.

Freud, S. (1917). Mourning and melancholia. *Standard Edition* 14:243–258.

——— (1923). The ego and the id. *Standard Edition* 19:3–66.

——— (1926). Inhibitions, symptoms and anxiety. *Standard Edition* 20:75–175.

——— (1933). New introductory lectures on psycho-analysis. *Standard Edition* 22:5–182.

——— (1940). An outline of psycho-analysis. *Standard Edition* 23:144–207.

Hayes, M. (1991). Personal communication.

Moore, B. E., and Fine, B. D., eds. (1990). *Psychoanalytic Terms and Concepts*. New Haven, CT: Yale University Press.

4

Ego Psychology

GERALD SCHAMESS

Structural theory was forged in the aftermath of the First World War, a cataclysmic event in human history. Between 1918 and 1936, Freud and his colleagues witnessed one unthinkable disaster after another: the war itself, the widespread destruction left in the aftermath of the war, the deadly flu epidemic of 1918, the dismemberment of the Austro-Hungarian empire, the Great Depression, the rise of Nazism, the beginnings of the Holocaust, and the preparations for World War II. Deeply pessimistic about human nature at its core, structural theory teaches practitioners about the primitive desires that drive human experience, about archaic codes of justice and retribution, and about the uniquely human struggle to transform amoral childhood wishes and fears into civilized adult behavior.

In contrast, ego psychology began to take shape in Vienna and England toward the end of the period between the two world wars, and it was elaborated after World War II, mostly by European expatriates who emigrated to the United States to escape Nazi persecution. Buoyed by their newfound political freedom and encouraged by the optimism that characterizes American society, they were considerably more hopeful in their fundamental view of human nature and more pragmatic in their approach to understanding mental processes. They shared certain beliefs with the Freudians about the powerful forces in the id, but were far more interested in the ego, which they saw as the preeminent psychic agency. For the most part, they studied and theorized about how the mind accomplishes particular tasks. As a result, ego psychology encourages practitioners to think about developmental processes across the life cycle, about the unfolding of human capacities in response to the interaction between environmental influences and inborn developmental potentials, about the internal forces that propel individuals toward ever more complex and goal-directed patterns of organization, and about the ways individuals either adapt to their social and physical environments or modify those environments to make them more compatible with personal needs and wishes. Because ego psychology focuses attention on the mind's development in interaction with the social and physical world, it provides therapists with a theoretical framework for (1) repairing the effects of arrested, incomplete, or distorted psychosocial development, and (2) facilitating a better fit between the psychological needs of the individual and the normative expectations of society.

CONCEPTUALIZATIONS OF THE EGO

The ego has been conceptualized in different ways over time. Freud's (1923) original formulation was, simultaneously, the most elegant and the most constricting.

> In its relation to the id [the ego] is like a person on horseback, who has to hold in check the superior strength of the horse; with this difference, that the rider tries to do so with his own strength while the ego uses borrowed forces. The analogy may be carried a little further. Often a rider, if he is not to be parted from his horse, is obliged to guide it where IT wants to go; so in the same way the ego is in the habit of transforming the id's will into action as if it were his own. [p. 25]

In this quotation, Freud emphasizes the ego's relative lack of strength in relation to the id. He notes that the horse (id) has most of the energy and power, and that the rider (ego) must depend on the horse's power if he hopes to arrive at his chosen destination. The metaphor suggests that most of the time, but not always, the ego is capable of harnessing the id's energy toward its own purposes.

Eloquent though the imagery is, Freud's view of the ego's relationship to the id and to the external world does not adequately convey how the ego is organized or how it functions. Because the metaphor assumes that the ego's fundamental job is to regulate id impulses, it does not recognize that other ego activities such as perception, cognition, judgment, reality testing, and affect regulation also play vital roles in helping individuals achieve their chosen objectives, that is, if we wish to preserve Freud's imagery, direct the horse where the rider wants it to go. In other words, the metaphor does not recognize that the rider has strength, knowledge, goals, and a range of inborn capacities that contribute to his effectiveness in regulating the horse's behavior.

Contemporary conceptualizations focus on the ego's executive and synthesizing functions. These conceptualizations assume that the ego performs a variety of different tasks that, when combined, allow it to organize and manage mental experience and functioning. The ego attempts to stabilize mental equilibrium, in much the same way as a gyroscope orients and stabilizes the path of a rocket in flight. Since each individual gradually constructs an idiosyncratic style of ego organization over the course of his/her psychosocial development, each individual's ego has idiosyncratic strengths and weaknesses. These particular strengths and weakness reflect the techniques and processes the ego utilizes to manage internal and external stimuli. Over time, the ego organizes the techniques into a stable, repetitive pattern called character structure. This pattern makes it possible for individuals to think, feel, and act in predictable ways throughout the life cycle.

Conceptualizing the ego in terms of its organizing and synthesizing functions focuses attention on the large number of specific tasks that must be accomplished, which people take for granted as they go about their day-to-day lives. The most important of these are (1) perceiving, filtering, and selectively remembering the enormous amounts of information that originate both inside and outside the mind; (2) organizing (editing) the filtered information in ways that allow individuals to think, feel, and act coherently; (3) finding socially acceptable ways of satisfying the conflicting demands of the id and the superego; (4) facilitating all of the routine mental activities (loving, learning, playing, acquiring new skills and capabilities, etc.) that characterize human experience; (5)

mastering the developmental and social challenges that arise normatively over the course of the life cycle; (6) developing capacities that make it possible to deal adaptively with the ordinary stresses of everyday life; and (7) finding ways of minimizing the disruptive effects that trauma has on overall functioning.

While a number of specific ego functions are listed in the section that follows, it is important to keep in mind that the concept of *ego* cannot be understood simply as the sum of its component parts, or even as the sum of its many functions. Contemporary ego psychologists assume that the ego has successfully accomplished its organizing and synthesizing functions when individuals experience themselves as coherent, functional human beings with an enduring sense of personal identity. When viewed from this perspective, the concept of *ego* closely resembles Erikson's concept of *ego identity* (see Chapter 6), and Kohut's concept of the *self* (see Chapter 7).

The following vignette illustrates adaptive, synthetic functioning under stress:

> A 47-year-old divorced woman moved to a new job in a new community where she had no friends or family. Her 22-year-old son, an only child, had decided to pursue his career in their home town, several thousand miles away. She was the oldest child in a large family that had always celebrated Christmas with ceremony and enthusiasm. The Christmas following her move she decided not to go home, fearing she would realize how lonely she was in her new community. To cope with her loneliness, she invited a number of acquaintances to her home for Christmas dinner. She chose people who she knew did not have other plans for the holiday. The dinner was pot luck, and she advised her guests to bring one present to be given to another guest after dinner. When the time for gift giving arrived, she stipulated that none of the guests could open a gift until they had answered a personal question asked by another guest. Her guests, many of whom barely knew each other, were delighted by the game and enthusiastically engaged in asking and answering questions. By the end of the evening the party had generated considerable good feeling, much to the hostess's delight. The lively interaction and good cheer temporarily overcame her loneliness and reminded her of the family gatherings she had enjoyed so much. She also realized that she had gotten to know quite a lot

about her various guests. Although she still missed her son and siblings, she felt she had begun to make a place for herself in her new community.

EGO FUNCTIONS

The ego's ability to organize and synthesize mental activity is based on the interaction of a number of interrelated capacities called *ego functions*. The most important of these are described below. A working understanding of ego functions is enormously helpful both in evaluating client's strengths and weaknesses, and in predicting how they are likely to respond to different therapeutic interventions. In addition, periodic review of a client's ego functioning provides the therapist with a systematic way of evaluating treatment progress.

Reality Testing

This function involves the individual's capacity to understand and accept both physical and social reality as it is consensually defined within a given culture or cultural subgroup. In large measure, the function hinges on the individual's capacity to distinguish between his/her own wishes or fears (internal reality) and events that occur in the real world (external reality). The ability to make distinctions that are consensually validated determines the ego's capacity to distinguish and mediate between personal expectations on the one hand, and social expectations or laws of nature on the other. Individuals vary considerably in how they manage this function. When the function is seriously compromised, individuals may withdraw from contact with reality for extended periods of time. This degree of withdrawal is most frequently seen in psychotic conditions. More frequently, however, the function is mildly or moderately compromised for a limited period of time, with far less drastic consequences. The following vignette describes someone whose reality testing was severely compromised:

A young volunteer entered a locked, padded, seclusion room in a state mental hospital. The room was occupied by a 10-year-old boy who crouched, trembling, in a corner. An aide explained that the boy had become violent that morning, attacking everyone who approached him. Having placed him in seclusion, the staff thought it might com-fort him if someone kept him company. Since the boy conveyed nonverbally that he did not want to be approached, the volunteer sat quietly in the corner furthest away from him. After an hour, the boy asked why the volunteer was there. The volunteer answered frankly and asked if the boy was frightened. The boy asked why the volun-teer wasn't afraid of the snakes. Startled, the volunteer looked around the room. The boy volunteered that the room was crawling with poisonous snakes, which were trying to kill him. The only safe place was where he was sitting, since he was saying "magic words." How-ever, he didn't see any snakes where the volunteer was sitting and asked how the volunteer kept the snakes away.

A second example describes a less severe loss of reality testing:

A young professional woman, Mary, had been living with her aged mother, who died suddenly. The estate was not large, and the will divided the assets equally among Mary and her siblings. Mary mourned her mother intensely. In addition, she needed money des-perately since she had not worked during the years she lived, rent free, with her mother. She had cared for her mother, and with her mother's approval, had pursued an interest in painting. Among her mother's possessions was an heirloom chest that the siblings de-cided to sell to raise cash. Citing her knowledge of antiques, Mary estimated the chest's worth. Much to everyone's surprise, two pro-fessional appraisers evaluated it at half of Mary's estimate. For the next six months, Mary refused to accept the professional evalua-tions, thereby making it impossible to sell the chest. It was only after her grief had moderated and she had found a full-time job that she accepted the "realistic" appraisal and allowed the chest to be sold. Her temporary loss of reality testing was a result of her ego's depletion in the process of mourning her mother.

Judgment

This function involves the capacity to reach "reasonable" conclusions about what is and what is not "appropriate" behavior. Typically, arriv-ing at a "reasonable" conclusion involves the following steps: (1) correlating wishes, feeling states, and memories about prior life experiences with current circumstances; (2) evaluating current circumstances in the context of social expectations and laws of nature (e.g., it is not possible to transport oneself instantly out of an embarrassing situation, no matter how much one wishes to do so); and (3) drawing realistic conclusions about the likely consequences of different possible courses of action. As the definition suggests, judgment is closely related to reality testing and the two functions are usually evaluated in tandem.

I placed the quotation marks around "reasonable" and "appropriate" because sound judgment is a social construct. Clinicians who understand the contextual nature of judgment think carefully about their own cultural values, as well as about the particular social and cultural contexts within which their clients live. For example, the "appropriate" response to a schoolyard threat from peers is quite different for middle-class, suburban high school students than for inner-city students. The middle-class students would, at worst, have to consider the possible implications of being drawn into a fist fight. The inner-city student with good judgment would have to consider the possibility of being shot. The "appropriate" action for the two teenagers would be quite different, and would depend not only on their internal (psychological) organization, but on the realistic dangers they face and the social norms that characterize their particular communities.

On a day-to-day basis, judgment plays a central role in deciding whether one has drunk too much to drive safely; whether one is adequately prepared to pass a test at school; whether the man or woman one has fallen in love with is likely to be a loving, reliable partner; or, at the most basic level, whether one is dressed warmly enough to go out in the cold (you and your mother might disagree about whether you are properly dressed).

Modulating and Controlling Impulses

This function is based on the capacity to hold sexual and aggressive feelings in check without acting on them until the ego has evaluated whether they meet the individual's own moral standards and are acceptable in terms of social norms. Adequate functioning in this area depends on the individual's capacity to tolerate frustration, to delay gratification, and to tolerate anxiety without immediately acting to ameliorate it. Impulse control also depends on the ability to exercise appropriate judgment in situations where the individual is strongly motivated to seek relief from psychological tension and/or to pursue some pleasurable activity (sex, power, fame, money, etc.). Problems in modulation may involve either too little or too much control over impulses.

A group of adolescent male gang members were on a therapeutic camping trip and were cooking shish kebab for dinner over an open fire. Having delayed preparing the fire until they were famished and desperate to eat, they were only able to cook the meat until it was lightly browned on the outside, before they tried to eat it. With each bite, they yelled and cursed, blaming the counselors because the meat was raw. This sequence was repeated several times, and the boys were never able to control their appetites long enough to cook the meat adequately. The only gang member who enjoyed his meal was a boy accurately nicknamed "Joe Fats" because of his love of food. Of all the boys, he alone listened carefully to the counselor's instructions and waited patiently until the meat was cooked. He feasted royally while his friends cursed.

Therapists who work with eating disorders regularly see problems that arise from excessive impulse control. A common but extreme example involves the anorexic teenager who, on eating half a carrot, feels compelled to exercise for several hours to burn off the calories she has consumed. Clients who are severely anorexic cannot tolerate any kind of oral pleasure, feeling that food will make them fat and ugly, and that they have to punish themselves severely whenever they eat.

Modulation of Affect

The ego performs this function by preventing painful or unacceptable emotional reactions from entering conscious awareness, or by managing the expression of such feelings in ways that do not disrupt either emotional equilibrium or social relationships. To adequately perform this function, the ego constantly monitors the source, intensity, and direction of feeling states, as well as the people toward whom feelings will be directed. Monitoring determines whether such states will be acknowledged or expressed and, if so, in what form. The basic principle to remember in evaluating how well the ego manages this function is that affect modulation may be problematic because of too much or too little expression.

As an integral part of the monitoring process, the ego evaluates the type of expression that is most congruent with established social norms. For example, in dominant American culture it is assumed that individuals will contain themselves and maintain a high level of personal/vocational functioning, except in extremely traumatic situations such as the death of a family member, very serious illness, or terrible accident. This standard is not necessarily the norm in other cultures. For example, when Middle-Eastern Arabic women mourn the death of a loved one, their culture expects them to scream and wail publicly, tear their garments, and pull out their hair. Women who do not publicly express intense grief are viewed with suspicion. Their restraint is thought to be inappropriate, suggesting they may not have really loved the family member who died. Compare the Arabic norm for mourning among women with the vignette cited below, which describes an American man who is mourning his mother's death. In doing so, keep in mind the gender differences within American culture; men who mourn are expected to behave differently from women who mourn. Using a cultural standard, the behavior described in this vignette would have been even more problematic had the client been a woman. This first vignette illustrates constriction in the expression of affect:

> A man calmly told his therapist that he was relieved about his beloved mother's death. He noted that she had suffered greatly from a degenerative neurological illness during the last years of her life. He added that his religious beliefs assure him that she has passed on to her "just reward" in Heaven. During the memorial service and funeral he did not shed a tear and after the service he disposed of her household possessions without the slightest conscious awareness of grief. Some weeks later he entered treatment. He was perplexed about the reasons for his reduced work effectiveness and for his difficulty concentrating, even on such simple tasks as reading the newspaper.

The second example involves excessive and inappropriate expression:

A photographer felt his supervisor had unjustly reprimanded him. Consumed with anger, he told the supervisor, "You're not fit to be a pimple on a real photographer's ass." He told friends about this incident who worried about his future, yet he was the only one surprised when he was fired. On being asked to reflect on this behavior, he commented that he had every right to be angry and to express it openly. His only regret was that the remark overestimated his supervisor's competence.

In evaluating this man's overall ego functioning, it would be necessary to consider not only his capacity to modulate affect, but also his reality testing, judgment, and capacity for impulse control. As the example illustrates, all of these functions were seriously compromised.

Object Relations

This function is discussed as a separate theory in Chapter 6. For now it is sufficient to say that this function involves the ability to form and maintain coherent, loving, and/or friendly ties with significant others. The concept refers not only to the people one interacts with in the external world, but also to significant others who are remembered and represented within the mind. Adequate functioning implies the ability to maintain a basically positive view of the other, even when one feels disappointed, frustrated, or angered by the other's behavior. Disturbances in object relations may manifest themselves through an inability to fall in love, emotional coldness, lack of interest in or withdrawal from interaction with others, intense dependency, and/or an excessive need to control relationships.

Self-Esteem Regulation

This function involves the capacity to maintain a steady and reasonable level of positive self-regard in the face of distressing or frustrating external events; anxiety, depression, shame, guilt, and other painful emotions; and triumph, glee, ecstasy, and other exhilarating emotions. Generally speaking, in dominant American culture a measured expression of both pain and pleasure is expressed; excess in either direction is a cause for concern. White Western culture assumes that individuals will maintain a consistent and steady level of self-esteem, regardless of external events or internally generated feeling states.

A 35-year-old professional man who had grown up with rejecting parents had always assumed that his wife sometimes ignored him because she didn't love him. His perception caused him enormous emotional pain and confirmed his private view that he was less than fully human. His idea that he was basically a "loathsome" creature reflected his serious problems in self-esteem. After discussing his feelings in treatment, he asked his wife whether she was avoiding him, and if so, why. To his surprise, he discovered that during childhood she had suffered from a serious learning disability, and still had difficulty focusing her attention when she felt "overstimulated." Since she knew that she loved him and he loved her, she had always assumed he would understand if she was sometimes inattentive. He responded to these revelations by further examining his reasons for viewing himself as a person "with whom no one would voluntarily associate." Thereafter, he found it easier to maintain a positive sense of self-esteem, even when his wife was distracted and temporarily unavailable to him.

Mastery

When conceptualized as an ego function, mastery reflects the epigenetic view that individuals achieve more advanced levels of ego organization by mastering successive developmental challenges. Each stage of psychosexual development (oral, anal, phallic, genital) presents a particular challenge that must be adequately addressed before the individual can move on to the next higher stage. By mastering stage-specific challenges the ego gains strength in relation to the other structures of the mind and thereby becomes more effective in organizing and synthesizing mental processes. Freud expressed this principle in his statement, "Where id was, ego shall be."

An underdeveloped capacity for mastery can be seen, for example, in infants who have not been adequately nourished, stimulated, and protected during the first year of life, in the oral stage of development. When they enter the anal stage, such infants are not well prepared to learn socially acceptable behavior or to control the pleasure they derive from defecating at will. As a result, some of them will experience delays in achieving bowel control and will have difficulty in controlling temper tantrums, while others will sink into a passive, joyless compliance with parental demands that compromises their ability to explore, learn, and become physically competent. Conversely, infants who have been well gratified and adequately stimulated during the oral stage enter the anal stage feeling relatively secure and confident. For the most part, they cooperate in curbing their anal desires, and are eager to win parental approval for doing so. In addition, they are physically active, free to learn, and eager to explore. As they gain confidence in their increasingly autonomous physical and mental abilities, they also learn to follow the rules their parents establish and, in doing so, win parental approval. As they master the specific tasks related to the anal stage, they are well prepared to move on to the next stage of development and the next set of challenges. When adults have problems with mastery they usually enact them in derivative or symbolic ways.

> Over a two-year period, prior to each of her therapist's three vacations, an intelligent, well-educated client from an upper-class family, canceled the last appointment prior to the therapist's departure. She had been abandoned repeatedly by her parents and other caregivers during childhood and had unconsciously established a pattern of leaving relationships before the person she cared about could leave her. Well in advance of his next planned vacation, the therapist pointed out the pattern of missed appointments. She was surprised by the therapist's comment since she was totally unaware both of what she had done and of the feelings connected with her behavior. As a result of the interpretation, she kept all her appointments, including the last one before the therapist left. After the therapist's return she commented that it had taken her more than two years to believe he would actually come back. Moreover, in his absence she realized she had never believed he would want to see her again, even if he did return. The interview material suggests that, over the course of treatment, she had begun to master the separation anxiety that had, until then, interfered with her attempts to establish intimate relationships. From that point onward she could talk more openly about her fears of loss and abandonment. Over time, her attention gradually turned to issues of sexuality and intimacy.

THE USE OF DEFENSE MECHANISMS

Up to now we have discussed the ego in terms of the specific functions it performs. In doing so, we have paid particular attention to the superordinate functions that involve organizing and synthesizing mental processes. We now consider the ego's role in protecting the self from both real and perceived danger, and the methods (defenses) by which it fulfills that task. Defense mechanisms are among the most important of the ego functions.

The self requires protection from four kinds of danger: (1) conflict among the different agencies of the mind (id, ego, superego); (2) conflict in interpersonal relationships; (3) conflict in relation to social norms and institutions; and (4) the disruption of psychological equilibrium that occurs in response to trauma. As noted in Chapter 3, conflict among the agencies of the mind arises when there is a clash between developmentally early, unconscious, sexual, and aggressive wishes (emanating from the id), and the ethical and moral standards represented by internalized conscience (emanating from the superego). Interpersonal conflict arises when an individual's unconscious wishes and fears are incompatible with the behavioral expectations and needs of caregivers, family members, friends, and/or lovers. Social conflict arises when unconscious wishes or fears and the behaviors associated with them challenge consensually accepted social norms. Trauma occurs when psychological equilibrium is disrupted (at least temporarily) by an inescapable need to cope with terrifying external events.

When faced with one or more such dangers the ego uses defense mechanisms to protect the self. Defense mechanisms automatically and unconsciously modify the individual's perception of and/or reaction to danger. The specific mechanisms that are employed reflect the ego's evaluation of the perceived danger and the level of psychosocial development the individual has achieved. Ego psychologists believe that the conscious self feels threatened whenever it becomes aware of unconscious wishes and fears, regardless of whether they originate in the id or superego. Every defense mechanism is designed to keep unconscious content from entering conscious awareness. However, each defense mechanism accomplishes the task in a different way.

While defense mechanisms protect the self from perceived danger, they do so at a certain cost. The cost varies, depending on the mechanisms employed. As one would expect in a hierarchical theory that emphasizes the mastery of stage-specific developmental tasks, it is assumed that individuals employ defense mechanisms that are congruent with their achieved levels of ego organization. At the lower levels of ego organization, the ego uses defenses that significantly interfere with reality testing. Defenses such as denial and projection interfere with overall ego functioning even though they protect the self to a limited degree. At intermediate levels of organization, the ego employs defenses that interfere with impulse control and judgment, turn wishes and fears into their opposites, redirect feelings away from their original objects, impede cognitive functioning, and/or undermine memory. Defenses such as acting out, reaction formation, displacement, and repression interfere less with overall functioning and usually provide the self with better protection. However, the cost of utilizing them may still be considerable. At higher levels of organization, the ego uses defenses (e.g., sublimation and humor) that protect the self quite well and enhance rather than interfere with overall functioning.

Although the distinctions between the defenses used at higher and lower levels of ego organization are important, clinicians should remember that individuals *always* use the *most adaptive* defenses available to them. The unconscious choice of a defense or set of defenses depends on the individual's developmental history, the nature of his/her significant relationships, and the stresses and supports inherent in his/her social environment. Within that context, the defenses reflect the best choices the individual is capable of making. Descriptions of defenses in the literature and in the classroom often sound pejorative, almost as if the person employing them were doing something bad or weak. Nothing could be further from the truth, since defenses are always attempts (often gallant attempts) to preserve psychic integrity and survival under the pressure of stress and fears. It is important for clinicians to remember this principle when deciding how they will deal with specific defenses that interfere with overall functioning.

Anxiety and Defense Mechanisms

Before listing and describing the defense mechanisms used by the ego, it is important to explain how they relate to anxiety. Defense mechanisms are automatically triggered when the ego becomes conscious of anxiety, an inherently distressing emotion that individuals experience along a continuum ranging from mild discomfort to intolerable panic. Unpleasant though it is, anxiety serves a necessary and useful function in regulating mental processes. In much the way that pain alerts us to problems that are likely to affect our bodily functions, anxiety alerts us to problems that are likely to affect our emotional well-being. It is effective as a warning precisely because most people find it so painful and unsettling. When the ego perceives anxiety, it responds by mobilizing the defense mechanisms available to it with the aim of preserving emotional well-being and limiting the degree of functional impairment.

In his monograph "Inhibitions, Symptoms, and Anxiety," Freud (1926) identified five types of anxiety. Each type is associated with a particular stage of psychosexual development and with a normal developmental task that must be mastered if the individual is to progress to the next, more advanced, developmental stage.

Freud thought that the first and most overwhelming kind of anxiety was experienced in early infancy, particularly during the initial twelve months of life. He named it *automatic anxiety* to distinguish it from *signal anxiety*, which he viewed as developmentally more advanced. Automatic anxiety arises in response to excessive levels of frustration, such as hunger, or threatening kinds of stimulation, such as fever, loud noises, or noxious odors, which the infant can neither escape nor modulate. When faced with such painful stimulation, infants have no recourse except to cry, kick, and flail about. Fortunately, they can usually be consoled by an attuned caregiver, even when they are extremely distressed. If outside help is not forthcoming, they can only cry until they exhaust themselves and fall asleep. By doing so they shut off both outside stimuli and internal mental processes.

Contemporary ego psychologists assume that infants experience these terrifying moments at the level of excruciating organic distress, accompanied by inchoate fears that overwhelm them. If this type of anxiety is reevoked in adulthood, it frequently leads to psychotic decompensation. However, some traumatized individuals are able to limit the degree of decompensation, even when so stressed, by utilizing dissociation as a defense. Dissociation, which also shuts off internal and external stimulation, has serious but far less drastic consequences (see Chapter 15 on the anxiety disorders). Because this type of anxiety threatens the total loss of ego functioning, contemporary theorists refer to it as *annihilation anxiety*, a term chosen in an attempt to capture the depth of the overwhelming, disorganizing terror involved.

A second, developmentally more advanced level of anxiety often referred to as fear of loss of the object is originally experienced during the second and third years of life. It involves the fear of being abandoned by a primary caregiver. Since young children depend on adults both for survival and for emotional well-being, abandonment anxiety is quite terrifying. In spite of the degree of terror that the threat of abandonment evokes, therapists should remember that abandonment anxiety is an important marker of developmental progress. Abandonment anxiety can only occur when normal development has progressed far enough for the child to recognize that the primary caregiver exists separately in the world, and therefore is not under the child's omnipotent control. Generally speaking, if this kind of anxiety is reevoked in adults, it is enacted through intensely dependent and/or clinging behavior, or through acting out, which may be antisocial in nature. Acting out unconsciously asserts that the individual does not need a caregiver, is not anxious, and is capable of taking perfectly good care of her/himself without any assistance from anyone else.

The third level of anxiety, called fear of loss of love of the object, is associated with the threat of losing the caregiver's love and esteem. Children ordinarily become aware of this danger during their third and fourth years of life. It is evoked by their attempts to: (1) curb childhood sexual and aggressive desires and (2) accept the behavioral rules and constraints their parents endorse. This type of anxiety is allayed when children can maintain a stable internal representation of the caregiver (object constancy) and are willing to change their behavior in order to win the caregiver's approval.

At a still more advanced level of development, we see an anxiety that is specific to the phallic and oedipal stages of development. This type of anxiety, unfortunately still often referred to as castration anxiety, involves a fear of bodily harm or of the loss of a valued physical or mental capacity. It is based on the child's projected fear of retribution for hostile wishes against a parent. The theory postulates that such wishes are directed against the parent who prevents the child from conceiving a baby with the other parent. Adults who reexperience this kind of anxiety tend to use neurotic defenses and to function at a neurotic level of intrapsychic organization (see Chapter 15). In spite of the psychic pain associated with castration anxiety, its appearance indicates that the individual has successfully mastered the previous stages of psychosocial development and has achieved a high level of ego integration.

And finally, during latency, children may selectively experience anxiety associated with any or all of the earlier stages of psychosexual development (annihilation, abandonment, loss of the caregiver's love, bodily injury, or loss of valued capacities). Different levels of anxiety are evoked because the internalized parental representation, the superego, has assumed responsibility for making moral judgments and meting out punishment. In this role, the superego threatens the ego with phase-specific punishments, based on how it views particular wishes, feelings, and memories. Ego psychologists believe that after latency, if development has progressed reasonably well, the superego will be less punitive in responding both to forbidden wishes and to situations that threaten its moral standards. The mature superego's increased flexibility reduces pressure on the ego, thereby making it possible for the ego to consider a greater range of options in attempting to resolve intrapsychic and interpersonal conflict. Since contemporary theory states that the ego continues to mature during latency and thereafter, people who have mastered the developmental tasks intrinsic to the oral, anal, phallic, and genital stages of development tend to experience anxiety in more transient ways, to employ healthier (higher-level) defenses, and to become less dysfunctional in the face of perceived psychological danger.

Defenses are activated by anxiety in the following way. When the ego perceives anxiety, it responds automatically, first by evaluating the nature of the danger, and second, by reviewing its repertoire of defenses. It chooses a defense or set of defenses that had been effective in managing a similar threat earlier in life. Since all defenses are unconscious, individuals do not ordinarily recognize either the danger they are defending against or the protective mechanisms that have been activated. If the chosen defenses work as intended, anxiety disappears from conscious awareness. However if the defenses fail and do not eliminate or at least diminish the threat of danger, anxiety increases and additional defenses are called into play. Generally speaking, the most threatening perceived dangers are those that reevoke real and/or imagined childhood fears. To illustrate how this process works it is useful to reconsider Mr. Johannson, the power plant engineer who was discussed in Chapter 4.

Mr J. obsessed endlessly over whether he had actually turned off the water outtake valves he was responsible for turning off. During treatment he remembered that he had been very angry at his wife because she had sided with his son in a family disagreement. With considerable shame, he also remembered his feeling that his wife preferred his son to him. This incident reevoked childhood experiences of his own with an indulgent mother and a stern, punitive father. When, some months later, he became impotent for the first time, his childhood anxieties returned. Unconsciously, he viewed his impotence as the punishment he had feared when he was 5— castration. In thinking about his impotence, he was consciously aware of concerns about his sexual functioning, but not of his childhood memories or anxieties.

In attempting to deal with both the current and historical threats to his manhood, his ego employed several different defense mechanisms that had previously protected him from similar dangers (the defenses italicized here are explained in more detail below). When his anger at his wife threatened his childhood defense of *repression* (he remembered nothing about his childhood oedipal wishes and fears), he *regressed* to a developmentally earlier level of psychosexual organization, replacing the wish for genital intercourse with a compensatory wish to exhibit his phallic prowess by creating an enormous flood. (There is a wonderful description of a similar fantasy in Rabelais' [1532] classic book *Gargantua and Pantagruel*, 1946 edition, pp. 41–43.) Realizing that the compensatory wish was also unacceptable, he defended against it through *reaction formation* and *undoing*; that is, in his conscious mind he was determined *not* to cause a flood (*reaction formation*), even if he had to turn the valves on and off for hours at a time (*doing and undoing*). Given the strength of the wish and the intensity of his castration anxiety, the combination of defenses available to him did not work adequately. His levels of anxiety and functional impairment increased, and he finally entered treatment.

Defense mechanisms are easy to understand once their unconscious content has been revealed. However, before the client has acknowledged unconscious content, the underlying meaning of any given defense mechanism is, by definition, unclear. In fact, there is no way a therapist can be certain that a defense mechanism is being utilized until the client acknowledges the defense in some fashion. For example, if the client does not remember an event or a feeling (repression), how can the therapist know that something is missing from the patient's memory? Similarly, if a client says she loves her mother, how can the therapist determine whether she does, in fact, love her mother, or whether she unconsciously hates her mother (reaction formation)? While it is useful for therapists to develop hypotheses based on other information the client has presented, it is important to remember that hypotheses are no more than informed speculations, until they are confirmed or disconfirmed by the client. This way of approaching the unconscious material encoded in defense mechanisms encourages therapists to be respectful of the protective role that defenses play and to remember that clients voluntarily (albeit unconsciously) give up defenses when they feel it is safe to do so. From an ego psychological viewpoint, patience, respect, and careful observation are the crucial elements that permit clients to feel safe enough to recognize the underlying meaning of the defenses they employ.

A HIERARCHY OF DEFENSES

We can now consider specific defense mechanisms and how they operate. Of the twenty or more defense mechanisms identified by Anna Freud (1936) and George Vaillant (1992), we will present eleven. In doing so, we will follow the well-established tradition of categorizing defenses hierarchically. Vaillant (1992) classifies defenses as developmentally early/psychotic, immature, neurotic, and mature/healthy. These categories parallel the stages of psychosexual development that have been discussed previously. Note that the classification reflects a continuum. It begins by describing defenses that drastically impair functioning, continues with defenses that are less disruptive, and ends with defenses that enhance functioning.

Although we will use Vaillant's classification system, we do so with a proviso. Vaillant contends that people who function at the higher levels of ego organization always employ higher-level defenses, the ones he classifies as neurotic or mature/healthy. In contrast, clinical reports suggest that highly functioning clients actually employ a wide range of defenses, including some that are categorized as developmentally early or immature. It seems likely that the ability to call on, as needed, a wide range of different defenses is an indication of emotional health. Vaillant's hierarchical system seems slightly more reliable in describing clients who function at lower levels of ego organization. Such clients seem to have fewer choices available to them, and therefore rely almost exclusively on developmentally early and/or immature mechanisms; however, clinicians have seen many examples of clients with poor ego organization who also have a rich array of defenses at their disposal depending on the level of anxiety they are experiencing.

Developmentally Early/Psychotic Defenses

Denial

The ego ignores or disavows a painful event or the meaning connected with it. When denial is operating, the ego simply does not acknowledge the existence or implications of threatening aspects of external reality. In its most extreme forms, denial contributes to the development of psychotic delusions and hallucinations. However, in most instances it simply blocks out specific events or stimuli that are overwhelmingly threatening to the ego. Denial is ubiquitous among alcoholics and drug abusers who, even in the face of overwhelming evidence, refuse either to admit their addictions or to acknowledge that the addictions interfere with their functioning. For example, in an inpatient alcohol rehabilitation program, it was customary to videotape the original intake interview with every client. Two weeks later, when the clients had "dried out" and regained their health to some degree, they were shown their own videotapes. Approximately a third of them insisted they were not the person who appeared in the videotape. They could/would not believe they had ever looked so desperate, so down and out.

　　Like every other defense mechanism, denial can be adaptive under certain circumstances, especially in realistically dangerous situations where there is no means of escape. Soldiers in combat use denial adaptively to minimize their terror and to keep fighting. Patients suffering from slow, debilitating, and fatal illnesses often use adaptive denial to sustain their will to live.

Projection

The ego deals with unacceptable impulses and/or terrifying anxieties by attributing them to someone in the external world. In this defense, individuals do not experience or acknowledge the projected impulses or anxieties as their own. They feel victimized by some other person who, inexplicably, wishes to injure them, or who blames them for some terrible deed. In its most extreme form, projection dominates the mental life of psychotic or paranoid clients whose relationships with external reality may be seriously compromised. Even when it is utilized by healthier people, projection can be a startling and disconcerting defense. For example, a Caucasian recreation worker tells of having to restrain a 6-year-old African-American boy who had been throwing pool balls around the game room. When the boy had finally been carefully restrained, he turned around, spat in the worker's face and said, "You black boogie bastard." The worker, who was quite fond of the child, later told his supervisor, "I was near tears. I don't know much psychology, but I do know that if one of us sees himself as a 'black boogie bastard,' it's not me."

Because projection can have such a profound negative effect on the people toward whom it is directed, it is important to emphasize the important constructive role it plays in everyday human interactions. Projection makes it possible to fall in love, to care for children, and to empathize with people whose inner lives and cultural experiences are different from our own. All of these quintessential human activities are based on the ability to put one's own thoughts and feelings into someone else's mind and to retrieve them as needed. The process can be more or less healthy, depending on the degree to which the projected thoughts and feelings are congruent with the other person's actual thoughts and feelings.

Immature Defenses

Acting Out

This defense involves the direct expression of wishes, impulses, and fantasies through overt behavior. Immediate action makes it possible for individuals to avoid conscious recognition of distressing feelings they unconsciously experience as intolerable. "Acting out involves chronically giving in to impulses in order to avoid the tension that would result were there any postponement of expression"(Vaillant 1992, p. 245). Addicts who drink because they cannot tolerate depressive feelings, patients who engage in self-mutilation because they feel unsure of whether they are actually alive, and the adolescent who steals a leather jacket because he can't tolerate wanting but not having a jacket of his own are all using acting out as a defense.

Dissociation

In dissociation, a painful idea or memory is separated from the feelings attached to it, thereby altering the idea's emotional meaning and impact. It is a core defense among incest survivors and among adults who were abused as children.

> A 38-year-old woman who had been sexually abused repeatedly as a latency-age child could remember the details of the abuse but did not experience any feelings in relation to the abuse. She knew intellectually that she must have bad feelings, but could feel nothing. After a period of treatment she became aware that when she started to experience feelings connected with the abuse she simply disappeared emotionally, even in the middle of a conversation. "I just go away in my head. Sometimes when I'm driving, I look around and realize I've lost half an hour. I don't know where I am, how I got there, or what's been going on in my head. I've just been gone even though I've been driving the car. I get scared about that. I wonder whether some day I'll have a serious accident."

Regression

This defense involves a retreat to an earlier level of psychosexual functioning and/or ego organization. Typically, it appears when a specific developmental challenge cannot be mastered or when an environmental stressor creates high levels of anxiety. While it usually makes its first appearance as a defense during the anal stage of development, it is utilized throughout life regardless of the individual's level of ego organization. In childhood, regression is frequently seen after the birth of a sibling. For example, an older child temporarily loses bowel or bladder control, even though control had previously been well established. In such instances, the regression is caused by jealousy of the new baby and by the older child's fantasy that s/he would be equally loved and fussed over if s/he was a baby.

Regression may also take place "in the service of the ego." When adults become physically ill and need care, they frequently take to their beds, asking to be fed, bathed, and pampered. While such behavior reflects a transitory wish to be a baby again, it may also facilitate healing. When regression is temporary, as in this example, it enhances ego functioning by providing individuals with a moratorium during which they do not feel they have to act in mature and responsible ways. As a result they are able to reassess their emotional problems, recover their strength, and return more rapidly to prior levels of functioning. When this occurs, stress on the ego is reduced, and the degree of functional impairment is limited. Under such circumstances regression not only protects the self from danger but also enhances the ego's adaptive capacity. However, in circumstances where regression continues over long periods of time, the defense significantly impairs ego functioning. In the case of regression, the duration and degree of regression markedly affect the "cost-benefit" ratio because the use of the defense becomes counterproductive.

Neurotic Defenses

Repression

This defense simply involves complete forgetting. Thoughts, memories, and feelings that are repressed simply do not exist in the person's conscious mind. Repression protects the self from unwelcome knowledge such as the awareness of desires that defy moral standards, or fears that are too terrifying to contemplate, or disappointments that are too difficult to bear.

> One young woman in treatment began talking about how much she had suffered in school from her serious, yet undiagnosed, learning disabilities. She described not only feeling stupid and ashamed but also alone and unprotected because no family member or teacher paid enough attention to help her figure out what was wrong. As the patient described those painful feelings and events, the therapist was thinking rather smugly about how vigilant and active she had been regarding her own children's learning disabilities and what excellent help she had gotten them. After the session, the therapist expected to feel compassionate toward the patient and pleased with herself, and was therefore surprised when she felt very frightened and ill at ease. She was even more surprised during the next session when she sat there nervously, hoping the subject of learning disabilities would not come up. Her anxiety grew until several days after the second session she suddenly remembered that she too

had struggled with learning disabilities as a child and that no one had been aware of her difficulties or helped her with them. Like her patient she had learned to get decent grades by paying very careful attention in class and compensating in every way possible for her visual-motor impairment. She had repressed these painful memories because she had not wanted to realize how angry and hurt she was at her parents for their neglect. During the first session in which her client talked about learning disabilities the therapist remembered how good she was with her own children so that she could forget how bad her parents had been with her. But the repression did not work for long since the patient's story brought the therapist so close to the memory and the truth.

Reaction Formation

This defense transforms an unacceptable wish into an acceptable one, a "bad" wish into a "good" one. When individuals employ reaction formation as a defense, the wishes of which they are consciously aware are the exact opposites of the wishes they actually want to fulfill. To understand this defense one must recognize that expressed love can conceal hatred, expressed mercy can conceal cruelty, and expressed obedience can conceal defiance. For example, parents who are very angry at their children will often be overly solicitous about the child's health and well-being, sometimes to the point of emotionally suffocating the child. Similarly, people who feel sexual desire for an unavailable partner will often describe publicly, at great length, in very derogatory terms, how sexually unattractive the object of their desire is. Although such talk may be part of a conscious strategy to challenge and attract a partner, when the underlying attraction is unconscious the negative comments serve a defensive purpose.

Displacement

In this defense unacceptable sexual and aggressive wishes are directed away from one person and redirected toward another. Usually, wishes and impulses are directed away from a person who is perceived as inappropriate and/or dangerous, and redirected toward a person who is perceived as appropriate and/or safe.

A young therapist working in a mental health clinic was unconsciously angry at his supervisor. He was unaware of his anger, in part because he was afraid the supervisor would evaluate him poorly. During his supervisory meetings, he complained bitterly about the clinic administration. Even though he was expressing intense anger he was unconcerned about his supervisor's response, since he knew she shared many of his negative opinions. He was quite surprised one day when his supervisor quietly asked him whether he might also be angry at her. At that point, he could no longer maintain the displacement, and he became consciously aware of his angry feelings for the first time.

Displacement occurs predictably and normatively during adolescent development. One frequently sees adolescents of both genders dating people who bear a distinct resemblance to the parent they had most loved when they were young children. Since one of the fundamental developmental tasks of adolescence is to find a partner, outside the family, toward whom one can feel passion, and with whom who can share one's most private thoughts and feelings, the adolescent's use of displacement is an essential and constructive component in his/her attempt to master this essential stage-specific task. Displacement is also the mechanism that takes place in transference and countertransference. Greenson (1965) described it best when he said that transference is "a new edition of an old relationship . . . an anachronism, an error in time. A displacement has taken place; impulses, feelings and defenses to a person in the past have been shifted onto a person in the present" (p. 201).

Undoing

This defense involves acting in ways that symbolically or actually make amends for prior thoughts, feelings, or behaviors that one feels guilty about and/or that threaten punishment. Mr. Johannson's inability to decide whether he had closed the water outtake valves at the power plant is a prime example of undoing. Having actually closed the valves, his unconscious wish to create a flood undermined his certainty about whether they really were closed. To make sure he had closed them, he had to reopen them. Having reopened them, he needed to close them again. On proceeding to the next valve, his unconscious wishes again made him feel uncertain about whether the last valve was open or closed, so it was necessary for him to start over again. As with Mr. Johannson, this process can go on for very long periods of time. Undoing is a defense most often seen in clients with obsessive-compulsive symptomatology (see Chapter 15). When it operates to a limited degree it can be quite adaptive. For example, accountants and computer programmers who are expected to make as few errors as possible are often praised for their use of doing and undoing, which is viewed as evidence of carefulness by their supervisors. When the defense gets out of hand, however, it disrupts ego functioning in profound ways.

Mature Defenses

Sublimation

This defense involves a process in which the ego transforms asocial sexual and aggressive wishes into derivative behaviors that are socially acceptable, or valuable.

> A gangly adolescent, who at 15 is six and a half feet tall and weighs a hundred and forty pounds, feels awkward, unattractive, and unlovable. He hates his peers, all of whom are better looking and more popular than he is. Three years later, he has learned how to dress, and by emphasizing his height, has made himself into a striking figure. He has worked on his coordination by studying dance and has developed some undiscovered talents as an actor. Instead of avoiding people and hiding in shame, he now participates in public theater performances and has become popular with his peers. He has quite literally transformed himself, and the self-hatred he thought he would carry to his grave has metamorphosed into a healthy, if somewhat exhibitionistic, appreciation of how wonderful he has become.

Another example shows how socially sanctioned behavior can demonstrate sublimation.

> Professional football players routinely display levels of aggression that, if enacted anywhere but in a football stadium, would quickly

bring them to trial for assault and battery. As professional athletes, however, they are extremely well paid for their talents. As long as they follow the rules, they are encouraged to knock people down and run over them in a kind of controlled mayhem. If they are good at the sport, they become role models as well as sex symbols for a sizable percentage of the population. The kind of aggressive behavior that, under other circumstances, would cause them and society enormous trouble has been transformed into a socially desirable activity.

Humor

This defense permits the overt expression of painful or socially unacceptable wishes and feelings without discomforting the individual who is being humorous or (in most instances) offending the listeners. Like sublimation, humor frequently enhances overall functioning.

> An extremely intelligent 7-year-old boy whose parents were engaged in a bitter custody battle was referred for treatment because of problems with peers and poor school work. On settling in for his first treatment interview, he asked whether the therapist had heard the story of the "Titchenstein monster." The therapist had not, and the boy told the following story. "Long ago and far away, nine children were playing on top of a high dam that was holding back a huge reservoir of water. Suddenly the dam began to crack, and the children realized they could not save themselves, since they had been playing in the middle of the dam. Their parents, half of whom were on one side and half on the other, could not reach them either. Just when they feared they were doomed, out of the water rose the Titchenstein monster, an enormous beast with red eyes, and flames coming out of his mouth. With one great, hairy claw he scooped up all the children, depositing half on one side of the dam, and half on the other. The children and parents were delighted to be reunited." At this point the child stopped, and asked the therapist if he had guessed the moral to the story. The therapist had not, and the child said, "You should have! . . . The moral is, a Titchenstein saves nine."

THE AUTONOMOUS EGO FUNCTIONS

Any serious discussion of ego psychology requires careful consideration of the work done by Heinz Hartmann. Among his other contributions, Hartmann (1939) articulated the view that a number of important ego functions are genetically programmed (inborn), and that these functions normally operate outside the sphere of intrapsychic conflict. This formulation made ego psychology into an independent, free-standing theory with important theoretical and clinical practice implications. When Hartmann first proposed it, the formulation was startling and innovative. It revised the prior view that at the beginning of life all psychic energy is concentrated in the id. The earlier formulation stated that it was necessary for the ego to acquire energy from the id, as id impulses were tamed during the course of psychosexual development. In that formulation, the ego's capacity to influence mental life depended entirely on its ability first to neutralize id energy, and then to use that energy for its own purposes. In constructing the horse and rider metaphor cited earlier, Freud tried to show that the rider (ego) could only pursue life goals only if he could control, direct, and manage the horse's (id's) superior strength and energy.

By postulating an autonomous, conflict-free sphere of ego functioning, Hartmann revised Freud's view, persuasively arguing that from birth onward the ego is endowed with energy and power of its own, allowing it to perform a number of essential mental functions, independent of id wishes or superego constraints. The functions that have primary autonomy include intellectual ability, perception, and motor activity (motility), as well as inborn capacities that facilitate the acquisition of language and make it possible to plan and initiate goal-directed behavior. Under ordinary circumstances, the autonomous functions are not affected by conflict of any kind. The ego is capable of maintaining and further developing these functions during the various phases of psychosexual development, except in instances where children are born with genetic limitations or have been subjected to severe and persistent mistreatment (neglect, abuse, rejection, or other trauma) early in life.

In this context, Hartmann proposed the view that autonomous ego functions develop within normal limits if the infant's genetic endowment is adequate, and if the infant's caregivers provide an "average expectable environment." Because the infant is totally dependent on its caregivers, normal development unfolds in the context of a human environment that recognizes and meets the infant's basic needs for nurturance, protection, care, and stimulation. Hartmann suggested that the "fit" between an infant's inborn temperament and the caregivers' ability to understand and address the infant's idiosyncratic ways of conveying need states is crucial in determining the infant's subsequent developmental course. The concept of an average expectable environment assumes that when there is a reasonably good fit between infant and caregiver, and the caregiver provides the infant with a reasonably protective and gratifying environment, the infant's physical and psychological capacities will develop within what are consensually considered to be normal limits. As noted above, however, in instances where the child's genetic endowment is compromised, or when the social environment is less than average and expectable, even autonomous ego functions can be disrupted. When this occurs, children experience significant emotional distress and suffer from serious functional impairments.

> Shovanna, the 9-year-old African-American girl who had seen her mother kill her father when she was 4 years old, (see Chapter 3) had a well-developed language ability for a child her age. However, when her spontaneous play unexpectedly reminded her of her father's murder and of her overwhelming fear for her own and her mother's safety, she instantaneously lost the capacity to speak coherently. She could say nothing about what she was experiencing and began to make the sounds an infant would. Because the killing occurred when Shovanna was 4, her capacity to use language had developed adequately before the trauma occurred. When the trauma was reevoked, however, she temporarily lost the function, even though it had previously been well established. Had the original trauma occurred at an earlier age, she might well have become mute, an outcome that could have permanently compromised her language development. Without language, her overall ego functioning would have been seriously, and perhaps permanently, impaired.

In considering the concept of the average expectable environment, consider how children are affected when they grow up poor, ill-fed, ill-housed, ill-educated, with inadequate medical care, and with little or no protection from the violence that permeates their communities.

Shameful though it is in a society as rich as ours, this litany of deprivation describes the average expectable environment for the substantial number of American children (25 percent) who grow up in poverty. Consider how parents are affected when they face the reality that they cannot provide adequate food and shelter for their children. Consider what it means when parents have to acknowledge to themselves that the environment in which they live not only deprives their children of adequate food, shelter, and health care, but may also be life threatening on a day-to-day basis.

Given what we know about the effects of severe deprivation and trauma, it is remarkable that so many children who grow up poor and who are surrounded by violence throughout childhood and adolescence reach adulthood with their ego functioning intact. The capacity for adaptive functioning that we see in these children is a tribute both to their innate resilience and to the efforts of caregivers who, against all odds, somehow provide them with a human environment that is good enough to promote healthy growth. Certainly, the conditions under which they live do not provide them with an average expectable environment as defined by middle-class standards. And just as certainly, the environment these children live in is not the one their parents would choose for them, if their parents had a choice.

Hartmann's other major contribution to ego psychology was the concept of *adaptation*, a term clinicians use regularly to describe behavior that allows individuals to cope advantageously with the environments in which they live. In Hartmann's view, adaptation can involve *alloplastic behavior*, behavior through which individuals change the external environment to better fit their own wishes and needs. Adaptation can also be *autoplastic* in nature. In autoplastic adaptations, individuals change how they feel and act to better fit the demands and expectations of the external world. In either case, adaptation is desirable when it creates a more harmonious relationship between the individual and the external world. Clinicians assess adaptive capacity by evaluating the client's ability to be productive in love and work, to enjoy life, to maintain mental equilibrium under stress, and to change when change is called for in ways that preserve an inner sense of ego integrity. Adaptive capacity is a fundamental attribute of healthy ego functioning. Successful adaptation is well illustrated by the parents and children described above who achieve high levels of ego integration in spite of dangerous physical and social environments that are unsupportive at best, dangerous most of the time, and deadly with disconcerting frequency.

MASTERY RECONCEPTUALIZED

In a significant elaboration of the concept of autonomous ego function, White (1959, 1960/1971) proposes that mastery be viewed as a primary motivational force, equal in importance to sexuality and aggression. He argues that there is an inborn human need to master developmental, interpersonal, and environmental challenges. From his perspective, human beings work toward achieving higher and higher levels of competence for the sheer pleasure of doing so. People who study, learn, theorize, challenge themselves, overcome difficulties, and change their environments to conform better to personal wishes and needs are simply being true to their species-specific basic nature.

White (1959) emphasizes that humans are born with a strong desire for "effectance" and "competence." Those concepts can be understood in terms of "what the neuromuscular system wants to do when it is otherwise unoccupied or is gently (rather than intensely) stimulated by the environment" (p. 321). Through this definition, White emphasizes that as a species we are intrinsically motivated to do a great many things that are not directly or indirectly related to need states. When we are not actively seeking gratification or avoiding pain and punishment, we work, play, interact, explore, and learn things. In White's view we engage in these different activities because we belong to an intelligent and curious species, which experiences pleasure in exercising and developing the capacities we are born with. White is eloquent in arguing for "effectance" as a basic motivating force. He states:

> The infant's play is indeed serious business. If he did not while away his time pulling strings, shaking rattles, examining wooden parrots, dropping pieces of bread . . . when would he learn to discriminate visual patterns, to catch and throw, and to build up his concept of the object? . . . [Infancy is] a time of active and continuous learning, during which the basis is laid for all those processes, cognitive and motor, whereby the child becomes able to establish effective transactions with his environment and move toward a greater degree of autonomy. Helpless as he may seem until he begins to toddle, he has

by that time already made substantial gains in the achievement of competence. [p. 326]

OVERVIEW AND SUMMARY

Ego psychology has markedly expanded the range of psychodynamic formulations that attempt to explain motivation. While childhood sexual and aggressive wishes are still viewed as primary, this expanded theory adds the autonomous ego functions and the desire for "effectance" to the list of variables that motivate behavior. This is a very significant change in that it encourages a fuller, more balanced view of human activity and provides support for assessments of human behavior that emphasize the importance of positive, growth-inducing capacities. In evaluating the problems a client brings to treatment, cognitive capacities, goal directed behaviors, and the desire to overcome difficulties are all viewed as indications of health. An appreciation of the client's strengths and latent capacities makes it possible to approach treatment in an optimistic and respectful way without losing sight of the underlying problems in ego functioning and adaptation.

By focusing on specific ego functions, carefully examining defense mechanisms, and placing anxiety in a developmental context, ego psychologists have emphasized the ego's supraordinate role as the organizing and synthesizing agency within the mind. It is the agency that manages what we think, what we do, and how we feel. This theoretical framework tells us that clinical treatment is best directed toward strengthening the ego both in its relationship to reality and its relationship to the other agencies of the mind. In this context, ego psychologists have reaffirmed the complementarity between individuals and society. The concept of adaptation makes it unmistakably clear that individuals do not exist separately from their social and biological contexts. As a species we are not only capable of changing our own behavior to suit a range of different environments, but are also capable of changing the environments we live in, to better suit the wishes and needs we bring to them.

The theoretical changes outlined above have had a profound effect on therapeutic practice. Given the extent to which they have changed practice, it seems fitting to end this chapter with a case example.

Some years into treatment Ms. R., a 47-year-old woman suffering from a serious depression, feelings of being "unreal," and the conviction that she was "crazy" in spite of the "normal" facade she maintained at work and in her social relations, began to talk about how worried she was about the safety and well being of her 34-year-old, drug-addicted brother, Colin. Colin no longer was in contact with her or with any other member of her family, having disappeared at least a decade before after a violent argument with her father (who had died in the interim). Ms. R. had information that suggested that Colin was living in an impoverished neighborhood of a large city, and she often thought about visiting that city in the hope of finding and helping him.

When Ms. R.'s male therapist commented on her love for and concern about Colin, Ms. R. went on with her plan to rescue him for a moment or two and then stopped in mid-sentence, staring intently at the therapist. After several minutes of silence, she continued by saying, "I don't think I've ever talked to you about this. When I was 13, Colin was born. My mother stayed in the hospital for at least a week, and my father invited me into his bed to sleep with him. I don't think he did anything overtly sexual, but I was very uncomfortable being there, and after a night or two, I told my mother. She must have talked with my father that same day because he told me that I needn't come to bed with him that night. After that, my relationship with my father changed drastically. Until then, he and I had always been close. From that time onward, throughout my adolescence, he criticized me constantly, calling me a slut and a whore. In front of the entire family, he would ask me who I was sleeping with now. Of course, as a good Catholic, I was hardly dating. I wasn't even kissing boys, let alone sleeping with them. My mother never said a word on my behalf, and as you know, by the time I was 17, I felt my survival depended on getting away from the family. When I left for college, I was certain my father and mother were both glad to see me go.

"Whenever I've tried to think about this time in my life, it was like stepping into a black, swampy pit where I would be sucked down and drowned. I don't know why, but when I heard you say that I love my brother, I suddenly imagined you would take my hand and walk with me into the pit, so I wouldn't be alone anymore. I thought if you held my hand the pit would still be horrible and dangerous, but that somehow I would be able to get out alive; I wouldn't drown. Looking back on all this, it seems strange. My mother was so exhausted after taking care of all my other sisters and brothers, that, being the oldest child, I raised Colin almost as if he were my own. I think that taking care of him made it possible for me to survive those awful years until I left home. During all of that time, I never knew whether my father's accusations were true. Mostly, I think I believed him."

This vignette is noteworthy because the client spontaneously remembered the traumatic events of her adolescence after she was convinced that the therapist understood and accepted the love she felt for her brother. That knowledge gave her hope that the therapist would stand by her during her worst moments of terror. The growing strength of her relationship with the therapist, and the image she created in her mind—of his taking her hand much as a parent takes the hand of a frightened child—gave her the courage to remember that her father had not only invited her into his bed, but had also abused her psychologically throughout adolescence. In subsequent sessions, she could talk in a feeling way about how the changed relationship with her father and mother (who, she felt, had not protected her from her father) had affected her view of herself. She recognized that she felt crazy in the face of her father's accusations and that she has felt crazy ever since, no matter how she has tried to conceal it.

If we assess Ms. R.'s functioning, using insights derived from ego psychology, we can make the following comments. Ms. R's social and vocational functioning seemed relatively intact in spite of her underlying view of herself as crazy. She experienced serious problems in maintaining self-esteem, as well as some encapsulated difficulties with reality testing, evidenced by her continuing uncertainty about whether she actually had been/still is a whore and a slut. Judgment, affect regulation, and impulse regulation were all intact, with some tendencies toward constricted expression. Her capacity for mastery was well developed in the intellectual, social, and vocational spheres. Under ordinary circumstances her primary anxiety focused on the dangers inherent in losing the love and esteem of a significant other, but when she remembered her adolescent abuse she briefly regressed to fears of annihilation. By the end of adolescence when she left home to go to college, her ego had regained its capacity for synthetic functioning and had successfully defended against the memories of abuse by repressing them.

Ms. R.'s capacity for relationships was well developed in a superficial way. On a deeper level, relationships were problematic for her because she could only relate to people by molding herself to their expectations. This made it possible for her to avoid the danger of subsequent abuse, but it foreclosed the possibility of genuine intimacy. Her experience in treatment made it possible for her to imagine a relationship in which another person would be interested in and attuned to her needs and feelings, without exploiting her.

As the treatment process indicates, the ego psychological approach did not focus on uncovering her unconscious sexual and aggressive desires, but instead encouraged the development of a new relationship that strengthened her overall ego functioning. This is the most important contribution ego psychology has made to contemporary treatment technique. It is no overstatement to say that the effects have been profound.

The next chapter considers the work of ego psychologist Erik Erikson, who expanded the concept of the ego to include self and identity and who described how the ego develops over the course of life.

References

Freud, A. (1936). *The Ego and the Mechanisms of Defense*. New York: International Universities Press.

Freud, S. (1923). The ego and the id. *Standard Edition* 19:3–66.

——— (1926). Inhibitions, symptoms and anxiety. *Standard Edition* 20:75–175.

Greenson, R. (1965). The working alliance and the transferences nemesis. In *Explorations in Psychoanalysis*, ed. R. Greenson, pp. 199–225. New York: International Universities Press, 1978.

Hartmann, H. (1939). *Ego Psychology and the Problem of Adaptation*. New York: International Universities Press.

Rabelais, F. (1532). *Gargantua and Pantagruel*. New York: Dutton, 1946.

Vaillant, G. E. (1992). *Ego Mechanisms of Defense*. Washington, DC: American Psychiatric Press.

White, R. W. (1959). Motivation reconsidered: the concept of competence. *Psychological Review* 66:297–333.

——— (1960/1971). The core of personality: fulfillment model. In *Perspectives on Personality*, ed. S. R. Maddi, pp. 85–146. Boston: Little, Brown.

5

Psychosocial Ego Development: The Theory of Erik Erikson

JOAN BERZOFF

In Chapter 4, we considered the functions of the ego: to organize, synthesize, defend against unwanted impulses, feelings, and anxiety, and to adapt to internal demands and societal realities. We looked at how the ego tries to master the forces within the internal world and the external environment. We considered some of the ways in which the ego functions independently of psychological conflict and we saw how the ego provides some coherence and continuity to the self.

ERIKSON, THE EGO PSYCHOLOGIST

Erik Erikson was a particularly important ego psychologist who examined how the ego maintains coherence over the course of an average expectable human life cycle. He theorized that the ego is shaped and transformed not only by biological and psychological forces but also by social forces. Erikson thus developed a *psychosocial* theory, modeled on Freud's psychosexual theory, which joined principles of ego psychology with Freud's epigenetic principles from drive theory.

Erikson made a lasting impact on our understanding of human function and dysfunction by expanding the principles of psychological development beyond childhood. He linked erogenous zones with particular modes of ego functioning and demonstrated how self and identity operate within a widening radius of social relationships.

In this chapter we examine how Erikson's theory expanded Freud's premise that psychological development occurs within the first fifteen years of life. Erikson's theory explored the ways in which social relationships and social institutions foster or hinder ego development throughout the life span. Erikson defined ego identity as a sense of personal continuity and sameness, personal integrity and social status, that occurs as a result of the interactions between self and the environment. He emphasized the importance of sociocultural environment in fostering or hindering ego development. He was the first psychoanalyst to articulate the interaction between the person and her environment and to consider the influence of culture and society on identify formation. Erikson was also the first life-span developmentalist who maintained that personality development is not fixed in childhood, but involves an unfolding of ego psychological developmental tasks over the life cycle. He wrote, "If everything goes back to childhood then everything is someone's fault and trust in the power of taking responsibility for oneself is undermined" (Evans, 1981, p. 27).

Like Freud's, Erikson's theory of ego development was epigenetic. Each developmental stage unfolds from infancy through old age; each stage builds on previous stages and affects later stages. Development is invariant, sequential, and hierarchical. Every individual negotiates basic developmental tasks and basic biopsychosocial crises from birth to death in a predictable developmental sequence. Erikson clustered these tasks into "eight ages of man," which he defines as infancy, early childhood, play stage, school age, adolescence, young adulthood, adulthood, and old age.

A Strengths Perspective

As an ego psychologist, Erikson's interest was not so much in pathology as it was in health; and so he identified the ego strengths as well as vulnerabilities that a person faces at each junction of life-cycle development. Erikson defined health in terms of the ways in which a person (1) masters her environment, (2) has a unified personality, and (3) perceives herself and her world accurately.

Identity

Identity was as central to Erikson's thinking as sexuality was to Freud's, his theory influenced by his own identity struggles. Born in Frankfurt, Germany, in 1901, Erikson had been abandoned by his biological father, who was Danish. He was raised by his mother, a German Jew, and his stepfather, a German-Jewish pediatrician, neither of whom told him about his biological origins until he was 18. In fact, his mother acted as if his biological father never existed, although Erikson clearly had some awareness of him based on his own sense of difference. As a child, then, Erikson suffered a series of identity crises. He was a blond, blue-eyed son of a Jew, thought to be Jewish by non-Jews and non-Jewish by Jews. His sense of not belonging, within his community or within his own family, became a central theme in his work. Interestingly, in adulthood he reinvented himself with a Danish name, that of the son of Erik or "Erikson." When he fled to America in the 1930s to escape the Nazis, he first attempted to emigrate to Denmark. Refused entry there, he subsequently came to America, once again having had the experience of being an outsider who had been excluded from what he considered his real homeland.

Erikson did poorly in school and, in fact, dropped out for a time. He would later conceptualize such periods as "psychosocial moratoria" during which adolescents temporarily suspend their identities, to discover and define themselves before making adult commitments. During his own psychosocial moratorium at age 17, he traveled around Europe as an artist. In 1927, he met Peter Blos, another ego psychologist, who was then tutoring the children of analyst Dorothy Burlingham. Anna Freud and Dorothy Burlingham worked together, and Erikson became a teacher in their Montessori school. Soon after, he was analyzed by Anna Freud. With neither a medical degree nor any formal training beyond high school, he was invited into the Viennese analytic circle. Without professional credentials, however, he continued to be an outsider. Although his marginal identity was costly to him, it was also beneficial as it afforded him a certain degree of flexibility within psychoanalysis and propelled him toward interdisciplinary pursuits (Monte 1980).

In 1933, taking with him the theoretical viewpoints from both ego psychology and drive theory, Erikson moved to Boston, Massachusetts, where he collaborated with anthropologists Margaret Mead and Ruth Benedict. This led to his cross-fertilization of anthropological, psychoanalytic, and ego psychological ideas. After teaching at Harvard and at Yale, he traveled to South Dakota where he worked with anthropologists to try to understand Sioux and Yurok Indians from both psychological and social perspectives. It was in this collaboration that he began to articulate how identity development occurs as a *psychosocial* phenomenon.

With these biographical footnotes as a backdrop, let us examine Erikson's most lasting and important contribution: that of his theory of the eight ages of man. Each developmental stage is defined by an individual's facing an age-specific crisis, at an age-specific time, with an age-specific concern. The past and the present crystallize into a new developmental task. In the negotiation and resolution of a developmental crisis, each person has the opportunity for development. Psychological and social crises increase a person's vulnerability but heighten his or her potential. At each stage of psychosocial development there is the potential for the emergence of a unique kind of ego strength, or what Erikson called a "virtue," although he did not use this word as it is most commonly used. Erikson (1964a) has written, "I'm not speaking of values; I only speak of a developing capacity to preview and abide by values established by a particular living system" (p. 113).

At each stage of development there is the possibility for a negative outcome, but Erikson cautioned against viewing the stages of psychosocial development as achievements with simply negative or positive outcomes. "Actually," he wrote, "a certain ratio of [positive and negative outcomes] is the critical factor. . . . [For example] when we enter a situation, we must be able to differentiate how much we can trust and how much we can mistrust in the sense of a readiness for danger and anticipation of discomfort" (Erikson 1968, p. 105).

Erikson's first five stages incorporate Freud's model of psychosexual development. Although Erikson did not challenge Freud's formulations, he changed the focus of attention, making them more relevant to distinctive social values and emphasizing the adaptive, positive character traits that can emerge when particular developmental tasks are mastered. He also expanded the original psychosexual model of development by adding ego psychological concepts, such as ego strengths, adaptation, mastery, and identity, and by emphasizing the importance of the person in her environment. He brought time as a construct into his theory and with it the idea that everyone relates to themselves and others at different stages of the life cycle in unique ways depending upon their different intersecting life stages and identities.

Let us turn now to his theory of psychosocial development to illustrate how ego identity emerges over the life cycle.

THE EIGHT AGES OF MAN

Erikson's psychosocial developmental timetable roughly corresponds to Freud's theory of psychosexual development until adolescence. However, whereas Freud thought that psychosexual development ended with adolescence, Erikson added three more important life stages that shape identity over the life cycle. He thus created a developmental theory that suggests that people grow, change, and develop throughout their entire lives (Table 5–1).

At each stage of physical, psychological and social development Erikson proposed that there are psychological and social tasks to be mastered and conflicts to be negotiated. Like Freud's psychosexual stages, Erikson's stages associate the tasks of ego development with dominant biological organs or zones of pleasure. Erikson, however, also presented the ways in which individual development took place in the context of interactions with larger social institutions, societal values, and social and cultural expectations. For the early stages, he kept Freud's original concept of erogenous zones. Once he went beyond adolescence and into adult development, however, he identified biological processes that shape psychosocial tasks and outcomes, but no longer defined them as erogenous because Freud's concepts of erogenous zones ended with adolescence.

Let us consider each of Erikson's eight epigenetic stages.

Infancy: Trust vs. Mistrust (0–18 months)

In the first stage of infancy, a baby's mouth is her source of nourishment as well as her medium for relating to caregivers. Erikson describes infants as social, interactive, and incorporative from the beginning. A baby drinks in her mother with her eyes and her skin. The baby comes to expect to be nurtured and taken in, as caregivers come to expect to give love and to be loved. Erikson views the infant as developing her

Table 5-1. Erikson's Epigenetic Stages

Basic Stages	Psychosexual Stages and Modes	Psychosocial Crisis	Significant Relations
I. Infancy	Oral-Respiratory, Sensory Kinesthetic (Incorporative Modes)	Basic Trust vs. Basic Mistrust	Maternal Person
II. Early Childhood	Anal-Urethral, Muscular (Retentive–Eliminative)	Autonomy vs. Shame and Doubt	Parental Persons
III. Play Stage	Infantile-Genital, Locomotive (Intrusive, Inclusive)	Initiative vs. Guilt	Basic Family
IV. School Age	Latency	Industry vs. Inferiority	Neighborhood
V. Adolescence	Puberty	Identity vs. Confusion	Peer Groups and Outgroups/Models of Leadership
VI. Young Adulthood	Genitality	Intimacy vs. Isolation	Partners in love, friendship, competition, cooperation, sex
VII. Adulthood	(Procreativity)	Generativity vs. Stagnation	Divided Labor, and shared household
VIII. Old Age	(Generalization of Sensual Modes)	Integrity vs. Despair	"Mankind"/"My Kind"

identity in the context of a relationship in which she learns about being cared for and loved. The reciprocity that occurs between the child and her caregiver ultimately forms the basis for basic trust. We saw in Freud's description of a baby that the mouth is the central organ and the zone of pleasure, which is also true in Erikson's epigenetic plan. By nature, infants take in the outside world through their mouths. They also bite, which reflects aggressive aspects of their interactions with caregivers. Ultimately infants need to form relationships with caregivers in which they can manage both their incorporative and sadistic modes. Sufficient trust in a caregiver's recognition and affirmation leads to what Erikson calls the virtue of hope. Without sufficient basic trust, a child develops an enduring mistrust and pessimism. The challenge of this stage is to achieve some balance between trust and mistrust. If this developmental task cannot be mastered, the negative outcome will be dependent, unthinking, rigid adulation of others, or its opposite, the pervasive mistrust of others. Although Erikson defines more than biological factors significant in this stage, he notes that basic trust develops from the interaction between the self and the social world, and forms the foundation for all other stages of development.

As an example, we will examine the case of Frances, whose identity was shaped during her earliest years in ways that left her both dependent upon and mistrustful of others.

> Frances was a 50-year-old white occupational therapist from a working-class background who could not develop even the most basic trust with others. While having gone on to complete many life-cycle tasks, including commitment to an adult relationship and a career, she felt a deep sense of hopelessness and mistrust. She described her relationship with her own mother as fraught with confusion. As early as she could remember, her mother, who was alcoholic, would swear at her, break lamps, and "be crazy." When her mother was finished with one of her outbursts, she would tell Frances that she (the mother) had a twin sister, and that it was the twin who had been raging and not herself. Frances grew up with a very deep mistrust of others, which she tried to overcome by seeing those in authority as always being correct and as having her best interests at heart. When, however, her boss transferred her to another part of the hospital for what she thought were capricious reasons, she felt hopelessly betrayed. Incapable of mastering her own disappointment, and unable to reconcile the belief that her boss was watching out for her with the feeling that he had betrayed her, she became so mistrustful that she left her job and never worked again.

While Frances' earliest childhood experiences of mistrust culminated in a profound psychological disorganization, Maxine, by comparison, also suffered great fear in early childhood, which resulted in a different outcome.

> Maxine was a 51-year-old white Jewish music critic and mother of two children. She survived World War II by being hidden in a cellar in Austria. For the first eight months of her life, she had little food or light and lived with a family that feared being sent to a concentration camp and killed.

To this day, Maxine feels physical fear when faced with dangers on the subways or on the streets. In a visceral way, she is hyper-vigilant, noticing even a menacing look and always aware of acts of violence around her. While she does not have memories of what it meant to be cold, hungry, or in severe peril, she carries a bodily feeling of mistrust within herself. But given a life context peopled with family members, teachers, and mentors, given her strong and abiding spiritual faith, and given her community, in which physical, psychological, and social needs were met, her mistrust has evolved into a healthy skepticism that mostly serves her well in her life career as a critic.

Early Childhood: Autonomy vs. Shame and Doubt (18 months to 3 years)

This second stage of child development corresponds with Freud's anal stage. While Freud's "anal" baby took sexual and aggressive pleasure in the retention and the expulsion of feces, Erikson's toddler learns to control his or her sphincter muscles in relationship to others and to the social world. The toddler tries to master his or her environment by controlling caregivers and others in her world. Biologically, a toddler needs to negotiate two muscular actions: holding on and letting go. Children at this stage need to achieve a sense of independence over their own bodies, including some control and autonomy over what is inside and what is outside of them. This includes not only the ways a toddler retains or eliminates feces, but also the ways in which toddlers hold on to and let go of toys, food, or other objects (in ways that often exhaust even the most patient caregivers). If a child experiences some autonomy in walking, exploration, and sphincter control, she may gain some confidence and pride, which becomes a part of her ego identity. If she experiences herself as overcontrolled, she will feel excessive shame and doubt.

Evan, a white 26-year-old lawyer, was recently reminded by his parents of his initial delight in an especially large production of feces. At age 2½, he had called his mother and father into the bathroom to examine and admire his opus. Both parents exclaimed with pride about its size and quantity. But when he called in his brother to look, the brother responded by saying, "That's not very big at all. In fact, that's one of the tiniest poops I've ever seen!"

Evan's mother also recalls preparing a family dinner when, as she watched in horror, 2½-year-old Evan peed all over the newly cleaned floor. His mother remembers her look of disgust and his of shame as he slinked away from her and hid in the bathroom. But given many other factors that supported his self-esteem—a sustaining day-care situation, a cultural milieu that encouraged the more playful and creative aspects of his willfulness—Evan developed an identity of independent self-assurance rather than one of self-constriction, shame, and doubt. In fact, Evan continues to be admired for his achievements, having chosen work that allows him to engage in struggles and battles for which he is paid. These battles are now fought in courtrooms and not in toilets or on the kitchen floor.

Ideally, a child at this stage develops a sense of identity based on social experiences of cooperation and self-expression. But a child filled with doubts will not feel autonomous; he or she will feel compelled by the will of others.

Michael was the seventh child in a lower-working-class, Irish-Catholic family. Both of his parents were financially and emotionally overwhelmed. They were living far from extended kin, which increased their isolation. Michael's father worked a day job as a security guard and his mother cleaned office buildings at night. Michael had little sense of protection and little supervision.

Michael remembers not being able to defecate until his mother returned home from work. As he grew older, he became concerned about encopresis (involuntary defecation). He would soil himself at school or worry that he would soil himself with friends. He felt exposed and without inner or outer control.

These feelings became manifest later in a number of adult feelings and behaviors. As an adult, Michael chronically doubted himself. He felt potentially invaded by others and felt he needed to protect himself from others. Friends and family were barred from his apartment or his workplace. Any time he was in public places he felt exposed. He was unable to use the bathroom at his girlfriend's house or at his workplace, as any toilets other than his own made him feel at the mercy of others, exposed and ashamed. These symptoms constricted his bodily, psychological, and social functioning.

The virtue at this stage is will: "The unbroken determinant to exercise free choice as well as self restraint" (Erikson 1964a, p. 119). Where Evan's willfulness became transformed into a strong and determined will, Michael experienced himself as without good will or free will.

Play Stage: Initiative vs. Guilt (Ages 3–6)

Like Freud, who depicted an oedipal stage, Erikson notes how children between 3 and 6 years of age enter into a period rich with imagination and creativity, ushered in by locomotion and language. This is a time of family romance and of conflicts between what a child may want in fantasy, and what he or she may have in reality. It is during the oedipal stage that Erikson sees children's modes of action as "On the make, the attack and the conquest," and it is within this stage that children face the ego-psychological tasks of identifying with their parents' and their society's values. In their social worlds, children who successfully negotiate both internal psychological demands and social expectations learn to plan and to discover. But they must also learn what they may and what they may not do. The virtue in this stage is the development of a sense of purpose, that is, "The courage to envisage and pursue valued goals uninhibited by defeat of infantile fantasies, by guilt or by the foiling fear of punishment" (Erikson 1964a, p. 122). In this stage, children begin to develop the ability to make enduring commitments.

Raoul, age 4, was a purposeful and delightful working-class Hispanic boy. At his day-care center, he'd initiate the building of enormous block structures, which he'd lead his friends in knocking down. On the playground, he'd boldly slide down the steepest slide, delighting in and conquering this scary structure. Each night he'd play a card game with his dad, who would often allow Raoul to outwit him and win. "I'm really good! I'm great," he'd say.

Where Erikson's theory has the most value is in considering Raoul's sense of initiative if he had been living in, let us say, Kuwait, growing up in a culture where 65 percent of Kuwaiti children have seen dead bodies of people they knew. What if he had seen corpses hanging from lampposts or on the doors of former houses, or lying in the streets? What effects, Erikson would ask, might the social surround have on the development of Raoul's initiative? Likewise, what if Raoul had grown up in the Henry Horner Housing Project, only one of many notorious projects in South Chicago (Kotlowitz 1991)? By age 5, virtually all children there have seen a shooting or known someone involved in one. In fact, 30 percent of children in American inner cities have witnessed a killing by the time they are 15 years old, and more than 70 percent have seen someone beaten. Erikson would expect the clinician to attend to the *interaction* between the child and his environment. Pathogenic environments do not create pathological children. Rather, Erikson would exhort the clinician to note Raoul's ego strengths and their effects on mediating his environment for him.

It is important to note that Erikson's life stages and the potential for psychopathology do not have a direct correspondence. However, serious difficulties during one of the first three stages of life may form the basis for enduring and serious dysfunction. Without basic trust at the anal stage, a child may bring that experience of excessive doubt into all subsequent life stages, doubting himself as a learner, as a sexual partner, as a worker, parent, or friend. The child who feels excessively guilty will lack initiative not only in this stage, but all the stages to follow.

School Age: Industry vs. Inferiority (Ages 6–11)

This stage corresponds to Freud's psychosexual stage of latency. As children enter school, their social worlds widen. Developmentally, they begin to reason deductively, to use adult tools to complete tasks with steady attention and with diligence. They are invested in making things and making them well. Children now move beyond the bounds of the nuclear family and develop play skills, cognitive skills, and skills about group life, including learning to express and integrate their own feelings. If a child's efforts are thwarted, for example, by inhospitable schools or by social conditions such as racism or homophobia, then his relationships with parents, teachers, or peers may be threatened, and an enduring sense of inferiority can become a feature of the child's identity. If a child can learn to work and play successfully in a supportive culture and social milieu, the groundwork can be laid for an identity based on a sense of industry and achievement. The virtue that may emerge at this developmental stage is competence, which Erikson (1964a) defines as "the free exercise of dexterity and intelligence in the completion of tasks unimpaired by intellectual inferiority" (p. 124).

Learning disabilities may present children with particular challenges in latency, where educational support from schools or lack thereof can make a profound difference.

> Eric was a wonderfully busy and industrious 8-year-old boy. But when he was faced with the task of understanding the printed word at school, he was unable to comprehend or decode the symbols. He began to feel stupid in the classroom and to kick and hit other children. Whereas this behavior could have been defined as pathological in and of itself, his school recognized that his was not a behavioral problem, but a reaction to frustration in mastering reading tasks. With a tutor and resource room to provide some academic support, as well as with emotional support from his single mother, he was able to reenter group life easily, without his sense of competence with peers being undermined. Here the social milieu was necessary to counter his identity as an incompetent learner and to help him achieve a more positive identity as a growing master of his learning.

Other kinds of societal pressures can lead to a sense of inferiority unless counteracted by other supports and forces within the family and the community.

> Lucy was an industrious and competent 7-year-old daughter of a divorced lesbian mother who had been in a relationship with a female co-parent for six years. Her family lived in a politically conservative, working-class rural community. Her mother could not reveal her sexual orientation at work, in Lucy's school, or to the larger community, as she was embattled in a custody case and feared losing her daughter if her sexual orientation were known. When

Lucy broke her arm at school, her co-parent was invisible as a significant other. There was no place to identify Lucy's second mother on the hospital forms. Only her biological mother was invited to attend parental conferences. Lucy was careful about whom she invited home. Despite the fact that there was no socially approved language to define the role of co-parent, and in spite of the homophobia Lucy faced when dealing with social institutions, her own identity as a competent student and friend was stable. This stemmed largely from her co-parents' clarity about their own identities as well as the support her family drew from an extended friendship network of other lesbian families.

Here again we see Erikson's emphasis on how the social milieu mediates and supports an individual's identity.

Adolescence: Identity vs. Role Confusion (Age 11–18)

Almost universally, adolescence is a difficult time. Adolescents face rapid hormonal changes. Their reference group shifts from parents to peers. They are deeply concerned with themselves. Erikson sees their efforts to fall in love as efforts to also define themselves. Adolescents are engaged in painful struggles over self-acceptance and acceptance from others. They are deeply concerned about who is "in" and who is "out." Adolescence provides a time of achieving individual identity through group identity.

In Erikson's schema, adolescence presents a pivotal crisis around the development of a sense of a personal identity. Adolescents are often in a state of suspended morality, as they begin to formulate personal ideologies based upon values that differ from those of their parents. The psychosocial task of this stage is that of identity vs. role confusion. The task of adolescence is to achieve a stable sense of self, which must fit with an image of the individual's past, present, and future and of larger possibilities. The ego identity that may be achieved in adolescence is the accrued confidence that one's identity will remain stable.

Erikson did not set a standard for the development of a "healthy" identity. Again, he always argued that the meaning of an adolescent's behavior had to be understood within the sociocultural and historical contexts in which the adolescent develops. In his studies of the Sioux Indians, he explored how an adolescent's identity may be shaped in the context of a disenfranchised culture. Erikson was careful to state that simply because an adolescent was socially or economically disenfranchised, she should not be seen as deviant. If adolescents, as was true for many Sioux Indians, engage in seemingly pathological behaviors such as truancy or passive aggression, these should be understood as adaptive responses to the disruption of their continuous identities and communities.

Sometimes an adolescent may develop what Erikson calls a negative identity. A negative identity may be forged around those "identifications and roles which at critical stages of development had been presented to them as most undesirable or dangerous and yet also as most real" (Erikson 1959, p. 131). Some adolescents form socially deviant identities with groups who may be dangerous, such as antisocial gangs or cults. A negative identity may also develop in opposition to the excessive idealism of a parent. While an adolescent may turn to antisocial groups, cults, or gangs, not all gang membership results in a negative identity. In fact, gangs can provide community, fraternity, fidelity, and loyalty.

> Mark was a 13-year-old Chicano boy in an urban housing project, who began to hang out with the Warlords. Their leader was a drug dealer who under less socially impoverished conditions would have been a positive role model in the community. Mark was drawn to the drug dealer's savvy, strength, and leadership skills. His identification with the dealer had aspects that were both positive and negative, as he learned to assess his situation and protect himself.

Erikson proposed that as adolescents struggle with who they are, they may need, as he did, a psychosocial moratorium—a period of time in which it may be adaptive to drop out and explore one's identity without making premature commitments. But if adolescents are not supported in forming coherent identities through their personal strengths and societal supports, they run the risk of losing themselves in fanatical or exclusive commitments or through negative identifications. If an individual's strengths and social world support the emergence of a coherent identity, fidelity can be the virtue. Fidelity is defined as the ability to sustain loyalties freely pledged in spite of differences in values.

Young Adulthood: Intimacy vs. Isolation

To achieve intimacy in relationships in young adulthood, a solid sense of identity is needed. Intimacy involves mutuality, which requires the ability to lose oneself and find oneself in another without losing one's own identity. When identity is shaky, attempts at intimacy "become desperate attempts at delineating the fuzzy outlines of identity by mutual narcissistic mirroring: to fall in love often means to fall into one's mirror image" (Erikson 1964a, p. 18). Without the capacity to share with loved ones, including friends, there can be a tendency toward isolation. In a sociocultural time such as the 1980s and 1990s, when individualism is so highly valued and the narcissistic pursuit of self-gratification is sanctioned, isolation may represent a socially sanctioned feature of what in fact are poorly consolidated identities of many young adults.

As part of intimacy, Erikson also identified the role of genitality, which he defined as the capacity for orgasm with a partner who is loved, trusted, and competent, and with whom one is willing to regulate one's work and play for the purposes of procreation. Real intimacy requires both having strong ego boundaries and being able to temporarily suspend them. For people whose identity is fragmented, rigid, or brittle, the capacity for real intimacy may be limited or impossible. The virtue of this stage is love, which Erikson (1964a) defined as "the strength of the ego to share identity for mutual verification of one's chosen identity while taking from this supportive relationship the opportunity to be a separate self" (p. 129).

Adulthood: Generativity vs. Stagnation

Loving and working adults need to feel concern for, and interest in, the next generation if they are to maintain their continuous identities. The abilities to extend interests both within and outside the home, and to establish and guide future generations, are particular challenges to men and women in midlife. To be generative, however, does not mean that one must produce biological children. Consider the coaches, troop leaders, clergy, and teachers who serve and work in their communities. Then reflect upon the ways in which they have shared their interests, coached, organized community or church activities, mentored, cured, and showed concern for others. Generativity ultimately involves finding one's place in the life cycle of generations. The opposite of generativity is stagnation and self-absorption, pseudo-intimacy or self-indulgence.

In this developmental stage the virtue is care. Care is "the widening concern for what has been generated by love, necessity, or accident" (Erikson 1964a, p. 131). The guiding parent, friend, teacher, mentor, or even storekeeper needs to have the conviction that "I know what I am doing and I am doing it right" (p. 131). The opposite may be authoritarianism, self-indulgence, or insensitivity to the needs of others.

> Dorothy is a 42-year-old African-American schoolteacher and single parent. The mother of two boys, she has worked since her sons were infants. In the school in which she teaches, Dorothy spends long afternoons, evenings, and weekends with her students, working on community issues, giving freely of her skills by tutoring, and by providing encouragement, guidance, feedback, and love. Her colleagues benefit from her effusive and generous nature. She wrote an important and widely used handbook on working with minority adolescents, she provided major leadership in curricular development, and she is consulted widely and often. Her generativity extended far beyond her nuclear family, although her two children also seem to thrive within the richness of her life.

By contrast, T. S. Eliot's poem, "The Love Song of J. Alfred Prufrock" (1917) captures some of the self-absorption, somatic preoccupations, self-consciousness, and stagnation of a midlife man who is not generative. It is interesting to note that Eliot wrote this poem when he was an undergraduate, containing within it his own concerns about a stagnant identity that had already begun in adolescence. J. Alfred Prufrock laments:

> "Do I dare?" and, "Do I dare?"
>   Time to turn back and descend the stair,
>   With a bald spot in the middle of my hair. . . .
>   Do I dare
>   Disturb the universe? . . .
>   Should I, after tea and cake and ices
>   Have the strength to force a moment to its crisis? . . .

Do I dare to eat a peach? . . .
I have heard the mermaids singing, each to each.
I do not think that they will sing to me.
(T. S. Eliot 1917, p. 18)

Here, we see how the difficulty negotiating earlier stages (initiative, intimacy), contributes to Prufrock's midlife experience of stagnation, fear, and a lack of capacity to care beyond himself.

Old Age: Integrity vs. Despair

Old age requires acceptance that death is an inevitable part of life. Whether having lived as a Sioux, an African-American, or an Irish Catholic, the finality of death in old age is inescapable. Each culture mediates the meaning and significance of old age differently. Asian cultures venerate the old and accord a great deal of respect and wisdom to people at this life stage. Many Western cultures respond to old age with fear and denial, warehousing old people in substandard nursing homes and isolating them from their communities and social supports. How a person negotiates this stage of life in the face of death is mediated by the individual's ego strengths, the culture, and the historical time.

In this stage, adults who have been cared for and who have cared for others may now care for themselves. In this last stage of life, integrity is the opposite of self-centered love. Integrity is a sense of acceptance that this is one's only life. This is the time (and last time) for emotional integration. An infant first learns to trust herself as she trusts the world, so in the beginning relies on another's integrity. With the achievement of integrity, the life cycle is complete. Erikson wrote that healthy children should not fear life if their elders are integrated enough not to fear death.

> If, at the end, the life cycle turns back on its own beginnings so that the very old become again like children, the question is whether the return is to a childlikeness seasoned with wisdom or to a finite childishness. The old may become (and want to become) too old too fast or remain too young too long. Here only some sense of integrity can bind things together. . .and by integrity we do not mean only an occasional outstanding quality of personal character, but above all, a simple proclivity for understanding or hearing those who understand

the integrative ways of human life. . . . [With integrity] there emerges a different, a timeless love for those few others who have become the main counterplayers in life's most significant contexts. [Erikson 1950, p. 46]

The virtue of old age is wisdom, defined as a "detached concern with life itself in the face of death itself." The opposite is disgust and despair, which implies a sense of futility about one's life, a meaninglessness, and ultimately an inability to care for oneself or for others. Consider the ways in which Mrs. Frank approached the end of her life:

Mrs. Frank was an 86-year-old woman who had lived in the same neighborhood most of her life. She had been married at 20, widowed at 60, and had raised two daughters who had families and careers of their own. Every week she attended a book group comprised of women of different ages. She often had young neighbors in for tea and was deeply interested in their relationships and their lives. Local kin would be invited for Sunday dinner. She was still involved in social action and she attended musical events regularly. Although her children and grandchildren were geographically distant, she maintained regular contact with them. She even came to speak to a psychology class on Erikson's final life stage and enjoyed her own presentation immensely!

While Mrs. Frank was in relatively good health, save rheumatoid arthritis, she also recognized that her own life was nearly over. She had prepared for her home to be sold when she became unable to function independently and had arranged for residential care when necessary. She had decided which books she hoped would go to which grandchildren, and which furniture would go to which daughter, had been able to talk with her children about her life and impending death, and appeared to accept her death as an ultimate finality.

While Mrs. Frank was able to approach the end of her life with wisdom and responsibility, integrating the many successful earliest resolutions of identity crises, Ira Marks, by contrast, met the psychosocial tasks at the end of his life with pessimism and despair.

Ira Marks was 70 when he developed Parkinson's disease. A formerly dapper shoe salesman whose personal attractiveness had been essential to his work and life, he now had a disease that made him unable to eat without spilling his food on his clothes. He was also incontinent.

Ira had been deeply involved in his Orthodox Jewish congregation and knew most of the members of his community. His wife had recently died of cancer and his children were living far away. Now isolated despite his religious community, he was cared for by strangers in his home. His speech was impaired, and when his children came to visit or when members of the congregation did stop by, he would turn away, put his head in his hands, and wail. Deep guttural sounds of despair, like those of a wounded animal, would emerge from him.

Prior to his wife's death, he had relied heavily on his own mother, and later on his wife. He had always felt unprepared to make any life decision without consultation with his rabbi. In the absence of any current relationship in which he could feel taken care of, either within his family or within his community, he was depressed and despairing. Ira could not evoke memories of past achievements or take pleasure in the achievements of his children or many grandchildren. Ultimately his lack of interest in his life culminated in anorexia. When he got a cold, it quickly became the pneumonia from which he died. He appeared to have died without feeling that his life had been worth living.

CRITIQUES OF ERIKSON

In the last decade Erikson has been faulted for the gender biases in his theory of life cycle development. While we will discuss these critiques more fully in Chapter 10, it is important to note that Erikson proposed that male and female life cycle development differ in childhood, adolescence, young adulthood, and midlife.

In describing childhood, Erikson identified gender difference in the spatial organization and play of boys and girls. He noted that boys' play tends toward creating high towers and protrusions, and is independent and aggressive. Girls at play tend to be preoccupied with interior, closed space, and their play is more receptive. Erikson understood these differences to be a result of the interface between anatomy, social roles, and psychosexual tasks. His underlying assumption of female passivity and receptivity, however, also reflected the sex role stereotypes and expectations for women in the 1950s and early 1960s, the decades in which he wrote.

Erikson proposed that, in adolescence, women lag behind men in the development of a gendered identity. In fact, he wrote that for a woman, identity is not actually achieved in adolescence but rather occurs in early adulthood, and is defined by the man she will marry, who will fill her inner space. This idea captures another gender stereotype—that women are defined by their relationships with men—then normalizes the stereotype and makes it a developmental goal. His theory also implies that female identity is less articulated and less differentiated than is male identity, with the disconcerting suggestion that this might result from a deficiency in women, rather than from the unequal social world in which women are raised.

In describing the state of generativity, Erikson suggests that female identity is defined by motherhood. Once again, the gender stereotype of a woman caring for children at home is designated as a developmental goal. If female identity in midlife is defined by motherhood, then why is male identity at the same stage not defined by fatherhood? Feminist life-cycle theorists have proposed alternative models for female identity, and these will be discussed at length in Chapter 10 on psychodynamic theory and gender.

Erikson has further been faulted for overemphasizing the role of separateness, autonomy, and individuation in the life cycle, while neglecting attachment issues at every stage of development. Many of his stages, such as autonomy, initiative, industry and identity, reflect the values of a Western male-dominated competitive industrialized culture (Berzoff 1989).

A second critique of Erikson elucidates a problem that every theorist has faced: all theorists are embedded in their unique culture and moment in sociohistorical time. Hence, when Erikson refers to intimacy, he refers only to heterosexual intimacy and he defines it as occurring through mutual, genital, heterosexual orgasm. But is this the only form of adult intimacy or love? We would argue emphatically that *genital* orgasm with a heterosexual partner is *not* the hallmark of intimacy, but that the ability to lose oneself and find oneself in another, in mutually regulated ways constitutes the highest form of adult intimacy and love. We hope that someone who paid such close attention to cultural variance as Erikson did would have been more inclusive of variance in sexual orientation, were he writing today.

Despite these two critiques, it is important to recognize that Erikson was one of the first developmental theorists to add gender to the definition of identity. Erikson was also one of the first to emphasize the importance of a person's location in the social structure and to recognize that a person's identity is influenced by culture. His theory is more open to critique precisely because it is more inclusive.

A third critique comes from the current discourse in postmodernism. Many theorists are beginning to question the value of stage theories such as Erikson's, which are both linear and hierarchical. They question the validity of a continuous construct such as "the self" and "identity." They ask whether a core self truly exists, or rather do our "selves" continue to develop in the contexts in which we live and work. In this latter view, we are multiple selves, with multiple identities, in multiple situations (Mitchell 1993). Postmodern theorists question whether a coherent and continuous identity is possible or even desirable in a technological world that requires multiplicity (Gergen 1991). Our multiple identities include ourselves as fax numbers, E-mail boxes, parents, workers, siblings, bosses, children. We must become multiple selves in the instant when the telephone rings, the fax machine intrudes, or when we step onto an airplane that within hours will transport us into entirely different contexts that call for different parts of our selves and identities. In a postmodern view, the self is continuously oscillating, based on the many social and relational contexts in which it is expressed.

SUMMARY

In spite of these critiques, Erikson's life-cycle model of ego development is important to psychodynamic practitioners. First, it brings child development out of the narrowly defined bounds of the nuclear family and into a social world in which developing children interact not only with parents but also with peers and teachers, in the context of larger social and cultural expectations. Second, it provides a developmental framework that projects personality development beyond infantile sexuality and concentrates on development past puberty and throughout the adult life cycle until death. Third, it focuses on the centrality of identity as opposed to sexuality as a central determinant of psychological well-being. Fourth, it begins to unite ego psychology with object relations so that an individual is seen as increasingly mastering inner and outer reality as she moves through the life-cycle tasks, individual stages, and relationships crucial to the developmental tasks of those stages. Finally, Erikson's theory is more psychosocial than Freud's or that of any other ego psychologists. His theory is the first and still the strongest to expand the discourse on development by adding the variables of culture, race, class, gender, and time to how a person develops a coherent sense of identity.

While Erikson was constrained by his own cultural constructs and values, his beliefs about the self, his era, and by a linear view of development, still his work has provided us with a theory that takes race, class, and gender into consideration far more than any previous psychodynamic theory. His inclusion of the sociocultural surround in which individual identity develops makes a profound contribution to clinical practice. While Erikson sought to explain the confluence of gender and identity, it is an ongoing task of our current and future theories to continue to articulate the ebb and flow and separation and connection as they occur in the identities of girls, boys, men, and women in differing sociocultural contexts.

References

Berzoff, J. (1989). Fusion and heterosexual women's friendships: implications for expanding adult developmental theories. *Women and Therapy* 8(4):93–107.

Coles, R. (1970). *Erik Erikson: the Growth of His Work*. Boston: Little, Brown.

Crawford, S. (1987). Lesbian families: psychosocial stress and the family building process. In *Lesbian Psychologies: Explorations and Challenges*, ed. Boston Lesbian Psychologies Collective. Urbana, IL: University of Illinois Press.

Devore, W., and Schlesinger, E. (1987). *Ethnic Sensitive Social Work Practice*. Columbus, OH: Merrill.

Eliot, T. S. (1917). The love song of J. Alfred Prufrock. In *T. S. Eliot: Poems, 1909–1925*, pp. 11–20. New York: Harcourt, Brace, 1926.

Erikson, E. (1950). *Childhood and Society.* New York: Norton,

———— (1959). Identity and the life cycle: selected papers. *Psychological Issues Monograph*, vol. 1, no. 1. New York: International Universities Press.

———— (1964a). *Insight and Responsibility.* New York: Norton.

———— (1964b). The inner and outer space: reflections on womanhood. *Daedalus* 2:582–606.

———— (1968). *Identity, Youth and Crisis.* New York: Norton.

———— (1980). Elements of a psychoanalytic theory of psychosocial development. In *The Course of Life: Psychoanalytic Contributions*, ed. S. I. Greenspan and G. H. Pollack, *Infancy and Early Childhood*, vol. 1. Washington, DC: National Institute of Mental Health.

Evans, R. (1981). *Dialogue with Erik Erikson.* New York: Prager.

Franz, C. E., and White, D. (1985). Individuation and attachment in personality development: extending Erikson's theory. *Journal of Personality* (53): 2.

Gergen, K. J. (1991). *The Saturated Self: Dilemmas of Identity in Contemporary Life.* New York: Basic Books.

Gilligan, C. (1982). *In a Different Voice.* Cambridge, MA: Harvard University Press.

Goleman, D. (1992). Attending to the children of all the world's zones. *The New York Times*, December 6, p. 7.

Kotlowitz, A. (1991). *There Are No Children Here.* New York: Doubleday.

Loevinger, J. (1974). *Ego Development.* San Francisco: Jossey-Bass.

Miller, J. B. (1990). The development of women's sense of self. In *Essential Papers in the Psychology of Women*, ed. C. Zanardi. New York: New York University Press.

Mitchell, S. J. (1993). *Hope and Dread in Psychoanalysis.* New York: Basic Books.

Monte, C. F. (1980). *Beneath the Mask.* New York: Holt, Rinehart.

Williams, J. (1987). *The Psychology of Women's Behavior in a Biosocial Context.* London: Norton.

6

Object Relations Theory

LAURA MELANO FLANAGAN

Object relations theory continues the study of psychological development and contributes its own special lens with which to look into the inner world. The focus of object reactions theory is not on the forces of libido and aggression or on the adaptive functions of the ego. Rather, it is on the complex relationship of self to other. Object relations theory explores the process whereby people come to experience themselves as separate and independent from others, while at the same time needing profound attachment to others. Melanie Klein (1952) summarized the core tenet of this theory: "There is no instinctual urge, no anxiety situation, no mental process which does not involve objects, external or internal; in other words, object relations are at the *center* of emotional life" (p. 53).

WHAT IS OBJECT RELATIONS THEORY?

Object relations theory is based on the belief that all people have within them an internal, often unconscious world of relationships that is different and in many ways more powerful and compelling than what is going on in their external world of interactions with "real" and present people. Object relations theories focus on the interactions individuals have with other people, on the processes through which individuals internalize those interactions, and on the enormous role these internalized object relations play in psychological development. The term *object relations* thus refers not only to "real" relationships with others, but also to the internal mental representations of others and to internal images of self as well. While other theories have attended to how libido and aggression may seek discharge, expression, and satisfaction or to how the ego copes with life stressors and adapts to conflicts between intrapsychic structures, object relations theory adds an inner mysterious world, with its own story, plot, drama, and above all, cast of characters.

When thinking about object relations in psychodynamic theory it is important to remember that the term is not synonymous with the commonly used term *relationships*. Object relations does refer, in part, to the complexity of external relationships with others, but it also includes the whole internal world of relations between self and other, and the ways in which others have become part of the self. This can be seen in peoples' fantasies, desires, and fears, which invariably include images or representations of other people. One's internal world, then, includes the mental representations of self and other. When object relations are assessed in the process of diagnosis it is to examine both the quality of real, interpersonal relationships and the internal self and object representations as well.

When confusing *object relations* and *relationships*, people may say "Mr. Smith must have good object relations because he has been married twenty years" or "Ms. Jones must have poor object relations because she is not involved with anyone." The mere fact that someone has been married for twenty years or that someone is not involved does not necessarily tell the clinician much about object relations. For instance, Mr. Smith could have remained married for twenty years because his object relations are troubled, because he believes that others are dangerous or bad. His self representation, his view of himself, could be that of a weak man desperately needing the protection of one good object, his wife. Ms. Jones, on the other hand, might have healthily and adaptively come to know herself as a person who benefits from solitude and separateness. Her self-representation could include a balanced view of both her strengths and needs, and her internal world might be filled with benign object representations that keep her from being too lonely while not involved.

The use of the word *object* to mean *person* is traditional in psycho-analytic literature. This choice may seem odd and is perhaps unfortunate because *object* usually refers to a *thing*. Each of the authors has had the experience of giving a lecture on object relations with students and colleagues from other fields who eventually, incredulously ask: "When she uses the word *object*, does she mean a person?" When the answer is yes, the response is always some variant of "What a *weird* choice of words for professionals who are supposed to be interested in *people*."

Object, when used in reference to a person, can sound depersonalizing and static. In fact, the word has been chosen to capture an important facet of human relations—that people outside the self can be many things including *objects* of desire and fear, rather than be just simply the people they are. The word *object* is also chosen because it clearly differentiates object from subject. In this way it becomes clear that the subject is the self and the object is the thing outside of the self that the self perceives, experiences, desires, fears, rejects, or takes in. A definition Webster offers for object is "what is aimed at."

In Freudian drive theory and in ego psychology, the term *object* is usually but not always used in reference to people. Yet the word *object* in drive theory can be somewhat depersonalized. Sometimes the word actually does refer to a thing: the object of an oral impulse can literally be the breast; the object used by a shoe fetishist is literally the shoe. Even when drive theory refers to objects as people, it is referring to people as representing the targets of the drives, and as such they become the means or object by which a drive can be satisfied or frustrated.

In object relations theory the person aspect of the object becomes more fully fleshed out. Object no longer refers to the person or thing outside of the self as the gratifier of an instinctual wish. Object refers much more to the person, real or internalized, with his or her qualities, with his or her contribution to the interaction.

Another distinction between object relations theory, drive theory, and ego psychology is that object relations theory looks more closely at how needs are met or not met in relationships, rather than at the satisfaction or frustration of particular impulses. In fact, this theory is the first to make a very clear and important distinction between need and impulse, with need being understood as a far broader concept.

D. W. Winnicott (1956), a major object relations theorist, believed that a drive or impulse can be gratified without the relationship being all that important, whereas a need has to be met by a person, thereby placing the relationship at the center of the experience. For optimum development to take place, important needs have to be met including the need to be seen and valued as a unique individual, to be accepted as a whole with both good and bad aspects, to be held tight and to be let go, and to be cared for, protected, and loved.

Object relations theory postulates that human beings are incorporative by nature, both physically and psychologically. Just as the body takes in food and drink and then metabolizes it, so too does the psyche take in what it experiences with others and process it to become part of the psychological self. In the physical realm what happens when a body takes in food depends in part on the individual body. So, too, in the psychological realm, there are individual variations in what happens to what is taken in emotionally. Ten people eating the same amount of salad or steak or chocolate cake will not gain or lose the same amount of weight or extract the same kinds and amounts of nutrients. What happens will be determined by each person's complex physical condition at the time. Ten people being criticized or being given a hug will similarly react in ten different ways depending on what psychological strengths, vulnerabilities, past experiences, and cultural influences have made them unique.

> Rose, a successful professional 35-year-old businesswoman, feeling ill, dreads the thought of asking her boss for some time off. She not only imagines the boss rejecting her request but is also convinced she will be shamed and humiliated. For several nights she dreams that she is "bleeding to death from the heart" on her boss's desk while the boss chats and laughs with friends on the phone. When Rose actually asks for the time off she is surprised and confused by the gentle, concerned manner in which she is encouraged to take a few sick days.

This example shows us how a person's internal representations of object experiences from the past can dominate the present inner world to such a degree as to render life painful and confusing by distorting present relationships. Rose is a person who often cannot tell what is inside and what is out, or even what is present and what is past. She was raised by a family that consisted of rigid, controlling, often sadistic grand-parents, a schizophrenic mother, and a severely depressed father. The family lived in crushing poverty and therefore offered limited economic and cultural opportunities, which caused further frustration and despair. There was a great deal of illness as well, and Rose suffered as each fam-ily member was hospitalized for serious physical and emotional break-downs. All of her caregivers were dead by the time she was 20. Nothing ever seemed stable, clear, clean, or safe. Therefore, Rose now carries within her the expectation that bad things will come *at* her (fearing the boss's rejection) and that life will come *out* of her (bleeding to death). Although Rose is very bright and has a quick, perceptive mind, which she uses successfully in her work, her judgment fails her when it comes to herself and her needs. She still experiences herself as being a bad little girl in that chaotic, hostile, frightening world in which she grew up.

Led by social work, which has always valued the biopsychosocial approach, all of the mental health disciplines are becoming ever more aware of the importance of looking not only at the person, but also at the person-in-situation. The striking, invaluable contribution made by object relations theory is that it helps the clinician to understand the power of the situation in the person. In other words, what is "outside" often gets "inside" and shapes the way a person grows, thinks, and feels.

BEGINNINGS

In Chapter 2, we saw that Freud's genius lay in his appreciation of the passions that "drive" humankind, passions both sexual and aggressive. However, he was also aware of the role that real objects play in develop-ment. In 1917 he published "Mourning and Melancholia," a paper that for the first time addressed the role of the object as much more than simply the target of the drives and stressed the importance of the object in psychological development. Freud distinguishes the process of nor-mal mourning from that of melancholia. In mourning, the sorrow is about loss and, once the loss is worked through, the self remains basi-cally unchanged or perhaps even strengthened through internalization of the lost "good" object. In melancholia, which looks like a mourning that doesn't end, harsh or negative feelings toward a lost loved one become internalized, are turned against the self, and actually change the self into a self-hating human being. This is the first time in psychoanalytic theory that change in psychic structure is seen as coming from an object relation rather than from the success or failure of the gratification of a drive.

In the time immediately after someone's death, the person in mourning is dejected, full or sorrow, and uninterested in present-day life. But that same person will often be passionately interested in memories of the dead person, who may seem more vividly alive and important than anyone else. The memory of the loved one's voice or of her smile, of the way she loved spaghetti or woke up in the morning—all these details are present, sometimes unbearably so. Places become filled with meaning, beauty, and pain because of past experiences with the dead person. It is as if the mourner makes one last desperate attempt to keep the person alive, to defy and deny the reality of loss. In time, however, as each memory is seized and cherished, reality ultimately requires letting the object go, allowing the mourner to return to the present, to the self, and to new objects.

Melancholia looks the same at first. There is the same dejection, the loss of energy and interest, but in melancholia these things do not pass. There is no sense of anything being worked through. The mourner remains in mourning, unable to move forward and, strikingly, in addition to being sad about the loss, seems full of complaints about the self. The mourner seems to be suffering from a disturbance in self-regard that often reaches the level of self-hatred.

What accounts for this melancholia, this drop in self-esteem? Freud postulated that the complaints about the self were actually plaints about the lost person turned against the self. In this condition, the loss of a significant other, occurring through death, abandonment, or emotional unavailability, is accompanied by strong feelings of ambivalence. To preserve a positive image of the other, the mourner takes in and identifies with the ego of the abandoned object and then directs feelings of anger and disappointment toward that internalized image. Self-reproach and self-punishment become ways of dealing with anger toward the ambivalently held other, as that anger is now turned against the self. Rather than letting the loved one go and creating inner space for new objects and experiences, the melancholic turns her energies away from the world and toward the self.

To explain this process, Freud (1917) wrote one of the most dramatic sentences in psychodynamic literature: "Thus the shadow of the object fell upon the ego" (p. 119). Here we encounter for the first time the potent idea that the nature of the relationship with an object influences the nature of psychic structure. We can see how the mental representation of another is created in the self and how it serves to shape a person's sense of self and ability to attach to others. The concept of the shadow of the object falling upon the ego, of something in a relationship beyond instinctual gratification or frustration profoundly affecting the structure of the self, represented an enormous expansion of psychodynamic theory and eventually became the heart of object relations theory.

The process of how and why a person identifies with others, takes in others, and turns feelings about others into ways of feeling about the self is being examined, discussed, and debated about by object relations theorists to this day.

BASIC CONCEPTS

In the rich and varied field of object relations there are several schools of thought or theoretical groups. From the beginning there has existed a lively tradition of dialogue, interaction, and even argument within and between the schools. The simplest division of the schools is into the British and the American traditions. Main proponents of the British school are Melanie Klein, W. R. D. Fairbairn, Harry Guntrip, D. W. Winnicott, and John Bowlby. Chief among the Americans are Margaret Mahler, Otto Kernberg, Thomas Ogden, and James Masterson.

Primary, Basic Attachment

Object relations theory fundamentally addresses the absolute, primary need for attachment and the harm that can come if that need is not met. Several theorists have explored this concept through direct observation of infants and children.

Bowlby (1969) was one of the first to conclude that attachment is a primary, biological, and absolute need in human beings, necessary for the survival of the species. Unlike the theoreticians who believe that the mother or primary caregiver becomes important because she takes care of the child's needs, Bowlby believed that she is important from the very beginning in an absolute, built-in, biological way that is part of the "archaic heritage" of the race. He argued that children can suffer true mourning due to loss of the caregiver (rather than merely frustration because wishes are not gratified) because the primary caregiver is crucial to their very existence. Before Bowlby, Winnicott had recognized the importance of not using the word *gratify* for the *needs* of the infant. As he says, needs can either be met or not met. It is instinctual wishes that are either gratified or frustrated. What Bowlby proposed from his extensive and voluminous study of behavior across many cultures is that attachment is an absolute *need*.

Earlier, Spitz (1946) published a study describing the psychological harm that can come to children who are deprived of adequate emotional care. He observed approximately 100 infants of mothers in a penal institution. For the first six to eight months the babies were cared for by their mothers. Then there ensued a three-month separation from the mother, during which the infants received adequate physical care from the nursery staff but were not cuddled or held in the same way as they had been when they were with their mothers. Slowly but surely the babies began to withdraw into themselves. They lost interest in and responsiveness to the world around them. A sizable proportion developed what is called "anaclitic depression"—a severe, total withdrawal from the environment, characterized by turning away from objects, and a going inward somewhere so far away that there can be no return. Suffering this kind of severe depression, some of the infants became anorexic and simply lay in their cribs, inert and drained of energy. A few actually died. Of those that survived, many showed severe developmental abnormalities in the use of motor skills and language even at 18 months.

Spitz's work helped to document how much human infants need ongoing interactional relationships to develop and even to survive. By observing the role of the mother–child interaction in shaping normal development, he noted that there were developmental steps, which he viewed as "organizers" of the self. At 2 months an infant follows the moving face of an adult; at 3 months she reacts with a smile to a face. At 6 to 8 months she shows "stranger anxiety," becoming wary and frightened of anyone unfamiliar and being very attached to one or two people, trusting only them to meet her needs. By 12 to 13 months, she begins to shake her head "no" to express disagreement, which also stimulates the beginning of the use of language. Currently some of Spitz's work seems outdated, not because any of it is inaccurate, but because more recent infant observation has added a detailed wealth of information about the richness of the infant's experiences and capabilities. A vignette from the treatment of a 45-year-old professional woman illustrates the theory of the universal need for attachment and the enduring emptiness and sorrow that can result from a paucity of early attachment:

> Sandy, a 45-year-old African-American woman, entered treatment complaining of an inability to take care of herself properly despite a seemingly successful and well-organized life. The truth of the matter was that she almost never cooked for herself, rarely even went to the market, and was quite unable to clean her house or keep her clothes in order. She lived alone and her dinner often consisted of buying a can of franks and beans and eating it out of the container barely warm. She slept in her underwear and took quick showers in the morning, but only out of necessity. She had been left alone and neglected a great deal as a child, and the therapist correctly determined that she lacked self-parenting skills because of that deprivation. Together therapist and patient worked on helping her learn to market, cook, clean, and take long, luxurious baths. Despite good progress Sandy still seemed very sad. When asked what was wrong she said, "I am really glad I have learned to take care of myself better. Every evening now I buy good food and cook it well and set the table with pretty things. I read a good book and bathe in my bath salts and powder myself and put on a soft nightgown and nice face cream. *And then I sit on the edge of my bed and wonder when the grown-ups are going to come home.*"
>
> Sandy had learned all about the comforts and joys of physical care, but still felt pathetically lonely inside because of never having had enough inner attachments. Sandy was born to a 16-year-old, single black mother who was in many ways still a needy child herself. Her mother became clinically depressed and unable to care for her when she was 6 months old. The child welfare system intervened, but, having neither the policies nor the resources to help keep mothers and babies together, the system placed Sandy in the first of a long series of foster homes. Sandy's great-grandmother fought

fiercely to be allowed to raise her, but was deemed "too old" at 59. Profound connections were therefore severed that were not to be replaced in the foster homes where Sandy lived for varying periods of time, always feeling like the outsider despite what often was adequate care.

In object relations terms we would say that Sandy's inner loneliness is due to her lack of soothing introjects. Introjects are the result of what one has taken in from others. They are the inner people we all carry within us. Their quality and quantity can vary tremendously. They can be helpful or harmful or absent or any complex combination thereof. Sandy teaches us that attachment is necessary for more than simple physical survival. The fullness and quality of a person's inner world is greatly influenced by the quality of early relationships and Sandy's had left her feeling too alone and unattended to.

THE NATURE AND QUALITY OF ATTACHMENT: "HOLDING" AND GROWTH—WINNICOTT

We now turn to the importance of the quality of attachment and how the nature of object experiences influence development. We will also evaluate the way in which this theory stresses the need to balance attachment with the capacity to be separate.

Winnicott was especially interested in the capacity to be together as a prerequisite for the ability to be alone and to enjoy solitude. His work explored the complex interplay between the need for attachment and the need for separateness in development. He realized that both needs are profound and that, because they are almost opposites, there is a tremendous amount of tension between the two. Louise J. Kaplan, in a book entitled *Oneness and Separateness* (1978), captures some of the intensity of this basic dilemma:

> Where does the dialogue begin? In his first partnership outside of the womb, the infant is filled up with the bliss of unconditional love— the bliss of oneness with his mother. This is the basic dialogue of human love. The next series of mother–infant dialogues concerns the

way the infant separates from the state of oneness with the mother. All later human love and dialogue is a striving to reconcile with our longings to restore the lost bliss of oneness with our equally intense need for separateness and individual selfhood. [p. 27]

Regarding the "bliss of oneness," Winnicott did place a rather heavy burden on the shoulders of mothers. He postulated that at the very beginning of life the infant thrives with a mother (or other caregiver) who can allow herself to merge into the kind of blissful union and total merger that, if it were not so healthy and fundamental to development, would be seen as abnormal. Winnicott (1956) calls it "primary maternal preoccupation" and, in fact, describes it as a "normal illness" (p. 302). By this he means that a healthy mother can allow herself to lose herself completely in her baby. The state described is akin to being totally, consumingly in love, and, as such, eases the shock of the transition from the perfect state of oneness in the womb to separate, extrauterine life. In fact, Winnicott says that this merger with the baby ideally needs to start during pregnancy so that this almost totally safe surround is ready for the infant when she is born.

This period of mother–child union shifts as the infant begins to recognize her separateness and her individuality grows. Her sense of being in a good-enough *holding environment* continues to be necessary, but it must be subtle enough to be protective without being overly impinging or limiting. By holding environment Winnicott did not mean merely literal holding, but the capacity of the mother to create the world in such a way for the baby that she feels held, safe, and protected from dangers without and protected as well from the danger of emotions within.

The critique of this theory is that it is highly culture bound, placing at its center the idealized stay-at-home mother of the 1950s. Taken too literally, it can sound as if the child's healthy psychological development is doomed unless the child's mother can achieve that state of primary maternal preoccupation. Taken in perspective, however, the value of this concept is that it can help the clinician appreciate the kind of closeness and attachment that needs to occur at least some of the time in treatment for development to proceed well. In other words, it is probably true that all babies and all people need to feel some moments of complete safety, union, and love.

It must also be remembered that it was Winnicott himself who qualified all his statements about mothers by saying that the mother does not have to be perfect for healthy development to occur. She just has to be "good enough," and the most important quality the good-enough mother possesses is a capacity for attunement to the baby's changing developmental needs, a daunting task in and of itself.

Now that we have looked at the state of blissful attachment to the object, we need also to understand how the child moves toward a state of separateness. In looking at children's strivings to reconcile the two needs, Winnicott observed that children turn to the use of what he called "transitional objects." The worn, scruffy teddy bear, the beloved chewed-up piece of blanket, the humming of Mom's favorite tune—these are the things that children literally carry with them in order to begin to cross that great gap away from complete union toward the sense of self as a separate entity. These transitional objects offer ways for the child to hold onto the internal representations of others when she is not yet able to do so on her own. In other words, when the capacity for internal representations is not yet formed, a separation can be experienced as a disappearance, as a ceasing to exist, as a permanent void. The transitional object then is literally the only bridge to the possibility that a person continues to exist even if absent.

Clinically the concept of transitional objects is extremely useful in helping those clients who have trouble holding onto the mental representations of others in their absence and cannot, like the healthy child, create a transitional object from within. When there are no internal representations of the therapist, vacations or even the time between sessions can leave the client with a sense of complete emptiness. The strengthening of the client's capacity for internal representation during a separation from the clinician can often be achieved if the clinician offers the client a picture, an address, a postcard—anything that will represent the object of the clinician while she is away. The purpose of the offer is to create a bridge, a transition to the time when the object can be retained in its absence without the need for pictures or cards.

When one client tearfully said, "I don't remember that you exist at all on the days when I don't see you," it was suggested that she call the therapist's phone machine once a day, not to talk or leave a message, but simply to hear her voice. After a few weeks of using the machine as a transitional object, the client became able to remember and experience that the therapist existed without making the call. "I have you inside me now whether I see you or not," she said, "and it makes the world a much easier place to be in."

From a cultural point of view it is interesting to note that the need for a transitional object to facilitate separation is by no means a universal phenomenon or a sign of emotional health. Not surprisingly, the phenomenon is found chiefly in groups that value independence and privacy and therefore encourage their children to tolerate being alone at a very early age. Jeffrey Applegate (1989) reports on several fascinating studies about the use of transitional objects that factor in such variables as sleeping arrangements, feeding patterns, and the extent of rhythmic physical conduct. In one study he observed Italian rural families, Italian city families, and Anglo-Saxon families living in Rome. In the rural group 77 percent of the children slept either in the same bed or same room as their parents and only 5 percent of them developed transitional objects. In the city group almost as many children slept in the same room as their parents but they were rocked and patted much less frequently and 31 percent turned to toys or blankets for comfort. In the Anglo-Saxon families only 17 percent of the children slept in their parents' room and 61 percent developed attachments to transitional objects. Having reminded the reader of the inevitable ethnocentricity of theory formation, Applegate urges clinicians to pay close attention to culture in developmental achievements. He recalls his training in which he was taught that the failure to develop transitional objects was an indicator of probable developmental arrest and subsequent psychopathology.

Winnicott (1958a) gave a great deal of thought to the capacity to be alone. He came to believe that the ability to tolerate, enjoy, and make use of healthy solitude could only be developed, paradoxically, in the presence of another. If aloneness is experienced as too separate, empty, or bleak, it becomes unbearable. This can happen if a child has been left alone too much either physically or through gross misattunement to psychological needs. Aloneness and loneliness become synonymous. The inner world is not peopled with enough comforting figures. Conversely, it can also happen that aloneness becomes painful or intolerable if the inner world is too crowded with threatening, controlling figures who offer neither safety, comfort, nor peace. The ideal, then, is for the growing child to experience being near someone while also being separate and apart, to be allowed to simply *be* in the presence of someone who is neither too stimulating nor too frustrating.

Regarding the quality of attachment, Winnicott (1960) made one additional important point. He believed that attachment needed to be flexible and genuine enough to nurture what he called the "True Self," which is at the core of the personality. The True Self is the repository of individuality, uniqueness, difference. In relationships characterized by genuine attachment, the separate individuality of both persons is seen, respected, and encouraged to flourish. But if the child's thriving for separateness is thwarted, the holding environment can become a prison, a limiting rather than an expansive force. The True Self cannot emerge if the child feels she must be exclusively attuned to the needs of others in the family system and if she needs to be a certain way in order to be recognized and acknowledged. The highly individuated True Self will not emerge when the environment fails to be genuinely attuned to the child's uniqueness. What happens instead is that the child may develop a False Self, one that seeks to suppress individuality and molds itself to the needs of others. This False Self, trying so hard to be responsive and to take care of others, ultimately becomes overly compliant. Uniqueness, vibrancy, idiosyncrasy, difference are all submerged. In this debilitating, constricting process the energy, the power, the "wildness" of the True Self is lost.

> Adam entered treatment for mild but chronic depression. In his early forties he had what he called a "seemingly perfect American life— a lovely wife, two great kids, and a successful career as a lawyer." It turned out, however, after months of exploration, that Adam hated being a lawyer. He had never liked it. The aggression, organization, and linear thinking that are so useful in a law practice had always "felt foreign" to him. With encouragement and acceptance he was able to come to know himself as a much gentler, more creative person. He discovered/remembered that what he really wanted to be was a florist, but that such a wish could not even be "known" to him, much less mentioned in his upwardly mobile family. At the current time, Adam is trying to figure out ways to leave the law and eventually work as a horticulturist. He has realized that he developed a False Self

to comply with family expectations and to protect the family from disappointment if he did not realize *their* dreams.

THE INTERNAL OBJECT WORLD— KLEIN, FAIRBAIRN, GUNTRIP

The British object relations theorists Melanie Klein, W. R. D. Fairbairn, and Harry Guntrip present us with very specific and useful ideas about what the internal object world can be like. The internal world is comprised of representations of self and other, representations formed by ideas, memories, and experiences with the external world. A representation has an enduring existence, and although it begins as a cognitive construction, it ultimately takes on a deep emotional resonance. For example, memory images of a mother feeding, hugging, cooing, and so forth, coalesce into an object representation of the mother. Similarly, the various images of the self as it is experienced within, for example, warm and loving, or selfish and repulsive, make up the self representation. These representations are not observable and may not reflect the actual situation, but they are the content of the internal world and the building blocks from which relationships are ultimately formed.

Although a drive theorist, Melanie Klein was most interested in the internal *relatedness* of infants from birth. She saw the drives as "inherently and inseparably directed towards objects" (Greenberg and Mitchell 1983, p. 136) from the earliest moments of neonatal life, and not merely for the reduction of bodily tensions but for fuller passionate relatedness to another person. In Freud's view, no fantasy will take place if real gratification is available. Klein offered a radically different view. She did not see fantasy as a substitute for real gratification, but as a basic characteristic of human beings. And for her, fantasies were always *peopled*, were always full of yearning for objects and object relations.

Klein's theory about the internal world was also developmental. However, unlike Freud, who postulated the oral, anal, phallic, and genital phases, Klein talked about internal positions. The term *positions* made it clear that she was not simply describing a phase or a stage to be passed through, negotiated, and resolved, but rather internal states, ways of perceiving the world, ways of feeling that can and will be experienced throughout the life cycle. The two positions presented by Klein are the paranoid-schizoid position and the depressive position. Each describes a state of object relations that occurs early in life but can also be present in adult life.

Before commenting further on Klein's theory, let us reflect again on a way to understand the concept of *position*. Because of the problems that arise from the fact that developmental theories depend on the idea of phases or stages or positions, Pine (1985) proposes the useful concept of *developmental moments*. If a child in the second year of life is said to be in the anal phase, does that mean that every moment of her existence is focused on anal issues of clean versus dirty, of giving and withholding? Surely not. And what about the fact that age 2 is considered to be the separation-individuation phase by Mahler? How many phases or stages can a child be in at once? Surely more than one. Pine suggests the idea of *moments* to solve this dilemma by trying to capture the fact that during certain times in life there are periods of "peak intensity and peak developmental significance of certain phenomena" (p. 40). Therefore, although the so-called anal child has many other important things going on in her life, there are probably more moments at age 2 when issues of surrender and control are of compelling interest to her than at other times in her life.

Pine's concept of developmental moments is also useful as we look at Klein's description of positions. The first position she defined, the earliest way of being, is the paranoid-schizoid position. The name itself is frightening and describes a terrifying period that can be filled with feelings of fragmentation, surprise, and fear. Even the most cherished, protected, and nurtured baby cannot feel safe and connected all of the time, simply because it is so little, delicate, and dependent in a stimulating and startling world. The child in the paranoid-schizoid position lives in a land of shadows and pieces, of noise and light, of moments that feel blissful and moments of great fear.

The main anxiety of this paranoid-schizoid position is that persecutory parts of objects will get inside the self, overwhelm it, and even annihilate it. Again, a baby's experiencing persecution is hard to understand; but if a baby gets very hungry, waits too long, gets panicky, then gulps down the milk so fast as to choke, then one can begin to understand how even something good on the outside can feel like an attack inside.

Klein postulated that there was no such thing as a totally objectless autistic phase. The early world of the infant is full of impressions of "things out there" and "things inside" without clarity or accuracy of what's where or what's what. The things out there are not even remotely experienced as what adults can come to know as whole objects or real people, but they are nonetheless present and important. Klein named objects as they are experienced in the paranoid-schizoid position *part objects* in order to capture the fragmented way the world looks when a person is, or feels, too little to perceive the whole.

An 8-year-old boy away from home at sleep-away camp for the first time writes to his mother:

> Dear Mom I miss you. a lot of times I think about you I almost always cry. I wish you were here. Miss Flule always try to kiss us good night so does miss lever. I wish you could kiss me good night. I'll love you even blu even wen you're spaced out. Oh if I could just see a part of your face then I would be OK. Your son Brian Dantona Kelly.

Under the painful pressure of separation, 8-year-old Brian is trying desperately to get enough comfort from the counselor's good night kisses, but it isn't quite enough to soothe away the pain and fear. He then remembers some of the mother's bad qualities ("blu" and "spaced out") and declares himself capable of loving her even with faults—interestingly, faults of distance. Then, with the strongest cry from the heart, he states that he would be OK if he could just see a part of her face. By age 8 Brian has achieved some sense of wholeness of others (which he demonstrates with the "I'll love you even blu"). However, in his vulnerable state, he has regressed to the world and the longings of a much younger child. A whole, complex, real object is not needed—just a piece, a fragment, a part will do. During a subsequent camp visit, his mother asks what part he would liked to have seen. He ponders awhile and the answer is not easy because at first he couldn't decide between her mouth or her eyes, but then said, "Oh, it doesn't matter, any old part would have helped."

Brian also makes sure that he signs his full name (as if his mother wouldn't know who just "Brian" was), probably to reassure himself about his wholeness, his solidity, and substance on this earth. He will not fall apart in fragments. As we will see later in the chapter, this is a good description of a person trying to hold on to what Mahler called "self and object constancy."

In describing the second position, the depressive position, Klein tried to capture some of the sadness that can occur, paradoxically just at the time that there is growth in the internal world. She saw the depressive position starting when the toddler begins to have enough experience to realize that the good person and the bad person are one and the same and, perhaps even more upsetting, that the person, the self, who loves is also the person who hates. The loss that comes from this developmental step of seeing both objects and the self as complex and multifaceted, is basically a loss of innocence, a loss of the belief in the possibility of perfection.

For many, this theory is disconcerting because the thought of a depressed 18-month-old is not a particularly welcome one, especially when the depression comes from normal development itself, rather than from any misfortune. However, the developmental phases of infancy do harbor these intense feelings. Even for mature adults there can be pain in trying to reconcile being both full of love and at the same time full of hate for the same person. It is a struggle and at times depressing not to experience oneself or an other as simply and totally good or bad.

The clinical utility of Klein's work lies in understanding that the 18-month-old is beginning to experience the first faint traces of one of life's most difficult and enduring dilemmas—that of both wanting and fearing to be whole.

> Melissa, a 20-year-old daughter of an alcoholic father, describes vowing three things to herself as a little girl: (1) that she would always "totally and completely" hate her father, (2) that she would "always be utterly different from him," and (3) that she would never need anyone and would never cry. With a stony face and great tension she reports that she has succeeded, but her presenting problem is that she is so tense and rigid that she feels "made of stone." A few meetings into treatment, when she is asked what would happen if she finds out that she does have some softness in her and does love her father a little, her answer is a terrible cry of despair: "First I would want to hit you and then I would get so depressed. I wouldn't be able to live."

Melissa is trying hard to keep her internal world very simple, with only the seeming clarity of black and white. She is struggling to ward off the depression that would ensue if she had to face both goodness and badness in her father and therefore in herself. The only way she had found to survive and distance herself from the traumas of her home was to think of herself as totally different from her "bad" father. Until entering therapy she believed it would be too confusing, too sad, and ultimately too unbearable to face the complexity that she and her father were each both good and bad. Her conflict, as it is for all of us, is the dilemma inherent in wholeness. To be whole one must give up the purity of ideal goodness and total badness. As a patient of Klein's said to her, "With wholeness you gain a lot. But some of the luster is gone."

Despite the loss of luster, Melissa eventually learned the benefits of wholeness and concluded, "I can love myself as a real person with some faults as well as lots of goodness." Her internal world, then, became peopled with images of self and others that were complex, full of goodness and badness, love and hate. This captures the essence of how the depressive position is mastered through the development of tolerance for an integrated sense of self and others. This concept is central to object relations theory.

An important critique of Klein's theory is that it collapses and condenses too many later feelings and experiences into preverbal infancy and ascribes to babies clear-cut internal experiences that they probably do not actually have in the form that Klein postulates. While there is validity to this critique, Klein's insights into the fears and desires, connections and disruptions at the beginning of life are both evocative and clinically useful. If a client is struggling with some of these feelings it does not matter in exactly what month they first felt them or whether they have words to describe them. It is also important to remember that Klein is not giving diagnostic labels to these positions (although the terms chosen can sound pathological), but rather describing normal, universal states.

Fairbairn

More than any of the other object relations theorists, Fairbairn believed that what is inside the self, what actually becomes part of the internal world and the structure of the self, is taken in from experience with "outside others." He saw the ego itself as composed of parts: the central ego of everyday living, the libidinal ego, and the antilibidinal ego. While the terms are awkward, they describe a complex self composed of many aspects both conscious and unconscious.

The central ego is primarily conscious and assumes the responsibility of the ego functions. The primarily unconscious libidinal ego refers to the part of the self that is loving and expansive, and grows in relation to good, positive experiences with others. The even more unconscious antilibidinal ego is the repository of bad object experiences that have now been introjected to become part of the self.

Dreams often reveal how internalized object relations express a person's internal world.

A 29-year-old secretary dreams she is walking on "a dark and evil plain." In the distance she sees a group of hoboes sitting around a fire and at first she is drawn to the warmth and the light. As she goes closer, however, she realizes that the hoboes are engaged in a brutal task. They are roasting puppies ("adorable, innocent, little puppies") on the fire. Some seem already dead and some are still struggling. Controlling her fear and horror, the woman figures out how much money she has and begins to bargain with the hoboes for the lives of the puppies that can still be saved. She does this with considerable mathematical skill, arriving at a precise amount per puppy. Even while still dreaming she is quite impressed by her skill, because she has always considered herself to be a "weak moron at math." As the dream ends she is carrying a bunch of living puppies to safety.

Working with this dream transformed the woman's therapy and has been an enduring metaphor for who she is and what she means to work toward. She understands all the characters in the dream to be parts of herself. The puppies were her "baby self," full of innocence and potential (libidinal ego). The cruel hoboes, *now within her*, were introjected from her parents who were, in her memory, extremely harsh toward anything infantile, weak, or tender (antilibidinal ego). What was most useful, however, was not another reminder that she had experienced her parents' rejection, but seeing that part of her was now similarly cruel toward her own weakness and babyishness. Helped by this dream, she became much more aware of the times when she was harshly lacking in compassion toward her own vulnerability and neediness. She began to alter her relationship to herself at those times by saying "my hoboes are at it again." This allowed room for true growth, and also enhanced the functioning of her more adult self, which the dream had also revealed to be more competent that she had known (central ego of everyday living). Her view of herself as a "poor little math idiot" diminished as she joyfully began to acknowledge her skills and strengths.

This example shows us how potent the positive and negative internalizations of others can be, how they can rule the internal world, and how they can change through new object experiences and the growth of consciousness.

Guntrip

Harry Guntrip added yet another dimension to the drama between internalized and actual relationships. He shed light on a different part of the internal world—the part that is terrified that if littleness and need were to be known, if hunger and even greed were to be revealed, they would destroy love. Guntrip's particular sensitivity was to the most vulnerable and weakened parts of the self. He described what he termed the struggle with "ego weakness" and the "regressed self" that takes place in everyone as they attempt to develop and thrive. Guntrip believed that "the core of psychological distress is simply elementary fear. . . . fear carrying with it the feeling of weakness and inability to cope with life" (Guntrip 1968). Much of the work done today on recognizing and healing the inner child comes from Guntrip's attunement to this "baby self" in all of us.

Although not completely disavowing the drives as powerful motivating factors in human motivation, Guntrip believed that they retained a central place in psychological theory only because people would rather think of themselves as filled with mighty instincts than face the greater universal truth of being tiny and vulnerable in a powerful and mysterious universe. He also believed that people can very easily become overwhelmed when they are loved.

Just as it is difficult to accept the Kleinian notion about the depressive position (that there is sadness in seeing the self and others as whole), so too it is painful to understand that people can be so frightened and needy that they cannot bear love when it is there. It is much easier to think of a needy person suffering because care and love are not available to him or her. Suffering because of the terror that love *is* there confronts us with a much more complex human dilemma.

> Tom, a 44-year-old CEO of a multi-million dollar corporation came for therapy because he "couldn't rest enough." A recent medical examination had revealed high blood pressure and a rapid heartbeat, and the physician had insisted on therapy. Tom was the kind of person who exulted in "never doing just one thing at a time." He was praised at work for his boundless energy, although his relationships at home were strained by his intensity and perpetual motion. He always arrived late for sessions and could barely sit still. After many months, which were spent trying to help Tom calm down a bit, he was finally able to respond to the therapist's request that he be still for a minute to see what that would be like. Since Tom had been pacing, he was standing at the time. When he remained still and closed his eyes, he began to rock ever so slightly and two silent little tears began to flow down his cheeks. In a tiny voice he said, "I feel like a nerd, I feel just like a nerd." The therapist was immensely moved by the sight of this powerfully built, well-dressed, self-described "captain of industry" revealing his suffering in such a poignant way. She was about to say something accepting and responsive when Tom added in a desperately tight tone "and please, please, don't be nice to me because then I will be nothing at all."

It took Tom a long time to accept and love the part of himself that, in the language of childhood, he called a "nerd." When he was able to make peace with his littleness, his behavior became much less driven. Eventually he also became less terrified at the loss of strength and autonomy, the loss of self, which he had believed would occur if he allowed someone to care.

One of the greatest contributions of object relations theory is a rethinking of independence and autonomy as developmental goals that define mental health and maturity. In the belief system offered by object relations theorists, connection is highly valued, whereas absolute independence is seen as unhealthy and not psychologically sound. Mature dependence is considered to be the ideal. Having achieved mature dependence a person could survive for a while without dependence on others, but would not actually want to. Development is understood to proceed from infantile (total) dependence to mature dependence, but never to the independence and autonomy so beloved by the ego psychologists and some of the American object relations theorists, or so valued in Western ideals of mental health.

EARLY PROCESSES AND DEFENSES

In the chapters on drive theory and ego psychology, we introduced the concept of defenses, defined some of the defenses, and described the role they play in development. We will now turn to the contribution of object relations theory to the understanding of the defenses. Since all the theorists discuss the defenses, we will not present each author's point of view but will look instead at the defenses that play the most important roles in object relations theory.

Object relations theorists wrote extensively about the defenses, paying particular attention to how they pertain to relational issues. Because of their interest in the creation of the internal world and the processes whereby object relations are organized, they worked most on defenses that start being at play in the earliest months and years of life. These defenses, known as the primitive defenses, are introjection, projection, projective identification, denial, splitting, idealization, and devaluation. As the names themselves imply, all these mechanisms exist to ward off and cope with anxieties inherent in object relations. These processes serve to manage fragments and parts of the self and others— to keep them in, to get them out, to control them.

There are, however, problems in using the term *defense*, and even more so, the term *primitive defense*, to define these processes. The term *defense* is most often used to describe the mechanisms people develop within themselves to ward off anxiety. Yet what is referred to especially when the words *introjection* and *splitting* are used, is simply the way the infant *is* at the beginning of life. Babies and young children simply do not have the capacity at first to know what is inside and what is outside, or even remotely to experience themselves or others as whole. They are too little and too new to do anything but live in a world of fragments and beginning impressions, so they are actually not warding anything off or "defending" against anything.

With regard to the characterization of certain defenses as *primitive*, the word itself is problematic because in everyday language it has a pejorative ring to it. Indeed, in modern anthropology and folklore, care is taken not to use the word *primitive* because of its connotations of being crude, unsophisticated, or inferior. In developmental theory, the term is meant purely descriptively as "pertaining to the beginning or the earliest time" (Webster). It is also meant to elicit compassion for the very young child trying to cope with a very complicated world with very simple inner mechanisms.

These issues become important when we attempt to do a full biopsychosocial assessment. When, for example, an adult is observed to be "doing a lot of splitting," we must assess whether we are looking at a constellation of primitive defenses (regression under stress), or a developmental arrest (failure to progress, either fully or in part, to a more advanced developmental level). It is an exceedingly difficult distinction to make since the words, feelings, and behavior of the client look and feel very similar. One way of trying to find out the difference is testing out whether the client welcomes the possibility of integrating fragmented parts of self and others.

For example, if it is pointed out to a client that the boss she is experiencing today as a "total devil" is the very same person whose kindness she was describing last week, and that observation is welcomed as useful, then one can speculate that the person was not previously helped to see others as complex and whole human beings and that the splitting was a developmental arrest.

If, on the other hand, suggestions that human beings contain good and bad aspects are not only unwelcome but actually rejected, one can begin to think along the lines of defense—that there is some reason why the person needs to keep various aspects apart and separate. There is a *desire* to avoid or control something. This is quite different from experiencing the world as being in bits and pieces. There is a real wish to keep the pieces apart to avoid the suffering that comes from seeing things as whole. The term *conflict model* is used when psychological dysfunction seems to be caused by maladaptive defenses. The term *deficit model* applies to those instances when the dysfunction is understood as being caused by developmental arrest.

We will now look in some detail at the contribution object relations has made to our understanding of the defenses, seeing them as both part of a normative developmental process and as mechanisms to ward off anxiety.

Splitting

Splitting is the term used to describe the process by which the good and bad or positive and negative aspects of the self and others are experienced as separate or are kept apart. The word *splitting* can be very misleading because it implies that something was once whole and was then split apart. Instead, splitting is meant to describe a way of seeing the self and objects *prior* to seeing them whole. It is central to the way in which infants first organize their world—into good and bad or frustrating and gratifying experiences. Infants make use of splitting to help order chaotic early life experiences. It allows infants to let in as much of the environment as they can manage when they still lack maturational ability to synthesize incompatible experiences into a whole.

When splitting becomes a defense it is an indication of an unconscious desire to keep things apart and separate. Splitting roughly runs along the lines of good and bad, but is often a very complex phenomenon and is not usually as simple, for example, as perceiving one's mother as all good or all bad at different times. Splitting can apply to one's self representation or to one's object representations. In either case the split is an enduring way of organizing the world.

A client describes experiencing her husband, a drug dealer, as having two modes of being. In one he is the strong, successful, occasionally even mean, talented, intelligent "king" of the street. At those times he looks muscular, handsome, and potent, and feels both quite superior and quite arrogant. In the other mode, the "split" way of seeing him, the same man seems to be virtually a baby. He looks small and weak. He seems to feel sick and stays in bed a lot, whining and begging for care. He is much sweeter at those times and even somewhat frightened.

There is evidence that the husband splits a great deal, also. His splitting applies to the way he sees others and probably to ways he sees himself. When he is feeling strong he sees his wife as weak and inferior, and when he is feeling needy and small he sees her as powerful and life saving. Both present us with examples of people who are splitting because they are unable to manage complex feelings that are not easily integrated.

Like all defenses, splitting has adaptive, useful functions. Splitting attempts to put some order into chaos, even if it is simple ordering into good and bad. Splitting can be the basis for the adult faculty of discrimination and the capacity to differentiate good and bad. It is also needed as the precursor to the more developmentally sophisticated defense of repression because it is a young way of keeping things apart, keeping away something that is feared as bad and unacceptable.

Introjection

The concept of introjection describes a process that is central to the object relations theorists' belief that human beings are incorporative by nature. Psychodynamic theories propose various kinds of internalizations, the three main ones being *incorporation, introjection*, and *identification*. These terms are often confused with each other and they are used in many different ways by different authors. We understand these processes to exist on a fluid continuum with introjection somewhere in the middle.

Introjection describes the process of internalizing aspects of the object or whole relationships with objects. We can think of introjects, for example, as the taking in of the warmth of a mother's joyful smile or the coldness of her angry frown, into the self. Introjection is a type of internalization that is more advanced than incorporation.

Incorporation, on the other hand, occurs when the distinction between self and other has only been barely achieved and when there is a sense of the object being swallowed whole. A schizophrenic man who cannot tolerate being separated from his mother says to his therapist that he has eaten her. Introjection is less advanced than identification, which is a much more selective process in which what is taken in are valued parts of another. An example of identification would be a man whose father was a Quaker activist in Latin America choosing to work among street gangs in Spanish Harlem. In introjection what is taken in from outside objects becomes part of the person's self representation. In identification, selective and valued parts of another are internalized. With introjection, the external object (or aspects of the external object) is taken in and assimilated as part of oneself.

Object relations theorists have focused primarily on how introjection helps us master our experiences with painful and disappointing objects in our lives in order to be able to bear the anguish that the people we love and depend on can also at times be hateful to us. The "badness" of the other is "taken in" in an attempt to control and master the situation, in an attempt not to feel so powerless and to preserve the positive image of the needed other. This part of object relations theory is of great use clinically and helps explain why the victims of abuse, crime, or brutality often end up by hating themselves. It would seem much more logical that the person being hurt would be angry at the person doing the hurting, but that is often not the case. Children who are taken away from abusing parents almost always ask to be allowed to return home, claiming that they are the ones who are bad. Surviving victims of the Holocaust have often described being filled with self-loathing rather than hating their torturers.

In *A Taste for Death*, P. D. James (1986) describes a character who shielded the object representation from possessing any "badness" at great expense to herself:

> Miss Wharton had been taught to fear in her childhood, and it isn't a lesson children can ever unlearn. Her father, a schoolmaster in an elementary school, had managed to maintain a precarious tolerance in the classroom by a compensating tyranny in his own home. His wife and three children were all afraid of him. But shared fear hadn't brought the children closer. When, with his usual irrationality, he would single out one child for his displeasure, the siblings would see in each other's shamed eyes their relief at this reprieve. They learned to lie to protect themselves, and were beaten for lying. They learned to be afraid, and were punished for cowardice. And yet, Miss Wharton kept on her side table a silver-framed photograph of both her parents. She never blamed her father for past or present unhappiness. She had learned her lesson well. She blamed herself. [p. 162]

To illustrate the power of introjection, Fairbairn (1952) wrote poignantly of how profoundly people needed to believe that "God's in His Heaven—All's right with the world"; of how crucial it is to feel that the world *outside* is good, even if the "badness" must be felt in the self in order to preserve that belief. At least then there is hope of redemption. A child can only survive believing that there are good objects because "it is better to be a sinner in a world ruled by God than to live in a world ruled by the Devil" (p. 66). In a world ruled by the Devil "the individual may escape the badness of being a sinner" but the world becomes a place without the possibility of hope, rescue, or salvation.

As always, there are adaptive and useful aspects to introjection, beyond that of warding off of anxiety. Introjection helps in the later, more sophisticated process of identification, as it is necessary to be able to take something in, in order to identify with it.

Projection

Projection refers to the process of expelling, sending outward, and getting rid of unwanted or bad feelings (parts of the self) and placing them in others. The purpose of projection is to disavow those aspects of the self. Projection is a defense that can cause a lot of trouble in a person's life since it distorts reality. It is at the heart of illnesses such as paranoia with the classic example being the murderously angry patient who goes through the world thinking everyone is going to kill her. The aim of projection is to make the self feel all right, devoid of badness. This can make the outside world seem very dangerous. It can also leave the self feeling empty, depleted, and sterile (for further explanation, see Chapter 4).

Projective Identification

Projective identification is one of the hardest defenses to define and understand. A complex phenomenon, it has several parts and serves a variety of functions. It is, in fact, not just a defense, but also the manifestation of a fantasied object relationship (Moore and Fine 1968).

The projective part of projective identification is the same as in simple projection in which the aim is to get rid of something within the self that is uncomfortable and unacceptable. But in projective identification the projector does not want to lose the projected part completely— hence the identification.

Ogden (1979) offers some definitive work on the subject. He proposes that projective identification serves four functions and, as such, plays a large part in much of psychic life:

1. A defense to distance oneself from an unwanted part of the self while in fantasy keeping the part alive in the recipient.
2. A mode of communication in which the projector hopes to be understood by making the recipient feel the same way.
3. A type of object relation in which the projector has achieved a certain degree of separateness but is still in some ways merged with or undifferentiated from the object.
4. An important pathway for psychological change and growth since the process is by no means static and the projector can learn much from the identification with the other.

The following are two examples of projective identification:

A wife talks constantly with her friends about her husband's intense anger and depression. She focuses in particular on the way he curses and then despairs when little things go wrong, such as the kids spilling their milk or a light bulb burning out, often screaming "God damn it—I can't stand it." In their arguments he always vehemently denies that he is depressed. In contrast, she describes herself as efficient, hopeful, and happy most of the time. A month after the couple separates the wife finds herself shouting "God damn it—I can't take it" over and over again as she frantically pounds the light switch to a bulb that has blown out. To her dismay she realizes in that moment that she too is depressed and that she had wanted to "place" all her frustrations and despair into her husband in order not to find it herself. However, she had remained intensely interested in her depression by constantly thinking and worrying about his. In subsequent marital counseling each partner learns to acknowledge and accept his or her own anger and depression, and the projective identification is no longer needed as a defense.

A client accuses her therapist of being a "greedy pig" when the therapist proposes a fee increase based on the fact that the woman's salary has doubled after a job change. Rather than feeling greedy the therapist is feeling quite virtuous because she has proposed only a moderate raise. She thinks that patient is greedy for not wanting to pay more now that she has more. The argument about who is greedy and who is not consumes a great deal of the therapy time and goes on for weeks. Only when the therapist's supervisor points out that perhaps she *is* feeling greedy and secretly desires a much higher fee does the impasse begin to be resolved. The therapist can then talk with acceptance of her own greediness to the patient enabling the patient to stop defending against that feeling in herself and to start exploring it instead. For the first time, the patient is able to recount how she felt growing up "on the edge of poverty" in a South American country where many of her friends and classmates flaunted considerable wealth. She had always hated "being a have-not among the haves" and now recognizes that she had "grown greedier and angrier every day"; hence, her projective identification with the therapist's request for more money.

Both these examples illustrate an important aspect of projective identification—that "it takes two to tango." If no one in the dyad can take responsibility for the unwanted feeling, it will be batted back and forth between the two like a hot potato. When one person can comfortably "own" the feeling, however, the pathway for psychological change can begin and the troublesome feeling can be integrated into both self and object representations. Another adaptive and useful function of projective identification is that of "staying in touch with" and "feeling with" the other person, capacities that later lead to the formation of mature empathy.

Idealization

Idealization is sometimes difficult to understand as a defense since the word itself has so many different meanings. For instance, we will see in the next chapter that self psychology views the capacity for idealization and the availability of objects to idealize as essential to the development of a vibrant, cohesive self.

Idealization is a defense when, like all the defenses, it is used to keep painful and unacceptable feelings out of consciousness. The feelings that are troublesome are usually the same ones that people want to disavow: anger, disappointment, envy, sadness, desire.

Dawn, at age 21, came to New York to study ballet with a renowned teacher. She had auditioned with him in the Midwest and been impressed by his knowledge and his rigor. Even before leaving her home town, she began to idealize her teacher as "the most wonderful ballet master in the entire universe." At this point she was idealizing him because she was afraid of such a big move and had to convince herself and everyone else that it was a good decision to go because her teacher would be "perfect." When she got to class in New York, she saw that the teacher had far too many students and was both unclear and sadistic in his way of conducting practice sessions. Because she could not yet face the painful truth of her disappointment, fear, and anger, she idealized him further, telling everyone that she admired his courage to be true to his art as he yelled at students and humiliated them. She spoke about the "purity of his standards." Only when several students quit the class because of his cruelty was she able to begin to face the fact that his behavior was abusive and unacceptable. Eventually she was also able to leave and find a more helpful and creative class.

Idealization is particularly maladaptive when it is used as a defense against envy. When someone idealizes a person in an attempt not to feel envy toward him or her, the idealization can actually make the envy grow, because the more wonderful the person is perceived to be, the more there is to envy.

Devaluation

Devaluation is the converse of idealization and is used as a defense for the same purpose—to disavow troublesome feelings such as neediness, weakness, insecurity, envy, or desire. Most people have at one time or another said, "I wouldn't go out with him if he asked me" or "She thinks she's so beautiful but I don't want her," when in fact they are very attracted to the other person but fear their advances would be rejected. If a person denies desire through devaluation they end up feeling smug and superior but quite alone.

In the previous example Dawn might have begun to devalue her teacher in an attempt to feel "I didn't want to study with him anyway," thereby denying the pain of dashed hopes. Both idealization and devaluation, when used as defenses, rob people of connection to their authentic feelings.

THE AMERICAN SCHOOL OF OBJECT RELATIONS: SEPARATION-INDIVIDUATION AND THE DEVELOPMENT OF SELF AND OBJECT CONSTANCY—MAHLER

Thus far in this chapter we have discussed some of the most central concepts of object relations theory: the need for attachment, the importance of the quality of attachment, the nature of the internal object world, and the role of the early defenses. Another important facet of object relations theory centers around how the self develops through relationships toward greater differentiation and individuation. Margaret Mahler, an American object relations theorist, added to the study of psychological development a schema that explains how a child makes attachments to significant others, internalizes those attachments and yet ultimately blossoms into a separate, autonomous individual.

Mahler called her developmental schema the process of separation-individuation. These are two different, but similar, interrelated and interwoven processes. She believed these led to the *psychological* birth of the human infant. Her work presents us with a Western, white middle class, male belief system of mental health. Autonomy and independence are highly valued and made synonymous with health and maturity. It is not a view of healthy development that would be shared by all cultures. We can harken back here to the example cited in the Chapter 1 of the Iranian students observing an Iranian and an American mother–child dyad. Mahler's conclusions would be exactly the opposite of the Iranian students'. The American child would be seen as growing appropriately in autonomy, becoming comfortable with separateness and independence. The Iranian child would be viewed as overly "clingy" and dependent and headed for developmental trouble. Hence, Mahler's image of the baby captures uniquely American themes. The baby, in Mahler's theory, is seen as "an explorer of the New World," even as "a conquering hero" (Shilkret, personal communication, 1994). Surely pathology and normality are in the eyes of the beholder.

Nevertheless, much can be learned about a child from Mahler's stages of separation-individuation, and her work has great clinical utility. Separation is defined as the process by which a growing child comes to experience herself as a separate, distinct entity who "stands alone," so to speak. It is the process of moving away from union/oneness with mother. Individuation is defined as the process of coming to experience oneself as the unique individual self one is. It includes very specific self-knowledge about the traits, qualities, characteristics, and idiosyncrasies that make one oneself and no one else.

Mahler delineated phases in the separation-individuation process that she tied to specific moments of a child's life and related to the physiological maturation of the child. Applied in too concrete a fashion, her theory can be linear and static. A similar problem can arise when particular pathologies are traced in a linear way to certain phases of development. Strict adherence to Mahler's phases are not useful and can lead to "cookie cutter" diagnosis. It would be better, once again, to think of them as Pine suggests, in terms of "developmental moments." What Mahler describes does not happen in set phases or only in specific months, but it does happen. Here then is a description of Mahler's phases of development.

The Autistic Phase (Birth to 12 Weeks)

It is important to note that Mahler's stages are not fixed and linear. Rather the ages for various phases often overlap. An autistic phase is postulated by Mahler (1975) as an objectless and, in fact, even self-less phase. If this phase exists, it would be a time of almost complete non-relatedness and nonmeaning. Mahler correlates problems during, or regression to, this phase with the development of psychosis later in life, which is highly problematic especially in view of the current state of knowledge about biological factors in the most severe mental disorders.

Many theoreticians reject the idea of an autistic phase since they believe instead in the infant's capacity to relate from the moment of birth. Mahler's conclusions about this phase in particular are also the most challenged by current infant research (Beebe 1993, Lyons 1991, Stern 1985). Their work reveals a subtlety and intensity of recognition, interaction, imposition of self, alertness, and relatedness in infants heretofore unknown. They refute that a baby is ever autistic or unrelated. Despite all this, it must be remembered that some children do suffer from autism and seem to be living away from relatedness in a land of mysterious shadow. There are also certainly autistic moments of nonrelatedness experienced by all adults.

The Symbiotic Phase (6 Weeks to 10 Months)

Mahler (Mahler et al. 1975) calls the symbiotic phase "the primal soil from which all subsequent human relationships form" (p. 48). *Symbiosis* is the term used to describe a time in life when caregiver and baby seemingly exist in one orbit. It is the time of the most complete union, of healthy merger. The holding environment is the most encompassing at this time and from it stems the feeling of being safe in the world. Symbiosis refers not only to the actual relationship with the caregiver in the first months of life, but also to the perhaps universal fantasy of a time of total omnipotent union and bliss. In Mahler's view the hallmark of symbiosis is "omnipotent fusion with the representation of the mother and, in particular, the delusion of a common boundary between two physically separate individuals" (p. 450).

Having looked earlier in this chapter at Winnicott's ideas about the quality of attachment, we can see how this phase coincides with his views about the need of the baby to experience "primary maternal preoccupation." However, we also know that this is the same time in life that Klein saw as the beginning of the paranoid-schizoid position. Again, there are undoubtedly moments of each—when the baby experiences blissful oneness, but also when she feels frightened by the bigness and chaos of the world around her.

Separation-Individuation Proper

According to Mahler, the baby begins to "hatch" out of symbiosis, entering what she calls separation-individuation proper. This includes the subphases of (1) differentiation, (2) practicing, (3) rapprochement, and (4) on-the-way-to-object-constancy.

Differentiation (5–6 Months to 10–12 Months)

This period is marked by the infant's beginning separation out of the symbiotic unity. Growing interest in the world outside of the primary caregiver is stimulated by the new ability to crawl or creep or roll, and eventually to stand. The chief caregivers are still tremendously important but they are no longer the center of the universe in the same way.

Practicing (10–12 Months to 16–24 Months)

Practicing coincides with increased locomotion and ever-increasing bodily skills. Learning to walk is of enormous consequence not just in terms of physical mastery but because it ushers in the psychological correlates of being able to stand alone and walk both toward and *away*. This era of new cognitive and motor skills is often filled with elation on the part of the toddler. It is a time of triumph, exhilaration, grandiosity, omnipotence, narcissism. "No" and "bye-bye" are often favorite words. The child feels like "the world is her oyster." She is "the gleam in her mother's eye." Sometimes, though, that new world out there becomes frightening or tiring; it is then that the caregivers need to be there for emotional refueling. It is best for the child if the adults in her environment can accept with good grace her omnipotence and grandiosity so that the child's eventual disillusionment can be gradual and so that some of the power and exhilaration of this phase remains available throughout the life cycle.

A group of adults is walking toward the ocean with an 18-month old-boy. As they reach the top of the dune they are all struck by the roaring of the rough ocean waves that day. The little boy looks momentarily startled but then squares his shoulders, holds up his head, and in a very imperious manner proclaims, "Stop, waves." He does it with such power that the adults almost expect the waves to stop. Naturally they do not. To really underscore the grandiosity of the toddler, he is not even fazed by it. Anyone else exerting such force to make something happen would be crushed, but not the child in this phase. He is perfectly happy with the power of the gesture and the fantasy, and so, ignoring the crashing waves, goes off contentedly to play in the sand.

Rapprochement

Rapprochement is probably the most complex and complicated of the phases for both parent/caregiver and child. This is because it is the time that the child has very opposing needs—the need to cling and be close as well as the need to separate, to be off on her own exploring the world.

Gone is the blithe exploring of the practicing days when separation seemed so triumphant. Yet the wish is not for total symbiosis either because that would mean giving up too much selfhood. Because of this complexity of needs, this phase can often be the most trying for care-givers. A needy parent might cling too hard when the child needs to be let go, while an overburdened parent might push the child away too soon when she needs to be held close a little while longer. From this phase is derived the idea that the parent needs to be both optimally frustrating and optimally gratifying, another of those daunting sounding tasks for parents.

> Sarah, a teenager whose parents were never comfortable with her emerging independence, uses a recurring metaphor to describe herself and her life. She sees herself as a pony in a corral with other horses. It is not a bad corral, but it is very boring. The "same old horses" are always in there with her and although warm and friendly, they are boring too. Outside the corral she can see prairies and riv-ers and mountains and yet she fears going out for two reasons. First, the corral has no gate—there is no way in or out—so she would have to jump the fence. Second, once out it seems as if she would be totally alone because there are no horses at all outside the corral and, although beautiful, the world looks sparse and lonely.

What Sarah has captured in this image is one of the developmental struggles of the rapprochement subphase called *ambitendency*, the term chosen in psychodynamic theory to capture the tendency to swing be-tween two intense wishes—the wish to be close and the wish to be sepa-rate—and the two enduring, intense fears—the fear of engulfment and the fear of abandonment. These twin fears arise most potently as chal-lenges during rapprochement but vestiges of this dilemma often remain present throughout life, and for some, ambitendency becomes central to psychological problems and dysfunction.

Ambitendency needs to be carefully distinguished from *ambivalence*, with which it is sometimes confused. Whereas ambivalence refers to one person's mixed or contradictory feelings toward another person, ambi-tendency describes one person's fluctuations of desires and fears within herself. In a state of ambivalence a person has simultaneous and oppo-site feelings, usually love and hate, about another. This can be difficult to bear and to come to terms with. Ambivalence causes discomfort because it represents the struggle to integrate good and bad feelings about another object. Ambitendency also causes discomfort but it is the discomfort of an earlier time developmentally. In ambitendency the developmental challenge is not to reconcile the positive and negative aspects of the other, but rather to overcome fears about the dissolution of the self. In ambitendency the developmental opportunity is to discover that one need not be engulfed and destroyed by closeness and that distance does not necessarily mean abandonment and unbearable aloneness.

People often experience a resurgence of ambitendent feelings at the beginning of falling in love. This proved to be the case with Richard, who came for brief, focused therapy due to the wild, intense mood swings he could not control at the beginning of his relationships with Peter.

Richard had felt ready for a serious, committed relationship for some time. He believed himself prepared to proceed wisely when he met Peter and realized that he liked him a great deal. He was dismayed when he soon "started acting like a nut case." On one date Richard would feel very loving and close toward Peter and talk with him about the possibility of a long-term, committed relationship. On the next date he would be aloof and distant and talk about himself as a loner with little interest in engagement or closeness. Despite these shifts, which he could not control, Richard was having a wonderful time with Peter and recognized that he was learning to love him deeply. In therapy, Richard kept talking about his "ambivalence" about Peter, but he soon realized that he did not have mixed feelings about Peter at all. What he did have was deep fears about what degree of closeness and separateness he desired and could tolerate. He could not find a comfortable way of being that included a good balance of union and separateness. When he felt close to Peter he wanted to "merge with him forever," but then that would scare him because he feared he would lose "all energy, individuality, and ambition." Impelled by these fears he would distance, but distance too much, and then become frightened about having gone too far away and being too alone.

Once Richard understood these fears he was able to confront them, realize how young they were, and work on achieving a comfortable way of being with Peter in a long-term partnership. Over the years Richard has returned to therapy occasionally for short term work on other issues, career changes, aging parents, and so forth. After 12 years he is still in a happy, fulfilling relationship with Peter. He states he still struggles occasionally with fears of engulfment and abandonment, but he recognizes what they are and works through them successfully.

In this example Richard has worked out and grown beyond rapprochement issues. These developmental tasks will be revisited in Chapter 12, where we talk about the borderline condition, since many of the developmental tasks and problems of rapprochement appear in people suffering from that disorder.

On the Way to Object Constancy

On the way to object constancy is the name chosen by Mahler to denote the last subphase of separation-individuation. The fluid nature of the title has been welcomed by many practitioners because it denotes that developmental achievements are not fixed and rigid but come and go depending on the various stresses and strains in different periods of a person's life.

Object constancy refers to the establishment in the psyche of a relatively stable, benign, and positive representation of the mother, and eventually of others, that "holds" even in the face of absence, disappointment, or anger.

Object constancy provides security and strength from the feeling that the self can endure and be well whether or not the object is meeting its needs at the moment. Object constancy is related to object permanence but is not the same thing. Piaget (1937) coined the term *object permanence* to denote a purely cognitive achievement, that is, the capacity to retain a mental representation of an object even when the object is not present. Object permanence has no affective coloration. Object constancy adds that affective dimension because its achievement introduces the capacity to retain belief in the goodness of the object even when it is not being gratifying in the moment.

Many people struggle with weak object permanence and wavering object constancy. Clinicians hear this from clients when they say, "I can't even remember that you exist when I am not in the office with you" (lack of permanence), or "I can't believe you are there for me and care about me if we disagree about something" (lack of constancy). In treatment the achievement of object permanence and object constancy are often worthwhile and attainable goals.

> Eileen suffered from the lack of a well-developed object constancy as well as from occasional lapses in object permanency. The world, therefore, was often an overwhelming and frightening place for her. If a friend or co-worker became annoyed with her, she could not remember that they basically liked her. Although she tried, she could not summon an image of the therapist to help her out internally when she was getting lost in the belief that no one liked her. Eileen came up with the idea that it might help her if she could call the therapist's answering machine every day, not to talk and leave a message, but to hear the outgoing message. Eileen meant this quite literally and said, "Perhaps if I really hear the message every day that you exist and are basically a decent, courteous person, I will finally *get* the message that there are good people out there in a constant relationship with me no matter what is going on." Eileen called the machine daily for approximately three weeks and discussed the changes occurring within her in her weekly sessions. One day she stated simply, "It's done; I've got it now, I don't need to call any more," and from that day forward felt transformed by her developmental achievement. For the first time in her life, she was able to form friendships and get along with supervisors.

As mentioned before in this chapter this also illustrates the use of what Winnicott called the *transitional object* to achieve object permanence and constancy.

A CRITIQUE OF OBJECT RELATIONS THEORY IN ITS SOCIAL CONTEXT

It is important, as with all theories we study, to place object relations theory in its historical and cultural contexts. The heart of object relations theory was developed in England and in the United States during a decade when belief in the existence and the value of the nuclear family was at its height.

It is no accident then that the theory focuses with great intensity and specificity on the mother–baby relationship, assuming not only that mothers would be the primary caregivers but also that mothers would be able to be at home during almost *all* of the early child rearing.

Like any other theory, then, this theory must be understood to be limited by when and where and by whom it was constructed. One of the most important critiques to bear in mind is that object relations theory can sound like, or actually become, a potentially mother-blaming theory. Since the vicissitudes of development are tied so closely to the quality of the mother–child interaction, there is a danger of interpreting this to mean that whatever goes wrong is primarily the mother's fault. This does not seem to have been the intent of the theoreticians, but in paying such intense, microscopic attention to mother and child, they did at times lose the forest for the trees. The forest encompasses other relationships within and outside of the family—the social, cultural, religious, and economic forces at play, and the innate temperament, personality strengths, weaknesses, (and therefore *input*) of the baby itself. When Winnicott said, "There is no such thing as a baby," he meant that there is no such thing as a baby without a mother. We would say there is no such thing as a baby without a mother, and/or father, siblings, grandparents, extended family, and, ultimately, a neighborhood, school, and religious and cultural affiliations. There is also no such thing as a baby who grows up without being profoundly influenced by the prevailing realities of and attitudes toward gender, race, ethnicity, and class. A baby always grows up in a specific country within its political system, and the values of that system have a profound impact on its development.

It is crucial to remember these parts of the forest in order to put object relations theory in perspective and to understand what it does and does not offer the clinician practicing in the 1990s and beyond. This is especially important because current demographics in the 1990 census (U.S. Department of Commerce, p. 50) tell us that only 21 percent of the population in the United States live within what is called the traditional nuclear family of a biological mother and father, and 2½ children! Everyone else lives in some other kind of family composition, and therefore a majority of children are growing up with stepparents, with single parents of either sex, with same-sex couples as parents, in multiple family arrangements, in foster homes, and in institutions.

Even more surprisingly, no matter what the family composition, only 10 percent of all mothers do not have some work outside the home and are able to raise their children full time. If to this 10 percent we add the 3 percent of the children with nannies and the minuscule number of fathers home full time, it still means that 87 percent of all children in the United States are being raised by multiple caregivers rather than one primary caregiver. The mommy or daddy (or anyone else for that matter) able to spend a lot of time gazing into the infant's eyes and partnering every developmental step simply does not exist anymore.

What is interesting about these demographics is that almost nobody wants to believe them. When the facts are presented in class there is always shock, disbelief, and strenuous protest along the lines of "that can't possibly be true." It seems as if there is a universal romanticized fantasy within our culture about the perfect "Father Knows Best," "Ozzie and Harriet" type family. It is probably the fantasy of the family we all wish we had grown up in—and that fantasy dies hard.

Another limitation of object relations theory (and, in fact, of all psychological theories) is that it was developed largely by white, Jewish or Christian, middle- to upper-class clinicians treating patients derived primarily from the same racial, socioeconomic, and religious backgrounds. These theories, then, are not derived by, or from, a study of the poor, the disadvantaged, or racial or religious minorities or non-Western cultures, and do not in any way capture the richness, heterogeneity, and diversity of the current population of the United States. For this reason great care must be taken to evaluate what aspects of these theories are irrelevant or actually harmful to the care and treatment of specific individuals or groups within our society.

In a *New York Times Magazine* article (Smith 1990) entitled "Mothers: Tired of Taking the Rap," a clinical social worker and mother writes poignantly of how a rigid, narrow adherence to the belief that mothers are responsible for everything can be misleading and damaging.

> As part of my work I have made many home visits to very poor women in housing projects. I witness the obstacles these mothers must overcome to arrange a day's worth of juice and pampers for their toddlers. They have no money, bad housing, no day care, no way to earn a living, no physical safety, few reliable relationships and no social

support. But when their children are evaluated at mental-health clinics the all-too-common requiem for the mother's effort is simply "neglectful and unmotivated." The fact that mothers have had primary responsibility for raising children does not mean they have had the power and the resources to protect children from the world's tricks and perils—nor from their own circumstances and limitations. Primary responsibility for raising children cannot be simply equated with primary responsibility for harming children.

Such fantasy notions of the good mother harm all mothers and cause them to assume too much blame for damaging their children. Mothers imagine irreparable psychological consequences whenever they yell, stay late at a meeting, use the TV as a baby-sitter, forget to serve a vegetable, let a child share a bed, or leave a bad marriage. I cannot remember ever working with a mother—wealthy, middle class or poor—who did not have secret theories about how behaviors, or choices, or feelings of hers had deeply harmed her children. While some part of such worry and guilt is appropriate to the task of child rearing, it is increased unfairly and exponentially by the pervasive and unremitting image of what a really good mother would have done in her place.

CONCLUSION

What then has object relations theory contributed to our knowledge of the client's inner world? Most simply, it has provided a number of basic concepts for understanding psychological development.

The first and most basic concept of object relations theory is that of the primary, absolute need of human beings for attachment. The second central concept is that the child's inner world is shaped by internal representations of others. The third important concept is that human beings need to be both alone and with others, and that the struggle to balance and meet these seemingly contradictory needs lasts throughout the life cycle. Fourth, object relations theory looks at why we need others, how we take them in, and how we relate to them internally. It looks at the consequences of loss on the development of selfhood. It looks at the influences of relationships on the internal world. Being very much a theory about psychological processes, object relations theory pays particular attention to the earliest experiences and defenses—those that have to do with trying to distinguish between self and other, between what is inside and what is outside, and eventually with accepting and integrating both the good and the bad parts of the self and others.

Object relations theorists have also given us a new way to look at the therapeutic encounter. One of the most useful tools for learning about a client's early object relational experiences is the relationship that develops between client and therapist. Here the clinician learns in her bones about the client's feelings about separateness; here the clinician comes to know (often through projective identification), how the client's difficulties and strengths in relationships are reexperienced in the present. Here the client and therapist discover how in the transference, the client may hide true wishes while trying to conform to her perceptions of what the therapist wants the client to be. Here the therapist may experience the client's fear that if the client is too different or too close, the therapist will no longer care. Here the clinician and client can begin to understand the costs and gains of separation and individuation and what these may have meant and now mean for the client.

Often the clinician cannot know and the client cannot express the complexity of her inner object world until both have experienced it together, in a relationship, over time. And although managed health care may push us toward solving problems using time-limited, intermittent treatment, it is ultimately object relations theories that remind us of the utter centrality of a relationship to psychological development and growth.

In Chapter 7 we turn to a quite different view about how relationships with others shape development—that of self psychology.

References

Applegate, J. (1989). The transitional object reconsidered: some sociocultural variations and their implications. *Child and Adolescent Social Work* 6(1): 38–51. New York: Human Sciences Press.

Bowlby, J. (1969). *Attachment and Loss*, vol. 1: *Attachment*. New York: Basic Books.

Fairbairn, R. (1952). *Psychoanalytic Studies of the Personality*. London: Routledge & Kegan Paul.

Freud, S. (1917). Mourning and melancholia. *Standard Edition* 14:237–258.

Greenberg, J. R., and Mitchell, S. A. (1983). *Object Relations in Psychoanalytic Theory*. Cambridge, MA: Harvard University Press.

Guntrip, H. (1968). *Schizoid Phenomena, Object Relations and the Self.* London: Hogarth.

Jacobsen, E. (1964). *The Self and the Object World.* New York: International Universities Press.

James, P. D. (1986). *A Taste for Death.* New York: Warner.

Kaplan, L. (1978). *Oneness and Separateness.* New York: Simon & Schuster.

Klein, M. (1940). Mourning and its relationship to manic-depressive states. (Unless otherwise stated, Klein references are from *Contributions to Psychoanalysis 1921–1945.* New York: McGraw-Hill.)

———— (1946). Notes on some schizoid mechanisms.

———— (1948). *Contributions to Psychoanalysis, 1921–1945.* London: Hogarth.

———— (1952). *The Origins of Transference.* In *Envy and Gratitude and Other Works, 1946–1963.* New York: Delacorte.

———— (1963). *Our Adult World and Other Essays on the Sense of Loneliness.* New York: Basic Books.

———— (1975). *Envy and Gratitude and Other Works, 1946–1963.* New York: Delacorte.

Lyons, R. (1991). Rapprochement on approachement: Mahler's theory reconsidered from the vantage point of recent research on early attachment relationships. *Psychoanalytic Psychology* 8(1):1–23.

Mahler, M., Pine, F., and Bergman, A. (1975). *The Psychological Birth of the Human Infant.* New York: Basic Books.

Moore, B. W., and Fine, B. D. (1968). *A Glossary of Psychoanalytic Terms and Concepts.* New York: American Psychiatric Association.

Ogden, T. H. (1979). On projective identification. *International Journal of Psycho-Analysis* 60:357–373.

Piaget, J. (1937). *The Construction of Reality in the Child.* New York: Basic Books.

Pine, F. (1985). *Developmental Theory and Clinical Practice.* New Haven, CT: Yale University Press.

Smith, J. M. (1990). Mothers: tired of taking the rap. *New York Times Magazine,* pp. 32–38, June 10.

Spitz, R. (1946). Anaclitic depression: an inquiry into the genesis of psychiatric conditions in early childhood. *Psychoanalytic Study of the Child* 2:313–342. New York: International Universities Press.

Stern, D. (1985). *The Interpersonal World of the Infant.* New York: Basic Books.

United States Department of Commerce, Bureau of the Census. (1990). *Census of Population: General Population Characteristics, United States.* Washington, DC: Department of Commerce.

Winnicott, D. W. (1951). *Transitional Objects and Transitional Phenomena.* London: Hogarth.

———— (1956). *Primary Maternal Preoccupation.* London: Hogarth.

———— (1958a). *Through Paediatrics to Psycho-Analysis*. London: Hogarth.
———— (1958b). *The Capacity to be Alone*. London: Hogarth.
———— (1960). *Ego Distortion in Terms of True and False Self.* London: Hogarth.
———— (1965). *The Maturational Processes and the Facilitating Environment.* London: Hogarth.
———— (1971). *Playing and Reality*. Middlesex, England: Penguin.

7

The Theory of Self Psychology

LAURA MELANO FLANAGAN

Until now, we have examined very different views of the self. In drive theory, the self is a cauldron of seething impulses composed of bestial impulses of sexuality and aggression. In ego psychology, the self is that agency that mediates between the drives, reality, and morality. In object relations theories, the self is made up of internal representations of relationships with others. This chapter presents the theory of self psychology, which attends with its own specificity to what kind of life experiences contribute to the formation of a vibrant, cohesive self, and describes the tenets of self psychology, which focus with a different lens on how the self develops in the context of relationships with others.

Throughout the history of philosophy, literature, psychology, and the social sciences, there have been many ways of defining and constructing ideas of self, no two exactly alike. Indeed, all psychodynamic theories talk about the self in one way or another. What distinguishes self psychology (and the reason it is called self psychology) is its focus on understanding the self as a cohesive whole. The emphasis is on the person's *subjective* sense of cohesion and well-being rather than on the supposedly *objective* functioning of various aspects or parts of the self, such as the id, ego, and superego. Self psychologists try to understand the experience of self from the inside out, rather than from the outside in.

In *Webster's New Twentieth Century Dictionary* there are many definitions of self. The two most congruent with self psychology are "the entire person of an individual" and "the union of elements (body, emotions, thoughts, sensations) that constitute the individuality and identity of a person."

The theory of self psychology was first developed by Heinz Kohut, who published the main body of his work in the 1970s and early 1980s. His work gave birth to what has become a separate and distinct school of thought and a specific way of conducting treatment. His followers are still expanding on his theories and publishing vigorously today. Self psychology has become one of what are known as the "four psychologies," (Pine 1990), the other three being drive theory, ego psychology, and object relations theory. In some ways self psychology flows out of and incorporates some of the ideas of those theories, but it also critiques, rejects, changes, and modifies many tenets of the other theories and makes its own unique and creative contributions.

At first Kohut postulated that the development of the self coexisted with the development of the ego as a separate but equally important line of development. However, by the end of his life he rejected classical structural theory altogether and placed what he called a tripartite self with its own structure at the center of the personality. In Kohut's final metapsychology, the self is a supraordinate configuration that exists from birth. It is the source "for our sense of being an independent center of initiative and perception, integrated with our most central ambitions and ideals and with our experience that our body and mind form a unit in space and a continuum in time" (Kohut 1977, p. 177). We will see later in the chapter that this supraordinate self as described by Kohut has its own structure, needs, and driving forces. Id, ego, and superego are replaced by the concept of the tripartite self driven by ambition, pulled by ideals, and needing to recognize itself in similar others. Also central to Kohut's theory is the belief that the self can best come to be understood through empathy rather than through insight. Indeed, according to self psychologists, the self can only develop within a manageable empathic matrix of relationships that offer a combination of optimal empathic responsiveness and manageable empathic failure.

INTELLECTUAL AND CULTURAL CONTEXTS FOR SELF PSYCHOLOGY

As was discussed in Chapter 1 and as has been true of all the other theories we have looked at, the themes of the theories are always congruent with the cultural themes of the time. It is important to remember that the very concept of *self* is itself a social construct rooted in time, place, and culture. The value placed on the development of an individuated, autonomous, flourishing self varies widely from culture to culture. The notion of an enduring individual self has always been central in Western Judeo-Christian tradition and is still very much a part of the ethos of the modern, Western, largely male-dominated, industrialized world, which values autonomy over community. Many other major systems of belief, such as Buddhism, to name just one, view the individuated self as an impediment to spiritual growth and enlightenment.

The historical context in which self psychology developed is the 1970s and 1980s, decades known for an almost fierce focus on individual self-definition, fulfillment, and well-being. This was a time of self-aggrandizement, overindulgence, excessive power, in which "perfecting" the self became its own goal. Magazines such as *Self* flourished; popular novels such as *The Bonfire of the Vanities* and movies such as *Wall Street* mirrored the society's preoccupations with greed. Christopher Lasch's *The Culture of Narcissism* (1978) describes Americans in that era as living in "a state of restless, perpetually unsatisfied desire" (p. xvi). The ascendance of self psychology coincides with the era when many people in the United States valued commitment to self-actualization above all else. Not surprisingly, the pathologies of the times became "self" pathologies: the empty self, the fragile self, the fragmented self.

Still, self psychology is considered to be one of the most useful clinical theories precisely because it is very open and positive in its view of human nature and focus on the individual. There are almost no dark forces in self psychology since the self is viewed as having a tremendous desire and capacity to grow if its needs are met. There are no drives or unruly impulses originating from within, but rather there is an innate, motivating "push" toward health.

Early in his career Kohut observed that he was treating a group of patients who were not helped by his interpretations of drive and conflict. They did not feel better about themselves, nor were their symptoms alleviated even though they gained a certain amount of insight.

Kohut suggested that many of these patients struggled with dilemmas of narcissism. On one hand, they were arrogant, aloof, and felt superior to others; on the other, they seemed not to have achieved a sound, cohesive sense of self or healthy, balanced self-regard. In the transference relationship, these patients needed either to be admired profusely or to find perfection in the clinician or sometimes both. In examining his own countertransference, Kohut realized that these patients often left him feeling listless, bored, and disconnected. They were so wrapped up in themselves that the therapist could not feel useful or sometimes even real. They seemed not to need anyone at all and yet paradoxically seemed very fragile and prone to shame. Later Modell (1975) was to write about narcissistic pathology as "the illusion of self sufficiency," a phrase that poignantly captures the narcissistic struggle to appear strong and invulnerable while hiding tremendous neediness and lack of cohesion.

Because of these observations, Kohut began to rethink the question of what constitutes the healthy self. Eventually he abandoned the drives as the motivating force in growth and personality formation, and placed the impetus to become a cohesive self at the center of psychological development. He also rejected the Freudian notion that psychological structure is composed of the id, the ego, and the superego, and the idea that the resolution of intrapsychic conflict produces health. Instead, a healthy self is derived from experiences in which caregiving others, known as selfobjects, meet the specific needs of the emerging self. Rage and aggression are no longer seen as flowing from distinct, innate drives, but rather as reactions to unmet needs.

At first Kohut believed that his new insights applied only to certain patients who suffered from narcissistic character problems. He still saw the validity of drive, ego, and object relations theories for problems of a neurotic nature. However, by the end of his life he believed that all psychopathology was based on flaws in the self and that "all these flaws in the self are due to disturbances of self-selfobject relationships in childhood" (Kohut 1984, p. 53). Here again we see the phenomenon that we discussed in the Chapter 1 and have pointed out already several times in the book: the apparently natural but unfortunate tendency of major theoreticians and their followers to come to postulate that their theories are true for everyone at all times. Again we reiterate our belief that this is not possible. Human nature is too complex and human experience too diverse for one theory to even begin to explain everything about development or psychological health and illness.

THEORIES ABOUT NARCISSISM

Before turning to the actual building blocks of self psychology, it is necessary to understand the profoundly new and different view of narcissism that is offered by Kohut and that lies at the heart of self psychology. Freud's view of narcissism was drive centered, based on energic concepts, and, as such, was both quantitative and linear. It was quantitative in that he believed each person has a finite amount of libidinal energy. What was directed toward another must be taken away from the self. If a person has only a certain amount of libido to divide between self and others, then she will need to replace self-love and self-involvement with object love in order to move forward in development. It was a linear theory for related reasons. In Freudian psychology narcissism has only one line of forward development—from self love to object love.

Freud also differentiated primary narcissism from secondary narcissism. Primary narcissism exists in the earliest phases of life when all libido is attached to the ego. For the infant, this state is considered natural; it is the starting point of development. Secondary narcissism occurs later in life when the libido that has been directed toward others is withdrawn from objects back into the self due to illness, trauma, or old age. Thus, in secondary narcissism an infantile state of self-involvement is re-created, and Freud considered this to be unhealthy and in need of resolution. Throughout Freudian theory narcissism has a mostly pejorative connotation; it is something to be outgrown or avoided.

Since Freud, debate and controversy have swirled around this subject. Many of the ego psychologists and object relation theorists have also described primary narcissism as a state of utter self-absorption and absolute infantile omnipotence to be modified or outgrown. But they are by no means in agreement with Freud or with each other about how, when, or why narcissism develops or what an ultimate, healthy resolution might be. To give just a few examples, Klein denied the existence of any period of primary narcissism whatsoever. The Blancks, major ego psychologists, wrote about the possibility of "sound" secondary narcissism and defined this as the acquisition of healthy self-regard wherein self representations are cathected with value (Blanck and Blanck 1979). In all these definitions, however, there still exists the implied belief that narcissism is something to be outgrown in favor of a more adult interest in others.

Kohut, on the other hand, eventually described narcissism in much less pejorative and much more expansive ways, differentiating between the crucial development of healthy narcissism and the pathology of narcissism. He postulated a separate and central line of development for normal, healthy narcissism. His view was less linear, polarized, and quantitative than that of the other developmental theories. Self psychology is based on the belief that the more attunement and love people have for themselves, the more they will have for others. Kohut did not view self love and object love as mutually exclusive. He did not posit object love or separation-individuation as primary goals of development or as important signs of health and maturity. On the contrary, he valued a much wider range of possible choices, seeing them as equally healthy and worthwhile ways of living.

> Although the attainment of genitality and the capacity for unambivalent object love have been features of many, perhaps most, satisfying and significant lives, there are many other good lives, including some of the greatest and most fulfilling lives recorded in history that were not lived by individuals whose psychosexual organization was heterosexual-genital or whose major commitment was to unambivalent object love. [Kohut 1984, p. 7]

Kohut did not view independence from others as a hallmark of maturity since he believed that we are all mutually dependent throughout life.

THE THEORY OF SELF PSYCHOLOGY

Despite devoting a considerable amount of attention to the concept of narcissism, Freud began the first section of his paper "On Narcissism" (1914) with the following statement: "The disturbances to which a child's original narcissism is exposed, the reactions with which he seeks to protect himself from them and the paths into which he is forced in doing so—these are themes which I propose to leave on one side, as an important field of work which still awaits exploration" (p. 92). To these themes Kohut devoted his life, in his study of what he called "the science of the self" (1978, p. 752). From his explorations he concluded that the plight of "Tragic Man" was at the heart of the human condition. "Tragic Man" describes the suffering that all individuals struggle with when empathic failures thwart their efforts to achieve self cohesion and self realization.

He contrasted his view to what he called Freud's notion of the pleasure-seeking "Guilty Man" who struggles with conflicts that arise between desires and prohibitions.

Several new, key concepts are central to Kohut's understanding of psychological development: (1) the importance of empathy not only as the main tool in clinical work but as the matrix within which all growth takes place, (2) the notion of the structure of the tripolar self, and (3) the existence and crucial role that selfobjects play in psychological development. The role of empathy in development and in clinical work is not a new concept, but Kohut elevated it to a position of supreme importance and considered it to be the primary clinical tool. Kohut did not use *empathy* according to the current, lay usage of the word, which often includes notions of warmth, sympathy, or approval. He meant something much closer to the dictionary definition of the word: "The projection of one's own personality into the personality of another in order to understand him better: intellectual identification of oneself with another." According to the dictionary definition one could have empathy for an ax murderer and that is precisely the way Kohut used it—to *understand* from within the experience of another, no matter what the experience. Much more than a feeling, empathy is a way of *knowing*.

Kohut wrote a great deal about the use of empathy or vicarious introspection as a tool in clinical work. He also described his belief that all human beings need an empathic matrix within which to grow and that only an empathic environment can provide the psychological nutriment and sustenance essential for mental health. Kohut did not envision the environment, however, as being always empathic. He knew full well that perfect empathy is impossible. Sooner or later human beings always disappoint or fail each other to some degree. What he did say was that there had to be an optimal balance of empathic gratification and empathic failure for the developing self to flourish and eventually experience itself as energetic and cohesive. Both in life and in clinical treatment, reactions to failures in empathy can be worked through if the disappointment and anger over unmet needs can be expressed and understood. This leads to a stronger and firmer sense of self. According to self psychology, empathic attunement is the necessary facilitator of development; repeated empathic failures are the roots of disturbance and thwarted growth.

A children's book that always gets a joyous response from youngsters is *I Hate It When . . .* (Preston 1969). The "when" refers to necessary parental endeavors such as "when you scrub my face" or "when you get soap in my eyes." This is an example of empathy for children because it acknowledges the truth of what children feel even when someone is doing something for their own good. The book does not say, "Because you hate it, I won't scrub your face" or "You shouldn't hate it when I do necessary things for you." It merely, through empathy, acknowledges what *is* and therefore validates something in the sense of self in the child. Caregivers scrub faces and sometimes children hate it; that simple reality offers true empathy to both. In some ways this is akin to Melanie Klein's beautiful point that if you can name troublesome feelings you can begin to master and transform them, because you have a fuller, more accepting knowledge of yourself. Empathy does not necessarily make a person feel good, but it does help people feel genuine and authentic.

The following example illustrates the inner impoverishment that can ensue when there is a lack of empathy.

> Lisa, a 37-year-old woman from El Barrio, a Latino section of New York City, joined a support group at a women's center. The group decided to focus on identifying and healing the "inner child." Participants encouraged each other to remember and tell their stories of neglect, mistreatment, and abuse. Lisa, who was the sixth child of an exhausted, struggling, poor single mother, became alarmed when she could summon no specific memories of her early childhood. Every time the group turned to her, she felt "gray and empty." She secretly feared that she had undiagnosed memory problems or that she was stupid. After many weeks she and the group began to realize that the gray empty feeling *was* the memory. Her childhood had been characterized by an absence of empathy for anything about her—good, bad, or indifferent. She realized that her sense of herself was vague and diffuse and lacked specificity. The group members realized that they did not have to help Lisa heal the wounds of overt trauma; rather, they had to help her explore what did not blossom in her due to years of inattention.

When it came to defining the structure of the self, Kohut made a radical departure from the Freudian view that a person's structure is made up of the id, ego and superego. He introduced a major new piece of metapsychology by postulating that the self is made up of three distinct poles. Just as the Latin words *id, ego,* and *superego* were probably not the best choices to identify parts of the self in English (see Chapters 3 and 4), so too the choice of the word *pole* for parts of the self is awkward. However, Kohut chose pole to refer to an aspect or a pathway of development within the self that has its own energy and needs. He initially identified two poles in the self, the pole of the grandiose self and the pole of the idealized parent imago, and so labeled the self bipolar. Toward the end of his life Kohut added a third pole, the pole of twinship, and considered the developmental needs of this pole to be equal in power and necessity to the other two. Confusingly, much of the literature of self psychology still refers to the bipolar self. But the full structure that Kohut eventually envisioned was tripolar.

Perhaps the best way to understand the tripolar self is to turn to Kohut's concept of selfobjects, for it is selfobjects that are needed to meet the needs of each aspect or pole of the self. In *A Dictionary for Psychotherapists*, Chessick (1993) defines selfobjects as follows:

> An object may be defined as a selfobject when it is experienced intrapsychically as providing functions in an interpersonal relationship that add to or maintain the cohesive self. This includes affect attunement, consensual validation, tension regulation and soothing, recognition of one's autonomous potential, and restoration of a temporarily threatened fragmentation of the self through a variety of activities and comments. [p. 357]

Self psychological theory postulates that selfobjects, understood as people or things outside of the self, are vitally necessary to every individual as sources of mirroring, as examples to be emulated, and as similar selves to feel at one with. Selfobjects are needed to fulfill these functions throughout the life cycle and are called selfobjects because they stand not as objects to be related to in and of themselves but as objects that give the self what it needs in order to become and remain energetic and cohesive.

Although selfobjects are most often other people, it is important to realize that other things such as art, literature, music, and a variety of symbols can serve selfobject functions. For example, a client who is particularly attuned to the weather, may use it as a selfobject.

Susan, whose sense of a well-functioning, cohesive self is very fragile, begins feeling "lost and panicky" if there are several rainy or
cloudy days in a row. When the sun returns, she experiences a restoration of hope and well being. For her, the sun as a symbol of
warmth and beneficence is a potent selfobject and her sense of
merger with it is one of the few sources of well-being in her life.

There is a new psychiatric diagnosis called seasonal affective disorder (known as SAD), which identifies patients whose brain function
is affected by the shorter amount of daylight in the dark winter months.
However, even that biologically based diagnosis would not preclude the
meaning of light and warmth in Susan's internal world. This particular
patient, who became quite attuned to the interweaving of psyche and
soma, was helped immeasurably by the combination of light therapy and
talking about what strengths blossom in her when she feels that the "light
and warmth" in her relationship with the therapist are sufficient to nourish her energy and hope.

To understand the main contribution of self psychology, we will
now turn to the selfobject needs of each of the three poles of the tripolar
self—the pole of the grandiose self, the pole of the idealized parent
imago, and the twinship pole. Each needs empathic responses from
selfobjects in order to flourish and grow. Each is necessary for the
development of a cohesive self. Again, although the language of self psychology is cumbersome, the theory describes poignant human needs and
yearnings. The word *pole* sounds rigid, but what it is attempting to capture is not a fixed tripartite structure but rather the idea of a flexible,
ever-changing, relational web of aspects or polarities of the self.

The first part or pole of the self described by Kohut, the grandiose
self, needs mirroring selfobjects, people who will reflect and identify its
unique capacities, talents, and characteristics. The grandiose self is the
self that wants to feel special and full of well-being. It is the repository
of natural, healthy exhibitionism. It also includes a great deal of specificity about characteristics of the self and therefore forms the core of
identity and individuality. People with sound grandiose selves are
vibrant, full of confidence, hopeful, ambitious, and productive. They
don't quite believe they can do anything but they often have the courage and the vision to try. There are echoes here of Mahler's practicing
child crowing that the world is her oyster, being the gleam in everyone's

eye. There is also a similarity to Winnicott's concept of the "True Self," full of raw vitality, fantastic feelings, and fervent wishes.

If we think back to the story of the little boy in Chapter 6 who needed to feel he could stop the waves when he was frightened, we can see how harmful a lack of empathy for grandiosity could be. If the adults had said, "Don't be silly—you can't stop the waves," he might have experienced his littleness or helplessness as overwhelming or, at least, as humiliating. Empathic attunement to his need to feel powerful, on the other hand, allowed him to go off and play with a sense of whole-ness and well-being.

The concept of the grandiose self can best be illustrated in clinical examples where there has been an absence of delighted mirroring or an active thwarting of the child's wish to shine on the part of the selfobject.

Mary, a 42-year-old woman beginning treatment, was surprised, moved, and a little scared when her therapist reacted with delight at the way she described an event of the previous day. With a keen sense of observation and a twinge of humor, she recounted how her meditation teacher, who had been sitting on the floor dressed in a sweat suit humming a mantra, suddenly jumped up, changed into a ball gown, and went rushing off to meet her diplomat husband at a white-tie event for dignitaries of the United Nations. The therapist laughed at the humorous description and smiled warmly at Mary as she recounted this tale. She observed that Mary seemed very stirred by this attention. Mary responded to this mirroring by stating sadly that no one in her family ever seemed to identify or care about any of her qualities, except if she was bad. No one had ever noticed or enjoyed her humor, her way with words, or her vitality. She then began to tell the tale of her childhood in a very rigid army family. The standards of behavior for the children cen-tered around silence and self-effacement. "Children should be seen and not heard" was actually embroidered on a sampler hanging in the living room. Grandiosity was not only seen as unhealthy, but was feared as unruly, disruptive, and possibly leading to evil. Boast-ing and pride in oneself were "works of the devil"—traits to be tamed, controlled, and, if possible, rooted out. Naturally, through the course of her life, Mary had become a good listener, but she felt that she "had lost myself in paying attention to others." She

had entered treatment after reading a book on shamanism and realizing that she could "no longer find my soul." She felt that, "The
flame of my spirit was flickering out because no one recognized or
cared what it was like."

Subsequent treatment has revealed to Mary many specifics
about herself that she now thoroughly enjoys: she is very funny, she
can be sarcastic when she wants to be, she has a true gift of imagery, she sometimes would rather talk than listen, and she likes
being the center of attention.

Because self psychology is not a drive theory, one still needs to ask
about what energies or forces fuel the wish or need for a healthy, grandiose self. Kohut never fully offered a substitute for the drives, but did speak
of the pole of the grandiose self as "driven by ambition." This fits in with
his general concept that there is something in each person akin to a biological growth force that pushes the individual toward the completion
of maturational tasks. Kohut believed this inner motivation, or tension,
to be the innate, embryonic push every individual has toward the development of a cohesive self.

Anxiety is also understood differently in self psychology than in
drive, ego, or object relations theories. As in interpersonal theory (see
Chapter 8), anxiety is not seen as arising from intrapsychic conflict, but
rather from loss of contact with the self or selfobjects. It is experienced
not so much as tension or nervousness, but rather as fear and dread. In
the pole of the grandiose self there can be fear of loss of contact with
one's authentic self if grandiosity becomes too exaggerated and unreal.
The authentic self feels special or strong in a genuine way based on real
qualities. A person who has become overly grandiose may feel so filled
with energy and power that these become painful and frightening. The
anxiety is akin to that experienced by people in manic states who feel
they might burst or disintegrate.

When Yvonne, a hard-working, talented, inner-city teenager earned
a full scholarship to a prestigious college, she received so much
attention in her school and from the media that she began to feel
"high and wild." She no longer paced herself well in her studies,
becoming obsessed with getting higher grades even though they
were no longer necessary. She began to daydream of getting straight

A's in college and "becoming famous on campus." With just a little help she realized she had become overstimulated by all the admiration. She learned to meditate as a source of needed self soothing and within a period of weeks was considerably less anxious. In this example, Yvonne recaptured the mature qualities that derive from the pole of the grandiose self, which are enthusiasm over appropriate goals and the ability to pursue these ambitions with joy and self confidence.

The second pole that Kohut described is that of the idealized parent imago. By imago he meant an internal, sometimes unconscious, object representation of an idealized other, usually from the early history of an individual (Chessick 1993). Again, the choice of words is unfortunate and misleading. First, the word *imago* is awkward, unfamiliar, and not used in common parlance. Second, calling it a *parent imago* is misleading because it implies that the experience is limited to childhood and that the representations are limited to early caregivers. This contradicts one of the strengths of self psychological theory, which postulates that selfobject needs can and should be met by a variety of people throughout the life cycle.

The idealized parent imago aspect of the self contains what Kohut proposed as the second, universal, selfobject need—the need to have someone strong and calm to idealize and merge with in order to feel safe and complete within the self. Just as the pole of the grandiose self needs to feel that the beauty and the splendor within is mirrored by others, the pole of the idealized parent imago needs to see strength and wonder outside of the self, in others, in order to merge with their growth-enhancing qualities. The pole of the grandiose self needs to be shown qualities within the self that are wonderful, while the pole of the idealized parent imago needs to find qualities in others that are wonderful.

Annie, a 54-year-old Caucasian woman, came to treatment because of a depression so crippling she could barely function. The therapist had been highly recommended to her by a trusted friend and had been described as a caring, skilled practitioner. Annie was very pleased with the first meeting and said she experienced the therapist as "warm and smart." By the second session Annie was paying close attention to the therapist, gazing at her intensely in the hope of seeing something good, which because of her need (and because the therapist is a genuinely nice person) she found. By the third session she would start speaking about the therapist while coming down the corridor before even entering the office. She would say things like, "Oh, you look so pretty today. You look so calm. I feel better already" or "You're so smart. I just know you are going to be able to help me today." She always said these things with a piercing childlike sweetness and her whole being seemed filled with the hope of having found someone wonderful to merge with. In speaking about her early experiences, she described a family she was ashamed of. Her father was an alcoholic tyrant and her mother a "witty socialite with no substance." As her treatment progressed, Annie often remarked on what a difference it made to her that she now had "someone special who makes me feel calm and hopeful."

Kohut described the energy that motivated this part of the self as a "pull." The pole of the parent imago is "pulled by ideals." By merging with the calmness and competence of the selfobject, those qualities can be established within the self.

There can be anxiety in this pole also and one form is the potential loss of self. This may happen if the merger with the idealized selfobject becomes total. Anxiety arises from trying to maintain the delicate balance between merger experiences that enhance the self because one feels protected and strengthened by the power and calm of another, and merger experiences that lead to loss of self cohesion because too much of the self has disappeared into the bigness and greatness of another. Probably everyone can think of a time when he or she needed to "sink into" the calm and strength of a parent, a spouse, a lover, a friend, or even a TV program at the end of a hard day. Finding such a selfobject to merge with is a wonderful experience that can, however, become frightening if the immersion in the other results in a loss of self so complete that disorientation or panic ensues.

A teenage African-American boy began to feel much better about himself once he started idealizing Michael Jordan's skill and prowess. He discovered a sense of power and possibility and applied himself much more diligently to his studies and to training for the basketball team. However, he scared himself at times when he realized that there were moments when he was thinking about Jordan's prowess so intensely that he "kind of lost it" and forgot who he himself was. He realized that he had to learn to balance seeing Jordan's skills as a source of strength with a realistic awareness of himself and without losing his own sense of identity.

Aside from problems of merger, self psychologists see other risks inherent in idealization. If others are idealized too much, the self can be left devalued, feeling little, worthless, and ashamed. This is a new way of looking at the psychological dangers of idealization. Drive theorists understood idealization primarily as a defense, as a way of denying hostile impulses against a loved one. "See, I don't hate you. I think you're great." Ego psychologists understood that idealization could potentially interfere with the regulation of self-esteem, but did not focus in the same way on the contribution healthy idealization can make to a person's very sense of self.

When there are sufficient selfobjects in a person's life to idealize, the mature qualities of the pole of the idealized parent imago can develop. These are the ability to delight in and grow from qualities in others and eventually to experience pleasure and pride in one's own qualities, standards, and values. The qualities of the idealized selfobject are taken into the self as a result of successful merger experiences.

The third pole, the pole of twinship, refers to the need to feel that there are others in the world who are similar to the self. This mutual recognition, this finding of a sameness in a pal or a soulmate, provides another kind of universal sustenance from selfobjects. The need for a twin is related to, but also subtly different from, the need for the grandiose self to be mirrored or the need of the pole of the idealized parent imago to have strong and wondrous selfobjects. Kohut came to consider the selfobject needs of the twinship pole to be as vital as the need of the other two poles for developing a vigorous and cohesive self and therefore he eventually designated it as a pole in its own right.

Peter, a 35-year-old Caucasian man from a working-class background, was immensely moved, and formed an instant, powerful, and permanent bond with his therapist, when he asked her what her major had been in college and it turned out to be the same as his—French literature. His family and his peers had ridiculed him throughout his childhood about his love of words and reading. He had been strongly advised against majoring in French, not only by his parents, but also by his guidance counselor in high school who had called his interest "an esoteric, useless pursuit." The fact that the therapist had also been a French major was seldom talked about in therapy. It just remained there as a precious and reassuring similarity and, by its power, enabled him to see how little his need to be understood had been met in the course of his growing up. Oddly enough, this same therapist had had an unusual number of patients over the years who turned out to have been French majors and to whom that bond had great meaning.

Because Kohut developed his ideas about the importance of the twinship pole toward the end of his life, he never did posit the energy that motivates that part of the self or the anxiety it experiences. We would say that the energy is born of the need not to be different or isolated or "weird," and that anxiety arises when there is no one "the same as me."

One young woman describes suffering greatly from the fact that all her siblings are retarded. She talks about the embarrassment she feels when she is out in public with them. She expresses how wonderful she would feel in the hospital where she is a physician if one of her siblings were a doctor also. Poignantly, she states, "If only one of them could walk beside me and be like me, I wouldn't be afraid of being inadequate anymore. I wouldn't feel so alone." Not being able to establish a feeling of twinship with her own siblings made her feel so "different and strange" that she did not realize she could establish a sense of twinship with colleagues. When this was pointed out to her in a support group, she was able to mourn her lack of twinship opportunities within her immediate family and start trying to find twinship selfobjects elsewhere.

Another example many people can identify with is how welcome it is to encounter a fellow citizen when traveling abroad, especially for an extended period of time. A graduate student engaged in folklore field work in Afghanistan described the pure joy he felt at meeting an American after living many months in a small native village. He laughed at the fact that the two would never have been friends back home in the United States because they disagreed wildly on many philosophical, cultural, and political issues. However, it was "worth its weight in gold" to be able to talk to someone who missed hot dogs, wondered what team had won the Orange Bowl, and remembered spending Sunday mornings in pajamas reading the *New York Times*. Too much time spent without a feeling of twinship can make people feel like they are unraveling and losing touch with themselves.

The mature qualities that develop when the selfobject needs of the twinship pole are met are security and a sense of belonging and legitimacy. These enhance the nuclear self and all its endeavors.

> Yoshi, a 28-year-old Asian-American man who played catcher on his Little League, high school, and college baseball teams, developed a great bond with other catchers, whether they were competing for his spot or playing for the opposing team. At tryout camps and baseball clinics he would always seek out the other catchers to talk about their mutual love of playing that particular position, so central to the action, so physical, dirty, and painful. They would compare notes about knee operations and the soreness after games and swap funny stories about what prima donnas certain pitchers were. Yoshi observed that it was almost as if the catchers had a secret language only they understood. Although as an adult Yoshi no longer plays baseball, he believes that these twinship experiences have made him very confident in the world. A successful salesman, he can walk into any company and feel "I am not alone or different on this earth." He is part of a brotherhood that provides him with sustenance and strength.

Self psychology does not postulate specific childhood developmental phases for the three parts of the self that are closely tied to certain months or years of life. However, Kohut did believe that there was a general sequence in development, with the needs of the grandiose self being predominant until around the age of 4, and the need for ideal selfobjects to be at its most intense from 4 to 6. He did not suggest an age-specific time for twinship needs, although we believe that they are particularly strong in adolescence. It is important to remember that his main belief about selfobject needs from the three poles is that they continue to exist in some form naturally and appropriately throughout the entire life cycle.

In all three poles, how does a person "take in" the qualities and functions of selfobjects? Kohut believed that what occurs when needs are well met is the process of *transmuting internalization*, which is defined as "the process through which a function formerly performed by another (selfobject) is taken into the self through optimal mirroring, interaction, and frustration" (Elson 1986, p. 252). As the self takes in the functions of selfobjects, they are gradually changed and made one's own so that the healthy self is not a replica of selfobjects but a unique self in its own right. The word *transmuting* was carefully chosen by Kohut to try to capture the transformative nature of internalization. The meeting of selfobject needs does not simply fill a person with well being and a sense of cohesion. Rather, the meeting of selfobject needs acts as a catalyst for development so that people can become more fully themselves. Some critics of self psychology hear the theory as advocating that they simply "give" to patients to help them heal, but a careful reading of Kohut and his followers contradicts this view. Empathic attunement to needs is not meant merely to fill or soothe; it is meant to stimulate the needed energy for clients to work and grow in their own way.

Thus, to follow up on some of the cases mentioned earlier in this chapter, Mary eventually grew to experience her skill in storytelling with delight, but with her own "take" on it. She was ultimately amused by different things than the therapist was, and became aware of her capacity for observation at different times and in her own unique way, which was always somewhat wry and subdued. Annie's pain was never fully soothed by her merger with the intelligence and calm of her therapist, but she found hope in the fact that a better selfobject was available to her. Peter derived a sense of legitimacy and "sameness" that allowed him to explore the specifics of what he was really like as a person in his own right, with his own special love of language and literature. All of these transmuting internalizations seemed to potentiate self-knowledge, growth, and cohesion in the nuclear self, and, very importantly, a sense of joy.

Kohut often used the term *microinternalizations* to capture the flavor of the myriad number of times the self needs to take in psychological nutriment from selfobjects. The empathetic attunement of selfobjects, including the willingness to admit and repair empathic failures, is the necessary groundwork for transmuting internalizations to occur.

A SELF PSYCHOLOGICAL VIEW
OF PSYCHOPATHOLOGY

When it comes to psychological suffering and illness, Kohut and the self psychologists speak of "disorders of the self" and offer various ways of classifying these disorders. Underlying all the disorders is the belief that psychological illness occurs when the legitimate developmental needs of the three poles are not met with optimal empathy and optimal frustration. This puts self psychology squarely in the *deficit model* of psychopathology rather than the *conflict model*. In the conflict model, psychological problems and illnesses arise when internal impulses and desires clash with prohibitions and guilt. In the deficit model, human beings are viewed as much more vulnerable to hurt, neglect, and deprivation than to being disturbed by tumultuous forces within. Self psychologists (Kohut and Wolf 1978) distinguish between (1) primary and secondary disorders, (2) a variety of typical self states, and (3) a variety of character or personality types. Notwithstanding the fact that they are offering a system of classification, they take care to point out that these are merely outlines and that no individual can ever be completely categorized by any of these classifications.

The primary disorders of the self include the familiar categories from *DSM-IV*: the psychoses, borderline states, narcissistic behavior disorders, and narcissistic personality disorders. The self psychological view of the etiology of these disorders is that severe deficits occur in the cohesion of the self when the mirroring, idealizing, and twinship needs of the developing individual have not been met due to chronic deprivation or severe trauma. Biological and social causes are not ruled out and are seen as contributing to the fragmentation of the inner world. More will be said about the self psychological view of these major diagnostic categories in the later chapters on psychopathology.

The secondary disorders that Kohut and Wolf refer to are "reactions of a structurally undamaged self to the vicissitudes of life" (p. 414), or the transient drop in self-esteem, depression, nervousness, elation, detachment, and so forth that individuals feel due to the inevitable stresses in life. These are called secondary because they do not shake the core of the person's sense of herself as an integrated, whole human being.

The self states identified by Kohut and Wolf do not follow psychiatric diagnostic criteria or categories. Instead they are descriptive categories of disorders of the self that are useful in clinical work especially in enhancing empathy and identifying the unmet selfobject needs of the client. The categories described are the understimulated self, the overstimulated self, the fragmenting self, and the overburdened self. These categories are not absolute. They refer to ways of experiencing oneself in the world that have become pervasive and enduring. Particular deficits are thought to have a tendency to lead to particular disorders but there is a great deal of fluidity among all the categories.

The understimulated self describes those individuals who often feel empty, bored, listless, or apathetic. Their selfobjects have not been able to mirror and nourish their grandiosity sufficiently. They feel flat, robbed of their buoyancy, their sense of aliveness and richness. Mary, whose case was presented earlier in this chapter, is, in fact, a painter who struggles mightily to "find something inside to put on canvas." She came into treatment describing herself as "arid, barren, and gray." She felt hopeless and inept about the prospect of ever finding selfobjects that would awaken her to life.

The overstimulated self describes those who have suffered from the opposite problem—intense, excessive, inappropriate, or erratic mirroring. Intense but not consistent behavior on the part of selfobjects can leave the developing self feeling overwhelmed and too full of feeling. There is not space or peace enough for transmuting internalization to take place because the person is always being crowded from the outside. In this case the person often feels robbed also, but robbed of the sense that her own unique strength and vigor resides within herself and is her own.

An overstimulated self can also develop as a result of idealized selfobjects being too powerful, vibrant, or famous. In such instances there is no ideal calmness to merge with, and learning self-soothing becomes a problem. Sometimes the result is a kind of flatness, underachievement in the service of keeping the self-system regulated. Sometimes the result can be an oversensitivity to anything new or stimulating.

Syrie, the daughter of a well-known, highly grandiose musician, feels constantly "full of ideas and projects and worries and pain." A performer in her own right, she can't shake either the wildly erratic praise or the self-aggrandizing attitudes of her father. She is often so overstimulated that she jumps if the phone machine clicks in the office or a car horn sounds in the distance. In treatment she hopes to develop a clearer, more realistic, sense of her own talents and resources. She already feels helped by the notion that it is possible to distinguish between real qualities or achievements and grandiose fantasies and beliefs. She is comforted by the example of the therapist's quiet, solid pride in her own achievements and would like to develop the ability to merge with the therapist's joyful yet appropriate sense of self-esteem.

While in healthy self states there is a basic cohesion, the fragmenting self has little sense of cohesion. Individuals with this disorder have not been related to as a whole by their selfobjects. They have received attention but it has been erratic, inconsistent, and unpredictable. The caregivers are often worried and distractable themselves, their attention flitting from one thing to another.

Vicki, the daughter of a very anxious mother, has trouble paying attention to one subject at a time in treatment. She will sometimes fly out of the office at the end of a session leaving the door to the building wide open. She experiences herself as a "bunch of pieces—like a puzzle thrown on the floor." She remembers with pain that her parents and all her older siblings would always interject "odd things" into conversations. One of them would say, "Your sweater is the wrong color" or "Your hair isn't combed" when she would be trying to tell a story about her day in school. She understands that it is hard for her to experience herself as a unified whole when people were always paying attention to random, scattered parts of her as she was growing up.

The overburdened self, on the other hand, has felt too alone and unsupported. Perhaps a person's problems or neediness were not accepted or even allowed. Perhaps her idealized selfobjects were not calm and reliable. Perhaps there were no twinship selfobjects who seemed to be going through similar difficulties. Whatever the case, the overburdened self feels he or she must "go it alone" in what is experienced as an unnerving, demanding, even hostile world. Neediness is experienced with guilt rather than with compassion.

Nancy feels she has to be responsible for all the problems of her family. "I have to take care of them—they need me to be strong." She is also hyperalert to "the pain and suffering in the universe" while very reluctant to reveal her own, believing that no one could possibly ever want to help her. Both her parents suffered from major depression throughout her life, and family interactions revolved around the parents' neediness and despair.

The character types identified by self psychologists are mirror-hungry personalities, ideal-hungry personalities, alter-ego-hungry personalities, merger-hungry personalities, and contact-shunning personalities. This way of looking at various personality types is self-explanatory and captures the poignancy of what can occur when the needs of each pole of the individual are not met or are met traumatically. The resultant yearning can shape personality and leave the person in a perpetual state of craving and/or fear.

A CRITIQUE OF SELF PSYCHOLOGY IN ITS SOCIAL CONTEXT

Like most other psychodynamic theories, self psychology does not pay much attention to specific issues of race, class, culture, gender development, sexual orientation, or even biology. That having been said, it must be noted that self psychology has been well received by those with feminist and sociocultural concerns. One reason for this is that mental health is defined by the subjective experience of well-being, cohesion, and vigor within the individual self. In the self psychological model, for instance, heterosexuality is not held out to be any more healthy than homosexuality. The goal of sexual development is for everyone to become more fully and vibrantly who they believe and experience themselves to be. This is a construct that allows greater fluidity in this area than many of the other theories, which postulate much more fixed psychosexual stages and outcomes.

For many feminists, self psychological theory is welcome because it broadens the parenting role to include fathers and all significant others. Kohut did not believe in the existence of a symbiotic phase between mother and infant and, unlike Winnicott, did not think mothers have to regress to form attachments with their babies. Thus, aspects of the mother–child bond become demystified, less sacred and magical, and more available to any person in the baby's life with parenting skills.

The oedipal drama is also reformulated in significant ways. It is seen as less of a drama and it is not necessarily a time filled with desire, competition, acquiescence, loss, guilt, or fears of revenge. For self psychologists the story can be one of joyful self-discovery. Having people of different genders to love and be loved by and to identify with is seen as offering wonderful opportunities rather than awful choices.

The impact of sociocultural factors can also be easily folded into self psychological theory. It can be used to understand the suffering to the self caused by social ills. Groups that are oppressed can be seen as suffering from selfobject failures on the part of society. People of color, the poor, many women, homosexuals, the disabled—to name a few groups—are rarely mirrored for their talents and sometimes do not have good, strong, calm role models to idealize and merge with. Hence, society can be seen as fostering a lack of self cohesion when it is oppressive. There are a growing number of opportunities for twinship experiences in grass roots organizations and support groups, but, for some young people, the only twinship ever offered is on the street in gangs. A thorough understanding of selfobject needs of the tripartite self would be a sound beginning in the formulation of better mental health and social policies as well as better clinical skills.

Some critiques of self psychology center precisely on the fact that the theory places such a high value on individual development. Although such a value fits snugly with certain aspects of current American culture, it is certainly not espoused by all cultures. There are many other constructs that place the good of the group or the community far above the good of the individual. In such cultures, the mirroring of individual qualities would be seen as less important than teaching individuals what they have to sacrifice in themselves for the benefit of the community.

Another critique of self psychology focuses on its belief about the nature of the human condition, which it sees as basically tragic. There is great compassion in the theory for the vulnerability and neediness of the human infant but for some this is too passive and empty a vision of what it means to be and to become a person. Self psychology does not seem comprehensive and complex enough to those who believe that there are innate negative and destructive forces within people that need to be acknowledged and worked with, and who do not want guilt to be removed from the range of experiences to be understood. While self psychology suggests that pathologies arise from deficits in the environment, it has been critiqued for neglecting the intrapsychic conflicts *within* human beings.

Nevertheless, despite what some see as its flaws or shortcomings, self psychology has made an enormous contribution to psychodynamic theory. Even those who do not see it as a comprehensive theory often make use of its concepts in their clinical work and find themselves enriched in their capacity for attunement and empathy.

CONCLUSION

What then does self psychology contribute to our knowledge of human psychological development? Self psychology offers a particular view of human nature and therefore of development. It offers new beliefs about the structure of the self. It offers a way of conducting treatment based on empathic attunement to selfobject needs. Self psychology posits that the achievement of a cohesive, well-regulated, empathic, and vigorous self is the goal of all psychological development. The health and well-being of the self derives from empathic attunement on the part of selfobjects, as well as the working through of empathic failures. According to self psychologists, the self is tripartite with each part of the self having specific selfobject needs. The grandiose part of the self needs mirroring. The idealized part of the self needs wonderful people and things with which to merge. The twinship part needs to experience others as similar and therefore comforting. Qualities and functions of selfobjects are taken in by the process of transmuting internalizations; these help the self grow strong and whole, enjoying a sense of genuineness, authenticity, and individuality.

In the absence of, or through excessive disappointments with, selfobjects we all experience difficulties with healthy self-regard, with ambitions, values, or goals. In the absence of a strong other with whom to merge, there may be a sense of frailness and emotional vulnerability. In the absence of mirroring selfobjects, there may be difficulty recognizing and valuing the self and valuing others. In the absence of twinship mergers, there can be difficulties in achieving a sense of connectedness.

As is true in object relations theory, empathic failures are necessary and are inevitable. Self psychology provides us with a way to learn about how selfobjects were or were not available to perform self functions. Self psychology provides a new lens to help us understand empathy's potential to promote emotional growth in the present. Self psychology offers a way of understanding not only what was missing, but what can be provided via new relationships (therapeutic and other) to make healing and growth possible. It is very much a theory of how the "outside" affects the "inside" and how the inside grows into selfhood.

Chapter 8 discusses interpersonal theories, some of which predate self psychology and some of which take it further. Sullivan's interpersonal theory was a forerunner of self psychology. He emphasized the importance of self-esteem and the value of the *real* relationship between client and therapist. He identified empathy as a therapeutic tool and stressed the role of interpersonal relationships in shaping development. More recently the interpersonal school is being enriched by theories of intersubjectivity, narrative, and constructivism—all of which try to go even more deeply and specifically "inside" both client and clinician.

References

American Psychiatric Association. (1994). *Diagnostic and Statistical Manual of Mental Disorders*, 4th ed. Washington, DC: American Psychiatric Association.

Blanck, G., and Blanck, R. (1979). *Ego Psychology II: Psychoanalytic Developmental Psychology*. New York: Columbia University Press.

Chessick, R. (1993). *A Dictionary for Psychotherapists*. Northvale, NJ: Jason Aronson.

Elson, M. (1986). *Self Psychology in Clinical Social Work*. New York: Norton.

Freud, S. (1914). On narcissism: an introduction. *Standard Edition* 14:67–104.

Kohut, H. (1977). *Restoration of the Self*. New York: International Universities Press.

———— (1978). *The Search for the Self*. New York: International Universities Press.

———— (1984). *How Does Analysis Cure?* Chicago: University of Chicago Press.

Kohut, H., and Wolf, E. (1978). The disorders of the self and their treatment: an outline. *International Journal of Psycho-Analysis* 59:413–425.
Lasch, C. (1978). *The Culture of Narcissism*. New York: Norton.
Modell, A. A. (1975). A narcissistic defense against affect and the illusion of self-sufficiency. *International Journal of Psycho-Analysis* 56:275–282.
Pine, F. (1990). *Drive, Ego, Object and Self*. New York: Basic Books.
Preston, E. M. (1969). *I Hate It When . . .* New York: Viking.

The Interpersonal School and Its Influence on Current Relational Theories

EDMUND DELACOUR

Drive theory, ego psychology, and object relations theories have all focused on what occurs *intrapsychically*, that is, within the mind of the individual. In drive theory, structural theory, and object relations theory, the unit of attention is the individual: the drives, id, ego, superego, life-cycle tasks, internalizations, and mental representations of self and others. Interpersonal theory changes the focus once again from a *one-person psychology* to a *two-person psychology*. Interpersonal and relational theories make central not the individual with his or her hypothesized internal forces and psychological structures, but rather the field between individuals. From this theoretical position, it is the relational field that ultimately defines personality and psychopathology.

This chapter traces the evolution of relational theories beginning with the work of Harry Stack Sullivan, and considers a number of Sullivan's key ideas that were forerunners to many current theoretical trends, all of which can be considered "relational." These include self psychology, narrative, constructivist and intersubjective approaches, and the school of interpersonal psychoanalysis.

If Freud was the product of his nineteenth century Victorian culture, then Sullivan was a product of the very different intellectual climate of the United States of the 1920s and 1930s. As we saw in Chapter 2, in the Vienna of Freud's time the reigning scientific paradigm was based on Newtonian physics with its elaboration of force, structure, and the flow of energy. Freud tried to make his new "science" respectable by formulating its language and models to conform to the prevailing notions of science of his age. He made the scientifically acceptable notion of biological drives the fundamental building block of his theory. The ultimate metaphor for his metapsychology was a hydraulic system with the individual's life forces flowing back and forth among the hypothetical entities of id, ego, and superego. The object of scrutiny, as we have said, was the individual, and not the social field in which the individual develops.

By contrast, Sullivan grew up in a post-Einstein world and, in keeping with the prevailing paradigm of his era, was much more oriented to systems and to the pattern and flow of energy among people. Freud saw the individual in opposition to the external world struggling to make peace between this world and the inherently asocial drives. For Sullivan what is formative is what transpires between people, not what is inherent in the individual. In a real sense, the individual in interpersonal theory exists only in the context of a real or fantasied interpersonal relationship. "For all I know every human being has as many personalities as he has interpersonal relations" (Sullivan 1964, p. 221).

Sullivan's theoretical language, which can sound so strange to us today, was, in fact, very much in step with the intellectual climate of his day. He was an intellectual product of what is known as the Chicago school of social science. This intellectual melting pot included such figures as George Herbert Mead in sociology, the linguist and anthropologist Edward Sapir, and Jane Adams in social work. Sullivan was also influenced by anthropology and he borrowed the idea of participant-observation from that field. Participant-observation research suggests that not only is it the subject of the research who is studied, but that the researcher influences the subject and the subject influences the researcher.

For Freud (and his culture) what is real is what lies below the misleading surface of things. In his classical version of psychoanalysis the true meanings, the deep meanings, are the hidden ones. For Sullivan what is real takes place *interpersonally* and the problems people have are due to their interpersonal realities. As Edgar Levenson (1985) has put it: "For the Freudian, the key question is, what does it truly mean? For the interpersonalist, the question is, what's going on around here?" (p. 53). Sullivan felt that as people come to understand their interpersonal realities, not their inner psyches, they cease to have "very great difficulties in living," in other words, to have psychopathology.

Freud and Sullivan also treated patients with differing problems and differing cultural definitions of what was wrong with them. Freud's bourgeois Vienna was preoccupied with sexuality in hypocritical, damaging, and secretive ways. The symptoms of his neurotic patients reflect their preoccupation with sexuality's ubiquitous meanings. Sullivan, on the other hand, began his career and developed his interpersonal theory while working with chronic schizophrenic patients. These were patients who Freud felt lay outside the scope of psychoanalytic technique. They were unable to develop a transference. Sullivan was undeterred by such therapeutic pessimism, and was eager to apply psychoanalytic ideas to schizophrenic patients because these ideas offered an alternative to the biological psychiatry of his day. He believed that intrapersonal ideas offered a way of making sense of seemingly bizarre schizophrenic behavior. He concluded that, far from being incapable of transference, schizophrenic patients could *only* relate through transference. In fact, these transferences are so literal that the job of the therapist is to make the patient aware of the therapist as a *real* person in her own right and not as a parent.

Nietzsche's aphorism that all theory is autobiography seems particularly apt regarding Sullivan. He was a colorful but extremely private person. The legends that surrounded him during his life depict him as having had significant emotional troubles during his adolescence, out of which he fashioned his view of mental illness. He was called or called himself at various points "schizophrenic," "psychopathic," and "alcoholic," and his biographers consider him to have been homosexual in an era that considered homosexuality deeply pathological. In the material that has been written about him, the influence of his lonely childhood is always stressed. He was born on a small farm in upstate New York in 1892, the only surviving child of a poor Irish farmer in a Protestant region. His mother was a semi-invalid who felt she had married beneath her, and was chronically resentful and aloof. According to Clara Thompson, from whom Sullivan received his training analysis, his mother was not interested in knowing the boy who was her son, but used him as a dummy on which to hang her illusions. . . . The closest friends of his childhood were the livestock on the farm. With them he felt comfortable and less lonely. There were no companions, and when finally he went to school he felt out of place, not knowing how to be part of the group. [Thompson, in Sullivan, 1962, p. xxxii]

We can begin to see the personal antecedents in the man who was to emphasize loneliness as central to psychopathology. Sullivan said of schizophrenics that he ignored their bizarre sexual preoccupations and concentrated on their loneliness. His own experience with loneliness led him to be optimistic about the prognosis of schizophrenics. He reportedly told colleagues that he had been hospitalized for a schizophrenic episode during his adolescence, though the truthfulness of this has never been established, and Sullivan was apparently often misleading or deceptive about his past (Perry 1982). In fact, he believed that a struggle with schizophrenia was a universal aspect of adolescence. This was part of his conviction, that "everyone is much more simply human than otherwise" (1953).

SULLIVAN'S THEORY OF INTERPERSONAL DEVELOPMENT

Sullivan hypothesized a series of developmental stages from infancy through late adolescence. Without going into the stages in great detail, it is worth noting what was innovative about them and how interpersonal developmental ideas have been echoed in subsequent developmental theory. For Sullivan, developmental stages are not defined by the progression of libido through erogenous zones, as in Freud's psychosexual theory or Erikson's psychosocial theory, but rather by the series of interpersonal configurations that characterize socialization. He emphasized the development, or lack thereof, of skills pertinent to these new interpersonal situations, much as the later ego psychologists, particularly Erikson, would do. Another feature of Sullivan's theory is that crucial development extends beyond the early childhood years. In this he resembles Erikson, who also recognized that personality development occurs throughout the life cycle. Sullivan's developmental stages are characterized as much by how they provide the context for the overcoming of earlier trauma or developmental failure as by how they describe what can go wrong. "I am much more interested in what can be done than in what has happened" (Sullivan 1956, p. 195). Again we see similarities to Erikson whose "identity crisis" is that point when cumulative developmental weaknesses can lead to breakdown, but also the point where there can be a reworking of earlier crises, leading to a new and stronger foundation for subsequent growth.

In interpersonal theory the fundamental unit is the initial developmental pair, the mother–infant dyad. Sullivan's first developmental stage is called *infancy*. It extends from birth to the maturation of the capacity for language development, which ushers in a new mode of interpersonal relating. From the first moment of his or her extrauterine life, Sullivan's conceptualization of the infant is that she is inseparable from her interpersonal field. She is dependent on the "mothering one" for food, warmth, and comfort. In fact, the relationship is physically symbiotic from the outset, since the mother needs the infant to relieve the pressure of milk in her breasts. This emphasis on mother–infant reciprocity brings to mind the later developmental contributions of Winnicott and Erikson. The infant's initial experience of herself, in Sullivan's language, is indistinguishable from her experience of the mothering one. It would be impossible to overemphasize the importance of this for Sullivan. For him there is no such thing as purely individual experience. All thoughts, feelings, dreams, and reveries reflect the *interpersonal* nature of an experience and involve relationships with others.

In the infant's life with the mother, a tension state arises sometime during the first 6 months, which Sullivan identifies as anxiety. It is unlike other tension states in the infant, such as hunger, in that there is no activity that will lead to a reduction of this state of tension. In fact, the presence of anxiety thwarts the satisfaction of other needs. The infant may be unable to eat or to digest food during a state of anxiety. The origin of this state of paralysis in the infant is, according to Sullivan, the child's experience of disapproval from the mothering one. It is via empathy, however, that the mother understands the needs of the crying infant, if the source of the tears is not apparent. Sullivan asserts that anxiety arises later in stages as loss of approval of significant others or loss of self-esteem or, more directly, from loss of interpersonal security. For the infant, however, there is no activity that she can engage in that will relieve the anxiety. Only a change in the *other* person can bring a return to a state of relative security, in which tension can be released. We see then that Sullivan's theory is no longer only directed solely toward examining the infant's needs and their satisfaction, but now directs attention toward how the interaction between the infant and her mother changes both people in the relationship.

Sullivan identified dissociation as the core concept. He has described how earliest experiences with others can be so traumatic that the baby experiences aspects of him- or herself as "not me." When an infant strives for interpersonal security, but is severely threatened, she may experience intense anxiety and dissociate areas of experience. Sullivan compared the sudden onset of intense anxiety to a blow on the head. The events immediately preceding the concussion are subject to a brief amnesia. The individual is only vaguely aware of the circumstances surrounding the event and thus is in a poor position to learn from it. The not-me or dissociated self organization remains with a person throughout life. This dissociated material is often linked to body image.

When dissociated material erupts into conscious awareness, we observe primary process, hallucinations, and delusions. In relatively healthy people, this material gets discharged in sleep. Here is an example of Sullivan's view that everything found in the schizophrenic can be found in different proportions in the normal person. Generally, psychopathology is proportional to the amount of dissociation the person has to contend with. The aim of psychotherapy is to integrate what has been dissociated. This is very congruent with current views on trauma and its treatment.

The second developmental stage, *childhood*, is ushered in with the appearance of articulate speech between the ages of 12 and 18 months. A child's communication with significant others now involves *consensual validation*, a shared and agreed-upon meaning. The child uses language increasingly to differentiate parts of the environment. The child begins to use language for the development of increasingly complex security operations. Finally, it is through language that the child begins to learn the really valuable verbal operations that involve consensual validation, a confirmation and a sharing with another of her experience.

Sullivan delineates the third developmental stage, the *juvenile* era, as the interpersonal context in which peer relationships develop. When the child is ready to begin school, she can truly begin to be social. Until now the interpersonal world was largely limited to the caregiving parental figures. Now a child relates to others similar to himself or herself. If not given the opportunity to have real playmates, the child will invent imaginary ones. During this era, a child learns to deal with authority figures other than the parents. She confronts the issues of competition and compromise with peers, the resolution of which will have important consequences for her interpersonal style. This is the child's first exposure to a reality other than the inevitably idiosyncratic one of her family. Sullivan believed children gain much by the opportunity this offers for the child to gain a perspective on her own family.

Sullivan's fourth stage, *preadolescence*, is relatively brief, from the ages of 8½ to 10 years. It ends with the onset of puberty. It is characterized primarily by the development of intimacy with someone of the same sex. For the first time the child is capable of love according to Sullivan's definition, that is, the valuing of another's welfare and happiness as dearly as one's own. Sullivan saw the "chum" as a valuable interpersonal relationship that allows both participants to experience consensual validation of their personal worth. Friendship provides the basis for future relationships with members of the same sex. Generally, Sullivan believed that intimacy with someone of the same sex in preadolescence is essential for the later intimacy in a heterosexual relationship. He is almost sentimental about the possibilities of the preadolescent stage of life. "I believe that for the great majority of our people, preadolescence is the nearest they come to an untroubled human life, that from then on the stresses of life distort them to inferior caricatures of what they might have been" (1954, p. 56).

While the characteristic interpersonal relationship in the preadolescent era is the dyad, Sullivan also stresses the importance of the group, the typical form of preadolescent society. It is in this larger group that pairs of chums come to terms with different kinds of leadership and with being led. Hours are spent in mutual fantasies. In the profound experience of accepting others and being accepted by them, a sense of personal worth can develop. This sense of personal value is based in part on how the person feels accepted and understood. This is a view of self development defined by a self-in-relationship. Sullivan wrote that the experience of loneliness is the most utterly bleak human emotion, worse even than severe anxiety. In fact, people will willingly endure severe anxiety in pursuit of intimate contact with another. The preadolescent has the first full experience of loneliness. This is the driving force behind finding a confiding other, which is characteristic of the era. In infancy there is the need for physical contact and tenderness. In childhood there is a need for activities with significant adults. In the juvenile era the need shifts its focus to the peer group. It is not until preadolescence that loneliness reaches its full significance and it remains a continuing force throughout life.

The physiological maturation of puberty disrupts the same-sex intimacy of preadolescence and ushers in the era of *early adolescence*. The adolescent experiences feelings of "lust" and her primary interest shifts from same-sex intimacy to genital satisfaction. An adolescent is now challenged by conflicting needs for genital satisfaction, intimacy, and interpersonal security.

Late adolescence, Sullivan's last stage, follows from the earlier stages (Sullivan 1953, p. 111). By now the personality has become a "relatively enduring configuration of interpersonal relations," and is established in its interpersonal contexts. This context is both real and imagined. Each person carries within herself imaginary persons who in fantasy either like or dislike her. Sullivan calls these "eidetic" people, while other theories would refer to them as introjects or internalized objects. By the end of adolescence, the self-system has evolved an elaborate system of security operations aimed at keeping the experience of anxiety to a minimum.

SULLIVAN'S APPROACH TO TREATMENT

Sullivan's theory was largely an outgrowth of his clinical practice and it can be argued that his primary goal in theorizing was to improve the effectiveness of clinical work. His reputation during his life was based on his clinical teaching, and he didn't write papers as much as give lectures, which were posthumously edited into book form. This is the reason for the rather informal, almost conversational tone of his work. He was, as we have seen, a practical theorist, who was guided by what is observable and what works. Sullivan especially emphasized the importance of language to the interpersonal field. He was the first theorist to emphasize how language uses the speaker, as much as the speaker uses language. For him, the individual is inseparable from his language, and thus his relationships to others. In fact, Sullivan defined health as a person's ability to put the interpersonal situation into words: "No one has grave difficulties in living if he has a very good grasp of what is happening to him" (as quoted in Levenson 1989, p. 544). Sullivan was also much more concerned with the *actual*, as opposed to the fantasized, aspects of his client's past and present experiences. He was apt to consider the patient's symptoms not as evidence of conflicting drive and defense factors, but rather as adaptations to the particularly deforming interpersonal circumstances with which the individual had to contend.

While Sullivan was initially excited by Freud's *theoretical ideas* as providing the beginnings of a psychological explanation for severe mental illness, he quickly became impatient with a number of aspects of the *technique* of psychoanalysis. He felt that psychoanalysts were in danger of erroneously or prematurely concluding that they satisfactorily understood their patients because of their belief in psychoanalytic ideas. He thought that the technique of free association frequently added the sin of passivity to that of dogmatism. The therapist might believe that he or she could simply wait and find the therapeutically useful, often symbolic, meaning in the patient's associations, without appreciating either how anxiety provoking the situation might be for the patient or how the patient might use the lack of structure in the psychoanalytic situation to avoid what is troubling her. In this way he advocated tailoring the technical approach to the specifics of the case, rather than trusting in a single theoretical approach for everyone. It is also true that he felt classical theory overemphasized the importance of sexuality. "Sex is important for the twenty minutes it may occupy from time to time, but it is not necessarily behind everything else that fills the rest of the time" (1954, p. 169). Regarding technique, Sullivan felt a stance more active than the classical one was generally needed. He might interrupt a patient to say "This seems to be *really* free association, but I wonder what on earth it pertains to" (1954, p. 84). He also was skeptical about an unquestioned reliance on the couch. He felt that this aspect of technique could lead to a therapist's intellectualizing and becoming preoccupied with symbolic meanings at the expense of attending to the patient's anxiety.

In his therapeutic work with schizophrenics, Sullivan stressed the importance of the therapist establishing himself or herself as both a real person and as *different* from the original figure in the patient's life. This is part of his general preference for greater activity on the part of the therapist than was the case in classical analysis. Otto Will, a prominent

Sullivanian analyst, gave an intriguing example of this from his own analysis with Sullivan when Sullivan was near the end of his life (1980, personal communication). During a session Will had been incredibly angry at Sullivan. He had said he felt like throwing him out of the window and, considering how unwell his therapist, Sullivan, looked, he felt it wouldn't be very hard to do. At the end of the session as he was getting ready to walk out, Will suddenly said, "I've just realized that the way I'm feeling about you is exactly the way I used to feel about my father." Sullivan replied: "I don't believe a word of that. I think you hate me and I want you to know that the feeling's mutual. I'll see you tomorrow." We can guess that Sullivan felt that his patient was escaping from the uncomfortable immediacy of his expressed anger at his physically vulnerable therapist, and was seeking refuge in a transference insight that would protect both patient and therapist at the moment of leave-taking. Sullivan's somewhat outrageous response dramatically restored the emotional intensity by keeping the focus on the immediate here-and-now interaction. It also embodied Sullivan's view that affects can be tolerated without the need to resort to denial. The patient does not need to fear that the therapist cannot survive the patient's or his own feelings.

Rather than emphasizing free association and the couch, Sullivan liked to speak instead of the therapist's careful exploration of a patient's interpersonal history and current situation as a *detailed inquiry*. In this way interpersonal technique is quite consistent with the now-standard psychosocial history. The detailed inquiry proceeds most productively when there is exquisite sensitivity to the patient's anxiety. This is because this anxiety is the motive for the patient's avoidance of the relevant material. While Sullivan didn't use the word *resistance*, this is what his interpersonal version of resistance would mean: the patient resists exploring what will be anxiety-provoking, that is, threatening to the maintenance of his or her self-esteem. This view of resistance differs from the classical view, in which resistance is seen as the patient's tenacious clinging to the unconscious instinctual gratification embedded in the symptom. The key in Freud's view is anxiety about unconscious, disapproved-of, instinctual wishes becoming conscious. In Sullivan's theory the key is anxiety over self-esteem. For Sullivan the therapist's job is to find a way to make the anxiety-threatening exploration as tolerable as possible. It is here that Sullivan's theory of empathy finds its clinical relevance: the therapist can only hope to gain the therapeutically necessary material if the patient feels the therapist's respect and sensitivity. Kohut, as we have seen in Chapter 7, put his own special emphasis on therapeutic empathy, not just as a way of providing a conducive atmosphere in which the patient may work, but also as the only method for changing the patient's past emotionally hurtful experiences via the therapist's providing a new interpersonal experience. This notion of empathy as a tool of investigation and treatment, and not just a tactful way of interacting with patients, was explicit in Sullivan's work. With greater empathy for the patient there is less of a tendency to see the patient's situation in terms of pathology, and more of a tendency to see it in terms of the patient's humanness and strength.

A relevant example of the failure of therapeutic empathy is the not-uncommon practice of revising a diagnosis to the more severe category of "borderline." This revision sometimes can be justified as the result of a therapist's deeper understanding of the client, an understanding that may only have been possible after prolonged therapeutic engagement. On the other hand, it may reflect the therapist's departure from an empathic stance (whether momentary or permanent) and the assumptions of a negative position, now rationalized by the new and more severe diagnosis. The therapist accounts for her troubling experience of the patient by concluding that the patient is more disturbed than previously thought. It is certainly not possible to avoid the negative feelings behind this kind of countertransference labeling of the patient; and Sullivan believed that much can be learned from these negative feelings about the patient's interpersonal history. What is crucial, however, is that the therapist consider the interpersonal context for the relabeling, in other words, that she sees it as emanating from something in the *dyadic interaction*, and not as a singular event.

SULLIVAN'S INTERPERSONAL THEORY AND ITS RELATION TO CURRENT RELATIONAL THEORIES

Having reviewed Sullivan's ideas about psychodynamics and psychotherapy, the question is how to place this theory of the 1930s and 1940s in our present theoretical context. It is clear that Sullivan's clinical insights and formulations have become an integral part of clinical understanding today. Generally, these insights have not been attributed to Sullivan himself. It is in this sense that Sullivan, as Leston Havens has put it, "secretly dominates" much of psychodynamic theory in America (Havens and Frank 1971, as quoted in Greenberg and Mitchell 1983, p. 80). But does Sullivan's interpersonal theory constitute a theory of equivalent scope and complexity as drive theory or ego psychology, for example? Or is it more useful to consider Sullivan mainly as a precursor to later relational theories? We now examine more specifically the relationship between interpersonal theory and current trends in theory.

Interpersonal Theory: A Two-Person Psychology

Present-day students and practitioners utilize many of Sullivan's ideas. Perhaps foremost among the tenets of interpersonal theory is Sullivan's stress on the interaction between the therapist and the client. This emphasis is captured by the now widely accepted notion that the clinical encounter requires a *two-person psychology* to replace the *one-person psychology* of classical theory.

Sullivan's attention to the emotional state of the therapist, especially to the inherent anxiety in being with another person, is by now such a central part of our clinical approach that we may not recognize what a shift of emphasis it reflects. The clinical moment, in the interpersonal view, no longer consists of an objective observer, the clinician, viewing, as through a microscope, a suffering or ill patient. The clinician is now seen as an inevitable part of the field that he or she is trying to observe. "Therefore, the psychiatrist [sic] has an inescapable, inextricable involvement in all that goes on in the interview; and to the extent that he is unconscious or unwitting of his participation in the interview, to that extent he does not know what is happening" (Sullivan 1954, p. 19). The clinician is no longer protected by the illusion that he or she is not a contributor to the interaction, that his or her anxieties, defenses, aggressiveness, seductiveness, and any other personal tendencies are not evoked or expressed in some way in the interaction. In this framework, it is the *interaction* that is the only source of knowledge of the client, and the clinician is unavoidably part of the interaction, one hopes a relatively observant part.

It is this acknowledgment of the clinician's participation in the interaction that anticipated the current, practically universal, appreciation of *countertransference*. This term, around which so much clinical and theoretical writing and discussion has focused in the last decade, has increasingly moved beyond its original narrow definition as those neurotic aspects of the clinician that are stimulated by the transference of the client. The term has increasingly come to refer to all the emotional reactions of the clinician in relation to the client. Its usefulness has moved beyond its important role in identifying problematic contributions of the therapist. Now the clinician's affective experiences become the primary tools with which to understand the largely unconscious aspects of the client that emerge in the interaction. Clients present themselves and their history through their interactions with the therapist, who must discover the client in his or her own countertransference experiences.

For example, a therapist might become aware of nagging feelings of revulsion and disdain for a patient, feelings seemingly incompatible with the therapist's professional ideals of acceptance and empathy. Through evoking such feelings, the patient may be conveying what she doesn't yet know in words, namely the most hated and defended against aspects of her own body image. The therapist's willingness to explore her own negative feelings for the patient thus becomes a tool for learning about the patient and, ultimately, the patient's interpersonal history, a history that is not available for verbal communication. This history instead is only communicable through a transference–countertransference enactment.

This perspective was for a long time resisted in traditional psychoanalytic thinking because theoretical priority was given to the *individual*. When the focus of inquiry is on the individual, as in the original formulation of drive theory and ego psychology, the clinician's position of objective observer makes more sense, and the contributions of the clinician to the interaction must be minimized and seen as negative. It follows then that the earlier definition of countertransference was limited to the presumably avoidable intrusion into the treatment of the clinician's neurotic response to the client. Our current, broadened view of countertransference is that it is the most informative source of data regarding the problematic aspects of the client's psychology. This represents a major shift of theoretical focus from the *individual* to the *interaction* between the client and the therapist. It is this interactional focus that is the starting point for current relational perspectives.

Sullivan also anticipated the current interest in the self by emphasizing the central role of *self-esteem*. By so doing, he anticipated Kohut's self psychology. Sullivan believed that anxiety, the noxious affect to which he attributed all of the "difficulties of living," was interpersonal in nature. Rather than being the result of conflict between drives and the internalized forces that oppose them, anxiety is the anticipated loss of esteem in the eyes of valued others. This anxiety, with its history in the client's interpersonal relations, is defended against in an effort to maintain self-esteem. The purpose of the defense is to maintain self-esteem.

Interpersonal theory was a forerunner of self psychology, but not because both theories prominently use the term *self*. Kohut's use of the term *self* means the total, unique personality, while for Sullivan, the self of *self-system* refers to the defenses against anxiety. Rather, both theories stress the central role of self-esteem in a person's sense of well-being. As we will see, Kohut, like Sullivan, insists that preservation of self-esteem is much more crucial and fraught with difficulty for his clients than their conflicts over drives. In this context, *narcissism* is described as the trait that is involved in the maintenance of self-esteem. Interpersonal theorists put the patient's self-esteem at the center of their clinical work, with the idea that little makes sense if the client's narcissistic vulnerabilities, as we would currently be likely to label them, are not kept in mind in a moment-to-moment way.

The Interpersonal World of the Child

We have described interpersonal theory's affinity with self psychology in the attention to both empathy and self-esteem. Daniel Stern's (1985) highly influential synthesis of infant research, titled significantly *The Interpersonal World of the Infant*, also stresses the more prominent role of the infant's interpersonal experience over drive experience. In Stern's view the child develops through interactive structures beginning in earliest infancy. He refers to "representations of interactions which have been generalized" (p. 97) as the building blocks for the child's personality. Much of current infancy research has identified mother–infant interaction, including disruptions in these interactions, as the formative nexus of personality development. Self and object representations are formed from these interactions. Again we hear a conception of the personality as "relatively enduring configurations," that concept that is now the current preoccupation of much psychoanalytically informed infancy research. This research has had increasing influence on practice, as clinicians stress the parallels between the mother–infant dyad, on the one hand, and the treatment dyad, on the other. Concepts such as *attunement* and *cueing* in the treatment situation derive from a view of treatment as re-creating moments of the mother–child dyad.

Interpersonal Psychoanalysis

Greenberg and Mitchell (1983), two prominent interpersonally trained analysts, in their important book *Object Relations in Psychoanalytic Theory* conceptualize psychoanalytic theories as adhering either to a "drive-structure" model or a "relational-structure" model. They argue that Sullivan's interpersonal theory constitutes, along with Fairbairn's object relations theory, the most complete relational theory. The term *relational* has begun to stand for contemporary approaches that share Sullivan's emphasis on the interpersonal, regardless of whether the approach is called interpersonal, intersubjective, self psychological, object relational, or ego psychological. As Mitchell has written (1991): "'Relational perspectives' . . . suggests our belief that all of the major currents within post classical psychoanalytic thought have grappled, to different degrees and each in its own fashion, with the replacement of Freud's drive metapsychology with a theoretical framework based most fundamentally on relations between self and others" (p. 5). Mitchell gives priority to the interpersonal world over and above the biological. This position now dominates all of the postclassical trends of psychoanalytic thought. While the term *interpersonal* denotes the psychoanalytic school founded by Sullivan and his colleagues, the more ecumenical term *relational* is meant to cover this general orientation as it is found in a variety of psychoanalytic schools today.

Current theorists trained in the interpersonal tradition, such as Bromberg, Aron, Hirsch, Greenberg, and Mitchell, are likely now to identify themselves as "relational." A trend among these writers has been to look for precursors to Sullivan in earlier psychoanalytic theorists. Currently Ferenczi has been rediscovered as an early analyst who stressed many of the themes interpersonalists have found important, particularly the value of countertransference and the actual, as opposed to the fantasized, nature of the patient's parents. There is a historically interesting story in this regard about Sullivan and his colleague, Clara Thompson, allegedly flipping a coin to decide which one of them would go to Europe to be analyzed and then return to analyze the other. The coin flip ended with Thompson going to be analyzed, and her analyst was

none other than Ferenczi. So, just as there has been greater acknowledgment of Sullivan's contributions to psychodynamic theory, many of
Sullivan's followers have been finding common ground with earlier
approaches that they feel are also relational in their essence.

Postmodern Theories: Constructivist, Narrative, and Intersubjective Approaches

Postmodern perspectives have clear affinities with interpersonal theorists. Postmodern theories oppose the natural science model of classical
psychoanalysis and the philosophical worldview of logical positivism
to which it adheres. Postmodernism can be thought of as a group of
approaches that hold that there is no fixed reality, only constructed
versions of reality determined by the perspective of the one doing the
describing. Perhaps more than anything, postmodern theories derive
from the notion that language does not objectively describe an ultimately
knowable world, but rather elaborates a worldview already contained
within the conventions of that language. Language in this sense is relational and depends on the consensual understanding of those using it,
rather than having a fixed, objective relationship to what it is intended
to represent (Gergen 1994).

One of the postmodern revisions of psychoanalytic theory has been
termed *constructivist* or, in the work of Merton Gill and Irwin Hoffman,
social constructivist. Gill's (1982) and Hoffman's (1991) reevaluations of
the concept of transference have emphasized the technical importance
of a here-and-now focus on the interaction between therapist and patient,
even when the clinical material is not manifestly about the treatment
relationship. This was quite consistent with an interpersonalist technical orientation. Gill and Hoffman have gone beyond technique to a critique of the scientific assumptions of classical psychoanalytic theory and
have proposed a *social constructivist* model for the treatment situation.
In this view, the therapist is no longer seen as a detached observer, objectively identifying the patient's transference *distortions*. He or she is an
inevitable *participant* in the therapeutic dialogue that is now seen as co-
constructed rather than originating solely in the patient.

A related theoretical development can be seen in Roy Schafer's
(1983, 1992) use of narrative as a theoretical framework for psychoanalytic theory and the treatment process. Like Gill and Hoffman, Schafer

has criticized, from many perspectives, the philosophical assumptions of traditional theory. He proposes variously a "perspectivist," "hermeneutic," or "narrative" viewpoint in which there are only "versions" of the past or of a clinical interaction, and no unassailable ground on which to stand in proclaiming one's own version to be the objective truth. Similarly, in this view (unlike the view of classical theory) there is no sharp line that one can draw between subject and object or between the two participants in the therapeutic dialogue, since they mutually influence each other and their views of each other contain their own constructions or projections. In this account of the treatment process, the psychoanalytic dialogue is co-authored by the two participants, so that the patient's life narrative is transformed by the analysis of transference and defense. By conceptualizing the clinical reality as co-constructed, Schafer, Gill, and Hoffman are increasingly locating themselves in an interpersonal, or, in the more current term, *relational* framework. Sullivan is not the sole or necessarily the most significant precursor to these related theoretical developments, but he made many of the same critiques of classical theory that have subsequently been elaborated in these highly diverse theories, and his view of development as founded in relationship rather than drive has been adopted by them. In this sense his influence is very wide indeed.

Another related theoretical trend that extends Sullivan's fundamental assumptions is associated with the term *intersubjectivity*. This concept, which originates in hermeneutic philosophy, has been increasingly utilized by psychoanalytic writers of varying persuasions, for example, Atwood and Stolorow (1984), Benjamin (1990), and Ogden (1994). In one sense, these writers are developing the implications of the two-person as opposed to the one-person model. Intersubjectivity is defined as "the field of intersection between two subjectivities, the interplay between two different subjective worlds . . . [and] postulates that the other must be recognized as another subject in order for the self to fully experience his or her subjectivity in the other's presence" (Benjamin 1990, pp. 34–35). In this view, then, the other is not merely an object of the self's drive or perceptions, as in traditional theory, but is a subject in her own right. The treatment situation becomes the area of intersubjectivity in which the patient discovers herself through her encounter with the subjectivity of the therapist.

In this view, the therapist is also no longer the arbiter of objective truth or reality. The client brings his or her own unique experiences and their meanings to the therapeutic encounter while the therapist, or observer, brings to the therapeutic encounter his or her own subjective reality. Between the therapist and client, a shared reality is co-constructed. The therapeutic relationship now is composed of "two people, both of whom are participating in a changed interpersonal interaction . . . that is layered by reciprocal unconscious, preconscious, and conscious" (Hoffman 1982, p. 407). From this perspective, there is an elaborate and complex interplay created between the intrapsychic worlds of both the therapist and the client that takes place in the interpersonal domain between them. What occurs is based not only on the client's life experiences, dynamics, subjective feelings, and associated meanings, but on the therapist's as well.

This intersubjective perspective, as is true of narrative and constructivist perspectives, de-emphasizes the division between the client's subjectivity and the therapist's subjectivity. From Sullivanian interpersonal theory onward, the client and therapist together form the psychological system so that the focus of the therapeutic work becomes the intersection between the subjectivities of each of them.

Mitchell (1993) has pointed out that the emphasis of this relational perspective shifts from uncovering the truth through insight (as was the case in drive theory and ego psychology), toward restoring the client's core subjective truths. Each partner in the therapeutic dyad brings her own meaning and experience to the encounter. Both sides of the subjective situation are then experienced and understood for new personal meanings to be created. All of these relational perspectives, from narrative theory, constructivism, and intersubjectivity, flow from interpersonal theory. Each of them de-centers the role of the therapist, questions the authority of the observer, and attends to the interaction between the observer and the observed. All of these relational formulations are a part of a meta-theoretical revolution in which psychological understanding is interpretive and where the curative factor is contained within the therapeutic relationship itself. While this conceptualization of the psychotherapeutic and developmental processes (Stern 1985) has its roots in European philosophy and finds common ground in psychodynamic writers other than Sullivan, it clearly shares with Sullivan a starting point in "relation" and not in "drive."

CONCLUSION

We return now to the question of how to evaluate Sullivan's place among the plethora of current psychoanalytic theories and perspectives. One answer is that his theory, while equivalent in scope to modern ego psychology, has contributed a lot to it. For example, Erikson's emphasis on the external world and the inevitable "others" who are contained both in our fantasy lives and in our external roles and relationships has its derivations in Sullivan. From this perspective Sullivan has been enormously influential in the shift away from what Erikson (1964) called Freud's "grandiose onesidedness," meaning the extraordinary elaboration of the individual's inner life and neglect of external factors, toward the inclusion of "outside" in understanding the individual.

A second answer is that Sullivan is simply not read as much as he was two or three decades ago. The reason for this, however, is not just that his terminology never quite caught on, or that his developmental theory is less comprehensive and almost completely ignores female development, though these are both certainly true. A more important reason why Sullivan is relatively ignored today is oddly a measure of his success in both steering and anticipating developments of American psychoanalysis. Ego psychology has incorporated enough of an interpersonal perspective to make Sullivan's contributions to developmental theory no longer so distinctive. Object relations theories always had more in common with Sullivan's interpersonal theory. The increasing popularity of these theories in this country has made it impossible to disentangle them from Sullivan's theory. We have seen Sullivan's influence on, or similarity with, self psychology, current infancy research, countertransference theory, and, of course, current interpersonal theory.

Perhaps another reason why Sullivan's ideas have not been given their due relates to his homosexuality during a period in which psychoanalysis proper was particularly homophobic. Perhaps his "oddity," his widespread distance from others, also contributed to his exclusion from mainstream analytic circles. Perhaps because his wisdom was disseminated through an oral tradition and not in writing, his ideas have more easily been appropriated by others.

And, finally, those recent trends in psychoanalytic theory (constructivism, intersubjectivity, and narrative approaches) that can be considered part of a general intellectual movement called postmodernism clearly have extended and elaborated upon the main ingredients of Sullivan's interpersonal theory. Sullivan seems to have anticipated where the field would go in this regard.

Finally, Sullivan contributed the value and importance of the therapeutic relationship, including the therapist's subjectivity, to promoting psychological growth. He contributed pioneering ideas about the role of needed others in promoting self-esteem. In fact, because so many diverse trends in psychoanalytic theory have recently been meaningfully grouped together as "relational," this alone says a great deal about how the most significant movements in theory development have been heralded by the shifts in emphasis that interpersonal theory began.

References

Alexander, I. E. (1990). On the life and work of Harry Stack Sullivan : an inquiry into unanswered questions. In *Personology*, pp. 199–260. Durham, NC: Duke University Press.

Atwood, G., and Stolorow, R. (1984). *Structures of Subjectivity*. Hillsdale, NJ: Analytic Press.

Bateson, G., Jackson, D. D., Haley, H., and Weakland, J. Toward a theory of schizophrenia. *Behavioral Science* 1:251–264.

Benjamin, J. (1990). An outline of intersubjectivity: the development of recognition. *Psychoanalytic Psychology* 7 (suppl):33–46.

Chapman, A. H. (1976). *Harry Stack Sullivan: His Life and Work*. New York: Putnam.

Chatelaine, L. (1981). *Harry Stack Sullivan: The Formative Years*. Washington, DC: University Press of America.

Erikson, E. H. (1964). The first psychoanalyst. In *Insight and Responsibility*, pp. 17–46. New York: Norton.

Fromm-Reichmann, F. (1952). *Principles of Intensive Psychotherapy*. Chicago: University of Chicago Press.

Gergen, K. J. (1994). Exploring the postmodern. *American Psychologist* 49: 412–416.

Gill, M. M. (1982). *Analysis of Transference*. New York: International Universities Press.

Greenberg, J., and Mitchell, S. (1983). *Object Relations in Psychoanalytic Theory*. Cambridge, MA: Harvard University Press.

Havens, L., and Frank, J. (1971). Review of P. Mullahy, psychoanalysis and interpersonal psychiatry. *American Journal of Psychiatry* 127:1704–1705.

Hoffman, I. Z. (1982). The patient as interpreter of the analyst's experience. *Contemporary Psychoanalysis* 19:389–422.

—— (1991). Discussion: towards a social-constructivist view of the psycho-analytic situation. *Psychoanalytic Dialogues* 1:74–105.

Levenson, E. (1984). Harry Stack Sullivan: the web and the spider. *Contemporary Psychoanalysis* 20:174–189.

—— (1985). The interpersonal (Sullivanian) model. In *Models of the Mind*, ed. A. Rothstein, pp. 49–67. Madison, CT: International Universities Press.

—— (1989). Whatever happend to the cat? *Contemporary Psychoanalysis* 25:537–553.

Mitchell, S. A. (1988). *Relational Concepts in Psychoanalysis*. Cambridge, MA: Harvard University Press.

—— (1991). Editorial philosophy. *Psychoanalytic Dialogues* 1:1–7.

—— (1993). *Hope and Dread in Psychoanalysis*. New York: Basic Books.

Ogden, T. H. (1994). The analytic third: working with intersubjective clinical facts. *International Journal of Psycho-Analysis* 75:3–20.

Perry, H. S. (1982). *Psychiatrist of America: The Life of Harry Stack Sullivan*. Cambridge, MA: Belknap.

Schafer, R. (1983). *The Analytic Attitude*. New York: Basic Books.

—— (1992). *Retelling a Life: Narration in the Psychoanalytic Dialogue*. New York: Basic Books.

Sullivan, H. S. (1953). *The Interpersonal Theory of Psychiatry*. New York: Norton.

—— (1954). *The Psychiatric Interview*. New York: Norton.

—— (1956). *Clinical Studies in Psychiatry*. New York: Norton.

—— (1962). *Schizophrenia as a Human Process*. New York: Norton.

—— (1964). *The Fusion of Psychiatry and Social Science*. New York: Norton.

Stern, D. A. (1985). *The Interpersonal World of the Infant*. New York: Basic Books.

Stern, D. B. (1983). Unformulated experience. *Contemporary Psychoanalysis* 19:71–99.

Thompson, C. (1962). Introduction. In *Schizophrenia as a Human Process*, ed. H. S. Sullivan. New York: Norton.

Tompkins, S. S. (1979). Script theory: differential magnification of affects. *Nebraska Symposium on Affects*, vol. 26. Lincoln, NB: University of Nebraska Press.

9

Coloring Development: Race and Culture in Psychodynamic Theories

LOURDES MATTEI

"You are made of chocolate, and I'm vanilla."
A 3-year-old boy comments while playing with an adult

Psychodynamic theories have a long and contradictory relationship to issues of race and culture. As has been pointed out throughout this book, psychological theories are embedded within the particular worldview of their time. Hence the insights and preferences and the biases and stereotypes of their sociohistorical context are voiced through their concepts and ideas. Psychoanalysis is no exception.[1]

From Freud onward, a number of psychoanalysts have presented us with ways of understanding the relationship between society and the

---

1. In this chapter the terms *psychoanalytic* and *psychodynamic* are used in the following manner: *psychoanalytic* refers to early theory and writings as well as a specific technique; *psychodynamic* is used as a more generic and encompassing concept, embracing a more contemporary and diversified field of psychoanalytically informed theories and practices.

individual. Paradoxically, although psychoanalysis from its inception aspired to universality (culture-free, color-blind principles), a culturalist tradition exists. This tradition encompasses a series of psychoanalysts who have used psychoanalytic ideas to culturalize or help explain how a social context affects personality development. In addition, psychodynamic principles have been used to explain malignant social dynamics such as racism, bigotry, and ethnocentrism.

This chapter examines the relationship between psychoanalysis, race, and culture; reviews key interpretations of racism and ethnocentrism from drive theory, ego psychology, object relations, and self psychology; presents a developmental framework with which to understand racial/ethnic identity; and discusses some of the possibilities and challenges faced in doing cross-cultural psychodynamic work. I do not see psychological theories—in this case, psychodynamic perspectives—as *the* explanation for such complex and multiply determined processes as racism and ethnocentrism. At the same time, I firmly believe that psychoanalytic insights can help illuminate, deepen, and open up debate about racial dynamics and their impact on human development. This chapter represents my synthesis of some of the strengths and significant insights contributed by these theories.

RACE AND CULTURE IN
THE PSYCHOANALYTIC TRADITION

Psychoanalysis' interest in culture has taken many paths. Since its inception, psychoanalysis has been interested in culture and society. Beginning with Freud himself, we see the writings of his later years—the "cultural books" (*Totem and Taboo, Civilization and its Discontents, Group Psychology and Analysis of the Ego* and *Moses and Monotheism*)—characterized by a preoccupation with the application of psychoanalysis to larger groups, communities, and social issues (Paul 1991). In addition, anthropologists have long been interested in the debate over the universality of psychoanalytic concepts across cultures (e.g., Geertz 1973, Kurtz 1992, Malinowski 1927/1953).

Psychoanalytic writers interested in the ethnicity have used psychoanalytic principles in various ways. Freud claimed from early on that his theories were universal. His claim notwithstanding, the impact of Freud's ethnicity in his theory has been a long-standing source of interest and controversy (see Brunner 1991, Gilman 1992). Like many European thinkers of his time, Freud held the ethnocentric belief that Western civilization represented the most advanced stage of human history. The comedian Dick Gregory aptly captures this view in this joke: "You gotta say this for whites, their self-confidence knows no bounds. Who else would go a small island in the South Pacific, where there's no crime, poverty, unemployment, war or worry—and call it a 'primitive society'" (Watkins 1994, p. 502). Frosch (1989) comments on the *misuse*, or ethnocentric application, of psychoanalytic principles as follows:

> Using an evolutionary framework of highly doubtful validity, this involves an assumption that the current patterns of culture to be found in non-industrialized peoples can be regarded as fossilized versions of the actual pre-history of Western culture; . . . Indeed the strongest ideological determinant of this work is an assumed equivalence between so-called "primitive" people, children, and the insane. . . . A related tendency common to many psychoanalytic studies is to view Western culture as the pinnacle of development, with non-industrialized societies representing either or both a fixation at childhood points of development, or pathological regressions. [pp. 212–213]

This view of other societies as primitive, as psychologically underdeveloped and/or sick, has been a persistent interpretation of psychoanalytic theory. This simplistic and ethnocentric use of psychological principles to understand social processes, or psychological reductionism, has resulted in well-deserved criticisms of psychoanalytic theory. Unfortunately, psychoanalytic writings are still plagued with the (mis)use of the term *primitive* when referring to infantile and pathological manifestations and interpretations.

It is also worth noting that the attempt to examine the relationship between the "social" and the "individual" has frequently led to a *deemphasis* of culture in psychoanalytic inquiry. Culture comes to be perceived as an outward layer as opposed to the more important core of the psyche. In its extreme, some psychoanalysts have dismissed social dynamics as a screen or stage for the playing out of intrapsychic, biologically determined conflicts. Consequently, psychoanalysis has often been criticized for neglecting the sociocultural context in which the psyche develops in favor of an extreme individualism. Most recently, postmodern views in psychology such as social constructivism have questioned the very existence of the concept of the "individual" (Gergen 1994; see Hoffman 1991 for a social constructivist view in psychoanalysis).

Keeping these critiques in mind, let us now look at the four psychologies and how each perspective illuminates and/or obscures our understanding of racism and bigotry.

DRIVE THEORY

Freud believed that humans were inevitably shaped by a fundamental, inherent antagonism between the id (wishes and desires) and societal prohibitions. Social values, its rules and prohibitions, become "individual," or internalized by the individual, as part of superego development. In Freud's tripartite model of the mind, the superego is the psychic subsystem that "carries" our group's rules. As an agent-within, the superego is often in conflict with other parts of the psyche, namely the id, while the ego acts as a mediator between instinctual forces and cultural norms. The id is the psychic container of the deeper motivational forces and it is essentially fueled by our beastly past. Psychoanalysis singled out two irreducible forces in human development: the sexual and aggressive drives. These forces, particularly sexuality, are seen as entering into lifelong conflict with the demands of social life. Development is thus defined by drive theory as a series of *conflicts* faced in a stage-like progression or what has been called the psychosexual theory of development. Problems encountered in our passage through these stages lead to *fixations*, which are expressed or manifested in *symptoms* or *compromise formations*.

Within a drive-theory perspective racist dynamics can be understood as psychosexual conflicts or fixations; in other words, racism has been seen as an expression of unconscious conflicts. In this theoretical context, blackness "colors" powerful fantasies: the black body is psychically equated with the repressed. Kovel (1970) in his book *White Racism* places in historical context the legacy of these fantasies, fantasies that we all have inherited and share. When Africans were brought as slaves to American shores, contact with Europeans fueled racial fantasies and myths: "These people were black; they were naked; they were unchristian: ergo, they were the damned" (p. 63). Using blackness and whiteness as "cardinal symbols," Kovel makes the following psychoanalytic interpretation:

> Spurred by the superego, the ego designates the id, which is unseen, as having the qualities that come from darkness; as being black. The id, then, is the referent for blackness within the personality; and the various partial trends within the id, all repressed, make themselves symbolically realized in the world as the forms of blackness embodied in the fantasies of race. [p. 66]

The unconscious itself becomes associated or symbolized by the psyche as darkness. Our deepest fears and anxieties—which in drive theory are, at their root, sexual conflicts—get enacted through racial struggles. Thus Kovel argues, racism can embody anal as well oedipal conflicts and anxieties; the black body comes to be perceived as dirty and/or castrated, both hated and desired.

Frantz Fanon, a pioneer psychiatrist from the Antilles, wrote passionately about this *embodiment*, applying a psychoanalytic perspective to understand racial dynamics in colonized societies. The threat for the white person *is* the black body, he argues: "The Negro is a *beast*, a phobic object, the personification of The Other" (1967, p. 170, emphasis mine). Thus the black body *activates* anxieties of the most dreaded (and the most desired): the black person "symbolizes the biological danger . . . To suffer from a phobia of Negroes is to be afraid of the biological. The Negroes are animals" (p. 165). Focusing on the centrality of sexual impulses, Fanon highlights the confrontation and conflicts with difference. In this case skin color difference, a physical difference, arouses genital anxieties in the white man; the black body comes to symbolize both sexual potency and danger.

In sum, drive theory has been used to understand racist dynamics by suggesting the following interpretations: racism is a symptom indicative of underlying psychosexual conflicts based on the unconscious association of darkness—the black body—with our beastly impulses (sexual and aggressive drives). These racial fantasies then are reactivated and reenacted through the various psychosexual stages. Furthermore, in a racist society, racism can be understood as a compromise formation resulting from psychosexual anxieties and conflicts, a socially acceptable "solution" to the inherent conflictual relationship between the individual and society.

Drive theory in general has been widely criticized by its ethnocentric reductionism; social as well as psychological dynamics are reduced to sexual conflicts (conflicts particularly salient to European, nineteenth century "civilized" society). Furthermore, explanations grounded in oedipal anxieties have been deservedly critiqued as having a pervasive male bias (with its concomitant pathologizing of female psychology; see Chapter 10). At the same time, important insights can be derived from this perspective, including the central role of unconscious conflicts in racist dynamics; more specifically, the association of blackness with the repressed, whiteness with the rational. Racial fantasies are seen as *embodied* in dark skin (black body), fantasies that shape and express a variety of powerful fears and conflicts, particularly anxieties related to sexual and aggressive wishes and impulses.

EGO PSYCHOLOGY

In the United States, psychoanalytic theory developed its own emphasis on Freud's structural theory of the mind. We have come to know this particular theoretical framework as ego psychology.

In contrast to Freud's tragic or pessimistic views of human nature, the development of psychoanalysis in the United States flourished with triumphant optimism with its emphasis on the ego's capacity for mastery and adaptation (Hartmann 1958). In an ego psychology framework, the ego's functions and defects move to the foreground. The assessment of the ego's multifaceted mechanisms—in particular, the ego's defensive maneuvers—in the formation of *character structure* is a prominent feature of our clinical lens. In addition, the developmental thrust of this perspective shifts our focus to the importance of achieving an integrated identity.

How does ego psychology understand prejudice and bigotry? Let us begin by highlighting the insights derived from a significant, and now classic, study of ethnocentrism by Adorno and his colleagues, *The Authoritarian Personality* (1950). Following the Holocaust, a group of social psychologists sought to explain the emergence and dynamics of anti-Semitic attitudes applying psychoanalytic principles. Combining ego with social psychology, Adorno and his team established a relationship among a sociopolitical climate (fascism), family dynamics (authoritarian parenting style), and personality development (prejudiced individual). The authors explain:

> A basically hierarchical, authoritarian, exploitative parent–child relationship is apt to carry over into a power-oriented, exploitatively dependent attitude towards one's sex partner and one's God and may well culminate in a political philosophy and social outlook which has no room for anything but a clinging to what appears to be the strong and a disdainful rejection of whatever is relegated to the bottom. [p. 971]

Thus parenting that relies primarily on domination and subordination through the exercise of a rigid and punitive discipline significantly shapes a certain type of personality—the authoritarian personality. In turn, this type of personality is especially susceptible to ethnocentric, nondemocratic ideas. The authoritarian family environment forms a personality with a tremendous amount of hostility and ambivalence toward authority. This character structure struggles with fears and conflicts typical of the anal stage of psychosexual development, such as extreme need for order, cleanliness, and control, as well as limited tolerance for ambiguity and ambivalence. The intensity of hostility fueling these dynamics result in an excessive reliance on projection and displacement. These defensive maneuvers protect this personality from conflict, and ultimately from psychotic disintegration. Minority groups (e.g., Jews, blacks) become the perfect targets or substitutes for the externalization of aggression. Consequently and paradoxically, Frosch (1989) reminds us, "the prejudiced person *needs* her or his hated object in order to survive" (p. 234, emphasis added).

In this application of ego psychology, we see the critical importance of childhood experiences in the generation of hostility and hatred underlying racist dynamics. Furthermore, defenses against these aggressive impulses—particularly projection and displacement—are seen as holding the bigoted personality together. These dynamics are exacerbated by the complexities and alienation of modern life.

Another contribution to the psychoanalytic debate on the impact of race and culture in development comes from Erikson's work. Erikson (1963, 1968) placed *identity* at the center of psychoanalytic inquiry. Expanding Freud's theory of psychosexual development to include the sociocultural realm, Erikson sees development as a lifelong progression of stages in the context of the individual's culture. From this perspective, all of us pass through the same developmental sequence, with our particular culture offering its unique possibilities and challenges for resolving universal conflicts (see Chapter 5).

Erikson's writings include observations of minority groups in the United States such as the Sioux, the Yurok, and the "Negroes." His observations in this area are an example of a common understanding of the psychodynamics of race: cultural beliefs such as racial stereotypes are internalized through negative identifications:

> No individual can escape this opposition of images, which is all-pervasive in the men and in the women, in the majorities and in the minorities, and in all the classes of a given national or cultural unit. Psychoanalysis shows that the unconscious evil identity (the composite of everything which arouses negative identification, i.e., the wish not to resemble it) consists of images of the violated (castrated) body, the ethnic outgroup, and the exploited minority. [1963, p. 243]

A psychological consequence and dilemma of this type of internalization is the inevitability of low self-esteem for a minority identity. That is, identification with the dominant group prepares the way for identity conflicts, thus compromising healthy, "normal" development for members of minority groups. This view of the impact of minority status in development is part of decades of debate and research on the relationship between self-esteem and racial/ethnic identity. We see this view as vulnerable to a type of *social reductionism*. From this perspective, lack of social esteem is assumed to be categorically absorbed or psychologically translated into low self-esteem by the individual. Psychic damage resulting from the internalization and identification with minority status is neither inescapable, inevitable, nor simple. We now know that the relationship between self-esteem and racial/ethnic identity is magnificently richer and more complex than initially conceived (see Cultural Identity and Self-Esteem, below).

With ego psychology's emphasis on ego functions, racism and bigotry are psychologically understood as a defense against anxiety. These defensive maneuvers consist primarily of projection and displacement of aggressive impulses onto minority group members. In addition, Erikson's focus on identity, including minority identity, expanded psychoanalytic attention to the impact of culture in psychological development.

OBJECT RELATIONS

> Racial prejudice is, after all, a problem in object relations.
> Marjorie McDonald, 1970

> The place where cultural experience is located is in the *potential space* between the individual and the environment (originally the object).
> D. W. Winnicott, 1971

We have looked at how drive and ego psychological theories view difference and prejudice. Contemporary thinking in psychoanalysis has shifted its emphasis from concerns over the beastly struggles of civilized life to the developmental needs of the individual through her relationships. The growth of the individual psyche is seen as unfolding within a relational matrix. Many relational theorists now believe that experience in relationships form the basis for our internal lives as well as our perception of the external world. The relationship between the inner and outer worlds is more fluid, open, and reciprocal than earlier psychoanalysis implied. These recent perspectives were discussed in Chapters 5 and 6 and include schools of thought such as object relations, self psychology, and interpersonal and intersubjective psychologies. Interestingly, relational schools were foreshadowed by Freud (1921):

> In the individual's mental life someone else is invariably involved, as a model, as an object, as a helper, as an opponent; and so from the first individual psychology, in this extended but entirely justifiable sense of the words, it is at the same time social psychology as well. [p. 1]

How can we understand racial dynamics from a relational perspective?

Object relations focuses on the infant's struggle with the emerging awareness of separateness and thus difference. Our psychological birth follows a slow and eventful differentiation process with a primary other around the recognition and establishment of a core sense of identity. This developmental process is patterned by the pulse of what we perceive as being me and not-me experiences—the pleasures and anxieties of separateness.

Skin color difference shapes a major sense of difference. Our awareness and experience of skin color difference in our relational context give form and meaning to our racial identities. Even before we are born, our parents' fantasies, thoughts, wishes, and anxieties about the color of the infant, affect how we "put together" who we are (Bowles 1988). We know that a child's discovery of skin color difference is neurologically possible before the first year and it can generate *skin-color anxiety* (McDonald 1970).

Initially, a difference is psychologically experienced as "not-mother," subsequently, as "not-me"; a difference comes to symbolize what we recognize as Other. We also know from psychoanalytic experience that a recognition of a difference in early life—particularly if it is suffused with emotional intensity and/or cultural significance—will be "charged" with basic affective shadings of good and bad. In fact, *stranger anxiety* has been regarded as "the original emergence of the other as enemy" (Fornari in Volkan 1988, p. 18).

The following dialogue from a therapy session between a clinical social work student and Joey, a 7-year-old, demonstrates how color comes to be symbolized and expressed:

> *J.:* What's your favorite color?
> *Th:* I like lots of colors.
> *J.:* I don't like black. Black jelly beans are nasty.
> *Th:* Black jelly beans are licorice. So you don't like licorice?
> *J.:* White ones taste okay, though.
> *Th:* You like the flavor of the white ones?
> *J.:* (pause) My teacher's white.
> *Th:* (pause) And I'm white.
> *J.:* Well, kind of.

Experiences in relation to skin color become part of the internal image of the self, and eventually become integrated in the child's developing racial identity. The internal representations of self and other are colored by racial tones and will become an important part of the child's overall self system. For psychological well-being, the child must internalize, in relationship to her primary caregiver, a loving feeling toward her own skin. These sensations become part of a general sense of self—a unique, special, loved person (Bowles 1988). Anxieties and defenses related to developmentally specific stages or ways of relating can come to be expressed, fought, tangled, and/or confused with the anxieties of racial difference (McDonald 1970). For example, in the case of Joey, color differences in food symbolically represent his issues and concerns related to the earliest stages (oral in the psychosexual model) or most dependent stage (object relational), in addition to expressing basic concerns about his self-worth.

We noted earlier how psychoanalytic drive theory suggested that racism and bigotry reflected both anal anxieties (excessive preoccupation with order and with dirt) as well as genital fears (dark body as castrated). In her racially integrated nursery, McDonald (1970) came to the following conclusion:

> Separation anxiety can have many determinants, from many developmental levels and many different kinds of personal experiences. In our clinical experience we found that no matter what the individual developmental or traumatic focal point for the separation anxiety, the dark-skinned child revived it, for *all* the children. [p. 134]

Racism—the association of white with what is good and black with badness—remains an area of vulnerability for psychological splitting. We *all* remain at risk for the distortions and fragmentation of identity based on primary and unconscious racial dichotomies, especially when we are frightened, vulnerable, threatened, and angry.

Cultures introduce the child—initially through the mother, and later by other significant people in the child's life—to symbols that help in the externalization of both good and bad feelings about the self, or unintegrated representations of self and/or others (Volkan 1988):

> In externalization, elements of factual circumstances are invested with psychological magic that represents aspects of the child himself. These may include his own mental images and/or previously formed and internalized images of others, with their attendant feeling states. I call such reservoirs "suitable targets of externalization" and hold that they play an important role in the genesis of the concept of political and social enemies and allies and concepts of ethnicity and nationality. . . . Such targets are often determined by one's ethnicity or nationality. Familiar aspects of a child's environment—the taste of food, odors, sounds, or even oft-repeated songs or other shibboleths indicative of bonding . . . become targets on which the child externalizes aspects of himself. For example, an Italian child may hang a poster picture of Rome in his room, whereas his American counterpart may hang up a cowboy hat. Both objects are psychological pillows. [p. 31]

These psychological pillows change and, one hopes, acquire more complexity as we grow older. These psychological cushions can be used (to buttress identity integration or self cohesiveness) as well as misused (in the activation of prejudice) selectively throughout our lives.

In this section I have integrated insights from relational perspectives in order to understand some aspects of racial psychodynamics. Our experiences of, and in relation to, primary caregivers internalized through early childhood lay the foundation for our sense of identity. Moreover, early anxieties about *separateness* "color" our awareness and perception of *difference.* Our cultural group plays a major role in helping us organize the good and the bad in all of us. A "malignant spiral of racial misuse" results when certain groups become "seductive repositories" for our devalued sides (Sherwood 1980).

I will elaborate further on the development of a racial/ethnic identity later.

SELF PSYCHOLOGY

A prominent feature of this psychology is its emphasis on *self experience* (Pine 1990). In this perspective, experiences that foster *self cohesion* are the most critical for growth and development. These types of experiences depend on the responsiveness—the *emphatic attunement*—of our environment to our developmental needs. These needs are fulfilled and/ or thwarted through the formation of *self-selfobject mergers,* where we experience important people in our lives as part of the self. Failures in responsiveness or attunement are seen as leading to developmental deficits and thus to pathology.

Another distinguishing feature of this psychology is its reconceptualization of the psychodynamic understanding of narcissism. In contrast to earlier notions of narcissism, self psychology considers narcissistic needs of the self as key to a sense of wholeness, vitality, and well-being. The empathic recognition of the child's developing needs for mirroring and idealization are pivotal elements in self-esteem.

Given these assumptions, what is the impact of race and culture in the development, vulnerability, and cohesiveness of the self? Donner (1988) offers us some ideas:

> Everyone experiences assaults on his or her sense of self-worth and self-cohesion. However, everyone does not experience the same

opportunities for self-enhancing self-object experiences. Assaults on the self often occur selectively according to sociological categories of gender, race, ethnicity, class, age, and sexual preference. . . . Clinical social workers must ask how the larger society contributes to or interferes with opportunities for growth-producing mirroring or idealization. [pp. 20–21]

Hence, the social environment's choices of what to admire and what to devalue have impact selectively on processes affecting self-esteem. Thus, experiences of racism and bigotry are interpreted as assaults on the self. In addition, Donner (1987) provides us with some questions for reflection based on this psychology. For example,

> Who is or is not worthy of idealization and admiration, and who has access to group membership whose leaders society will mirror and admire? . . .
> Who is encouraged to pursue goals and ambitions, and whose ambition is more apt to be thwarted? [p. 21]

Like other relational theories, self psychology places the individual and her society—our inner and outer worlds—on a more mutual, interdependent plane than earlier psychoanalytic accounts. Our relationships with others shape and sustain our well-being throughout our lifetime. At the same time, self psychology's primary emphasis on the self makes it vulnerable to the same critique held against most psychological theories in the West: its underscoring of individual experience make it problematic when we attempt to apply it to groups that hold different values and conceptions of the person (see *Therapeutic Encounters of a Cross-Cultural Kind*, below).

The key insights on the psychodynamics of racism and ethnocentrism derived from the four psychologies include the following:

- the association in the unconscious of darkness (the black body) with beastly impulses (drive theory) or "badness" (object relations);
- the importance of aggression (hostility, hatred) and the excessive use of defensive mechanisms such as projection and displacement (ego psychology), and/or splitting and projective identification (object relations) to ward off identity conflicts exacerbated by the complexities and alienation of modernity;

- the relationship between child-rearing practices—punitive, hierarchical (authoritarian) parenting—and intolerance and bigotry in adulthood;
- social devaluation can be internalized through negative identifications (psychosocial/ego psychology);
- the tendency to (mis)use devalued racial groups, which act as "containers" for disavowed and unwanted aspects of the self (object relations);
- racist experiences—assaults on the self—impinge on self cohesion; minority group members' self needs such as idealization and mirroring are thwarted (self psychology).

We have seen a variety of ways in which psychodynamic theories have been used to explain the relationship between society and the psychological development of the individual. In the first section of this chapter we highlighted the problems of racism and ethnocentrism in light of psychoanalytic insights and interpretations. In the following section, we elaborate on the developmental paths of a racial/ethnic identity.

A DEVELOPMENTAL FRAMEWORK
FOR UNDERSTANDING PATHS OF
RACIAL/ETHNIC IDENTITY

> Can you see through your blue eyes like I see through my brown eyes?
>> Anna, a black adolescent, asks her white therapist

> Why is your face painted brown?
> Jim, a white 3-year-old, asks his Puerto Rican child care worker

How do we understand the development of racial/ethnic identity from a relational perspective? How do Anna and Jim's awareness of their race shape who they are and how they see others? Like other developmental experiences, the experience of skin color is based on the child's cognitive and emotional capacities in the context of her unique relational world. Skin color difference is not simply a biological fact. The meanings given by the family and the community to a difference significantly color the experience. In fact, research by developmental psychologists show that children have an awareness of racial (black/white) differences as early as the age of 3 (Katz 1987, Milner 1983). Nonetheless, racial categories remain relatively fluid until middle childhood. It is not until latency (8–10 years of age) that it is possible for children to acquire an accurate and a relatively stable understanding of race and ethnicity as a permanent characteristic of themselves and others—what is called *ethnic constancy* (Aboud 1987). In contrast to the preschooler, who can frequently identify correctly skin color differences but thinks they can be washed away or are painted on, the older child begins to recognize that her race stays the same throughout time and place.

By adolescence the self goes through a second major restructuring, an internal as well as external reorganizing with its attendant rebalancing of the need for autonomy and attachment (Blos 1962). Significant psychic organizations—clusters of internalized self and object representations—are expected to "loosen" and consolidate into a socially functioning and relatively stable identity as the adolescent self prepares to join the adult world. The cohesiveness of the self, including the relative integration of its various parts—its gendered and ethnic identities—is considered an important hallmark of adult mental health. The adolescent's conflicts with her identity, struggles that have come to characterize adolescence in industrialized societies, are considered normative and critical in the putting together of the various aspects of an individual's personality (Erikson 1963).

In sharp contrast to minority adolescence, scant attention has been paid to the issues confronted by a white identity during adolescence. There seems to be an implicit assumption that a white identity is simpler, less conflicted, or better adjusted. The assumption of an unproblematic white identity presents its own particular challenges, dilemmas, and risks. Since a white identity remains typically unexplored and unarticulated, it robs the adolescent of opportunities for a healthy (non-split) representation of herself as white. Consequently, the adolescent remains potentially at more risk of sustaining distorted aspects of self (grandiose or all-good) and other (devalued or all-bad), and thus of reenacting social biases and prejudices. To consolidate a mature racial and ethnic identity, the white adolescent will need to narcissistically "adjust" or mature her sense of omnipotence and grandiosity stemming from being part of the dominant group. In fact, we suggest that the white adolescent has typically less opportunity for the integration and growth of the ethnic line of development. In our social context, an unexplored racial identity—both white and black—remains vulnerable to early dichotomies of good and bad; in psychodynamic terms, the self stays at the mercy of distorted or unintegrated self and other representations.

The challenges and possibilities presented by adolescence have been avidly commented on (Blos 1962, Erikson 1968, A. Freud 1958, Nicholi 1988). At no time is the confrontation of cultural values, beliefs, and attitudes more acute than during adolescence (Sluzki 1979). Although entry into school is considered to be the first challenge for many minority families (the first systematic exposure to the dominant group), by adolescence the child is developed enough to *act* on the choices and alternatives to which she is exposed.

Once conscious awareness of the social meanings associated with racial and ethnic differences is achieved, the adolescent usually goes through several phases. This awareness and its concomitant phases can, and do, resemble adult racial identity phases (Phinney et al. 1990). The early stage of awareness generates much dissonance. Clashes with other values, such as equality and justice, trigger psychological conflict and anxiety. This dissonance is accompanied by feelings such as anger and rage (for the minority youth) and guilt (for the majority youth). For both identities, feelings of disappointment, betrayal, a disillusionment with authority (previously idealized) also surface. Several defensive maneuvers and strategies can be set in motion: denial ("race is not an issue any longer"), avoidance ("these issues do not apply to me"), split reverse identifications (everything ethnic is good, virtuous, and morally superior; everything white is bad, oppressive, and malignant). Eventually, we expect a mature integration to take place, a more autonomous and engaged identity evolves where selective identification guides the choice of values and ideals (see Helms 1993, Phinney et al. 1990, Sue and Sue 1990 for a comprehensive review of research in this area).

CULTURAL IDENTITY AND SELF-ESTEEM

Researchers on race and ethnicity have explored extensively the relationship among cultural identity, self-esteem, and mental health (e.g., Milner 1983, Phinney 1991, Rosenthal 1987, Spencer and Markstrom-Adams 1990). There has been a long-standing assumption that a minority or bicultural identity is riskier, more problematic than "normal" (dominant) identity. After several decades of debate and study, simple or clear conclusions remain elusive and contradictory (see Spencer and Markstrom-Adams 1990 for a review of this literature). There is no question that cultural discontinuity, ethnic or racial devaluing, and assaults present significant challenges for minority youth. At the same time, we know that minority children are not *inevitably* less adjusted, nor do they invariably experience lower levels of self-esteem (Cross 1987, Milner 1983, Powell 1985). The minority adolescent's knowing and experiencing more than one world not only presents significant challenges, it also offers richer possibilities—more flexibility and a different set of alternatives and choices given a supportive family and community resources. In fact, Latino adolescents who sustain an integrated *bicultural identity* show the best levels of psychosocial adjustment (Ho 1992).

As our social climate and historical times change, so does our research. The solution to the identity conflicts confronted by the confluence and clashes of cultures in the United States was viewed at one time as assimilation; the ideal was considered to be a monocultural (white) identity—American. Since the 1960s, we have seen a shift to a different ideal of identity, the hyphenated identity (e.g., African-American, Asian-American).

We now explore differences in structure (shape, design, and pattern) of the ideal self through a cross-cultural lens.

THERAPEUTIC ENCOUNTERS OF A CROSS-CULTURAL KIND

> The Western conception of the person is . . .a rather peculiar idea within the context of world cultures.
>
> Clifford Geertz, 1984

How would we describe the ideal person? What are our implicit or unconscious assumptions and values about who that should be? What traits does our group give praise and recognition; which ones are despised and condemned? What ways do we usually use to encourage or dissuade a person to acquire and follow certain paths and not others? As anthropologists know, learning about another culture is one of the best ways of knowing one's own.

Throughout the first half of this century, industrialized countries in the West, such as the United States and England, emphasized self-reliance and rational control. Like an animal's cage, the boundary around the self was expected to be tight and sturdy. By adulthood, this bounded individual was expected to regulate and master himself, including the conflicts and frustrations of civilized life. Child-rearing practices that were centered on strict discipline and hard work were seen as the most conducive to this ideal (Aries 1962, Vincent 1991). In the postmodern world attention has shifted; the mutually regulating world of many kinds of relationships now captures oscillating views of the self. Creativity and imagination, not rationality, fuels our healthy, vibrant, ideal self (Kohut 1971, Mitchell 1993). Accordingly, our group's child-rearing activities and rituals give prominence to the unfolding of the child's unique emotional, imaginative, and cognitive needs in an ever changing, highly technological society.

One distinguishing characteristic of the West is its emphasis on the individual. As Geertz observes in our opening epigraph, in the context of world cultures, this emphasis is indeed quite unique. In this century, the emphasis on the individual achieved its utmost expression through the quest for identity (Taylor 1989). This identity was supposed to be the essence of the person, an essence untarnished or uncontaminated by the demands of others (society). In sharp contrast to this individualistic essentialism, most past and current cultures stress the contextual role of a person in her group and in her society. Let's take a look at the contrast.

The conflicts of the individual—particularly the relationship to authority and the struggles of balancing dependence and autonomy needs—are areas that have long engaged psychoanalytic thinking. The psychoanalytic ideals give tremendous importance to the development of the individual and one's needs, conflicts, and desires. We will call this type of ideal self the individual self or *I-self* (Roland 1991). Figure 9–1 illustrates this type of self. The circles represent self (S) and other (O) as a single unit with integrated good (+) and bad (−) representational components, that is, a self that has achieved the stage of whole object relations. In this type of self, the ideal—a mature, healthy person—is expected to function as a bounded structure, illustrated here as a closed circle enclosing a clearly defined inside and outside. This inside has been the focal point of the psychoanalytic lens. The enclosure of this inside space—the achievement of an individualistic identity—is encouraged

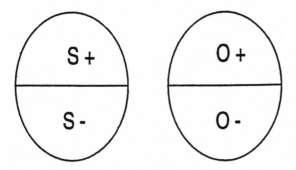

Figure 9–1. Model of "I-self."

through social norms such as our culture's child-rearing practices. For example, early weaning is intended to foster independence in self-care, which eventually is expected to lead to the regulation and management of affect, thinking, and behavior from inside the individual. Sleeping alone, early toilet training, the limiting of physical contact, the overriding value placed on autonomy, the denial and devaluing of dependence— all encourage this ideal. Cross-cultural research on the development of transitional objects suggests similar conclusions; cultural variations in feeding practices, level and duration of physical care between caregiver and infant, and sleeping arrangements seem to structure the kind and quality of transitional phenomena that emerge. Children from urban, industrialized, white, middle-class communities tend to develop an attachment to inanimate objects more often than other groups (Applegate 1989, Hong and Townes 1976, Litt 1981).

Other cultures draw the line differently. Roland (1988, 1991), a Western psychoanalyst who has worked with both Indian and Japanese patients, has made the following distinctions. In contrast to the Western individual self, Indian and Japanese selves can best be described as "a 'we-self' that is felt to be highly relational in different social contexts" (1988, p. 8). Consequently, narcissistic issues, conflicts, cognitive and ego functions, boundaries, and modes of communication form a different pattern and take different meanings. Familial-community and familial-group selves take precedence over an individual self. Our experiences working with Puerto Rican, Caribbean, and Latin American patients parallels Roland's (1991) psychodynamic observations:

In a "we-self" with more permeable outer ego boundaries, the inner representational world is also different from the individualized self of Westerners. There is far less separation of inner representations of self and other. Thus, self- and object-representations are in closer proximity in the familial self, and are more suffused with affect. [p. 166]

Dependence on others is not *the* conflict area (as in the *I-self*); in fact, autonomy and separateness become the primary source of anxiety. In these cultures, personal boundaries are more open and flexible. A diagram of a *we-self* may look like the one represented in Figure 9–2. In this diagram the ideal self is experienced as inextricably embedded in relationships with others. Personal boundaries are expected to remain porous and open (dashed lines around the structures). In addition, the relationship among the structures—the connections to others—is typically hierarchical, as prescribed by social tradition.

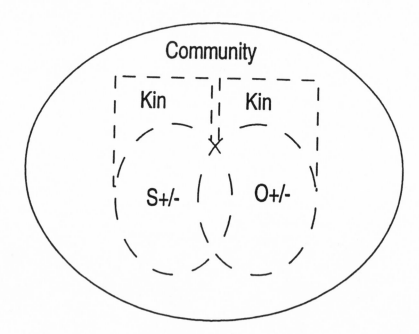

Figure 9–2. Model of "We-self."

Keeping in mind that cultures are "holding environments" (Winnicott 1971) that sustain a variety of self-structures, psychotherapy can be a place to reflect, explore, and create the vast areas of similarities and differences in the relationship. The following case vignettes illustrate some of the ways cultural identity comes to the foreground of the therapeutic encounter.

Case 1

María, a 13-year-old Puerto Rican girl, was referred by her teacher for psychotherapy. After being a steady honors student throughout elementary school, María's grades were declining rapidly. After an initial interview with the family, the therapist finds out the following: María has been refusing to speak Spanish at home, she rejects any Puerto Rican food served by her mother and aunts, and argues constantly about wanting to stay out with friends. The family is considering sending her to Puerto Rico to stay with the maternal grandmother. While the parents only speak Spanish, María refuses to speak to a Latina therapist.

Case 2

Antonio, a 25-year-old senior at a university, seeks therapy with a bilingual/bicultural therapist. As graduation approaches, he became increasingly depressed and anxious about his future plans. He has been in a relationship with an Anglo-American woman for three years. Although he reports that the relationship is satisfactory, he "confesses" that he cannot imagine a *familia* with a non-Latina woman.

Case 3

A Latina patient tells the following dream to her white therapist: a brown-skinned young woman lies at the bottom of a pool, her gleaming white bathing suit shining through the water. Bubbles of air begin to surface. "The woman is alive," whispers a voice.

In all these cases, racial/cultural identities form the framework for differences to be explored, re-created, and discussed. Thus, a difference, or the contrast between real and/or imagined similarities and differences, takes center stage in the space created between patient and therapist. As you enter the psychotherapeutic relationship, the conflicts and meanings of differences can be as rich and complex an area for psychoanalytic exploration and inquiry as any other mental structure we have discussed.

We have discussed several ways in which psychodynamic psychologies understand the relationship between individual development, race, and culture. As part of the dominant culture, psychoanalysis has mirrored many of its culture's prejudices and biases. Ironically, its theory and practice often replicated the same projections and displacements that it uncovered—seeing other races and nationalities as Other, as cultures more neurotic or less developed than itself. At the same time, psychoanalytic ideas have contributed significant insights into the psychodynamics of racism and ethnocentrism. Keeping in mind that theories about psychological development are not outside the culture that generates them, we conclude by proposing the coloring of development as an invaluable source of possibilities for drawing a plurality of selves.

References

Aboud, F. E. (1987). The development of ethnic self-identification and attitudes. In *Children's Ethnic Socialization, Pluralism and Development*, ed. J. S. Phinney and M. J. Rotheram, pp. 32–55. Newbury Park, CA: Sage.

Adorno, T. W., Frenkel-Brunswik, E., Levinson, D. J., and Sanford, R. N. (1950). *The Authoritarian Personality*. New York: Harper.

Applegate, J. S. (1989). The transitional object reconsidered: some sociocultural variations and its implications. *Child and Adolescent Social Work* 6(1):38–51.

Aries, P. (1962). *Centuries of Childhood: A Social History of Family Life*. New York: Vintage.

Blos, P. (1962). *Adolescence: A Psychoanalytic Interpretation*. New York: Free Press.

Bowles, D. (1988). Development of an ethnic self-concept among blacks. In *Ethnicity and Race: Critical Concepts in Social Work*, pp. 103–113. Silver Spring, MD: National Association of Social Workers.

Brunner, J. (1991). The (ir)relevance of Freud's Jewish identity to the origins of psychoanalysis. *Psychoanalysis and Contemporary Thought* 14(4):655–684.

Cross, W. (1987) A two-factor theory of black identity: implications for the study of identity development in minority group children. In *Children's Ethnic Socialization,Pluralism and Development*, ed. J. S. Phinney and M. J. Rotheram, pp. 117–133. Newbury Park, CA: Sage.

Donner, S. (1984). Self psychology: implications for social work. *Social Casework: Journal of Contemporary Social Work* 69(1): 17–22.

Erikson, E. H. (1963). *Childhood and Society*. New York: Norton.

——— (1968). *Identity: Youth and Crisis*. New York: Norton.

Fanon, F. (1967). *Black Skin, White Masks*. New York: Grover.

Freud, A. (1958). Adolescence. *Psychoanalytic Study of the Child* 13:255–278. New York: International Universities Press.

Freud, S. (1921). *Group Psychology and the Analysis of the Ego*. New York: Norton, 1959.

Frosch, S. (1989). *Psychoanalysis and Psychology: Minding the Gap*. New York: New York University Press.

Geertz, C. (1973). *The Interpretation of Cultures*. New York: Basic Books.

——— (1984). From the native's point of view: on the nature of anthropological understanding. In *Culture Theory: Essays of the Mind, Self and Emotion*, ed. R. A. Shweder and R. A. LeVine. Cambridge, England: Cambridge University Press.

Gergen, K. (1994). *Realities and Relationships, Soundings in Social Construction*. Cambridge, MA: Harvard University Press.

Gilman, S. L. (1992). Freud, race and gender. *American Imago* 49(2):155–183.

Hartmann, H. (1958). *Ego Psychology and the Problem of Adaptation*. New York: International Universities Press.

Helms, J. E. (1993). *Black and White Racial Identity, Theory, Research, and Practice*. Westport, CT: Preager.

Ho, M. K. (1992). *Minority Children and Adolescents in Therapy*. Newbury Park, CA: Sage.

Hoffman, I. Z. (1991). Discussion: towards a social constructivist view of the psychoanalytic situation. *Psychoanalytic Dialogues* 1(1):74–105.

Hong, K. M., and Townes, B. (1976). Infant's attachments to inanimate objects: a cross-cultural study. *Journal of the American Academy of Psychoanalysis* 15:49–61.

Katz, P. A. (1987). Development and social processes in ethnic attitudes and self-identification. In *Children's Ethnic Socialization,Pluralism and Development*, ed. J. S. Phinney and M. J. Rotheram, pp. 92–99. Newbury Park, CA: Sage.

Kohut, H. (1971). *The Analysis of the Self*. Madison, CT: International Universities Press.

Kovel, J. (1970). *White Racism: A Psychohistory*. New York: Pantheon.

Kurtz, S. N. (1992). *All the Mothers are One: Hindu India and the Cultural Reshaping of Psychoanalysis.* New York: Columbia University Press.

Litt, C. J. (1981). Children's attachment to transitional objects: a study of two pediatric populations. *American Journal of Orthopsychiatry* 51(1):131–139.

Mahler, M. F., Pine, F., and Bergman, A. (1968). *The Psychological Birth of the Human Infant.* New York: Basic Books.

Malinowski, B. (1927). *Sex and Repression in Savage Society.* London: Routledge & Kegan Paul, 1953.

McDonald, M. (1970). *Not by the Color of Their Skin: The Impact of Racial Differences on the Child's Development.* New York: International Universities Press.

Milner, D. (1983). *Children and Race.* Beverly Hills, CA: Sage.

Mitchell, S. A. (1988). *Relational Concepts in Psychoanalysis: An Integration.* Cambridge, MA: Harvard University Press.

——— (1993). *Hope and Dread in Psychoanalysis.* New York: Basic Books.

Nicholi, A. M., Jr. (1988). The adolescent. In *The New Harvard Guide to Psychiatry,* ed. A. M. Nicholi, Jr. Cambridge, MA: Belknap Press of Harvard University Press.

Paul, R. A. (1991). Freud's anthropology: a reading of the "cultural books." In *The Cambridge Companion to Freud,* ed. J. Neu. Cambridge, England: Cambridge University Press.

Phinney, J. S. (1991). Ethnic identity and self-esteem: a review and integration. *Hispanic Journal of Behavioral Sciences* 13(2):193–208.

Phinney, J. S., Lochner, B. T., and Murphy, R. (1990). Ethnic identity development and psychological adjustment in adolescence. In *Ethnic Issues in Adolescent Mental Health,* ed. A. R. Stiffman and L. E. Davis, pp. 53–72. Newbury Park, CA: Sage.

Pine, F. (1990). *Drive, Ego, Object and Self: A Synthesis for Clinical Work.* New York: Jason Aronson.

Powell, G. J. (1985). Self-concepts among Afro-American students in racially isolated minority schools: some regional differences. *Journal of the American Academy of Child Psychiatry* 24:142–149.

Roland, A. (1988). *In Search of India and Japan: Towards a Cross-Cultural Psychology.* Princeton, NJ: Princeton University Press.

——— (1991). The self in cross-civilizational perspective. In *The Relational Self: Theoretical Convergences in Psychoanalysis and Social Psychology,* ed. R. Curtis, pp. 160–180. New York: Guilford.

Rosenthal, D. A. (1987). Ethnic identity development in adolescents. In *Children's Ethnic Socialization, Pluralism and Development,* ed. J. S. Phinney and M. J. Rotheram, pp. 156–179. Newbury Park, CA: Sage.

Sherwood, R. (1980). *The Psychodynamics of Race: Vicious and Benign Spirals.* Atlantic Highlands, NJ: Humanities Press.

Sluzki, C. (1979). Migration and family conflict. *Family Process* 18(4):379–390.

Spencer, M. B., and Markstrom-Adams, C. (1990). Identity processes among racial and ethnic children in America. *Child Development* 61:290–310.

Sue, D. W., and Sue, D. (1990). *Counseling the Culturally Different: Theory and Practice.* New York: Wiley.

Taylor, C. (1989). *Sources of the Self: The Making of the Modern Identity.* Cambridge, MA: Harvard University Press.

Vincent, G. (1991). A history of secrets? In *A History of Private Life*, vol. 5: *Riddles of Identity in Modern Times*, ed. P. Aries and G. Dubys. Cambridge, MA: Belknap Press of Harvard University Press.

Volkan, V. D. (1988). *The Need to Have Enemies and Allies: From Clinical Practice to International Relationships.* Northvale, NJ: Jason Aronson.

Watkins, M. (1994). *On the Real Side: Laughing, Lying, and Signifying—The Underground Tradition of African-American Humor that Transformed American Culture, from Slavery to Richard Pryor.* New York: Simon & Schuster.

Winnicott, D. W. (1971). *Playing and Reality.* New York: Tavistock.

10

Psychodynamic Theory and The Psychology of Women

JOAN BERZOFF

"What does a woman want?" Freud is reported to have lamented in 1903 (Jones 1955, p. 421). Given that it has taken almost three quarters of the last century just to begin to answer the question, it is clear that the answer is anything but simple. In fact, the discourse on psychoanalysis and gender has produced a body of knowledge that is greater than Freud could have ever imagined.

Over the last seventy-five years, Freud has been both assailed and assimilated by feminists for his theories about women. He has been called misogynist and phallocentric for capturing the gender stereotypes of his Victorian times and labeling them normative. On the other hand, many of his ideas have been used by feminists, who have critiqued, revised, and improved upon his formulations and who have articulated different pathways for female psychological development.

This chapter considers the feminist critiques and the feminist revisions of psychodynamic theories. First, we look at drive theory and at some of Freud's problematic ideas about women as well as how these led to different conceptions of women's development in the social and cognitive domains. Next, we consider what feminists have said about object relations theory as well as how they have appropriated that theory to explain women's inequality in the social structure. We then discuss self-in-relation theory, which draws on concepts from object relations, interpersonal, and self psychological theories. Following that, we critique ego psychology, particularly Erikson's theory of life-cycle development, for its overemphasis on male developmental values. Finally, we consider postmodern feminist contributions to psychodynamic theory, which have begun to question whether there has ever been, or whether there can ever be, a psychology of women.

DRIVE THEORY

Let us begin then with drive theory. As we said in Chapter 2, Freud made some rather stunning statements about how psychosexual development occurs differently for little girls than for little boys in the oedipal stage of development. Freud began with the premise that little girls are really little men. He postulated that in early childhood girls are unaware of their own vaginas and actually see their clitorises as small penises. When they discover the anatomical differences between themselves and boys, they feel envy. Girls become heterosexual, he postulated, almost by default. They first turn away from their original love objects, their mothers, disappointed in them for not having provided them with a penis. Girls then turn toward their fathers in the hopes of restitution and with the fantasy that their fathers will provide them with a baby. Heterosexuality, in Freud's view, is a girl's consolation for not having a penis. Unlike boys, who renounce their oedipal desires for their mothers because of fears of being castrated, girls do not fear castration because, in Freud's view, they are already castrated. As a result, girls cannot ever fully resolve their oedipal issues and therefore develop weaker superegos than do boys. When girls do turn back to their mothers to identify with them, they identify with that which is feminine: passivity, masochism, and narcissism. These features, he suggested, are essential hallmarks of female identity.

It is difficult even to articulate such a theory in the 1990s because Freud's claims are so embedded in his Victorian society's devalued view of women. Nonetheless, he identified many important concepts that still contribute to our understanding of women's psychological development.

Karen Horney (1926) was one of the first of Freud's contemporaries to challenge his phallocentrism and to say that penis envy is not an intrapsychic event but rather a societal one. When a girl becomes aware of her anatomical difference, it is not the lack of a penis that makes her feel inferior. Instead it is the *symbolic* meaning of her difference from boys that makes her inferior. It is not the male anatomical apparatus that women want, but rather the access to what men have: power, opportunity, resources. This idea that women's psychological development is inextricably linked to their unequal place in the social structure has dominated almost all subsequent thinking about the psychology of women. Horney's critique is also the first of many to argue that there is no such thing as a woman "born." Instead a woman is "made." She is psychologically constructed by the society in which she develops (Rich 1976), as is her "inferiority."

A different and more contemporary critique of penis envy has come out of cognitive developmental psychology, and although it is not a psychodynamic theory per se, it helps us understand the development of female gender identity. Irene Fast (1984) has noted that "difference" has dominated most of the discourse on women. She has suggested that envy is a result of a child's cognitive awareness of difference. In her view, the recognition of difference is a cognitive achievement, not an intrapsychic one.

Cognitively, little girls and boys are aware of sex differences by the end of the first year of life. Between the ages of 1 and 2, little girls and boys begin to distinguish sex differences based on hair and dress. A little boy or girl might say, "He's a boy because he has short hair" or "She's a girl because she wears a dress." If a boy has long hair, or if a girl wears long pants or has short hair, the young child may have some difficulty identifying the gender. For the young child, the concept of gender is not fixed. Rather the young child still sees gender as reversible and fluid. By ages 3 to 5, however, boys and girls become aware that sex differences are not based on external characteristics but on genital differences, and then become curious about each other's genitals, and often explore the physical differences between them. However, the *meaning* of those anatomical differences does not actually develop until the child discovers that the genitals he or she has will remain constant forever. The awareness of gender constancy imposes limits. Having a penis means never giving birth to a baby; having a vagina means never having a penis. When children cognitively confront the limits of their own anatomy, they envy what they do not have. The awareness of the limits, and of gender constancy, leads to the development of a fixed gender identity. This view of envy as a cognitive developmental achievement depathologizes the concept.

Envy may have yet another social explanation. Rather than women envying what a man has, many feminists propose that men envy women. After all, since it is a woman who can give birth to a child, perhaps men experience womb envy. Indeed, in Freud's case of Little Hans (see Chapter 15), this 5-year-old boy insists he can have a baby. Although his father tries to dissuade him, Hans persists in the belief that he, like his mother, will give birth. Freud entirely ignores Hans' womb envy in this case and perhaps his blindness reflects his own defensive position. Denying his own envy of women, Freud may have needed to accord the penis a more central place in all of psychological development than it deserved.

OBJECT RELATIONS

Object relations theorists, in contrast, accord the mother, rather than the penis, a central place in human development. Recall that Melanie Klein described the infant as absolutely dependent on the mother; when a mother's milk is available, the infant feels loved. When the infant tries to drink too quickly and chokes on the mother's milk or when the mother is not available to the infant, the child can feel utter and complete hatred. The mother is the source of all of the infant's experiences of being worthy or unworthy. She can also be the source of the child's hatred, which may be experienced as an attack from without or within. The mother, in many object relations theories, is experienced as all-powerful. In fact, universal fears of an all-powerful mother may be the source of gender oppression. Dinnerstein (1976) contends that the rigid sex roles and sex role ideologies that are so prevalent in our culture stem from primitive fears about the power of women. Because neither boys nor girls develop a realistic sense of their own mothers as independent, autonomous agents, their fantasies about the power of their mothers become, paradoxically, greater. Because children need their mothers and are entirely dependent on them, they also wish to control them, so that the most pathological aspects of our current culture—violence against women, the denigration of women, humiliation of women—have their roots in earliest child-rearing arrangements.

Patriarchal societies create and maintain rigid gender roles as a societal defense against the power of women. Mothers can then both be viewed as the source of human creation and blamed as the source of human malaise (Dinnerstein 1976). When gender roles are perpetuated through child care arrangements in which only mothers care for children, women will continue to be feared, and men and women will be robbed of their fullest opportunities for human development (Chodorow 1978, Dinnerstein 1976,).

Nancy Chodorow (1974), a sociologist interested in the gender inequities in American society, has offered a similar critique, but she appropriates, rather than criticizes, object relations theory. She argues that in a society in which only women take care of children, boys and girls are socialized to develop gendered senses of self in the context of an unequal nuclear family. Boys develop their gender identities by first separating and individuating from their primary love objects, their mothers. To develop their sense of self boys have to develop strong ego boundaries between themselves and their mothers. Thus, boys develop a self that is more boundaried, more differentiated, and more autonomous than that of girls. In the process of their gender identity development, boys learn to repress or deny the parts of themselves that were forged in close contact with their mothers.

On the other hand, in the process of developing a female sense of self, girls never need break their preoedipal ties to their mothers. Their female sense of self develops in the context of a continuous relationship with their mothers. As a result of this continuity, girls develop different kinds of relational skills and capacities than do boys. Girls develop more permeable ego boundaries and with greater capacities for empathy than do boys.

Chodorow asserts that in a society in which women predominantly mother, differential relational skills become reproduced as asymmetrical gender roles. Boys are socialized toward autonomy, separateness, and individuation, girls toward a relational orientation and a more fluid sense of self. In a society that values autonomy over connectedness, this gender asymmetry does not serve women well. In the nuclear family, gender asymmetry perpetuates unequal gender roles. Like Dinnerstein, then, Chodorow asserts that gender inequalities will be perpetuated unless the functions of mothering are shared by both men and women.

Jessica Benjamin (1988) has also investigated the early object relations of boys and girls and has used that framework to understand their effects on gendered identities. She has suggested that for little boys, fathers represent the pure and idealized love that comes with independence and freedom. Boys recognize the freedom that their fathers have and identify with them and their separateness. For girls, the task of separation is far more difficult, because in Western cultures fathers represent separation and freedom to girls as well. But whereas boys identify with their fathers, girls must come to terms with being different from their fathers. What does a girl do with her own desire for freedom and separateness? Benjamin asserts that girls defensively learn to idealize men and to subjugate their own desires to the desires of men.

> Gina, a 21-year-old college student, describes her mother as "bland, ugly, fat, and frumpy." Her father (who, it turns out, is all of these things), she describes as "cool, brilliant, inventive, and creative." As treatment progresses, it becomes clear that Gina's mother is the more attuned and caring parent, whereas her father is quite self-involved and remote. Yet Gina finds herself in sexual relationships in which she tries to think the deep and profound thoughts she assumes men expect of her; invariably, she becomes silent with boys because she feels that they will and should control the relationship. She tries to dress seductively for men but has no idea what style of dress *she* likes. She expends much energy becoming an object of men's desires but says that she has little sense of who she is or what she wants.

For girls, men come to represent that which will control their own desires. A child who has some sense of personal worth does not need to be controlled by others. But girls, whose gender is devalued, learn to subsume their own desires. Perhaps this is why Margaret Mahler describes how little girls in the rapprochement subphase lose some of their enthusiasm, and become more depressed than little boys. Like Chodorow, Dinnerstein, and others, Benjamin has argued that if female self and object representations are ever to become more robust and alive for girls and women, then there will need to be changes in both the family structure and the social structure.

There are, then, a number of interrelated critiques. In nuclear family structures in which only one gender does the parenting, women may be feared. In a society that fears women, it is likely that they will be subjugated. In nuclear families, gender asymmetries may become codified as gender roles and become reproduced as social inequities. In family structures in which men represent freedom and separation, women may have to subjugate their own desires. In nuclear family arrangements, women are made powerfully responsible for the care of others, but are subordinate and powerless in the larger social world. As long as mothers remain the primary caretakers, they become the target of fear and loathing. Societies create patriarchy out of infantile fears.

FEMINIST INTERPERSONAL PSYCHOANALYTIC THEORIES: SELF-IN-RELATION THEORY

We have seen that theorists such as Chodorow have described female development as a self-in-relation paradigm. Interpersonal psychoanalytic theorists have elaborated on women's psychological experiences of being in relationships by analyzing the social structure in which women develop. These theorists from the Stone Center at Wellesley College (Jordan et al. 1983, Jordan and Surrey 1989, Miller 1976, Surrey and Kaplan 1990) have suggested that within American society, where women have been subordinate to men, women have found ways to act and react from their subordinate positions. Like any subjugated group, women have tended to form intense affiliations and relationships with other women in the workplace, the community, and the family. The kinds of relational bonds that they form, while in reaction to their subjugation, can be seen as fostering their identities and leading to stronger senses of self. Yet while women are socialized to make and sustain relationships, this activity occurs in a society that devalues relationships and overvalues personal productivity (Beroff 1989, Miller 1976).

Self-in-relation theorists argue that women are oppressed not because they are embedded in relationships, but rather because they are oppressed by the social structure. In this view, pejorative concepts such as female dependency and masochism are now turned upside down and are celebrated as cooperation and creativity. From this self-in-relation perspective (Jordan et al. 1983, Jordan and Surrey 1989, Surrey and Kaplan 1990) the female infant never separates but always develops a self in relation to others. But rather than pathologizing women's resultant dependency in relationships from birth on, the theory suggests that girls develop greater empathy and attunedness to others. A girl's sameness with her mother fosters her ability to see herself in her mother; her likeness catalyzes rather than impedes her development. In this analysis, there are echoes of self psychology—the belief that maternal empathy fosters psychological development. Yet while this perspective has tried to correct the devaluation of women, it has also tended to idealize them. Indeed, Stone Center theorists have repeatedly identified and valorized women's affiliative, nurturant, and maternal abilities. While self-in-relation theorists promote important ideas, these ideas have their antecedents in Chodorow's, Benjamin's, and Dinnerstein's writings, and surprisingly little credit has been accorded to these feminist theorists.

EGO PSYCHOLOGY

Another feminist psychodynamic critique has emerged from ego psychology. As has been true in so many of the psychodynamic theories we have studied, in ego psychology male development has been the prototype for all development and female development has been considered a deviation from the norm. Recall that Erikson postulated that normally (read "for men"), identity precedes intimacy. By the end of adolescence, a man has sufficiently separate and boundaried identity that he can form a relationship with a woman with whom he shares life's pleasures and with whom he can lose and find himself. On the other hand, a woman's identity occurs later. It is defined in early adulthood by the man she will marry and by the children who will fill her inner space. This theme—that men develop more separate identities than do women—has dominated most of the writing on men and women. Erikson's theory, like so many we have studied, finds women wanting.

Jean Baker Miller (1984) has argued that Erikson's theory neglects the role of relationships and attachments throughout the life cycle. In an effort to balance what she sees as an overemphasis on separation (with developmental goals such as autonomy, initiative, and industry), Miller has proposed adding a relational component to each of Erikson's eight stages of man. For example, in infancy, a girl develops not only trust but also a sense of herself in a relationship, giving her the capacity for emotional empathy. Miller challenges Erikson's second stage by noting that a girl does not ever become autonomous, but instead develops a sense of her own agency within a community of relationships with others. At the oedipal stage, girls in Western cultures begin to learn about their mothers' devalued place in society and to identify with them.

Lizzy, a 6-year-old girl, noticed that in her basketball games boys tended to shoot the baskets while girls were trained to pass the ball. She went to her school principal to tell her what she had discovered. Her principal responded that this was the "normal" way that girls learn to be girls. In effect, her principal codified that gender inequality was a normal part of Lizzy's development and that Lizzie should accept her devalued place in the game and in society.

In latency, a girl's relationships with female friends play an important part in her self definition. And yet, it has been noted that when girls on the playground who are engaged with female friends are asked what they are doing, they invariably reply, "Nothing" (Lever 1976). Clearly, girls in latency also learn to devalue, as their society does, their relational ties. By adolescence, Miller has noted, girls begin to see their own needs as conflicting with the needs of others. Gilligan (1982) has also noted that in adolescence girls begin to silence themselves academically, conforming to societal expectations to tend to the needs of men.

In a similar vein, Franz and White (1985) have criticized Erikson for his overarching emphasis on separation and individuation in his life-cycle theory. In fact, his emphasis on separateness privileges male development. Franz and White suggest, as does Miller, that Erikson's stages of development be viewed as two pathways—one of individuation and the other of attachment. For example, using Mahler's ideas about separation and individuation, they note that a 2-year-old child only becomes autonomous when she masters the relational achievement of object constancy. As a child develops within Erikson's stage of initiative, she develops greater relational complexity, taking the initiative to engage with others in play. By school age, a child develops the capacity for industry and also for collaboration with other children. Adolescence is a time when a child develops a separate identity, but it is also a time for interdependence. Like Miller, then, Franz and White offer a relational corrective for a theory that overemphasizes autonomy and separateness.

POSTMODERN FEMINIST PSYCHOANALYTIC CRITIQUES

Almost all of the feminist critiques of psychodynamic theories that we have studied so far have had common themes. Be they drive, object relations, interpersonal, or ego psychological, these theories have asserted that women are different, but not deficient, and that women's differences can best be understood in terms of their essential relational capacities and strengths. Women have been described as more empathic, more caring, more affiliative, more nurturant, and more maternal, and their relational skills have been said to alter their senses of self and of others.

In the last decade, however, from the postmodern frontier has come the critique that these so-called essential attributes of women (and of men) need to be challenged. Do all women (mothers) produce boys who are separate and autonomous? Are all girls relational? Is all of society reducible to the nuclear family? Is gender a stable construct?

Postmodern feminists have asked whether theorizing about women's differences in fact actually privileges one gender, while inferiorizing women as "other." Over the last decade, the very concept of gender has come into question as reifying and supporting the status quo. As long as psychological theories prescribe gender categories as dualistic or binary (i.e., males represent one set of behaviors, abilities, values, and capacities, and women another) we structure our realities accordingly and perpetuate gender stereotypes.

Deconstructing the concept of gender requires that we challenge the hierarchical oppositions that are embedded in our gender categories that legitimize power differentials. Hare-Mustin and Marecek (1990), for example, point to the alpha and beta biases in gender theorizing. Alpha biases exaggerate differences (e.g., all women are relational and nurturant; all men are autonomous and separate). Taken to the extreme, alpha biases valorize women for their relational skills while relegating them to the domestic sphere of caregivers for children. This leads us away from changing their unequal social conditions. Beta biases obscure differences (e.g., men and women are androgenous and there are no differences between them). Beta biases in gender theorizing can ultimately result in creating social policies that treat men and women exactly the same despite their differences (such as eliminating pregnancy leaves for women in the workplace). Both kinds of biases tend to dichotomize gender possibilities, reducing human complexity, ambiguity, and paradox.

As long as gender is conceptualized only as binary, gender conformity will be the goal. When gender is dichotomized, as is so often the case in psychoanalytic theories, a kind of relational "splitting" ensues. In the course of an individual's development, parts of self are encouraged for one gender, while other parts of the self are prohibited. Such splitting is regressive, prohibitive, and ultimately limits human possibility and human potential (Goldner 1991).

Postmodern theorists have further begun to ask, "Which women are we talking about anyway?" Do "female" qualities of nurturance and relationship apply to all women? Do they pertain to African-American single parents, to Asian women living in urban poverty, to Latina women, to single, married, lesbian, aging women, women with disabilities, privileged women, physically ill women, rural women, urban women, disadvantaged women? In fact, the question emerges again whether there should be a category at all such as "woman"? (Flax 1990, Spelman 1988, Unger 1979).

Peggy McIntosh (1988) has pointed out that "white privilege" has helped white feminist scholars assume that their own experiences are universal, normative, and representative. In the same way, white heterosexual women have assumed that all women are like them. As long as we assume that all women are nurturant, or empathic, or flexible, or affiliative, we lose sight of the ways that race, class, age, health, and ethnicity always mediate the meaning of being female. As long as ways of being are dichotomized only as female or male, we privilege some sexual arrangements and marginalize others. Many postmodern theorists, then, are calling for psycholog*ies* of women that are pluralistic, multicultural, contextual, and egalitarian.

Finally, postmodern theorists (Comas-Diaz and Greene 1994) reject that there is or should ever be a stable and continuous construction such as gender, just as there is no absolute identity based on race, ethnicity, or class. They focus instead on women as diverse and heterogeneous while warning of the political danger in identifying all women in essentialist terms. To do so runs the risk of further marginalizing women by reducing and oversimplifying their experiences.

The issues that postmodernists raise are not merely academic. If we are to truly try to understand women in clinical work, then we must be able to attend to the difference, the paradox, the ambiguity between and among them. While the concept of difference sparked the very psychology of women, it will be the appreciation of a complex multiplicity of gendered possibilities that will ultimately help our clients, both women and men, achieve their full relational potentials.

References

Benjamin, J. (1988). *The Bonds of Love: Psychoanalysis, Feminism and the Problem of Domination*. New York: Pantheon Books.

Berzoff, J. (1989). From separation to connection: shifts in understanding women's development. *Affilia: Journal of Women and Social Work* 4:45–58.

Chasseguet-Smirgel, J. (1964). Feminine guilt and the Oedipus complex. In *Female Sexuality*, ed. J. Chasseguet-Smirgel. Ann Arbor, MI: University of Michigan Press.

——— (1970). *Female Sexuality: New Psychoanalytic Views*. Ann Arbor, MI: University of Michigan Press.

Chodorow, N. (1974). Family structure and feminine personality. In *Woman, Culture, and Society*, ed. M. Z. Rosakdi, and K. Lamphere. Stanford, CA: Stanford University Press.

——— (1978). *The Reproduction of Mothering: Psychoanalysis and the Sociology of Gender*. Berkeley, CA: University of California Press.

Comas-Diaz, L., and Greene, B. (1994). *Women of Color: Integrating Ethnic and Gender Identities in Psychotherapy*. New York: Guilford.

Dinnerstein, D. (1976). *The Mermaid and the Minotaur: Sexual Arrangements and Human Malaise*. New York: Harper and Row.

Eichenbaum, L., and Orbach, S. (1983). *Understanding Women: A Feminist Psychoanalytic Approach*. New York: Basic Books.

Erikson, E. H. (1950). *Childhood and Society*. New York: Norton.

——— (1959). Identity and the Life Cycle: *Selected Papers*. Psychological Issues, Monograph No. 1, vol. 1. New York: International Universities Press.

——— (1964). Inner and outer space: reflections on womanhood. In *The Woman in America*, ed. R. J. Lipton. Boston: Beacon.

Fast, I. (1984). *Gender Identity: A Differentiation Model*. Hillsdale, NJ: Analytic Press.

Flax, J. (1990). *Thinking Fragments: Psychoanalysis, Feminism and Postmodernism in the Contemporary West.* Berkeley, CA: University of California Press.

Franz, C., and White, K. (1985). Individuation and attachment in personality development: extending Erikson's theory. *Journal of Personality* 52(2):224–256.

Freud, S. (1930). Some anatomical distinctions between the sexes. *Standard Edition* 20:241–258.

——— (1931). Female sexuality. *Standard Edition* 21:223–243.

——— (1932). Femininity. *Standard Edition* 22:1121–1135.

Gilligan, C. (1982). *A Different Voice: Psychological Theory and Women's Development.* Cambridge, MA: Harvard University Press.

Goldner, V. (1991).Toward a critical relational theory of gender. *Psychoanalytic Dialogues* 1(3):249–272.

Hare-Mustin, R., and Marecek, J. (1990). *On Making a Difference: Psychology and the Construction of Gender.* New Haven, CT: Yale University Press.

Horney, K. (1924). On the genesis of the castration complex in women. *International Journal of Psychoanalysis* 5:50–65.

——— (1926). The flight from womanhood: the masculinity complex in women as viewed by men and women. In *Woman and Analysis: Dialogues on Psychoanalytic Views of Femininity*, ed. J. Strouse, pp. 171–187. New York: Grossman, 1974.

——— (1973). *Feminine Psychology*, ed. H. Kelman. New York: Norton.

Jones, E. (1955). *The Life and Work of Sigmund Freud*, vol. III, pp. 420–456. New York: Basic Books.

Jordan, J., and Surrey, J. (1986). The self-in-relation: empathy and the mother–daughter relationship. In *The Psychology of Today's Woman: New Psychoanalytic Visions*, ed. T. Bernay and D. Cantor, pp. 81–105. Hillsdale, NJ: Analytic Press.

Jordan, J., Surrey, J., and Kaplan, A. (1983). *Women and Empathy: Implications for Psychological Development and Empathy.* Work in progress. Stone Center for Developmental Services. Wellesley, MA: Wellesley College.

Lever, J. (1976). Sex differences in the games children play. *Social Problems* 23:478–487.

McIntosh, P. (1988). White privilege and male privilege: a personal account of coming to see correspondences through work in women's studies. Wellesley College Center for Research on Women, Working Paper 189, 1–19.

Miller, J. B. (1976). *Towards a New Psychology of Women.* Boston: Beacon.

——— (1984). The development of women's sense of self. In *Essential Papers on the Psychology of Women*, ed. C. Zanardi, pp. 437–455. New York: New York University Press, 1990.

Rich, A. (1976). *Of Woman Born: Motherhood as Experience and Institution*. New York: Norton.

Spelman, V. (1988). *Inessential Woman: Problems of Exclusion in Feminist Thought*. Boston: Beacon Press.

Surrey, J., and Kaplan, A. (1990). Empathy revisited. Work in progress, no. 40, pp. 1–14. Wellesley, MA: Stone Center, Wellesley College.

Thompson, C. (1942). Cultural pressures in the psychology of women. *Psychiatry* 5:331–339.

Tronto, J. (1987). Beyond gender difference to a theory of care. *Signs* 12(4):644–664.

Unger, R. (1979). Toward a redefinition of sex and gender. *American Psychologist* 34(11):1085–1094.

Young-Bruehl, E. (1990). *Freud on Women: A Reader*. New York: Norton.

Young-Bruehl, E., and Wexler, A, L. (1992). On psychoanalysis and feminism. *Social Research* 59(2):453–483.

Commentary

JOAN BERZOFF, LAURA MELANO FLANAGAN, AND PATRICIA HERTZ

The preceding chapters have explored psychological concepts from a range of psychodynamic theories, and attempted to integrate biological and social perspectives with these theories. We looked at how forces from the inside and outside combine to influence development and shape individuals' lives. The content of these chapters can stand on its own, as it is often taught in separate courses on developmental theory or social theory in programs of social work, counseling, nursing, and psychology. However, in our experience as teachers and practitioners, this content is too readily divorced from the practice in which people then engage. Students learn about Freud, Mahler, and Kohut during one semester, for example, and then move on to a course in clinical practice or psychopathology with little integration of the theories they just studied. The theory then becomes a body of knowledge to memorize, but not to *use* in the room with clients.

How do we allow these theories to inform our practice in a meaningful, and possibly transformative, way? How do we hold in our minds a multiplicity of theoretical models without letting them clutter our

thoughts or our hearts, or without creating an agenda that may be irrelevant to the person with whom we are sitting? How do we organize what
we hear into meaning that does not foreclose other possibilities and other
interpretations? To address these questions, we must first acknowledge
the paradox inherent in this process. We must "know" and "not know"
simultaneously; we must strive to be both "full" of knowledge and theory
while being "empty" enough to be surprised, to learn, to appreciate the
uniqueness of every person with whom we work.

These theories, then, should ideally remain available and accessible
in our minds in order to teach us *why* a person may be presenting with
certain struggles and strengths at a given time and in a particular fashion. They can then help deepen our understanding of our clients' emotional turmoil, and help create options for healing and growth. They
must not, however, become guides or prescriptions for how the work
should proceed. If we "know" too much too soon, we stop listening
to the unique essence of our clients' lives; we run the risk of deciding
where the therapeutic journey will take us, rather than having it evolve
out of the interactions unfolding in the therapeutic relationship.

In the first half of this book, we noted that only by appreciating
external and internal dynamics can we more fully understand the pain
with which many of our clients present. Recall the two clients we described in Chapter 1—Martin and Michael. Both had been seen by post-
master's clinicians who had effectively intervened on their behalf
in the external environment, but who were bewildered by what their
clients experienced internally. Michael was a Latino man, raised in a
chaotic, physically abusive environment in which conflicting messages
abounded. Michael described himself as three Michaels: a good Michael,
a bad Michael, and a middle Michael, and his therapist was mystified
by the meaning of this. His history revealed severe and persistent physical
abuse at the hands of his stepfather and an early abandonment by his
mother, who had been abused by the same man.

The therapist who worked with Michael initially helped him adjust
to life outside the hospital, focusing on how discrimination, poverty, and
the stigma of mental illness affected his ability to function. With the
theories we have studied in this book, we can augment the therapist's
understanding of Michael's suffering. From object relations theory, for
example, we learned that people are not born with integrated senses of

themselves and that psychological integration develops over time; babies and young children often feel that they have good parts and bad parts, and that with time and care children can realize that they are a complex combination of both good and bad. We learned that there can be profound effects on a child's sense of self and ability to trust when the child has been neglected, abandoned, or abused.

Using this theoretical knowledge, we can start to make sense of the way Michael "carries" his suffering. His symptoms reflect the way he has integrated external and internal struggles, and found "solutions" to them. We can begin to develop hypotheses about how splitting the "good" and "bad" parts of himself helped him cope with the abuse and neglect of his environment, and with his internal rage and disappointment. We can see how this experience of himself remained fragmented in the face of oppressive and destructive forces from *without* and from *within*. The theoretical constructs in this book can then be bridged with the discussion of psychopathology that is to follow.

The story of Martin affords us a similar opportunity. Recall that Martin, a 28-year-old black Haitian man, came to treatment worried about what terrible thing would befall him next. He had become so preoccupied that he was unable to function in school, work, or his marriage. Martin had grown up in a Catholic Caribbean culture, raised by a father who was a policeman and who set extremely high standards for himself and his son. Prior to contacting the clinic, Martin had been capriciously arrested by white officers and had been the victim of racial assaults by fellow prisoners who had poured buckets of urine on him throughout his night in jail. Upon his release, he could not stop berating himself nor feeling that he deserved to be punished.

Each theory we studied can illuminate some aspects of Martin's symptoms and his internal struggle. A drive theorist might focus on Martin's own aggressive impulses, and wonder how they were discharged or checked both during and after his arrest. Had the anger he felt toward the white officers and prisoners been turned against himself? Or were Martin's feelings of unworthiness related to his sense that he had failed his church's and father's high expectations of him? A self psychologist might focus on how this frightening experience caused a tremendous injury to Martin's sense of self. How might his previous trust in his own emotional strength, or his belief in the wisdom of police officers like his father, been shattered by this racist assault? How might this have affected his goals and ambitions? Each theory advances a set of hypotheses about what may have led to the symptoms with which Martin presents.

In the rest of this book, we will offer a way to understand both Michael's and Martin's emotional struggles by focusing on several psychopathological syndromes. Before we move to a discussion of these diagnostic categories, however, we want to reflect for a moment on the concept to which we are devoting the remaining chapters—*psychopathology*. Webster defines *psychopathology* as "the science of dealing with diseases and abnormalities of the mind." The word *disease* implies illness or sickness, an entity to be treated—most likely by those who are "disease free." A division and boundary is then created between those who are allegedly "well" and those who are "sick." The notion that the definitions of health and illness themselves are largely social constructions gets lost, as does an appreciation that we all fall along a continuum of mental illness and health that is not static in nature.

If we can move to an understanding of pathology that is more closely linked to its Greek origin, with *pathos* meaning suffering, we can use the term *psychopathology* to connote suffering of the mind or soul. Other cultures, such as that of Native Americans, capture this condition with terms that suggest someone is "out of harmony." These descriptions of psychopathology force us to recognize that we are not necessarily so different than or separate from those who are labeled with mental illness. We all have elements of suffering and disharmony in our lives, with which we are able to cope with varying degrees of success at different points in our lives. Biological, psychological, and social forces will combine to determine where we fall in a given moment along the continuum from mental illness to mental health. As Harry Stack Sullivan (1940) noted: "In most general terms, we are all much more simply human than otherwise; be we happy and successful, contented and detached, miserable and mentally disordered or whatever" (p. 39).

In the following chapters, we review four major psychopathological syndromes using the theories we studied in the first part of the book. With a biopsychosocial perspective, we explore the complex interplay between nature and nurture in the creation of these disorders, and discuss the way the disorders themselves reflect the social contexts in which they emerge. We have chosen not to present these disorders exclusively according to the standardized nosology of *DSM-IV*, the diagnostic manual of psychiatric disorders recognized by the American Psychiatric Association, which is deliberately atheoretical. It offers a set of criteria that define disorders in terms of symptom lists; it offers an empirical way of ensuring that diagnosis be made on the basis of observable and describable behavior rather than on the basis of psychological ideology. It does not posit any particular reason for a given psychiatric problem, nor does it prescribe any one method for treating it. While this manual allows clinicians of all disciplines and theoretical orientations to make diagnoses based on common criteria, the richness of the internal, subjective psychological experience of "suffering" and "disharmony" is forfeited by this classification system.

Our goal in the following chapters is to demonstrate how a psychodynamic theoretical orientation can help us understand not just the symptoms of several disorders, but also the person with the symptoms. Using a biopsychosocial lens, we hope to illustrate how an application of theories we have studied deepens our view of the complexities of people's pain. From a biological perspective, we will explore how genetic and biological factors can predispose and/or lead to the development of particular disorders. From a psychodynamic perspective, we will look at how drive theory, ego psychology, object relations, and self psychology help explain the etiology and course of people's inner turmoil and outward dysfunction. From a social perspective, we will look at how gender, culture, class, and the forces of oppression can create the context for and fuel the development of emotional difficulties.

The mental disorders we have chosen to describe do not include the full range of psychopathological syndromes that affect people's lives. They represent an arbitrary and perhaps idiosyncratic selection of several major diagnostic categories, including the psychoses (with a special emphasis on schizophrenia), the personality disorders, the mood disorders, and the anxiety disorders. We chose to explore these four broad categories because they reflect a range of emotional problems with which people struggle, and because they illustrate how a biopsychosocial lens can help us fully assess people in the context of their inner and outer worlds. Unlike illnesses such as the cognitive disorders, they also lend themselves to exploration from a psychodynamic perspective.

In the following chapters, then, we will study psychopathology from the inside out and the outside in. In each diagnostic category, we will look at how what originates from the outside is experienced intrapsychically, and how what is experienced intrapsychically influences a person's perceptions of, and experiences with, the external world. Only then can we begin to appreciate the multiple levels of meaning in our work with our clients.

REFERENCE

Sullivan, H. S. (1940). Conceptions of modern psychiatry. *Psychiatry* 3:35–45.

11

The Psychoses, with a Special Emphasis on Schizophrenia

PATRICIA HERTZ

"You're CRAZY!" A simple, declarative statement whose meaning varies enormously depending on the context in which it is uttered. It may be used jokingly among friends mocking each other, or it may pass through the minds of pedestrians walking by a person who is muttering to himself. The "crazy" thoughts or behaviors of mentally disturbed people can alienate us, as we attempt to dismiss what we understand least yet often fear most. For beginning clinicians who seek to use logic and facts to assist them in understanding their clients, working with psychotic patients can be a frightening and overwhelming experience. In this chapter we attempt to diminish these fears by providing an understanding of the psychotic disorders using a biopsychosocial perspective. We briefly review several types of disorders before turning our attention to the most prevalent one—schizophrenia.

The term *psychosis* refers to a mental disorder in which there is a partial or complete withdrawal from reality. Psychosis, or a "break" from reality, can assume many forms. The two most notable symptoms are delusions, which are fixed, false ideas believed by the person that cannot be corrected by reason, and *hallucinations*, which are sensory experiences leading a person to see, hear, feel, or smell things that cannot be established in reality. Even in the absence of delusions or hallucinations, a psychotic person's capacity to evaluate reality is almost always severely impaired. Let us consider a sampling of people who present with psychotic symptoms. Each of the case vignettes below illustrates a person *experiencing* a psychotic episode yet suffering from a different mental illness.

> Sam, a 21-year-old man, came in for his second appointment. In the first meeting he had been well related and appropriately attired, and had been able to discuss his problems in a reliable, reality-based manner. In the second encounter he presented with a bloody and swollen face, stating that he had been in a fight with the devil the previous evening. The devil, he stated, had taken his head in his hands, yelled at him, and repeatedly banged his face against the bedroom floor. Sam reported that he had shot a quarter gram of cocaine shortly before the fight.

Sam experienced both auditory and visual hallucinations precipitated by his use of cocaine. He suffered from a cocaine-induced psychotic disorder. Street drugs, as well as prescribed medications, can precipitate psychotic episodes in which visual hallucinations frequently emerge as prominent characteristics. Caused by a transient or permanent dysfunction of the brain, this type of disorder has a biological etiology. Additional causes of psychoses that have an organic basis include dementia and delirium. When clients first present with psychotic symptoms, then, it is essential to have them worked up medically to determine if a general medical condition and/or substance intoxication or withdrawal have triggered their symptoms. Had Sam arrived at a clinic without either reporting his substance history or receiving a medical workup, he could easily have been misdiagnosed and hence mistreated. Mental health professionals are often the first people to evaluate such clients, and must recognize when to refer them for medical assessment.

Our next illustration is of a 33-year-old married woman who was hospitalized on an inpatient psychiatric unit due to her psychotic symptoms.

Carol brought her active, vibrant, and well-fed 3-month-old infant daughter into the hospital office. She noted tearfully that her daughter was not moving, was starving herself and was close to death. When the therapist commented on the medical reports documenting her daughter's good health, Carol angrily replied that the medical staff were actors involved in a plot to torture patients and to kill their babies.

Carol was suffering from a *postpartum psychosis*, which is estimated to occur in one out of every one thousand women following the birth of a child. This type of psychosis, usually brief but invariably upsetting in nature, is precipitated most frequently by the tremendous hormonal shifts that occur after childbirth. We do not yet know why some women are vulnerable to this condition and others are not; psychological, social, and biological theories have all been advanced to explain this phenomenon. Whatever combination of causes precipitate it, a postpartum psychosis is terrifying to all parties involved in what we generally expect to be an exciting and hopeful moment in a family's life. For Carol, delusions about her daughter initially robbed her of an opportunity to bond with her infant, and to rejoice in the miracle of this birth.

The last vignette we will consider illustrates a woman in the throes of a manic psychosis.

Susan, a 42-year-old mother of two, felt increasingly energized and high. She went on a spending spree, slept 2 to 3 hours a night, and had racing thoughts and pressured speech. She began hearing voices that told her to cover all the light bulbs in the house in order to keep out evil spirits, and to take over the treatment unit on which she worked as a psychiatric nurse.

Although Susan had no prior psychiatric history, she developed a bipolar mood disorder, which is discussed in Chapter 14. As is common with this disorder, the onset was gradual for Susan and occurred later in life than is usual in schizophrenia. Her psychosis emerged in a discrete episode and disappeared entirely when she began treatment with lithium. The majority of people who have mood disorders do not become psychotic; when psychotic symptoms do arise, they must be assessed in the context of the person's biological and developmental history, including current life stressors.

The conditions noted above by no means represent an exhaustive list of psychotic disorders or of conditions in which psychotic symptoms may appear. They reflect, however, a sampling of the many ways that people's minds can stray from reality, and their lives be disrupted from within. None of us is immune from these conditions, which must all be viewed along a continuum. Psychotic people are not necessarily psychotic all of the time; they may have moments or periods of great lucidity. Similarly, those of us who pride ourselves on being reality-based, may, at times of stress, become tangential and disoriented. "Crazy" is, after all, a relative term.

SCHIZOPHRENIA

Miguel, a 17-year-old boy with a good school record and many friends, gradually started to isolate himself from others, perform poorly in school, and talk to himself. He told other kids that Paul McCartney was planning to visit him for his birthday, and that because of his popularity in the music business, he could obtain front row seats to any concert in the United States. He became fearful that people were spying on him and trying to harm him due to his fame, and stayed awake and fully dressed for ten days in order to protect himself from others. He was then hospitalized on a psychiatric unit.

How do we understand Miguel's transformation from a well-functioning student to a client on an inpatient psychiatric ward? He developed an illness called *schizophrenia*, a mental disorder with frequently frightening, and disruptive, characteristics. From the work of Hall, Andrews, and Goldstein, Torrey (1988) quotes: "Schizophrenia is to psychiatry what cancer is to medicine: a sentence as well as a diagnosis" (p. 1). Like many cancers, schizophrenia afflicts people from all walks of life, and often has a chronic course. We are uncertain about its causes, unable to prevent it, and have limited success in treating it. Schizophrenia is a syndrome that alters a person's capacity to sustain coherent, reality-based thoughts, and that creates a disturbance in a person's affective life and behavioral patterns. For those afflicted, it can be experienced as a painful struggle for emotional survival. Although the nature vs. nurture debate about the cause of schizophrenia has raged for decades, almost everyone now agrees that biological vulnerabilities are at the core of schizophrenic disorders. In the absence of brain dysfunction and/or hereditary predisposition, social and psychological factors alone have not been shown to produce schizophrenia.

Schizophrenia was first classified in the late nineteenth century by the neuropsychiatrist Kraepelin (1896), who used the term *dementia praecox* to describe an illness that progressed toward a state of dementia and that began in adolescence (hence *praecox*) as compared to old age. In 1911, the Swiss psychiatrist Bleuler renamed the syndrome *schizophrenia*, a term broadly meaning "splitting of the mind." Although frequently and inaccurately confused with the concept of split or multiple personalities, this term referred to the splitting or fragmentation of various mental functions. Bleuler identified several traits common to schizophrenic patients, including inappropriate affect, loose associations of ideas/thoughts, and an autistic-like turning away from reality. It was Freud (1894) who first attempted to explain the psychodynamic etiology of this psychotic process. He initially explored how intolerable ideas, inadequately rejected by the ego, return in the form of hallucinatory wish fulfillments (Arieti 1974). Freud (1924b) later understood psychosis as developing from a conflict between the ego and the external world, leading to a total denial and reshaping of reality.

> Both neurosis and psychosis are the expression of a rebellion on the part of the id against the external world, of its unwillingness— or if one prefers, its incapacity—to adapt itself to the exigencies of reality. . . . [N]eurosis does not disavow reality, it only ignores it; psychosis disavows it and tries to replace it. . . . *Thus the psychosis is also faced with the task of procuring for itself perceptions of a kind which shall correspond to the new reality; and this is most radically effected by means of hallucination.* [pp. 185–186]

Although Freud's understanding of the causes of schizophrenia has been discredited in most clinical arenas, he offered valuable insight into the psychological mechanisms operative in these disorders. His description of the role of repression, projection, and symbolization remains extremely helpful in exploring the primary process thinking so central to the schizo-phrenic person's cognitive processes.

As research into the field of mental illness has flourished, we have refined, elaborated upon, and discarded different parts of the contributions made by various theorists. Social, psychological, and physiological paradigms have given us a more comprehensive understanding of the etiology and course of schizophrenia. In this chapter, we first look at the clinical/symptom picture of schizophrenia, then explore physiological and psychodynamic factors, and finally address relevant social, cultural, and environmental issues.

General Description

A staggering number of people in the United States have been diagnosed with schizophrenia. Approximately 1.5 million people suffer from this disorder (Torrey 1988). Most of us have known people with schizophrenia even though we may have been shielded from the reality of the diagnosis. How many of us, for example, have been told of a great-aunt Jane who had a "nervous breakdown" and was sent off to live "in the country," or of the high school senior Johnny who started acting strangely and never came back to complete his final semester at school? Euphemisms such as "nervous breakdown" have served to cloud our perceptions of this disorder and to prevent us from educating ourselves about it. Schizophrenia carries the "scarlet letter" of mental illness; the social stigma of this diagnosis often isolates those afflicted and further burdens their families.

The onset of schizophrenia usually occurs in late adolescence or early adulthood. Approximately three fourths of all people with schizophrenia are afflicted between the ages of 17 and 25 (Torrey 1988). Often the onset is gradual, with the most striking characteristic simply being that a person is not what he/she used to be. Sometimes the onset is acute, with a person suddenly becoming psychotic—having a "break"—with no clear prior indication of any psychological difficulties. Schizophrenia is usually triggered by a significant loss, the negotiation of a new developmental stage, or chronic feelings of frustration. The death of a parent, leaving for college, or moving can precipitate a break for the vulnerable individual. The course of the illness is similarly variable. Although all people with schizophrenia undergo an active psychotic phase at some point during the course of the illness, some recover with little residual deficit, some restabilize at a lower level of functioning, and others remain chronically psychotic. The most common course of the illness consists of a series of acute phases with increasing personality deterioration between episodes. A 55-year-old schizophrenic man, for example, may become psychotic infrequently, but appear to be a "shell" of his former being. His personality, not just his thoughts or affects, may be altered over time.

Once afflicted with schizophrenia, the prognosis is uncertain. Some factors that predict a more favorable outcome include an abrupt onset of the illness, the clear presence of precipitating events, and apparently good premorbid social functioning. Supportive networks, comprised of family members, friends, and mental health professionals, can also be important elements in influencing the course of the disease. According to the research compiled by Torrey (1988), the ten-year course of schizophrenia can be broken down as follows: 25 percent of people recover, usually within the first two years, and have no more than two psychotic episodes; 25 percent improve significantly; 25 percent improve moderately; 15 percent do not improve; and 10 percent die, mostly from suicide. This last figure is of importance because suicidal ideation and suicide attempts are a common and often overlooked occurrence in schizophrenia. Suicide is sometimes attempted during the first psychotic episode when clients feel bewildered and out of control, or during periods of depression when they feel despondent over the discrepancy between their early achievements and their current level of functioning. This figure is also important because the public frequently misperceives people with schizophrenia as homicidal. They are far more frequently victims of crime perpetrated by others, or, as tragically, by their own hands.

CLINICAL PICTURE

Max is a 37-year-old man who is paranoid and delusional, but bright and articulate. Christine is a 27-year-old woman whose speech is frequently incoherent and whose affect appears silly and inappropriate. Bob is a 45-year-old man who postures in a rigid, catatonic fashion. How can we understand how all of these patients can be diagnosed with schizophrenia? As we think of it today, schizophrenia is a *collection* of illnesses, with different types of schizophrenia highlighting different characteristics of the disorder. Schizophrenia, like all of the syndromes we will be studying, is not a static entity; it is a term that describes a constellation of symptoms and reflects a range of functioning. Indeed, the range of phenomena included in this diagnosis may suggest not only a varied and variable syndrome but also how little we really know about it.

Disturbance in Thought/Cognition

One of the most striking symptoms of schizophrenia is the disturbance in the cognitive processes of people with this illness. This disturbance may manifest itself in the *content* of thoughts, in the *form* of thoughts, and in *perceptions*. The content of a schizophrenic person's thoughts are frequently filled with *delusions*, fixed false ideas believed by the person that cannot be validated in reality. Delusions, as well as hallucinations, represent a failure to integrate cognitive, affective, sensory, and perceptual experiences as elements of the mind (Robbins 1993). It is always critical to place seemingly delusional beliefs in their cultural contexts before ascertaining that they are delusional, as the content of all delusions are culture bound. A Haitian man who complains that a curse was put on him through voodoo, or a U.S. political activist who states that the F.B.I. is tapping his phone, must be heard in the context of the norms and realities of their cultures. What sounds "crazy" may be so only to the ears of the uninformed listener.

Delusions are enormously varied in content and can at times have particular meanings in a person's life. They can emerge as a response to a physiological change caused by anxiety, as a means to avoid an experienced threat, and/or as an attempt to communicate with others. A person may believe, for example, that his thoughts are being broadcast to the world by an electronic device that was secretly planted in his ear. A person may have *ideas of reference*, believing things are related to or refer to him with no basis in fact. Watching TV and thinking that the TV commentator is mocking him is an example of this phenomenon. Delusions can be persecutory ("The C.I.A. is spying on me"), grandiose ("The peace postcard I mailed to you brought about a cease fire in Nicaragua and again in the war of Iraq and Iran"), somatic ("There is a knife growing in my stomach and it causes me pain"), and/or religious ("I am Christ"), in nature. Whatever the content of the delusion, primary process thinking usually prevails.

The following comments of a 34-year-old woman with schizophrenia illustrate this disturbance in thought content:

> I heard my name on the radio. They said the Christ child had been born. I am God, but would never admit it. I'd rather be a pathological liar. . . . I saw myself in a Michael Jackson cartoon. I saw my picture in the subways. How did they get it? I thought I looked good. It was scary. I sang and they applauded. I turned on the radio again and they offered me a Motown contract. They must have heard my voice in the underground.

The following letter written by a man with schizophrenia to his therapist offers us another illustration. Note his grandiose delusions, and how these delusions provide an explanation for the painful loneliness in his life.

> I am in true birth the living God child and son, kidnapped from Berlin, Germany, of Adolf and Eva Hitler. Yes, dear, Eva Braun Hitler and Adolf physically are my true Ma and Pa. Because I had been trying to save the American flag from being taken down since June 1959 daily at work, I have not been able to get a date with a girl. I am at war—Honest and True. . . . Please mail a copy of this letter dearest to a man I am very proud of President Richard Milhous Nixon.

Another area in which a disturbance in thought is manifested may be found in the schizophrenic person's perceptual difficulties. These are often in the form of *hallucinations*, which are perceptual experiences leading people to hear, see, taste, feel, or smell things that cannot be established in reality.

Auditory hallucinations are the most common type and can assume a range of forms: a repetitive sound ("I keep hearing a clicking noise"), a familiar voice ("My [dead] mother tells me to sleep"), or multiple voices of unknown origin ("I hear children's voices outside my window at night"). The hallucinations are often unpleasant, and dynamically may relate to intense anxieties and unresolved, conflictual thoughts. A woman with schizophrenia accused by her husband of infidelity, stated: "The smells are in my face. They are not around me but right in my face. I haven't done anything that wrong. God doesn't want me to have kids. I hear bells and a clamping sound in my stomach."

Perceptual difficulties can assume forms other than hallucinations. There can be an increased acuity of perceptions, a flooding of the senses with stimuli. Noises may appear louder, colors may look brighter, and odors may be more pronounced. This intensification of perceptual sensitivity can be very distracting. An adolescent client, for example, could not concentrate on his thoughts in the office because of how loud the ticking of the clock sounded to him. At the other end of the spectrum, there can be a dulling or blunting of the senses, so that a person appears oblivious to noises and activities in his/her environment.

In addition to the problems noted in content and perception, the form of a schizophrenic person's thoughts is also disturbed. The term *thought disorder* is used to describe this aspect of cognitive malfunctioning, which is manifested in a variety of ways. A *loosening of associations*, in which unrelated ideas are strung together with no awareness of their lack of logic, continuity, and purpose, is a prominent characteristic of a thought disorder. Words are sometimes associated by their similar sound (referred to as *clang associations*), or can be made up (referred to as *neologisms*). In the following excerpt from a letter written by a schizophrenic client, note her gradual loosening of associations.

It is my opinion that these three men belong in a Mental Institution. In fact I think all three of them act kind of funny and either belong in a jail or a Mental Institution. . . . [T]hey constantly make fun of me and my good name in fact all of them do and my name is McAuliffe same as Dick McAuliffe formerly of the Boston Red Sox and also General McAuliffe like General McArthur. McAuliffe, General McAuliffe that is said nuts when told to surrender to the Japs or Germans and is not nuts and neither am I.

Although these thoughts initially seem to make sense, they are strung together illogically as the author is unaware of the letter's faulty content and form.

Concrete thinking is another characteristic of schizophrenia, and represents a person's inability to move from a concrete to an abstract thought. This is seen most clearly in schizophrenic clients' literal interpretations of proverbs. When asked what "People who live in glass houses shouldn't throw stones" means, one client responded: "Rocks can break windows." At the same time things that should be taken literally can be experienced as having abstract, tangential, and elusive meanings.

Other, more subtle disturbances in thought processes are also evident in schizophrenia. Difficulty sorting out information and excluding nonessential data is common, as is the difficulty in responding to information appropriately. One patient, who clung to his daily routine of watching soap operas to help structure his world, became enraged at Dan Rather for interrupting his program to announce that the Berlin Wall had been torn down. Given the possible occurrence of delusions, hallucinations, loosening of associations, concrete thinking, and the like, we can better understand why many people with schizophrenia frequently choose to spend time alone, keep lights and/or the TV on all night, or struggle to follow seemingly simple directions. The world may seem a frightening place when it is impossible to determine what are external rather than internal stimuli, what are real versus imagined dangers, and what is the intended meaning of a vast array of communications.

Disturbances of Affect and Behavior

The cognitive disturbances described above are disquieting symptoms for the person with schizophrenia; their affective and behavioral abnormalities are frequently the more noticeable and alienating of the symptoms. Over the course of the illness, there is usually a loss of a subtle gradation of affect. People's emotions may become blunted (a severe reduction in the intensity of their affective expression) or flat (no signs of affective expression). A mother of a schizophrenic woman, for example, brought her daughter's therapist pictures of and letters written by her daughter before she became ill. She tearfully recounted how the expressionless woman the therapist had come to know was once a passionate, intense girl whose laughter and tears flowed easily; the disease had robbed her vibrant daughter of her emotional life. Affect can also be expressed inappropriately, when it is discordant with the content of a person's speech. A person may laugh loudly when describing a sad or terrifying event, for example, seemingly unaware of the discrepancy between the meaning of the words and the expressed affect.

Problems with the intensity and regulation of affect can also be seen in the schizophrenic person's experience of rage. Rage, understood by some theorists (Bion 1965, Robbins 1993) to be at the core of the schizo-phrenic person's emotional life, can be expressed globally in the language of destruction often seen in hallucinations. Poorly organized and often nonspecific, the rage can fuel a self-destructiveness, a kind of attack on one's thoughts, feelings, and perceptions. The following comment cap-tures this sense of destructiveness: "You try to save me from getting shot when these were my fears but the Middle East is not about war it's about oil and this state is going to lose its energy . . ."

Behavioral changes can be the most obvious of the disturbances brought about by schizophrenia. Inappropriate or bizarre postures, the reduction in spontaneous movements, pacing, and rocking can all appear as symptoms of the disease. Although these behaviors are often attributed to the antipsychotic medications, they may occur in patients who are not taking medication. When they do occur as a result of the medication, it is important to carefully weigh the risks and benefits of continued drug therapy.

Disturbance in a Sense of Self and Relation to the External World/Society

People suffering from schizophrenia undergo changes that profoundly alter their experiences of themselves and others. Although we will be studying these in greater depth when we look at schizophrenia in psycho-dynamic terms, this disturbance can be manifested symptomatically as well as intrapsychically. A loss of ego boundaries and a fragmentation of a sense of self can lead to extreme confusion about one's identity. This confusion is not an existential-like search to understand "Who am I?"; it is instead a disintegration of a feeling/sense of wholeness. Clients may become preoccupied with their body parts, or feel intruded upon by parts of others ("Your fist is stuck in my throat"). Their senses of themselves as having a coherent gender identity as a woman or as a man may also become unraveled; the content of paranoid delusions often includes a struggle with these gender and identity issues.

People with schizophrenia also have motivational levels that may be altered by the illness. Volition—the process of choosing, initiating, and actualizing—may become impaired, as patients present with a decreased capacity to actively engage with and take charge of their lives. There is a kind of "mental nihilism" (Robbins 1993), an urge toward mindless states of mental oblivion.

Coupled with this altered sense of self is a withdrawal from the outside world. Many people with schizophrenia undergo a process of desocialization, frequently related to a desire to withdraw from anxiety-ridden interactions with others. Fears of their own impulses, at times projected onto others, add to their need for distance. As noted before, the cognitive, affective, and behavioral disturbances associated with schizophrenia often render interpersonal contacts frightening and overwhelming. The use of private symbols and seemingly incomprehensible mannerisms can alienate others. Many people with schizophrenia retreat from society to a lonely and isolated, yet in some way safer, world. The bridge between that world and society can be rebuilt when a sense of relatedness is reestablished in the context of a caring, consistent therapeutic relationship. This process takes time, patience, skill, and a willingness to attend to the meaning of the person's sense of alienation.

NEUROBIOLOGICAL AND GENETIC THEORIES

As noted earlier in this chapter, there is general agreement that neurobiological vulnerabilities lie at the core of most, if not all, schizophrenic disorders. Scientific researchers have been unable to pinpoint the *exact* cause of schizophrenia, however, due in part to the range of conditions included under this umbrella term. Numerous neurobiological hypotheses have been advanced as possible causes, including neurostructural abnormalities, endocrine dysfunctions, immunological incompetencies, and viral infections (Creese et al. 1976, Parkenberg 1987). One of the biochemical theories currently debated is the dopamine hypothesis, which speculates that an excessive level of the neurotransmitter dopamine causes schizophrenia. This hypothesis explains why antipsychotic medications, which have been shown to block postsynaptic dopamine receptor sites in the brain, have been somewhat effective in treating this disease. Evidence supporting this hypothesis remains inconclusive, however, as questions have been raised about whether neurochemicals *cause* the disorder or are the *product* of the illness itself (Robbins 1993).

The role of heredity in schizophrenia has also been granted importance over the past several decades. Any clinician who has worked with the chronically mentally ill in one community for a length of time has invariably seen family members of different generations afflicted with this disease. Twin studies have shown a significantly higher concordance for schizophrenia among monozygotic twins than dizygotic twins; estimates suggest that identical twins have two to three times the rate of concordance for schizophrenia than their fraternal counterparts (Gottesman and Shields 1982). Similar results have been found in some adoption studies, which show that children of schizophrenic parents adopted away from the family develop schizophrenia at greater rates than adopted controls (Kety et al. 1972). Distinctions have been made within this group, however, with schizophrenia found to be more common in the biological relatives of people who have *chronic* schizophrenia. Robbins (1993), on the other hand, has noted that about 90 percent of people with schizophrenia do *not* have a schizophrenic parent, and that 81 percent have neither a parent nor a sibling who suffers from schizophrenia.

What do these genetic studies suggest, then, about this illness? It seems that a *predisposition* may be inherited for some types of the disease that, when combined with physiological and/or environmental stressors, may lead to the development of the illness. These studies certainly force us to remain humble about our still rudimentary understanding of the causes of schizophrenia.

Many medications have been developed over the years to treat this disorder. Antipsychotic medications, also known as neuroleptics, have been found most effective at reducing delusions, hallucinations, and overacuteness of the senses. For many people, they provide wonderful relief from the incessant voices and other debilitating characteristics of a thought disorder. They do not, however, cure the illness, and can produce a range of serious side effects. Tardive dyskinesia, a syndrome that causes involuntary movements of the tongue and mouth and jerky movements of arms, legs, and body, is estimated to have been drug induced in approximately 13 percent of those with schizophrenia (Torrey 1988). Clients and their families need to be forewarned about possible complications from medication, and must carefully weigh their risks and benefits.

The ways in which medications are dispensed to patients is also a frequently overlooked, yet in our view critical issue, in the treatment of clients with schizophrenia. One of the newer medications on the market, clozapine, costs $4,160 a year. Who in our society will have access to this medication? How will doctors decide to whom they can offer these prescriptions? With insurance companies reimbursing doctors for shorter visits with clients, the meaning of taking drugs is often inadequately explored. In many cases, symptoms are noted, side effects are reviewed, and follow-up appointments are scheduled. There is frequently little time taken to appreciate the fears, wishes, and concerns that clients understandably bring to their decisions to embark upon this pharmacological course. We believe that *prescriptions cannot substitute for care*; they should be given and received in the context of a relationship that requires time and attention if they are to help clients deal with the impact of psychological impairment on their lives.

The contributions made by medical research to our understanding of the cause and course of schizophrenia have been enormous. The disease model of schizophrenia has helped de-stigmatize the illness, and has offered patients effective treatment that "talking" psychotherapeutic interventions alone could not produce. However, we have concerns about exclusively biological theoretical models, because they can lead to an exclusive theory of practice. By understanding the disorder in solely neurobiological and genetic terms, the medical model has at times minimized psychosocial factors and rationalized assigning clients with schizophrenia to episodic 15-minute medication appointments while discontinuing other psychotherapeutic interventions. This often leads to the treatment of symptoms, and *not* the person with the symptoms. For many of the clients with schizophrenia, isolation and loneliness are all too constant by-products of their illness. Psychotherapy may not cure them; it does, however, offer a relationship in which their daily struggle is recognized and shared, and in which they can feel valued, safe, and understood. Along with medication, a therapeutic relationship can provide them with an opportunity to regain some mastery over their lives and to reduce their sense of alienation from others. The importance of this process will become clearer as we turn our attention to the psychodynamic factors in schizophrenia.

PSYCHODYNAMIC UNDERSTANDING OF SCHIZOPHRENIA

Even though certain behaviors of schizophrenic clients may seem "crazy" to others, they may be internally logical and rational to the people with schizophrenia. A person may wear sunglasses all of the time in order to block out the lasers he believes are blinding him; another person may wear a hockey goalie mask all day because he believes he is Jason of *Friday the 13th* movies; another may hold daily conversations with Queen Elizabeth in order to feel connected to a special, seemingly powerful individual. How we understand these *compromise solutions* to internal crises and external pressures will inform our capacity to work empathically with schizophrenic clients. Using the theories described in the first part of this book, we will explore the relevance of the role of the drives, the functions of the ego, the level of anxiety, and the quality of object relations in understanding schizophrenia.

Drive Theory

Freud (1911, 1914) initially postulated that schizophrenia resulted from a regression in the face of intense frustration and conflict with others, a literal turning of the energy attached to others (and the representations of others) back on to the self. When he advanced his structural theory (1924a,b), he revised his view and attributed psychosis to the development of conflict between the ego and the external world, resulting in a disavowal and remodeling of reality (Gabbard 1990). Although neither of these theories satisfactorily explains the etiology of schizophrenia, the impact of the psychic energies—in the form of the aggressive and libidinal impulses—emerges in the cognitive and affective states of people with schizophrenia. We must remember that because of schizophrenic people's difficulties sorting through and processing external stimuli, they are vulnerable to experiencing the world as a dangerous and frightening place. Internal stimuli also contribute significantly to this fear and confusion in the form of cognitive disturbances such as hallucinations and delusions. With these processing difficulties and the impaired defensive functioning of the ego, the schizophrenic person's sexual and aggressive urges are frequently poorly controlled and regulated. These impulses can also become fused, as loving relationships switch precipitously to hostile ones. Statements such as "You better put me in restraints because I'm dangerous" or "I am powerful enough to stop the war" can reflect an aggressive upsurge in the face of a feeling of helplessness or of a perceived (internally or externally generated) threat. This upsurge, frequently accompanied by intense anxiety, can lead to a regression to a primitive psychosexual stage of development. Themes of orality may emerge, as expressed in images of eating and swallowing others whole as evidenced in the comment "I swallowed his head."

The following example illustrates issues from drive theory, which we have just reviewed, and from ego psychology and object relations theory, which we will turn to next. Glenn was hospitalized after becoming increasingly psychotic, and wrote this letter to his much loved and feared therapist.

> Listen i am getting strung out about the whole thing [his attachment to his therapist] you just want to fuck yourself to death, then when your through see if i'm any good—then i thought i remembered the stern looks and when i'd come in your face would be shiny like you had vaseline on it i use to hate that you use to look like you worked there i like it better when you just look like somebody's wife but any way those things scared me I don't want to die.

Feeling abandoned by his therapist, Glenn felt enraged by his need for her and understood himself as discarded for being "no good." He projected both his loving and aggressive impulses onto his therapist, whom he then perceived as dangerous and stern. His fears of his therapist's and his own aggression threatened the very core of his existence. Consistent with the quality of many schizophrenic people's object relations, Glenn's intense longing for an attachment to his therapist was challenged by his terror of it. What he desired most he also most feared.

Ego Functions

Early writings on schizophrenia postulated that the ego of the person with schizophrenia was weak, and thus unable to withstand the dilemmas posed by reality (Freud 1924a). But what is meant by a "weak" ego? As with all the illnesses we will be studying, the impairment of ego functions depends on the severity of the illness, and on the stage of the illness. Before looking at two of the functions of the ego in greater depth—the management of anxiety and the defenses—we can make the following general comments about the ego functions of many people with schizophrenia. First, perception, memory, and the range of autonomous functions of the ego suffer some degree of impairment. Second, judgment is frequently poor, as is reality testing. Third, thought processes are hindered by the intrusion of primary process material. Fourth, the synthetic-integrative functions of the ego, which help organize and integrate the disparate aspects of one's personality into a coherent whole, are compromised.

As described in the first part of this chapter, the thinking of people with schizophrenia is characterized by what Searles (1965) describes as a lack of differentiation between the concrete and the metaphorical. Idioms are interpreted literally, and the richness of nuances and metaphor in language is lost. Searles suggests that this concreteness of thought in people with schizophrenia serves an important function; it helps to maintain various anxiety-laden affects under repression. He offers the following example in his work with a schizophrenic man to illustrate his point:

> When, for example, antagonized by his self-righteous demandingness, I told him abruptly, "You can't have your cake and eat it too!" I felt completely helpless when he responded to this at a literal, "concrete" level, by saying, "I don't want to eat any cake in the hospital! You can eat cake here, if you want to; I don't want to eat any cake here." One can see how his concretistic interpretation of my figure of speech enabled him to avoid the affective meaning of my comment. [p. 564]

SCHIZOPHRENIC ANXIETY AND ITS MANAGEMENT

Depending on how well it is managed, anxiety can motivate people to act or it can paralyze them. In developmental terms, we have said that anxiety can be experienced as threatening on different levels: people may fear losing the love of another; they may fear being abandoned by others; or in more primitive terms, they may fear losing themselves. For the person with schizophrenia, anxiety is usually experienced as the latter: as a *fear of annihilation*. The intensity of annihilation anxiety is so overwhelming that individuals may fear that they will cease to exist, or that their identity will be reduced to a part of a person rather than a whole. Themes of disintegration and engulfment often emerge in sessions with psychotic clients as manifestations of the rage previously discussed as well as intolerable anxiety. Comments such as "Nuclear war is here and the world is exploding into pieces" and "I saw myself in the center of the earth swallowed up and found by no one" express clients' experiences of annihilation anxiety. This anxiety is frequently precipitated by loss, by frightening interpersonal contacts, and by the experience of powerful affects. In the following example, note how Mark, a man with schizophrenia, expressed his anxiety in his first session with a new therapist.

> Mark, a Jewish man with schizophrenia, reported in his first session that his father owned a deli. He handed the therapist a bag, saying he had brought her a corned beef sandwich. He then hesitated, appeared anxious and said, "I thought I brought you a corned beef sandwich but maybe it was a piece of my arm." The therapist, using the higher level defense of humor to handle her anxiety, replied, "Hold the mustard."

Imagine the level of panic experienced by Mark during this first encounter. Most, if not all, of us would approach a first session with a therapist with some trepidation and perhaps fear. For this psychotically vulnerable individual, however, meeting someone new provokes fears of disintegration, if not annihilation, of parts of himself. Establishing a safe relationship with his therapist, in which these feelings could be tolerated and understood, was a crucial part of the therapeutic task.

How can we understand this level of anxiety in dynamic terms? Pao (1977) uses the term *organismic panic* to describe this state of fear. He notes that due to the great and overwhelming distress experienced by schizophrenic people early in their lives, "the predisposition to anxiety may become so enhanced that each time he should experience anxiety he experiences panic instead" (p. 394). Panic interferes with the development of healthy ego functions and relationships with others. When conflicts arise, the schizophrenic person uses the more primitive "tools" (denial, projection, and primary process thinking) to alleviate the panic he feels. Psychotic symptoms can be the end result. Pao acknowledges that the problems in the schizophrenic person's early years may be attributed to nurture and/or nature. The inadequate maternal "understanding and ministration" that leaves the child in a state of "organismic distress without relief" may be caused by problems inherent in the infant, in the mother, or in some combination of both. His emphasis on developmental difficulties in the early stages of a schizophrenic person's life, however, has unfortunately echoed other "mother-blaming" stances about the etiology of schizophrenic disorders. His description of the powerfully disorganizing and disruptive nature of the experience of anxiety, however, offers a valuable contribution to our understanding of the inner world of people with schizophrenia.

Semrad (1960) notes how psychosis may be the best possible solution for overwhelming anxiety and intense affect that cannot otherwise be borne. He believes that in the face of losses, life stressors, and unbearable affects, the "schizophrenia-vulnerable person" retreats from reality in order to avoid the painful experience and the affects associated with it. As Day and Semrad (1980) note:

> When onset is acute, the patient is faced with three alternatives for dealing with his unbearable pain: homicide, suicide, or psychosis. He chooses psychosis and withdraws from a reality he can no longer endure. Illness emerges as the only option available for the survival of a particular individual, given his genetic background, his early developmental history, and his current environment of pain and frustration. [p. 220]

Although this psychodynamic formulation is rarely offered now as the sole cause of schizophrenia (particularly as related to the issue of *choice*), the level of anxiety and distress described by Pao and Semrad captures the "subjective holocaust" (Semrad 1960) experienced by people with schizophrenia. Generated by biological and intrapsychic determinants, annihilation anxiety is a significant factor in schizophrenic people's interactions with others and in their inability to engage successfully with the demands of daily life.

THE DEFENSES

People with schizophrenia rely heavily on the defenses of denial and projection. These defenses lead the person to lay the responsibility for unacceptable drives (particularly aggression) and wishes onto others, and to misperceive reality. Both of these defenses can be identified in the following example.

A client with schizophrenia had a delusion that three attractive girls (whom he barely knew) were in love with him, and that other boys were "after him" because of his popularity. This delusion helped him construct reality to satisfy his wishes, as real relationships were too unbearable (i.e., denial), and to attribute his own intolerable aggressive fantasies to others (i.e., projection).

Another defense frequently used by people with schizophrenia is introjection. The woman with schizophrenia we mentioned earlier, angry and sad about the loss of a relationship that had ended ten years ago, reported that she had swallowed this man's head. She therefore heard his voice regularly, an occurrence that was alternatively pleasurable and annoying. This represented her symbolic taking in and retaining of the lost object as part of her internal psychological structure. It is important to remember that all of these defenses can be functional in some way. While they bring a heavy penalty, they also can help people construct a world in which their external reality is more tolerable and their internal reality is easier to bear.

Object Relations

As implied in our clinical description of schizophrenia, many people with this illness have difficulty negotiating relationships with others. Their aversion to contact with others often reflects their difficulty maintaining self-object boundaries and differentiating components of their minds from characteristics of other people and other things. Psychoanalytic theorists such as Searles (1965) suggest that this loss of ego boundaries is one of the most formidable mechanisms of the schizophrenic process, as it may help the person avoid experiencing potentially toxic emotions. Theorists such as Mahler (1952) trace these difficulties in self-object differentiation to a regression to, or fixation in, the symbiotic stage of development. The adult relationships of people with schizophrenia may become characterized by simultaneous longings for, and terror of, fusion; attachments to others are experienced as mergers, and separations feel like death to—or disintegration of—the self or the caregiver. The following comments of a man with schizophrenia and his mother capture this dynamic:

> *Son:* You can't go visit John. If you leave, I'll die. Or if you stay, maybe your spirit will swallow me up.
> *Mother:* You don't feel that way. You can't be angry now. I'm not.

These types of interactions can obviously occur between people functioning at various levels of development; when they occur with a person vulnerable to psychosis, however, they create the unbearable paradox that both separation and intimacy may lead to destruction. It is not surprising that poor differentiation between self and other undermines the development of a clear self image—a self-identity as a whole, intact being *separate* from others and distinct from one's surroundings. A sense of where one's thoughts or even body begins and ends becomes severely impaired. Robbins (1993) traces this to the extreme undifferentiation and unintegration of the schizophrenic mind, and notes:

> In schizophrenics there is no internalized mentally represented, abstracted, or conceptualized template or model of a symbiotic relationship analogous to the possession configurations found in primitive personalities. As a result the schizophrenic is unable to make a mental displacement or transference of a primary relationship pattern to other persons. . . . He cannot initiate a relationship with a person outside the family as can the primitive personality, either as a possession or as a possessor, that is, as one who actively invests that person with emotion, endows him with loosely integrated projections of aspects of self, and induces him to become a symbiotic partner. Hence, the schizophrenic is unable to separate physically, much less psychologically, from his primary family. [p. 157]

Although a disturbance in object relations is clearly characteristic of the schizophrenic process, we would hold that its causes are multi-determined. Problematic early interactions alone do not cause the illness. A more integrated perspective considers the constitutional and psychological vulnerabilities of the infant and the fit between this infant and parents, who may be ill-equipped emotionally and deprived of actual resources as they attempt to handle a troubled child.

ENVIRONMENTAL AND SOCIAL FACTORS

Social Class, Ethnicity, and Culture

Just as personality is shaped and molded by culture, ethnicity, gender, and socioeconomic status, illness itself is given form and meaning by these variables as well. Social factors such as poverty, discrimination, and inequality can deplete emotional and psychic resources, creating undue stress on people who are already genetically vulnerable to schizophrenia. Conversely, favorable social environments may compensate for or mediate against these vulnerabilities. This does not mean that social or psychological factors cause schizophrenia, only that they can influence its development and course.

Studies have repeatedly shown the highest incidence of schizophrenia to occur in the lowest socioeconomic strata of urban communities (Eaton 1985, Torrey 1988). Different theories have been used to account for this trend, including the migration of people with illness to cities where more services may be available; schizophrenia itself causing a decline in people's earning potential; and industrial urban centers providing less support and creating greater levels of hostility than rural agricultural areas. The disproportionately higher rate of schizophrenia falls along not only economic and geographic lines but ethnic ones as well. The incidence of schizophrenia reported among blacks and Hispanics is higher than the rate of diagnosis for whites (Strakowski et al. 1993, Torrey 1988). Questions about bias in the diagnosis of minority groups have been raised to account for this difference, as well as questions about the role of discrimination and prejudice in creating stressors that exacerbate psychic vulnerabilities (Kohn 1973).

Whether we are addressing poverty or discrimination as variables in the etiology of schizophrenia, both have an impact on the resources available for treating the disease. Options for the uninsured are far more limited than for those with insurance and/or other economic resources. Hospitalizations and follow-up care are frequently determined by financial resources. Although money provides no protection against *developing* schizophrenia, the lack of it creates great stress in people's lives, leaving fewer treatment options, which may then influence the course of the illness.

Transcultural studies (Torrey 1987, 1988) have shown several interesting differences in prevalence rates for schizophrenia in various parts of the world. Inadequate methodologies and uneven diagnostic criteria, however, have led to questions about the reported incidence of schizophrenia in many countries. Recent and more reliable studies have shown a low prevalence rate among the Amish and Hutterites in the United States, and in rural Ghana and Taiwan, and a high prevalence rate in northern Scandinavia and western Ireland (Torrey 1987). Further research is needed to explore and explain these confounding trends. Of note, as mentioned earlier, is that despite the worldwide presence of common symptoms of schizophrenia, the content of symptoms such as hallucinations and delusions is culture bound. Delusions of a religious or destructive nature have been reported to be common in Europe, but rare in Asia. In industrialized Western countries, delusions involving witchcraft and magic seem to have been replaced by those involving wiretapping, electronics, TV, and radio. As environmental conditions change, so too do certain outward manifestations of schizophrenia.

Gender

Numerous gender-related differences have been found in recent studies of schizophrenia (Angermeyer et al. 1990, DeLisi et al. 1989, McGlashan et al. 1990). Women tend to develop the illness later in life than men, to display more affective symptomatology, to respond better to neuroleptic medications and treatment, and to experience a higher level of functioning prior to its onset and upon recovery. More men than women are given this diagnosis, whereas more women are diagnosed with schizoaffective disorders. These gender-related differences raise many questions: Has the diagnosis of schizophrenia been based primarily on studies of men? What effects might women's greater affiliative behaviors and expression of emotion have on the diagnosis and course of illness? What differential interventions may be needed based on gender differences?

Availability of Resources

No full understanding of schizophrenic people's lives can occur without an appreciation of the resources, or lack thereof, available to the chronically mentally ill. Access to housing and to mental health and legal services is a critical variable in determining the quality of life of people with schizophrenia. In the wake of deinstitutionalization, many seriously mentally ill clients were discharged into the community, where community-based services were to provide alternatives to hospitalization. Housing, day treatment, and community mental health services were established to offer a comprehensive network for these clients. The positive outcomes of deinstitutionalization can be seen in the establishment of social clubs, transitional employment programs, and consumer groups such as the Alliance for the Mentally Ill. However, despite the generous and compassionate vision behind deinstitutionalization in the 1970s, adequate funds were not made available to realize many of its original goals. The long-term results of this failure are apparent in all parts of society: our city streets and shelters are crowded with homeless, chronically mentally ill individuals; our jails and prisons are overflowing with people who are psychotic; our community mental health centers are inundated with more persistently mentally ill clients than their beleaguered staffs can handle; the waiting lists for residential programs for the chronically mentally ill are months, if not years, long. In addition, funding for community mental health centers and state hospitals continues to dwindle at alarming rates to balance local budgets. While state hospitals close, private for-profit hospitals compete to serve this population in order to keep their beds full. The sickest people in our society are frequently "lost in the cracks," as they are discharged from institutions to poor and inadequate aftercare.

The shift to managed care in the 1990s is exacerbating these problems and leading to the "objectification" of people with schizophrenia. As health care becomes driven exclusively by cost containment, the most economical way for insurance companies to care for people with this illness is with brief hospitalizations, medications, and infrequent outpatient visits. The serious *psychological* dilemmas faced by people with schizophrenia are minimized; their complex inner worlds are left unexplored, as the focus of their care turns to the management of their behaviors. Robbins (1993) captures this state of affairs in the following comment:

> A consequence of viewing the mental manifestations of schizophrenia as expressions of an organic disease entity separate from the personality of the sufferer, manifestations that are meaningless and incomprehensible even to the schizophrenic himself, is the direction of so-called treatment measures to expunge these with "tranquiliz-

ing" drugs and to persuade the patient to conceal his thinking, symptoms, and limitations from others and try to function as if he were normal. . . . *But the preferred "treatment" of today mirrors and enhances the schizophrenic's basic alienation from others, and, regardless of the impression conveyed by his compliance, lends reality and substance to whatever mistrustful paranoid beliefs he may have that the world is a dangerous place and that others are basically inimical to his well-being.* [p. 187, italics added]

What solutions are there to this crisis? No simple answers exist. On one level, a commitment to the most disturbed members of our society is needed to provide funding for inpatient, outpatient, and outreach community psychiatric services, and for housing alternatives. On another level, a shift in our priorities must occur so that we *all* see the care of society's neediest as our joint responsibility.

CASE EXAMPLE

Let us end this chapter by moving from theories about schizophrenia to the human costs of the disease. The story of the life and struggles of a young man with schizophrenia follows. It is a sadly typical story in that it chronicles the gradual deterioration and impaired functioning so often seen in people with this illness. It is also a unique story, as is every schizophrenic person's, in that it reflects *his* expression of pain and suffering, and of the emotional demons in his life.

Karl is a 24-year-old man, who was referred to a community counseling center several years ago by a school guidance counselor. School personnel had grown increasingly concerned about his declining grades and obsessive preoccupation with his love for a 14-year-old girl. Karl was found stalking this young girl, whom he barely knew, writing her long love letters, and buying her excessively expensive gifts.

When Karl was 5 months old, his father died of cancer. His mother, who remained depressed for many months, remarried several years later and bore three more children. Karl identified strongly with his biological father's heritage, keeping his last name and maintaining ties to his father's family. A cousin, aunt, and grandfather on this side of the family have all been diagnosed with schizophrenia.

In latency, Karl began spending an increasing amount of time in his room playing with dolls, watching TV, and building houses with cards. The family began to hear Karl's voice from behind the closed door, as he talked to himself about the plot of soap operas and the best strategies for winning college basketball games. By the beginning of his senior year in high school, this academically average student was failing all his courses and isolating himself from his peers.

As the therapist became acquainted with Karl over the first few months of his psychotherapy, she was struck by his persistent inability to greet her, to make eye contact in the hour, and to display any affect regardless of the content of his speech. Showing little discomfort, he described the auditory hallucinations he had been having since his "rejection" by the 14-year-old "girl of my dreams." The hallucinations were most frequently made up of voices of children at play, laughing with one another, and were usually most pronounced at night. Karl slept with the radio or television turned on all night. More significant, perhaps, than these hallucinations was Karl's pervasive distortion of reality. He believed that he became Jason of the *Friday the 13th* movies, a character who was taunted and then drowned by his peers at a summer camp, and returned to seek violent revenge on his fellow teenagers. When angry or upset, Karl donned a goalie mask (to resemble Jason), grabbed an ax from a storage closet, and acted out his own violent homicidal fantasies in his room. On occasion, he walked the streets in costume, and approached passersby to ask them where he could buy a chain saw.

Karl developed numerous delusions in his life about random girls to whom he would become attached. If he briefly met a girl on a checkout line in a store, he would believe that she was madly in love with him. Love notes, engagement rings, and money would then be sent to her for months as his fantasy grew, although no further face-to-face contact would be initiated by him. He furthermore believed that his connections to the F.B.I. and Mafia would assist him in learning about and doing away with his potential rivals.

During the many hours spent locked in his room, Karl created something he called "my world." With dolls and cards at his disposal, he spent his time reenacting scenes from soap operas or sporting events, adding, changing, and deleting events as he pleased. He assumed a range of parts in each plot, which usually entailed a woman, her suitors, and a jilted lover.

Before we turn to the treatment Karl received, let us consider his emotional difficulties in the context of what we have studied in this chapter. Given the heavy genetic loading for schizophrenia in his family, we can suspect that Karl was constitutionally vulnerable to developing this illness. The onset of his difficulties was gradual, although the emergence of his most serious symptoms occurred following the rejection of his fantasized "girlfriend" in adolescence. Dynamically, both his aggressive and libidinal drives were poorly differentiated and neutralized, since his objects of love were quickly transformed into sources of rage. Given his sense of helplessness (in relation to his own mind and to the world), he was frequently flooded with murderous aggression directed alternately toward himself and toward others. During the first year of his treatment, he was chronically suicidal; he brought the therapist new wills he had written (in a black and white composition notebook) on a biweekly basis, in which he delineated to whom his records, tapes, and TV should be left. He had homicidal fantasies toward his stepfather and toward boys perceived as rivals.

Karl's object relations were impoverished, as actual contact with others felt threatening and overwhelming. His delusions and his world served to defend him against the despair and loneliness he felt. People were experienced as extensions of himself, and not as complex, separate individuals. They were most safely present in his fantasy life, over which he had greater control. Karl relied on primitive defenses (denial, projection, splitting, and externalization), and interpreted events in his life in a concrete, distorted fashion.

Working with Karl has been an alternately frightening, rewarding, boring, and interesting experience. He was given antipsychotic medication at the beginning of the treatment, which helped to diminish his auditory hallucinations. For the first several years of his therapy, he and his therapist constantly assessed how much of a risk he was to himself and to others. His family's help was elicited in this task, and they were referred to a support group for families of clients with major mental illness. As Karl came in week after week with the same details of imagined and real injustices committed against him, he and his therapist began to explore the disappointments, losses, and limitations in his life. He required two brief hospitalizations, the first following a suicide attempt, and the second when he became more psychotic (he believed he was Jason) and planned to harm another person. As he gradually felt safer in the treatment relationship and more aware of his sadness, he stopped writing wills and threatening to hurt other people. He repetitively shared the intricacies of his daily rituals, allowing the therapist to sense the depth of his despair and loneliness. For years in their work together, the therapist felt as if she were a nonentity, interchangeable with any individual and having no defining characteristics of her own in his eyes. When disruptions occurred in the treatment due to holidays and vacations, however, Karl responded with rage and increasing psychic disorientation.

Over the years, Karl has begun to use the therapist as an auxiliary ego, someone who could help him differentiate between fantasy and reality, between his feelings and his actions, and between the impulses arising within him from those expressed by others. He has relied on the therapist to help him control his impulses, modulate and differentiate his affect, and at times simply explain confusing aspects of life. They have shared the pain of his losses and of the limitations brought on by his devastating illness.

A student once asked the therapist if she thought therapy would "cure" Karl. If we define "cure" as Karl no longer suffering from schizophrenia, she would have to reply no. Karl continues to have delusions about various girls in his life, and to have limited social and vocational engagements. The concept of cure, however, may not be a useful one when applied to people like Karl.

We need instead to measure his gains in the context of his own life and his capabilities. We need to assess if therapy can assist him in returning to *his* optimal level of functioning. In this framework, significant changes have occurred in his treatment. When angered by a perceived rejection, he no longer becomes Jason complete with hockey mask and ax; he states instead, "I'm getting those Jason feelings," and then discusses what he is feeling and assumes others are feeling about him. Although wedded to the rituals with his dolls and cards, he now can be in the presence of others without feeling humiliated due to his behaving or talking in an obviously bizarre fashion. As he recently noted, "I can keep my crazy stuff in my room and in this office, so not everyone has to know about my emotional problems." This has enabled him to periodically sustain part-time work and to attend social gatherings with his family. As he has grown more accepting of himself, the therapist, too, is experienced by him as a more separate person with her own personality traits. Karl greets her when he enters her office, says "Bless you" when she sneezes, and even asks her if she had a good vacation following her absence.

Will society (and insurance companies) deem the work Karl and this therapist have done significant enough to warrant the time and money devoted to his case? We do not know. We are certain, however, that medication alone would not have healed his pain nor improved his sense of himself in the ways a consistent, caring treatment relationship has. Karl will have to carry the burden of his illness through the rest of his life. He has at least been able to share the weight of that burden for a period of time in a relationship that could also bear his pain.

References

American Psychiatric Association. (1994). *Diagnostic and Statistical Manual of Mental Disorders*, 4th ed. Washington, DC: American Psychiatric Association.

Angermeyer, M., Kuhn, L., and Goldstein, J. (1990). Gender and the course of schizophrenia: differences in treatment outcomes. *Schizophrenia Bulletin* 16:293–307.

Arieti, S. (1974). *Interpretations of Schizophrenia*, 2nd ed. New York: Basic Books.

Bion, W. (1965). *Transformations*. New York: Basic Books.

Bleuler, E. (1911). *Dementia Praecox or the Group of Schizophrenias*. New York: International Universities Press, 1950.

Creese, I., Burt, D., and Snyder, S. (1976). Dopamine receptors and average clinical doses. *Science* 194:545–546.

Day, M., and Semrad, E. V. (1980). Schizophrenic reactions. In *The Harvard Guide to Modern Psychiatry*, ed. A. M. Nicholi, Jr., pp. 199–241. Cambridge, MA: Belknap Press of Harvard University Press.

DeLisi, L., Dauphinius, I., and Hauser, P. (1989). Gender differences in the brain: Are they relevant to the pathogenesis of schizophrenia? *Comprehensive Psychiatry* 30:197–208.

Eaton, W. W. (1985). Epidemiology of schizophrenia. *Epidemiologic Reviews* 7:105–126.

Freud, S. (1894). The neuro-psychoses of defence. *Standard Edition* 3:45–61.

—— (1911). Psycho-analytic notes on a case of paranoia (dementia paranoides). *Standard Edition* 12:3–88.

—— (1914). On narcissism: an introduction. *Standard Edition* 14:67–102.

—— (1924a). Neurosis and psychosis. *Standard Edition* 19:149–153.

—— (1924b). The loss of reality in neurosis and psychosis. *Standard Edition* 19:181–187.

Gabbard, G. O. (1990). *Psychodynamic Psychiatry in Clinical Practice*. Washington, DC: American Psychiatric Press.

Gottesman, I., and Shields, J. (1982). *Schizophrenia: The Epigenetic Puzzle*. London: Cambridge University Press.

Kety, S., Rosenthal, D., Wender, P., and Schulsinger, F. (1972). Mental illness in the biological and adoptive families of adopted schizophrenics. *American Journal of Psychiatry* 128:302–306.

Kohn, M. L. (1973). Social class and schizophrenia: a critical review and a reformulation. *Schizophrenia Bulletin* 3:617–631.

Kraepelin, E. (1896). *Dementia Praecox and Paraphrenia*, trans. R. M. Barclay. Edinburgh: E. & S. Livingstone; New York: R. E. Krieger, 1919.

Mahler, M. (1952). On child psychosis and schizophrenia: an autistic and symbiotic infantile psychosis. *Psychoanalytic Study of the Child* 7:286–305. New York: International Universities Press.

McGlashan, T., and Bardenstein, K. (1990). Gender differences in affective, schizoaffective, and schizophrenic disorders. *Schizophrenia Bulletin* 16:319–330.

Pao, P. (1977). On the formation of schizophrenic symptoms. *International Journal of Psycho-Analysis* 58:389–401.

Parkenberg, B. (1987). Post-mortem study of chronic schizophrenic brains. *British Journal of Psychiatry* 151:744–752.

Robbins, M. (1993). *Experiences of Schizophrenia: An Integration of the Personal, Scientific and Therapeutic*. New York: Guilford.

Searles, H. (1965). *Collected Papers on Schizophrenia and Related Subjects*. London: Hogarth.

Semrad, E. V. (1960). *Teaching Psychotherapy of Psychotic Patients*. New York: Grune & Stratton.

Strakowski, S. M. , Shelton, R. C., and Kolbrener, M. L. (1993). The effects of race and comorbidity on clinical diagnosis in patients with psychosis. *Journal of Clinical Psychiatry* 54(3):96–102.

Torrey, E. F. (1987). Prevalence studies of schizophrenia. *British Journal of Psychiatry* 150:598–608.

———— (1988). *Surviving Schizophrenia: A Family Manual*. New York: Harper & Row.

12

Borderline and Narcissistic Personality Disorders

PATRICIA HERTZ

The study of the personality disorders is a challenging and rewarding task, full of its share of controversies. As we examine this classification of disorders, we will touch upon some of these controversies as we discuss the concept of character, the epidemiology and characteristics of several of the disorders, and the value of a psychodynamic lens in understanding their development. Before turning to these specifics, however, let us begin by looking at two brief anecdotes—one from a client and one from a movie—to see what they might teach us about the concept of personality styles.

Catie called a therapist for a first appointment after getting her name from an acquaintance. With a sense of urgency in her voice, Catie noted that all of her previous therapists were lousy, that everyone in her life had let her down, and that she felt desperately alone in the world and terribly depressed. Although the therapist was merely a name on a piece of paper she had gotten from a friend, Catie spoke to her with a kind of intimacy and insistence that left the therapist feeling she had two choices. She was going to be the one to "fix" Catie's life for her, or she would be yet another person who would disappoint and abandon Catie as everyone else had.

The next illustration comes from the movie *Goodfellas*, which depicts the life of the Mafia in Brooklyn. The narrator and protagonist, Henry Hill, explains why he chose to live a life of violence, taking what he deemed was his with no regard for the rights of others. Henry brazenly ridicules those who work honestly for their paychecks as "suckers" who have "no balls," and contrasts them to the men in his circle who simply take what they want when they want it. The life of crime to which he was drawn as a teenager—a life of stealing, lying, and killing with no remorse or regret—becomes routine for him. Over time, all of Henry's relationships and aspirations reflect a pattern of deceit, aggression, and disregard for others.

What might these examples illustrate about personality styles and disorders? People are generally *consistent* in how they deal with the world and with other people, and in how they react to life's stressors and demands. Behaviors, attitudes, interests, and aptitudes reflect particular personality styles and character traits, and form what is unique about each individual. When these characteristic patterns are shaped by problematic constitutional, psychological, and/or social forces, they can become maladaptive and ultimately disruptive to one's overall level of functioning. The result can be the development of the psychopathological syndrome called *personality disorders* (also known as *character disorders*, terms we will use interchangeably in this chapter).

For Catie, relationships had come to be equated with abandonment and betrayal. A thread of nonprotection and misunderstanding ran through her life, leaving her with the conviction that she would always be left disappointed and alone. She therefore approached others with anger and desperation, hoping for a different experience yet preparing for the worst. For the narrator in the movie, violence at home and in the streets had come to shape the norms of his culture. To "be someone," to "make it," meant learning how to "score" at someone else's expense and not to care about the pain inflicted on others. His worldview comprised the choices "be screwed" or "screw someone else." For both Catie and this movie's protagonist, the "disorder" in their personality structures influenced most aspects of their lives.

In our study of the personality disorders, we have chosen to devote more space to the borderline and narcissistic syndromes than to the others delineated in *DSM-IV*. We have done this for several reasons. Both of these disorders have received tremendous professional scrutiny, and have generated compelling and contrasting views of their etiology and treatment by leading psychodynamic theorists. The treatment of these clients can engender intense, complicated, and alternately loving and hateful feelings in both the transference and the countertransference. Therapists are frequently drawn into an enactment of the central conflicts and struggles in their clients' lives, challenging them to be "players" in old dramas while attempting to offer new relational experiences. The work with these clients can thus be excruciatingly challenging, but—given the psychodynamic underpinnings in the etiology of these disorders— remarkably productive and rewarding.

The concept of personality/character disorder originated in the psychoanalytic study of character. Before focusing on the development of a disordered personality, then, let us first define what we mean by the word *character*. The American Heritage Dictionary (1973) defines character as "the combination of qualities or features that distinguishes one person, group, or thing from another." Psychoanalytic theorists capture the more dynamic aspects of character formation in their definition. Fenichel (1945) describes character as "the habitual mode of bringing into harmony the tasks presented by internal demands and by the external world" (p. 467). Reich (1945) defines it as "an armoring of the ego" against the dangers of the outside world and repressed instinctual demands, and emphasizes that it represents "not only the outward form . . . but also the sum total of all that the ego shapes in the way of typical modes of reaction" (p. 171). Character, then, reflects a pattern of adaptation, *unique* to each individual; once formed, it is *relatively* constant and enduring. We use the word *relatively* because people's patterns of relating can appear remarkably different when the context for their behaviors is significantly altered. Although controversy remains about what actually forms character, we believe that constitutional factors, psychological influences, and societal conditions all contribute to character formation—both in its normative and pathological evolution. Newborn infants are clearly not blank screens at birth; they have the seeds of a personality that blossom differentially based on the influences of the external environment (family, culture, economic opportunities, forces of oppression) and the organization of their internal worlds. When problems exist in either or both of these realms, character structure will be affected.

Our characters are made up of numerous traits, some of which can be useful and adaptive in one context, and yet dysfunctional in another. Being obsessional, for example, may be an enormous help during tax season, but a hindrance during crises that require a spontaneous decision. At what point do traits become so problematic that a character becomes *disordered?* According to *DSM-IV*, a personality disorder exists when character traits are so inflexible and maladaptive that they cause either significant impairment in social or occupational functioning, or subjective distress. We are not referring here to a sudden change in a person's behavior, but to features typical of a person's long-term functioning. Character disorders reflect an *enduring*, dysfunctional way of experiencing nearly all aspects of life.

EPIDEMIOLOGICAL FACTORS AND CLASSIFICATION OF PERSONALITY DISORDERS

Although an estimated 15 percent of the population have personality disorders, there is little agreement about the causes of specific disorders. Studies of genetic factors (Livesley et al. 1993, Thaper and McGuffin 1993) have shown a higher concordance for personality disorders among monozygotic twins than among dizygotic twins, although they have not identified exactly what (predisposition, biochemical makeup, etc.) is inherited. Other studies (Chess and Thomas 1978) have suggested that certain temperamental traits identified in children under 3 years of age may predict the development of a personality disorder later in life. Psychodynamically oriented theorists (Akhtar 1992, Kernberg 1970, 1975, Masterson 1981) have focused on early childhood experience and the "fit" between child and parent in explaining the etiology of these disorders. Despite the lack of consensus about the causes of these disorders, all agree that in their most severe form, they exact a significant emotional cost to afflicted individuals and to their significant others.

Given the complexity of this psychopathological syndrome, how do we classify people with personality disorders? On a psychological continuum from health to major mental illness, they fall between the neuroses and the psychoses. Unlike people with neuroses, their problems are *not* confined to discrete aspects of their lives while other aspects remain free of psychological conflict (Waldinger 1986). Unlike people with psychosis, they are primarily oriented to reality; if they do have psychotic episodes, these lapses occur infrequently and are of short duration. For people with personality disorders, there has been some degree of integration, so that their personalities are relatively stable over time—even if their symptoms are not. This is, in fact, why the diagnosis of personality disorder is not generally made until late adolescence or early adulthood. Although traits may be evident in childhood, it is the relative stability—albeit dysfunctional—that is the hallmark of the disorder.

The authors of *DSM-IV*, interestingly, take a slightly different approach to this set of diagnoses than to most of the others in the manual. Reflective of its general classification system, *DSM-IV* offers descriptions of the symptoms characteristic of each personality disorder, and establishes diagnostic criteria by focusing on observable behavior. It also, however, refers more directly to psychodynamic concepts such as ego functions, object relations, and sense of self in describing this syndrome. *DSM-IV* groups the personality disorders into three clusters, and each reflects common general symptoms. These categories are (1) people who appear odd or eccentric, and fear social relationships; the associated character disorders are paranoid, schizoid, and schizotypal; (2) people who appear dramatic, emotional, or erratic, and who tend to act out their conflicts directly on their environment; the associated disorders are antisocial, borderline, histrionic, and narcissistic; (3) people who are primarily anxious, fearful, and careful, and have fewer problems with reality testing; the associated disorders are avoidant, dependent, obsessive-compulsive, and passive-aggressive. A residual category exists for people with mixed or unspecified conditions.

Whereas *DSM-IV* primarily offers a snapshot of various behaviors, a psychodynamic perspective adds a greater understanding of *why* a person may act in a particular maladaptive way. It explores a range of factors, such as superego development, quality of object relations, and defensive structure, to determine how particular styles of being, relating, and growing are developed and retained. This perspective has led theorists such as Kernberg (1970) to classify personality disorders into "higher, intermediate, and lower" levels of organization of character pathology. In lower levels of personality development, as in antisocial character disorders, there is an impaired capacity to experience guilt, a predominance of aggression, and a reliance on primitive defenses such as projection and splitting. In higher levels of organization, such as in histrionic character disorders, there is a well-integrated, albeit severe, superego, an ability to experience a range of affective responses, and a reliance on defenses such as repression and reaction formation. This form of classification describes the presumed *internal states* of individuals, rather than their symptom pictures, to determine diagnosis.

CRITIQUE OF THE DIAGNOSTIC CLASSIFICATION OF PERSONALITY DISORDERS

Regardless of the perspective used to classify personality disorders, many problems and much controversy surround the use of these diagnoses. Although they are conceptualized as objective diagnostic entities, they are inevitably defined by the prevailing social, cultural, and political norms. Views on what constitutes health and illness are rooted in implicit assumptions about "normal" roles for men and women, about "correct" displays of emotion, and about "reasonable" needs for dependency on others. Who defines these "objective" standards for "adaptive" levels of functioning? Can we fairly label behavior out of its social context as it emerges, for example, in response to chronic abuse or racism?

Kaplan (1983) captured the gender bias codified in *DSM-III* in her critique of the criteria for dependent personality disorder. She created the following fictitious personality disorder to satirize *DSM-III*'s assumption that women's dependency needs, and the way they express them, are unhealthy.

Diagnostic Criteria for Independent Personality Disorder

The following are characteristic of the individual's current and long-term functioning, are not limited to episodes of illness, and cause either significant impairment in social functioning or subjective distress.

A. Puts work (career) above relationships with loved ones (e.g., travels a lot on business, works late at night and on weekends).

B. Is reluctant to take into account the others' needs when making decisions, especially concerning the individual's career or use of leisure time, e.g., expects spouse and children to relocate to another city because of individual's career plans.

C. Passively allows others to assume responsibility for major areas of social life because of inability to express necessary emotion (e.g., lets spouse assume most child-care responsibilities). [p. 790]

Sound familiar? In another society and time, might these "normative" traits associated with "successful" men be labeled as disordered? Might dependency—a reliance on advice, collaboration, reassurance, closeness—be associated with health? As exemplified in this satirical illustration, pathology is determined in part by the assumptions and biases of those who define the diagnoses. The traits of the "Independent Personality Disorder" reflect the way many men have been socialized to function in our society, and have been rewarded for so doing. The characteristics of men, many have argued, have been used as the criteria to ascertain "healthy" psychological functioning, whereas those of women have too readily been deemed pathological.

Other feminist authors have challenged the diagnostic entity of personality disorders because the category does not adequately attend to the profound effects of trauma and oppression on psychological functioning. As Brown (1992) suggests, there are a wide range of conflicts that can result from being powerless, oppressed, and discriminated against in a repetitive, ongoing manner that do not reflect a disordered personality. These behaviors may be adaptive responses to experiences of interpersonal trauma, for example, that have become tenacious over time due to repeated exposure to traumatic experiences. "Certain forms of behavior which in isolation may appear dysfunctional or pathological, are actually appropriate and precise responses to other aspects of the interpersonal environment" (p. 217). A category such as "battered women's syndrome" (Walker 1984) would account for characteristic behaviors of battered women (e.g., guardedness, passivity), without pathologizing the women in question. Brown suggests that a new diagnostic framework is needed, one that describes how repetitive victimization and/or exposure to sexism, racism, and other forms of cultural oppression affect psychological functioning and personality development.

In addition to the feminist critique of this classification system, other concerns arise in the use of the diagnosis of personality disorder.

First, a stigma is often associated with these disorders, as they may be used to label people pejoratively. In some professional settings, the diagnosis of personality disorder is offered with an implicit judgment and warning—i.e., this client will be "trouble." People's individual stories are disregarded, and the diagnosis itself is reduced to a simplistic caricature. Second, the categories are established in a notably arbitrary fashion, as many people exhibit traits of several of the disorders. Third, as suggested in the previous paragraph, character structure is difficult to assess when significant trauma has occurred. Trauma can temporarily and/or permanently alter character structure, defensive functioning, and the quality of one's relationships with others; clients may therefore present with some symptoms of a particular personality disorder when they are suffering primarily from posttraumatic stress disorder. (See Chapter 15 for a further discussion of this.) Inappropriate treatment may then ensue if therapists focus exclusively on the internal world of character structure and not on the traumatic context in which problematic—and perhaps situationally adaptive—behaviors emerged.

The last cautionary comment to make about the use of this diagnostic category involves the issue of cultural context. Given every culture's unique norms in regard to socially acceptable expressions of conflict and pain, symptoms diagnosed out of context may erroneously appear to reflect a disordered character. For example, Mendez-Villarrubia and LaBruzza (1994) note that people in some Hispanic cultures may develop episodes in which they shout, cry, tremble, lose consciousness, and become nervous and angry. These symptoms may reflect an *ataque de nervios* (attack of nerves), a culturally acceptable way to respond to stress. Through this culturally condoned expression of pain, people mobilize the support of the family and community, and are temporarily relieved of their social roles. In a different culture, these very same symptoms may reflect characterological and/or organic difficulties, and warrant a notably different treatment intervention.

PERSONALITY DISORDERS AS A DIAGNOSTIC ENTITY

Each of the personality disorders we will be studying encompasses a unique constellation of symptoms and etiological factors. What generalizations, however, might we offer about the character disorders as a diagnostic entity? Broadly speaking, the following characteristics are associated with these disorders:

1. The ego functions (reality testing, capacity to tolerate anxiety and delay frustration, judgment, etc.) of character-disordered individuals are differentially impaired, although they may be relatively inadequate and immature. Responses to stress are usually inflexible and maladaptive, but may change over the course of the life cycle.

2. Individuals with a character disorder usually feel that their problems lie not within themselves but in the environment. How is this manifested? A worker, for example, may be having problems at his job. Rather than consider his own contribution to the problem, he may blame his boss, his co-workers, or his family. Winnicott (1965) explains this need to hold the "environment" responsible for one's failings as follows: "[The individual carries] a hope that never becomes quite extinguished, that the environment may acknowledge and make-up for the specific failure that did the damage" (p. 207). We say that the problems for these individuals are *ego syntonic*, that is, they do not create internal psychological conflicts. This is in contrast to neurotic people, who are more likely to locate the source of the problem within themselves; problems are *ego dystonic* for these individuals, that is, they create turmoil and conflict within the psychological life of the person.

3. The ability to sustain loving, consistent, and mutually satisfying relationships with others is impaired to varying degrees. Someone who is schizoid, for example, may choose to be alone, have little contact with people, and seem indifferent to the reactions of others. Someone who is narcissistic may constantly need others to bolster his self-esteem and affirm his value and competence. Some psychodynamic theorists (Adler and Buie 1979) suggest that the extent of the impairment in relationships will depend on people's capacities to sustain positive images of benign others in their absence (object constancy) and to maintain boundaries between themselves and others.

4. Individuals with a character disorder are usually not troubled by their behavior, and, in fact, perceive themselves quite differently

than others do. The manifestations of their difficulties, however, are invariably distressing to those in their environment. A man with antisocial personality disorder, for example, was referred for treatment by the court following one of his countless car thefts. He boasted of his accomplishments, claiming there was not a car alarm in existence that he could not dismantle in six seconds or less. He felt untroubled by his behavior, which, needless to say, greatly troubled his victims. As with many character-disordered individuals, the impetus to change did not originate with him, but with the friends, family, colleagues, and legal institutions that put pressure on him to alter his behavior.

5. Because the character-disordered individual's issues are so frequently acted out or enacted in the interpersonal realm, the countertransference reactions of the therapist in the treatment relationship are invaluable tools in diagnosing, assessing, and treating these clients.

These generalizations provide us with a backdrop as we turn our attention to the study of the specific personality disorders. As we review each of these disorders, we must remember that we *all* have some of the traits delineated. It is the *prominence*, *rigidity*, and *clustering* of these traits that lead to a diagnosis of personality disorder in some individuals.

BORDERLINE PERSONALITY DISORDER

Let us begin our study of the borderline personality disorder with an anecdote that illustrates several of its characteristics.

The therapist's phone rang at 12:45 A.M. Sandra, a young woman who had been in treatment for three months, was on the other end of the line. Through intermittent sobs she told the therapist that a man to whom she was attracted ignored her at a concert earlier that evening, and that she was sitting on the bathroom floor with a bottle of aspirin in her hands. "I can't hold onto anything good anymore," she said. "If I take all the aspirin, the pain will disappear real fast. . . . When I get close to guys, they leave me. Then the little hurt sets off the big hurts, and I feel like total shit. Like what's happening in me will destroy any relationship. When I look at myself, I see a crippled mess. Like I'm running a race with my feet tied. I don't have normal hurts. I feel I have all the outside things. Inside I'm crummy."

Sandra's pain was overwhelmingly acute in the face of her disappointment. She felt abandoned and rageful, became enormously self-loathing, and impulsively grabbed a bottle of aspirin to "blot out" the hurt. She also felt that she could not hold onto any positive sense of herself in the face of the rejection. On the other end of the phone line, the therapist responded with a range of feelings: helplessness, anxiety, concern, and anger at the intrusion. This experience captures some of the dynamics typical of a "crisis" for individuals with borderline personality disorder and their therapists.

Why has the concept of *borderline* received so much professional and popular scrutiny? The reasons for this attention are varied. Although the prevalence of this disorder is estimated at between 2 to 4 percent in the general population, people with borderline personality disorders constitute 15 to 25 percent of all patients seen in outpatient and inpatient psychiatric settings (Leighton et al. 1963). Most mental health professionals have thus been involved in offering treatment to individuals with borderline personality disorder, an experience that can alternately be challenging and rewarding, and draining and frustrating. Much discussion and supervision time is devoted to the work with these clients, who frequently engage mental health systems to help provide containment for their destructive impulses. Complicated and intense transference/countertransference reactions are engendered; clinicians may be alternately idealized and then devalued, and seemingly secure attachments may be precipitously disrupted. Much of the work toward change happens *in* the treatment relationship, and not in the displacement; if the therapists are loved or despised in the moment, they know it through the passion of the affect expressed verbally or nonverbally in the hour. And finally, some of the leading psychodynamic theorists have offered compelling and contrasting views of the etiology of this disorder, and of the treatment interventions they consider to be most effective.

The concept of *borderline* evolved in an effort to categorize a group of clients who seemed to exist "on the border" between neurosis and psychosis. Unlike people with schizophrenia, these clients seemed to recompensate despite transient psychotic episodes; unlike neurotic clients, they developed problematic transference reactions and manifested primitive defense mechanisms in analysis. The first author who formally used the term *borderline* was Stern (1938), who outlined ten characteristics of a group of patients who were too ill to be treated with the classical psychoanalytic method (Richman and Sokolove 1992). Other theorists followed with different labels to describe this ill-defined population, including "as-if" personality (Deutsch 1942), pseudoneurotic schizophrenic (Hoch and Polatin 1949), and psychotic character (Frosch 1964).

Despite the general acceptance of the label *borderline* in current literature, theorists continue to debate the etiology of the disorder and question who should carry this diagnosis. Much attention, for example, has recently focused on the misuse of this diagnosis for people who are actually suffering from posttraumatic stress disorder. This concern applies particularly to women, who are diagnosed with borderline personality disorder three times more frequently than men and who, in many cases, have significant trauma histories. The symptoms many of these women manifest, such as unstable relationships and labile affect, have been used to justify the diagnosis of borderline personality disorder. Little consideration has been given to the possibility that these traits may have been normal responses to traumatic events in their interpersonal world. When the trauma history of sexual abuse, for example, was acknowledged and worked through, the borderline symptoms abated for many of these women and an intact character structure was apparent—one that would not be classified as borderline. Molly Layton (1995) explains the importance of acknowledging trauma as follows:

> What is added to our treatment of so-called borderline functioning when we locate its roots in a history of trauma? It is a profound shift in focus from character to context, like uneasily observing a person on the crowded street who seems to be gesturing and talking to himself, and then, thankfully, spotting the person across the street with whom he is in conversation.
>
> Viewing borderline traits as the fallout of real suffering ineluctably shifts therapy from a mission impossible to a mutually constructed more empathically demanding task of naming and sizing the effects of trauma. [p. 39]

An accurate diagnosis of borderline personality disorder can only be made, then, through a process of ongoing assessment and attention to what the psyche has had to "metabolize" from the environment. For some, the assaults from the external world, coupled with internal vulnerabilities, create entrenched, dysfunctional patterns that lead to formation of character disorders; for others, psychological and constitutional strengths protect a woman's character even though she may be symptomatic. Sorting through these diagnostic dilemmas is an essential part of the challenge in the work with our clients. Our treatment interventions should be guided by our assessments, which work best when they are hypotheses that can be changed and revised as new information is acquired. With these diagnostic challenges in mind, let us now turn our attention to the clinical picture—the symptomatology—of people with borderline personality disorders.

Clinical Picture

The manifestation of borderline symptomatology can be dramatic and jolting. Because individuals with borderline personality disorder often engage people through intense attachments, those involved in their lives are invariably affected by their symptoms. In the following sections, we will explore the prominent features of this disorder using a psychodynamic paradigm. We will look at the traits of the borderline personality disorder in the context of a person's object relations, ego functions, and sense of self.

Object Relations

Individuals with borderline personality disorder usually have relationships characterized by *instability and great intensity*, as their need for attachment to others fluctuates with their need for distance. People in their lives can be idealized one moment then devalued the next, with no affective sense that the person they hate today is the person they loved yesterday. Relationships often end abruptly, while new attachments are made precipitously. How can we understand this dynamic in object relational terms? First, although these individuals have a differentiated sense of self and other, the *boundaries between self and other are quite permeable*. Closeness can be experienced as "merger," as people feel engulfed in a longed for yet feared union. This experience of "fusion" is captured in the following comment a client made about her relationship with her boyfriend. "We're so close I feel like we're one person. . . . Sometimes it feels so good—like we're handcuffed together; other times it feels like he's in my face so I can't breathe." With poor boundaries, an *optimal distance* is difficult to establish; closeness may be stifling, yet separation may feel abandoning.

Another reason for the relational problems of people with this disorder is their *difficulty integrating positive and negative self and object representations* (Kernberg 1975). Simply stated, people with borderline personality disorder tend to experience themselves and/or others as "all good" or "all bad." This splitting of object representations can be seen in a client's description of her mother: "When I hate my mother, I just hate her. I can't remember her ever being nice. Now she's nice, but I know I'll hate her again and never want to see her." Anticipating the therapist's attempt to help her integrate these split representations, the client added: "And when I only feel hate for her you'll remind me that I once thought she was nice!"

The therapeutic relationship provides fertile ground for the emergence of splitting and precipitous endings and reattachments.

> Leah, a 25-year-old woman who ultimately completed a five-year therapy, fired her therapist eight times during the first two years of their work. During a stable period of the treatment, she told her therapist, "You gave me words for my thoughts and feelings. I felt mute before. You just seemed to know me and understand me." Two weeks later, when she and her therapist disagreed about the contents of a letter sent to the Welfare Department, Leah shouted over the phone, "I'm never coming back to see you. You don't know a thing about me. You're as incompetent as the rest of them," and then hung up.

For people in the helping professions this type of help-rejecting stance can be enormously frustrating and painful—like a roller coaster ride over which one has no control. It is critical to understand, however, that these fluctuations are an inevitable part of the work, and may be an adaptive way for the client to survive the fear of abandonment and of engulfment, and to manage the intensity of the rage directed toward others.

The lack of integration of positive and negative representations occurs not only in relation to others; it occurs as powerfully in relation to the self. People with borderline personality disorder tend to experience themselves as all good or all bad, with little gray area in between. In one moment they may be angrily self-righteous and entitled, believing that all of their problems result from their victimization in a cruel world. In the face of a failure or disappointment, however, they can lose all sense of self worth and become enormously self-loathing. Prior experiences of competence and adequacy disappear completely, as they perceive themselves as worthless, damaged human beings.

Carmen described feeling on one day that she was the most attractive, competent woman in her workplace. Following a rejection from a man the following day, she said, "I looked in the mirror and all I saw was this disgusting face; it had bulging eyes and crooked teeth. That, I realized, was me. I wanted to tear me apart limb by limb." Only one reality existed for Carmen then: the reality of that moment. Any experience of herself as an attractive, competent individual dissipated and could not be retrieved; it was replaced by her experience of herself as inherently defective.

We have explored how the difficulty individuals with borderline personality have in sustaining consistent, mutually satisfying relationships relates in part to their permeable boundaries, in part to their difficulty negotiating closeness and distance, and in part to their inability to integrate positive and negative self–object representations. One more theoretical construct helps us understand the quality of their relationships with others. Many people suffering from this disorder have *not achieved object constancy*, that is, the ability to internalize a whole object as an emotionally soothing inner presence that sustains the person during the other's absence. Without a solid capacity for evocative memory, individuals cannot retrieve soothing, comforting images when alone. This leads them to feel terrified of being alone, a characteristic that Adler and Buie (1979) and Buie and Adler (1982) consider the central, organizing feature of their pathology. This terror is not simply a fear of being lonely; ordinarily, when people are lonely, they can picture or feel the presence of loved ones whom they are missing. When people with borderline personality disorder feel alone, they experience a total void, an emptiness that renders the world a frightening place. They become fearful of abandonment, and deal with this fear in seemingly contradictory ways. At times, they urgently cling to others to ward off their aloneness; at other times, they distance themselves from others to avoid the threat of attachment/abandonment completely. This struggle was manifested in the following therapy.

> Margie was raised by two alcoholic parents who frequently left her and her siblings home alone while they went bar hopping to all hours of the night. During the first six months of treatment, Margie often called between sessions, stating, "I just need to hear your voice to make sure you're still there." Although frequently seen in exclusively pathological terms, this struggle to engage her therapist can be understood to represent a "powerful, healthy energy . . . embodying her lifelong attempt to locate a protective spirit" (Layton 1995, p. 40). Following the therapist's vacation, she missed several appointments; when coaxed to come back into the office, she reported the following: "I was literally paralyzed when you were gone. I broke out in hives; I felt hollow inside. I couldn't picture your face, hear your words to reassure me. You might as well have been dead. I thought maybe if I did something desperate you'd come back sooner; then I just decided to stay away from you so I wouldn't have to worry about your leaving me again."

Margie could not comfort herself with the therapist's image during the break in treatment. She responded to her ensuing despair and rage by alternately becoming self-destructive (e.g., she made superficial lacerations on her arm), and then by rejecting those for whom she yearned, yet feared, an attachment. As Margie became more able to hold onto the image of the therapist during ensuing breaks in the treatment, and to develop a sense of trust that the therapist would indeed return when planned, these behaviors abated.

Given the central role of impaired object relations in the pathology of individuals with borderline pathology, it may be helpful (and hopeful) to trace a client's object relations through the evolution of a therapy. Cassie, a 30-year-old woman who successfully completed a treatment of several years duration, described her relationships with others, particularly her mother, in notably different ways during successive stages of treatment. The development of her object relations shifted from merged selfobject representations to a more differentiated sense of herself and others, as can be seen in the following vignettes.

In the first year of her therapy, Cassie reflected on her relationship with her mother as follows: "My mother is totally dependent on me. She copies my haircuts, takes my advice. I can't get angry at her because she'd fall apart. I can't leave my mother; could you leave a kid who's trying to learn a new dance step while her shoe laces are tied together? . . . [Turning to the therapist, who had recently returned from a vacation] "I couldn't picture your face when you were away. It was like you were dead—you were so removed from my life."

At this point in the treatment, Cassie's object relations were characterized by poor boundaries between herself and others, and by her lack of object constancy.

Two and a half years into the therapy, Cassie stated: "It used to be when my mother was upset I'd spend all night with her. I'm first realizing what the word *separation* means. I don't have to feel all of my mother's feelings. I will always choose to give to my mother, but I can't give her all of what she wants. It's scary—this could be the end of my relationship with her—she could flip out. During her hospitalization, I felt like we were the kids in *Sophie's Choice*, and I had to decide who'd live. . . . I sometimes dream that one day I'll wake up and my mother will be an adult."

At this juncture, Cassie was struggling to develop a separate sense of self. Although she feared that separation would lead to dire consequences, she fought against her fears and depression to establish her own identity.

During the last year of treatment, Cassie married, was promoted at work, and planned to move out of state. She reflected on her relationships as follows: "My mother taught me how to love as one [hands clasped] but not as my*self*. Now I love as much but from one step back, ya know? Like before it was like I looked at a painting and saw colors up close. I'd find a color I'd like, focus on it, and it was beautiful. But I couldn't see the *whole* painting. If I'd move my face I'd maybe see one other color—like black. Yes, black—it was scary and awful. Now I can see the complex whole."

During her last year of treatment, Cassie had clearly moved toward integrating positive and negative images of herself and of others, and toward a fuller, complex affective life. In a letter she wrote to her therapist following her move, she described the pleasure she felt from a visit from a friend who had not been good in keeping in touch with her.

> "I guess I've never had an opportunity for her [the friend] to show how loyal and loving she can be with me. I am so glad I took the time and went through the pain of adjusting my expectations of our relationship. With you standing by my side, I worked hard at and won a treasure I could never have imagined—a relationship that "stayed."

Cassie had achieved object constancy, and with it, a sense of hope and trust in how relationships could enrich her life.

Ego Functions

Although there is a range of functioning along the borderline continuum, the ego functions of people with this disorder are impaired to varying degrees. The rigid use of more primitive defenses characterizes the borderline person's defensive operations. The defenses used most prominently include splitting, projection, projective identification, denial, primitive idealization and devaluation (see Chapter 4 for definitions). The thoughts, perceptions, and memories of people with borderline personality disorder are also affected. Cognitive disorientation and transient psychosis may occur under stress, and the capacity for solid evocative memory may not be achieved. People with this disorder may have difficulty modulating their feelings and impulses, and can show poor judgment and a disturbed sense of reality. Let us look at some of these ego functions in greater detail, so we can better capture the complexity of this experience.

IMPULSE CONTROL

As evident in the anecdotes thus far described, people with borderline personality disorders tend to be impulsive and unpredictable. They frequently engage in self-destructive acts, such as self-mutilation, substance abuse, sexual promiscuity, gambling, and violence. These behaviors are usually ego syntonic during the act, but ego dystonic afterward. Nancy, who frequently engaged in sexually promiscuous behavior, described her impulsivity this way: "I was so mad that I said 'fuck it'—I drank, picked up a guy at the bar, took him back to my place, and had sex. It was fun at the time—I needed it. Now I'm worried I have AIDS."

As described above, impulsive behaviors often occur in response to the threat of abandonment. Suicidal and self-destructive gestures may erupt with no apparent forethought, and with little consideration given to potential consequences. Self-mutilation is a common form of expression for this impulsive behavior, and carries with it different meanings that need to be assessed and understood on a case by case basis. At times, for example, people may cut themselves with the hope that they will die; at other moments the act may be an attempt to engage others in their lives and to force them to take notice; at still other times people may cut themselves to feel alive—to counteract the emptiness and deadness they feel when alone. The blood and physical pain help them know that they exist, help create a sense that "I am bleeding and feel pain so I must be alive." An example of this type of self-mutilation, along with features common to borderline pathology such as rage, self-loathing, and the use of projection, can be seen in the following illustration:

> Cindy entered her therapist's office looking angry and sullen, and wearing a bandage on her arm where she had cut herself following the previous therapy session. She began the hour: "You made me feel like a fucking loser on Monday. I'm pissed. Don't look at me like I have three heads. Turn away! You think I'm some kinda failure. Well fuck you too. I'm such a loser. I feel unsafe, but I won't let you put me back in the hospital. [Looking at her arm] I didn't even feel the pain. Like one minute I was unloading the dishwasher and the next there was blood trickling down my arm. It kinda made me feel like a person again."

Cindy became overwhelmed with feelings of inferiority and rage. Cutting herself made her feel alive again; if there was blood, then she still existed.

When people with borderline pathology make these kind of gestures, they are frequently described as being manipulative. If we understand a "manipulative" suicide gesture as a person's desperate attempt to provoke a response from another person, we can respond to it more empathically as a significant form of communication. If the term is used pejoratively to dismiss the serious nature of the person's action, it may ultimately encourage an escalation in the acting-out behavior as the client feels further abandoned. We as therapists have a range of responses to this self-destructive behavior, including feelings of anger, helplessness, frustration, and anxiety. We must learn how to recognize these important countertransference responses, and to use them as diagnostic tools in the treatment of our clients.

REGULATION OF AFFECT

Another impairment in ego functioning that is a hallmark of the borderline disorder is the poor regulation of affect. Although we all experience depression, anger, and dissatisfaction in our lives, the *persistence, lability, and intensity of these affects* is what differentiates the borderline person's affects from everyday affects. Anger, in fact, is considered by many to be the dominant affect that individuals with borderline personal disorder experience (Gunderson and Singer 1975). Two aspects of its manifestation are noteworthy. First, anger is often not modulated or experienced with any degree of gradation; a "little anger" suddenly becomes rage, or, as a client explained, "I go from number one on the scale of anger to number one hundred in two seconds flat." Second, the anger is often not differentiated from other affects. Situations that may engender hurt, sadness, or disappointment in many people are experienced solely as anger. A range of patients, for example, were told that their therapist would be leaving the clinic. Most discussed feeling angry, scared, sad, and disappointed during the weeks leading to the termination. One woman with borderline pathology stated consistently, "I'm just pissed. What else is there to feel? It's black or it's white." There was no shading to her feelings, as they were experienced not just intensely in a given moment but *exclusively*. Borderline individuals tend to show little capacity to experience ambivalence, that is, to be able to hold mutually conflicting feelings simultaneously. The all-or-nothing phenomenon we described in people's interpersonal relationships is therefore also evident in relation to affects.

Helping people with this disorder differentiate among various affects, and integrate them, can be an important part of the therapeutic work. Feelings may not be recognized or modulated, as evidenced in the following exchange between Maria and her therapist:

> Maria was discussing her rejection from a previously sought-after college program, and noted that she was not feeling disappointed. In response to the therapist's look of surprise, Maria questioned: "You mean I may be feeling a little disappointed? You mean you can sometimes feel moderately disappointed? I don't get it. That sounds like being a little pregnant to me. I'm either overwhelming disappointed, or not at all." She then explained why she "chose" not to feel anything in response to the rejection. "If I feel disappointed, if I feel anything in fact, how will I know I won't enter that black hole of depression? I can't risk it. . . . It's like the Loch Ness monster—there's always danger lurking in the waters." In not being able to differentiate or modulate her affect, Maria often felt a numbness, a pervasive deadness in her emotional life.

REALITY TESTING: SENSE OF REALITY

Although people with borderline personality disorder have a capacity for reality testing that is relatively intact, they can be vulnerable to transient psychotic episodes and to distortions of reality. In the following example, Cecilia, who suffered from no prior or subsequent episodes of psychosis, briefly "lost touch" with reality.

> Cecilia left for vacation with great fears about being on her own, and tremendous guilt—reinforced by her parents—for leaving her children for several days. Despite her 33 years of age, she packed an entire suitcase full of stuffed animals to "keep me company" and help soothe her when alone. On the third day of her trip, she walked down the street and "saw" her parents at the corner. She ran over to these two strangers, calling them Mom and Dad. Over the next 24 hours, she had auditory hallucinations as her parents "continued to talk" to her, criticizing her for neglecting her children. Cecilia had never before been psychotic and recompensated fully upon her return home.

Brief and transient psychotic episodes such as Cecilia's can emerge in people with borderline pathology, but unlike in psychotic disorders, they are ego-alien and unsystematized. Except during psychotic regressions, individuals with borderline personality disorder retain the capacity for reality testing; they can distinguish between fantasy and reality, and between self and other. Their sense of reality can, however, become distorted. They may have experiences of depersonalization, dissociation, or derealization, develop distorted views of themselves, or misperceive others' intentions as malevolent. The following comments reflect some of these phenomena: "It's odd—like I can be in this room and suddenly the room changes," or "I touched my arm and couldn't feel anything; it seemed like it wasn't attached to my body." More persistent distortions of reality can be manifested in their suspiciousness of others, onto whom they may project their sense of "badness" or evil. When there is evidence of these kinds of distortions, it is particularly important to assess whether past trauma has led to a dissociative process.

LEVEL OF ANXIETY

Individuals with borderline pathology often have difficulty binding their anxiety, which can be experienced as chronic and diffuse, or episodically intense and overwhelming. Given their lack of object constancy, they can experience tremendous anxiety in response to real or perceived abandonment. This anxiety can be characterized as "fear of the loss of the object." Unlike people with schizophrenia, they do not usually fear either being annihilated or having the power to annihilate others; rather, they fear the emptiness, rage, and aloneness precipitated by the loss of a significant other. In treatment, disruptions in the work— such as when therapists leave for vacation—can often bring on experiences of intense anxiety. This experience was captured by a young man who became distraught and anxious during the weeks prior to his therapist's planned departure. He was unable to concentrate at work or to sleep through the night. He told his therapist, "When you're away, I become unglued because you don't exist for me. You might as well be on the other side of the planet—I can't even picture your face." Phone contacts, appointment cards, or letters can often decrease the anxiety that arises in the face of these frightening separations.

Sense of Self

Having explored the quality of object relations and the ego functions of people with borderline personality disorder, let us use a self psychological lens to examine their sense of self. Central to the borderline pathology is the *lack of an integrated, cohesive identity and sense of self.* Whether due to the lack of selfobjects from their childhood who could mirror and idealize them and provide optimal frustration, or due to their difficulty internalizing the functions of their selfobjects, borderline individuals often struggle with the development of healthy self-esteem, ambitions, and goals. Their early lives are frequently devoid of people who provided the relatively consistent soothing, nurturance, and validation necessary to create cohesive selves. This deficit may make them vulnerable to transient infatuations with, for example, cult-like or religious figures who hold the promise of love and guidance.

Since people with borderline personality disorder tend to experience themselves and others in "all good/all bad" terms, the subtle complexities of feeling and thought are often absent. The self is frequently experienced in fragmented pieces, not consolidated into an enduring, cohesive whole. A client described this state as follows: "I feel fragmented, like there are two parts of me that have nothing in common but that they're a part of me. . . . I used to feel like a tiny speck, surrounded by gelatin."

People may manifest their identity disturbances in a variety of ways, including being chronically confused about their future goals and sexual orientation, making frequent geographical moves, and having shifting, unconsolidated views of themselves and others. Without a coherent sense of self, they may not achieve to their full potential despite their considerable talents.

Gary, an extremely bright, engaging man, spoke of functioning well below his professional aspirations as he worked part-time for fifteen years as a home health aide, making $6 an hour. He spoke alternately of his wish to do more with his life, and of his sense of entitlement about what the world owed him. He was involved in two consecutive long term relationships with men, which were sexual only during the first few weeks of courtship. He noted that the men with whom he lived over the years provided him with the security of not being alone—but no more. At age 41, he stated, "I don't really know what I am—straight or gay. I don't have a clue about my sexual preference—I'm scared of closeness with both men and women. I don't even know what I want to be when I grow up, because I don't have a clue as to who the 'I' in me is."

Psychodynamic Understanding

Having explored the symptoms of borderline pathology, let us now turn our attention to a developmental understanding of this disorder. Several psychodynamic theorists offer us an explanation of the etiology of these traits. Depending on their theoretical orientation, each of these theorists traces the heart of the disturbance to different developmental factors. Each explores how tasks are mastered at various developmental stages, and then hypothesizes how the unresolved issues from these stages are manifested later in life. The work of these theorists helps us understand how poorly negotiated tasks from early developmental stages create a foundation from which problematic patterns may develop; the dynamics that emerge in adult relationships, they speculate, reflect the unresolved issues from interactions with primary caregivers. It is tempting but very problematic to look at these models in a linear fashion, and to decide, for example, that difficulties in the separation-individuation phase automatically lead to an inability to trust. The impact of friends, extended family, teachers, religious mentors, physical illnesses, and the like *all* influence psychological development. The following conceptual frameworks offered by several prominent theorists focus most on the preoedipal relationships of people with borderline personality disorder.

Kernberg (1967, 1970, 1975), operating from a "drive-defense" model, traces the fundamental pathology in the borderline disorder to problems in early object relations. He believes that due to a constitutionally based predisposition toward aggression as well as rage from conflictual early relationships, some children cannot integrate positive and negative self and object representations. Although their ability to differentiate between themselves and others is intact, their capacity for experiencing ambivalence and a cohesive sense of themselves is impaired. Their good, loving images of self and other are protected from their excessive aggression through the development of a primitive defensive structure. Splitting, denial, devaluation, projection, and projective identification are the defenses used to keep the positive images of self and/ or other from being destroyed by rage or "badness." They also serve to ward off the anxiety that would otherwise result from borderline individuals' contradictory experiences of themselves and others, and compromise their ability to achieve object constancy.

Due to constitutional vulnerabilities and possible neglect or abuse in their childhoods, people with this disorder have harsh, often sadistic superego introjects. Hostile, "bad" objects are both internalized and projected, and coexist with overidealized images that lead to unattainable goals. What emerges are punitive thoughts and behaviors alternately directed toward themselves as failures, or toward others whom they experience as persecutors. Kernberg's description of these pathological internalized object relations, as well as his description of their defensive structure, offers us a way to understand the development of many of the symptoms we associate with borderline pathology.

Masterson (1976, 1981), who draws on Mahler's (1975) separation-individuation theory, focuses on abandonment depression and the defenses against it as central to borderline pathology. He hypothesizes that during the rapprochement subphase, borderline mothers withdraw their emotional support as their children attempt to separate and individuate; when the children remain dependent and clinging, they are rewarded. Either way the children pay an enormous psychological price. Those who move toward autonomy are faced with abandonment and depression; those who remain dependent and regressed never develop a separate, boundaried sense of self. In adult relationships, these individuals subsequently seek intimate ties with nurturing substitutes. When those relationships are established, however, the unresolved issues pertaining to autonomy and individuation reemerge. A pattern of unstable relationships then develops, in which intense unions are followed by precipitous ruptures.

Unlike Kernberg and Masterson, Buie and Adler (1982, Adler and Buie 1979) focus on deficits, not conflicts, as central to borderline pathology. They integrate Piaget's (1954) theory of cognitive development, Mahler's (1975) theory of separation-individuation, and Winnicott's (1965) concept of the holding environment to develop their theory about this disorder. They believe that because of a lack of "good enough" mothering during the separation-individuation phase of development, a core deficit results—an impaired capacity for solid evocative memory. Without the capacity to evoke the positive mental representation of a soothing, holding caregiver, a profound sense of aloneness and emptiness prevails. In times of stress—often precipitated by abandonment—panic then rage emerge because individuals with borderline personality disorder cannot evoke a positive representation of another, nor rely on their own impoverished resources to soothe themselves. They believe that aggression is not primary in the development of borderline pathology; it is secondary to the despair and panic resulting from the lack of nurturing, soothing introjects. The inner world is impoverished and relationships are alternately experienced as life sustaining or nonexistent.

The dynamic issues in borderline pathology are complex and rich, and often need time for adequate exploration. The treatment relationships that unfold with this population can be frustrating and draining, but also moving and gratifying. We want to end this section with a comment by Cassie, about whom we wrote earlier, that captures the sense of peace she found in doing the work of therapy. In reflecting on the turmoil and distress of her life, she noted: "I now know what it must feel like to be more 'normal': to have hurts that don't destroy me or the people I care about, to see that I don't have to sacrifice my*self* to my parents, to get to know myself and find I can love and be loved over time. . . . So, how'd we do it???? I guess that's been our work in the therapy!"

NARCISSISTIC PERSONALITY DISORDER

Over the last twenty years, authors such as Lasch (1979) have described the emergence of a "culture of narcissism," characterized by self-absorption and the glorification of the self. Devoted to self-improvement at any cost, many people have become obsessed with attempts to perfect themselves. They concentrate on improving their public images, and turn to cosmetic surgeons and personal trainers to help prolong life and defy the aging process. Some of this preoccupation with self-improvement has tangible and meaningful benefits. When it reflects the cultural norm, however, individual greed may be valued above collective responsibility, and empathy may be lacking for those who are different or less fortunate. Lasch has described this period as a disordered social time, remarkable for its degree of social fragmentation and its absence of rootedness and connection. Perhaps the individual diagnosis of narcissistic personality disorder, so prevalent during the 1980s, reflects this cultural phenomenon—one in which people protect themselves against the pain of deprivation and disconnection through self-absorption.

In this section, we explore the concept of narcissism from a clinical vantage point, focusing on the characteristics of the narcissistic personality disorder. Before exploring its exclusively pathological manifestation, however, we must appreciate that this concept encompasses normal functions as well. All levels of psychological development include aspects of narcissism; healthy narcissism, an ability to love oneself and/or to regard oneself positively, is critical in the development of self-esteem. How narcissistic issues are displayed varies across the life cycle and across cultures; before being deemed pathological, they should be evaluated in these respective contexts. Imagine, for example, the pride we may feel in a 2½-year-old girl who spontaneously stands before a crowd of people and begins to sing, dance, and clap her hands in glee. Many of us might smile at this exhibitionistic display, delighted in this girl's pleasure with her own accomplishments. We would not perceive her as being pathologically narcissistic. If, however, a woman of 30 frequently burst into song and dance before a crowd of bystanders, constantly seeking their admiration and attention, might we most likely wonder about her arrogance and self-centeredness? Displays of narcissism, such as exhibitionism and grandiosity, assume markedly different meanings depending on when they occur in the life cycle, and in which culture they are embedded.

The term *narcissism* was drawn from the Greek myth of Narcissus, summarized by Cooper (1986) as follows:

> Narcissus was a physically perfect young man, the object of desire among the nymphs, for whom he showed no interest. One nymph, Echo, loved him deeply and one day approached him and was rudely rejected. In her shame and grief, she perished, fading away, leaving behind only her responsive voice. The Gods, in deciding to grant the nymphs' wish for revenge, contrived that Narcissus would also experience the feelings of an unreciprocated love. One day, looking into a clear mountain pool, Narcissus espied his own image and immediately fell in love, thinking that he was looking at a beautiful water spirit. Unable to tear himself away from this mirror image, and unable to evoke a response from the reflection, which disappeared every time he attempted to embrace it, he gradually pined away and died. [p. 112]

Which features present in this myth do we currently associate with the concept of narcissistic personality disorder? Cooper (1986) delineates some of the traits evidenced by Narcissus: arrogance, self-centeredness, grandiosity, lack of sympathy or empathy for others, poorly differentiated self and object boundaries, and lack of enduring object ties. Let us hold this evocative myth in mind as we now turn our attention to the clinical picture of the narcissistic personality disorder.

Clinical Picture

Toward the beginning of the movie *Sunset Boulevard*, William Holden comments to Gloria Swanson, the aged, well-past-her-prime silent screen actress, that she was once famous. Denying the reality of her fall from stardom and masking the humiliation she feels about her current life circumstances, Swanson responds with indignation, "I *am* big. It is the pictures that are small." Her desperate attempt to remain special and unique, her unrealistic self-concept, and her devaluation of all that has occurred in the film industry following her departure are captured in this poignant and painful moment on screen. These traits will be explored below as we look at the disturbances in the sense of self, in object relations and in ego functions characteristic of the person with this disorder. As in all the psychopathological syndromes we have studied thus far, it is the *pervasive pattern* of these traits that constitute the disorder.

Self-Concept

As evidenced by Swanson's character, people with narcissistic personality disorder have *difficulty maintaining a realistic concept of their own self-worth*. On the one hand, they can have an inflated and grandiose sense of self-importance. Fantasies of magnificent achievements or unrealistic goals may preoccupy them. Comments such as "I am better than . . . ," or "I know more than . . . ," or "I am the most important person in this room" may be implied or stated in their conversations with others. Sam, for example, repeatedly spoke about his colleagues in the following terms: "I can't stand their stupidity, their constant drive. I won't waste my time in their committee meetings when I have so many better things to do." On the other hand, the self-concepts of people with narcissistic personality disorder may include an unrealistic sense of profound worthlessness and propensity toward shame. These feelings of inadequacy, "unlovableness," and self-loathing coexist with arrogance and self-importance; in fact, the grandiosity is likely to mask a core sense of vulnerability. Sam, the man who seemingly felt superior to colleagues, asked in a moment of despair, "What would it mean to no longer feel worthless? It would mean not secretly resenting people for being better than me. I'd have to stop pretending to be competent, because there's nothing worse than being reminded of one's worthlessness."

In the following illustration, we see how these themes may emerge in the course of a therapy.

> Gerry frequently entered his therapist's office with a demeaning comment about someone in his life, or with a question to the therapist about whether she had read a certain article or novel. The therapist often felt stupid in his presence, wondering if Gerry would not be better served by a more intelligent, better-read clinician. On this particular day, Gerry began his session in silence, more aloof and distant than usual. After a period of time, he asked in a demanding tone, "Who was that professional-looking man you smiled at when he left your office?" The therapist momentarily felt guilty— as if she had done something wrong—then recognized how so much of her self-doubt in her work with Gerry was evoked through projective identification. She felt as incompetent and inadequate with him as he felt perpetually in the world. After some exploration of his thoughts, he stated, "I assumed that I was your favorite client— in fact, in my head I pictured myself as your only client." He became devaluing momentarily, defending against his hurt, "My last therapist would never have smiled at another client leaving her office," then added with a sense of sadness and resignation, "If I'm not your special client, I feel like a nobody."

Although Gerry usually presented as arrogantly self-assured, he had a fragile sense of self, a self that deflated—like a balloon full of air that is pricked—in the face of a perceived slight, hurt, or disappointment. His vulnerability was usually concealed by a condescending, critical attitude toward others. Morrison (1986) has described this seeming paradox as follows:

> This need for absolute uniqueness, to be the sole object of importance to someone else, symbolizes the essence of narcissistic yearning. . . . What are *the affective implications of this yearning for uniqueness?* We have noted that it may lead to an outpouring of untamed

aggression, or of reactive rage against the offending object. Internally, however, I suggest that such an experience leads to a sense of utter despair, profound depression, and reflects the paradoxical extremes of grandiose entitlement, on the one hand and vulnerability to mortification, on the other. [p. 4]

Implied in the traits we have thus far reviewed is the tendency of people with narcissistic personality disorder to be *self-centered and self-referential.* They may talk about the details of their lives constantly, and may charmingly capture the attention of everyone at the parties they attend. Without attention and praise from others, however, they are left with a sense of deadness, of emptiness inside. In spite of the constant affirmation and admiration they seek in order to feel "whole" and good about themselves, they feel like frauds. Beneath the boasts are profound self-doubts and self-reproaches.

Jake, a 27-year-old man, struggled with many of these character traits in his life and relationships with others. The youngest of four in his family of origin, he was raised by a distant, cold father, and a critical, depressed mother who gave him daily enemas until he was 12. Jake felt ignored by his parents, who he remembers attended his siblings' performances and school functions, but never his own. "I could've jumped on the table and they wouldn't have noticed. . . . I wanted my mother to love me, to stop saying I was the black sheep and to say instead I was her miracle child. . . . I preferred being hit by her with a paddle [which she did routinely] than ignored." When Jake was 27, he sought therapy because of feelings of emptiness and depression, and a pervasive sense of dissatisfaction with his life. He had begun a career as a stand-up comic, and alternated between thinking he was the next Lenny Bruce and believing he had no talent. He was obsessed by what others thought of him, and married an attractive woman because "she was beautiful, self-assured—and I thought she'd make me more comfortable with myself." Performing before crowds was the only way he could defend against the dreaded boredom he feared in his life. He noted that he needed the audience to feel alive, and likened the pleasure of anticipation before a performance to a tiger standing tall before the crowds at a circus. When the audience departed, he would "crash," feeling empty and having little direction in his life.

Despite the bravado practiced on stage, Jake had a fragile sense of self so typical of people suffering from this disorder. Although intensely ambitious, he felt chronically bored and unable to channel his intellect and talent into any vocational, academic, or personal pursuit.

Object Relations

People with narcissistic personality disorder have relationships with others that are frequently superficial and shallow, and lacking in emotional depth. Showing little capacity for empathy, they can be insensitive to others' needs and exploitative in their behavior. Although the boundaries between themselves and others are less permeable than people with borderline personality disorders, they see others as narcissistic extensions of themselves. Their self and object representations are differentiated, but intimately tied together: as noted previously, their self definitions are largely dependent on tributes from others. This can breed a sense of entitlement in their relationships, a feeling that the mundane details of life should be the purview of others, rather than of themselves.

A colorful illustration of this can be seen in the novel *The Prime of Miss Jean Brodie* (1961). The title itself captures a narcissistic woman's desperate need to feel perfect, as well as her denial and fear of the reality of her vulnerabilities. Miss Jean Brodie, a middle-aged teacher, insists she is in the prime of her life despite her failing relationships with others and the betrayal by one of her students. She arrogantly holds onto the belief that she holds the "truth" about life and love, and tolerates no imperfections in herself and others. The students in her class become extensions of her own need for affirmation and admiration; if she can make them "perfect," then she can feel competent and "whole." Miss Brodie refers to them as the "Brodie set," and tells them, "I am putting old heads on your young shoulders. . . . all of my pupils are the crème de la crème. . . . Give me a girl at an impressionable age, and she is mine for life" (pp. 11–12).

Despite their seeming imperviousness to others' opinions of them, people with narcissistic personality disorder can be exquisitely sensitive to perceived slights. An unempathic statement, a felt criticism, or an unmet demand can trigger a *narcissistic injury*, that is, the experience of feeling deeply wounded, humiliated, and hurt. When "injured" in this fashion, people with this disorder may respond with intense rage. Following a session, for example, in which a therapist made an unempathic transference interpretation, Josh noted angrily to his therapist: "I was furious at you after last week. I'm not the least bit interested in what you think of me. I have my own agenda here, an important one, that has nothing to do with yours. I know far more than what you learn in your psychiatry and social work texts about what human nature is about." Josh felt exposed and misunderstood by his therapist; he subsequently became enraged, assuming a grandiose stand while devaluing her. As we will see in the next section, this posture characterizes the defensive style of the narcissistically disordered individual.

Intimate relationships are also deeply affected by excessive narcissism. People may have difficulty perceiving their partners as having interests and needs that may be markedly different from their own. They may engage in numerous extramarital affairs as a way to deal with boredom resulting from the shallowness of their relationships, and with their needs for new sources of admiration.

Ego Functions

In contrast to people with borderline personality disorder, the ego functioning of those with narcissistic personality disorder tends to be relatively intact. Their judgment, reality testing, and cognitive processes can be distorted by emotional issues to some extent, but they tend to function with greater consistency and proficiency than individuals with borderline pathology. They are often extremely articulate and opinionated, traits that may boost their self-esteem while masking a sometimes superficial knowledge base. Their anxiety is often experienced at the level of "fear of loss of approval, of acceptance, of love of another." It emerges in thoughts such as "I'm worried you will be disappointed when you see the 'real' me," as compared with "I'm worried you will abandon me." Given how common this fear is, we can see how all of us share these traits.

The defenses of people with narcissistic personality disorder serve to protect their fragile self-esteem. A defense such as idealization helps create "perfect" others with whom they can merge; devaluation and projection help rid them of their own imperfections, which they then "see" in others in relation to whom they feel superior; denial and rationalization assist them in not having to contend with their own weaknesses and vulnerabilities. The use of some of these defenses, and the function they serve, can be seen in the following case:

Larry, a 27-year-old man who talked incessantly about his looks in his psychotherapy, reported that he felt obsessed about his appearance. He applied facial cream eight times a day, was drawn to mirrors on all surfaces to "check up" on his looks, and constantly sought to be sexier or more outrageous than other men. At the beginning of each visit to his therapist's office, he would offer a critical comment about what he saw: "The picture on the wall is crooked." "The tag on the rug is showing." "Your skirt doesn't match your top." When a therapeutic alliance had been established in the work, Larry and the therapist explored why he felt a need to be so devaluing. He noted: "I do say something critical every time I come in here. Maybe I'm trying to make this—and you—imperfect because I feel so insecure. If I saw you as okay, or even perfect, I'd have to deal with how shitty I really feel about myself." Larry was ultimately able to understand that his preoccupation with his appearance reflected his attempt to "fix" his more deep-rooted sense of inadequacy. As he developed a more cohesive sense of self and greater compassion, he became more comfortable with the reality of his physique and more tolerant of imperfections in others. He no longer projected his worst fears about himself onto others, and slowly developed an awareness of the impact of his comments on them.

Psychodynamic Understanding

Working from a range of theoretical models, different authors have offered remarkably varied accounts of the etiology of the narcissistic personality disorder. Freud (1914) attributed narcissistic problems to a withdrawal of libido from the outer world into the ego, that is, a retreat from attachments to others to a state of self-absorption. He noted that this regressive retreat could be caused by stresses secondary to trauma, disease, or the onset of old age, and/or by frustrations in relationships with others. Although recognizing that all people have residual aspects of primary and secondary narcissism, he believed that the amounts of libido directed toward the self accounted for the differences in psychological functioning. The person, then, who lavished excessive attention and love on himself or herself would suffer from a disturbance in narcissism.

In the last two decades, the principal controversy surrounding the theoretical understanding of the narcissistic personality disorder has revolved around the models proposed by Kohut (1977a,b, Kohut and Wolf 1978) and Kernberg (1974, 1975). Many people have suggested that these theorists developed their models based on two different client populations, with Kohut basing his theory on a healthier and higher functioning population than Kernberg. Nonetheless, each model offers an instructive accounting of possible causes of this disorder, and of treatment interventions that derive from them.

Kohut (as noted in Chapter 7) understood pathology in terms of deficits in self structure. He attributed narcissistic pathology to the failure of the environment to provide age appropriate empathic responses to the child's needs. Without relationships in which they are adequately mirrored, and in which they have someone to idealize and feel similar to, children lack the validation, admiration, and modeling necessary for the development of a healthy self-esteem. They become vulnerable to feelings of worthlessness and inadequacy, and turn to others for self-definition. A 3-year-old child who sings "Happy Birthday" off-key with incorrect words may need to see the gleam in his mother's eyes to support his healthy exhibitionistic display and positive self-regard. Consistent critical or neglectful responses to these types of displays may contribute to the development of the fragile self that is so central in a narcissistic personality disorder. Kohut also notes that the environment must provide children with an "optimal level of frustration" so that they can learn to cope with disappointments, anger, and frustration. After all, the 3-year-old child who sings off-key will have to recognize, when older, that he is not the next Pavarotti. If children chronically experience too much frustration, they cannot take in selfobject functions nor experience the world as a safe place; if they chronically experience too little frustration, they remain entrenched in grandiose omnipotence and self-absorption. Either state can lead to the development of the traits we have discussed in the narcissistic personality disorder.

Having briefly discussed Kohut's view of the etiology of narcissistic disturbances, how might we understand its application to practice? Kohut believes that narcissistic issues emerge in the transference, in which clients reactivate the need for mirroring, idealization, and twin-

ship. By assuming an empathic stance, the therapist helps clients recon-
struct and identify selfobject needs, understand their experience of
disappointment in themselves and others, and ultimately seek out appropriate selfobjects. Rage and entitlement on the part of the client are not
interpreted as shortcomings of the client, but as understandable reactions to the inevitable empathic failures of the therapist. Kohut believes
that when these empathic failures are acknowledged and repaired, the
deficits leading to narcissistic vulnerabilities can be addressed.

Kernberg (1974, 1975) offers a strikingly different view of the etiology of narcissistic disorders. Although he believes narcissistic individuals function at a higher level than those with borderline personality disorder, he sees narcissistic personality as a subtype of borderline personality organization. He describes the self in the narcissistic personality as
a "grandiose pathological self," a self that needs to devalue others who
are ungratifying so that dependency needs can be denied and the unacceptable parts of that self can be projected. Rather than feel the pain of
their sense of worthlessness and of the unmet need for support and love,
people with narcissistic personality disorder may become arrogantly dis-
missive of others. This narcissistic stance serves to protect them from
recognizing their envious, dependent, and needy self.

To what does Kernberg attribute this disturbance? He notes that
aggression, constitutionally or environmentally induced, creates an intense envy of others. Conflict arises between what people long to have
and to be, and how they actually experience themselves. The goals of
treatment follow from this understanding. Kernberg suggests that people
with a narcissistic personality disorder must renounce their yearning for
perfection and accept the terror inherent in true intimacy. Unlike Kohut,
he interprets clients' idealization of the therapist as a defense, and challenges them to acknowledge their envy, rage, and, ultimately, their dependency needs. Hence, we can see how theory can inform remarkably
different kinds of therapeutic interventions, as the way we formulate
clients' problems shapes our ideas about how to help them effect change
in their lives.

The prevalence of certain disorders, or perhaps the prevalence of
the use of certain diagnoses, will most likely change as social conditions
and norms evolve over time. We have devoted this chapter to the study
of the borderline and narcissistic personality disorders, which have gar-

nered much attention in the mental health literature over the past twenty years. In the next chapter, we will take a briefer look at the other person-alilty disorders recognized in *DSM-IV*.

References

Adler, G., and Buie, D. H. (1979). Aloneness and borderline psychopathol-ogy: the possible relevance of child development issues. *International Jour-nal of Psycho-Analysis* 60:83–96.

Akhtar, S. (1992). *Broken Structures: Severe Personality Disorders and Their Treat-ment*. Northvale, NJ: Jason Aronson.

American Psychiatric Association. (1994). *Diagnostic and Statistical Manual of Mental Disorders*, 4th ed. Washington, DC: American Psychiatric Asso-ciation.

Brown, L. (1992). A feminist critique of personality disorders. In *Personality and Psychopathology: Feminist Reappraisals*, ed. L. Brown, and M. Ballou, pp. 206–228. New York: Guilford.

Buie, D. H., and Adler, G. (1982). Definitive treatment of the borderline personality. *International Journal of Psychoanalytic Psychotherapy* 10:40–79.

Chess, S., and Thomas, A. (1978). Temperamental individuality from child-hood to adolescence. *Annual Progress in Child Psychiatry and Child Devel-opment* 223–244.

Cooper, A. M. (1986). Narcissism. In *Essential Papers on Narcissism*, ed. A. P. Morrison, pp. 112–143. New York: New York University Press.

Deutsch, H. (1942). Some forms of emotional disturbance and their relation-ship to schizophrenia. *Psychoanalytic Quarterly* 11:301–321.

Fenichel, O. (1945). *The Psychoanalytic Theory of Neurosis*. New York: Norton.

Freud, S. (1914). On narcissism: an introduction. *Standard Edition* 14:67–101.

Frosch, J. (1964). The psychotic character: clinical psychiatric considerations. *Psychiatric Quarterly* 38:81–96.

Gunderson, J. G., and Singer, M. T. (1975). Defining borderline patients: an overview. *American Journal of Psychiatry* 132:1–10.

Hoch, P. H., and Polatin, P. (1949). Pseudoneurotic forms of schizophrenia. *Psychiatric Quarterly* 23:248–276.

Kaplan, M. (1983). A woman's view of *DSM-III*. *American Psychologist* 37(7): 786–792.

Kernberg, O. F. (1967). Borderline personality organization. *Journal of the American Psychoanalytic Association* 15:641–685.

——— (1970). A psychoanalytic classification of character pathology. *Journal of the American Psychoanalytic Association* 18:800–822.

———— (1974). Contrasting viewpoints regarding the nature and psychoanalytic treatment of narcissistic personalities: a preliminary communication. *Journal of the American Psychoanalytic Association* 22:255–267.

———— (1975). *Borderline Conditions and Pathological Narcissism.* New York: Jason Aronson.

Kohut, H. (1977a). *The Analysis of the Self.* New York: International Universities Press.

———— (1977b). *The Restoration of the Self.* New York: International Universities Press.

Kohut, H., and Wolf, E. (1978). The disorders of the self and their treatment: an outline. *International Journal of Psycho-Analysis* 59:413–425.

Lasch, C. (1979). *The Culture of Narcissism.* New York: Norton.

Layton, M. (1995). Emerging from the shadows. *Family Networker* 19(3):35–41.

Leighton, D. C., Harding, J. S., Macklin, D. B., et al. (1963). *The Character of Danger: The Stirling County Study,* vol. 3. New York: Basic Books.

Livesley, W. J., Jang, K. L., Jackson, D. N., and Vernon, P. A. (1993). Genetic and environmental contributions to dimensions of personality disorder. *American Journal of Psychiatry* 150(12):1826–1831.

Mahler, M. (1975). *The Psychological Birth of the Human Infant.* New York: Basic Books.

Masterson, J. F. (1976). *Psychotherapy of the Borderline Adult: A Developmental Approach.* New York: Brunner/Mazel.

———— (1981). *The Narcissistic and Borderline Disorders: An Integrated Developmental Approach.* New York: Brunner/Mazel.

Mendez-Villarrubia, J. M., and LaBruzza, A. (1994). Issues in the assessment of Puerto Rican and other Hispanic clients, including *ataques de nervios.* In *Women of Color: Integrating Ethnic and Gender Identities in Psychotherapy,* ed. L. Comas-Diaz and B. Greene, pp. 141–176. New York: Guilford.

Morrison, A. P. (1986). *Essential Papers on Narcissism.* New York: New York University Press.

Piaget, J. (1954). *The Construction of Reality in the Child.* New York: Basic Books.

Reich, W. (1945). The characterological resolution of the infantile sexual conflict. In *Character Analysis,* 3rd ed., ed. M. Higgins and C. M. Raphael, trans. V. R. Carfagno. New York: Farrar, Straus, & Giroux.

Richman, N., and Sokolove, R. L. (1992). The experience of aloneness, object representation and evocative memory in borderline and neurotic adults. *Psychoanalytic Psychology* 9(1):77–91.

Spark, M. (1961). *The Prime of Miss Jean Brodie.* New York: Dell.

Stern, A. (1938). Psychoanalytic investigation of and therapy in the borderline group of neuroses. *Psychoanalytic Quarterly* 7:467–489.

Thaper, A., and McGuffin, P. (1993). Is personality disorder inherited? An overview of the evidence. *Journal of Psychopathology and Behavioral Assessment* 15(4):325–345.

Waldinger, R. J. (1986). *Fundamentals of Psychiatry*. Washington, DC: American Psychiatry Press.

Walker, L. E. A. (1984). *The Battered Women's Syndrome*. New York: Springer.

Winnicott, D. (1965). *The Maturational Processes and the Facilitating Environment*. New York: International Universities Press.

13

Other Personality Disorders

JOAN BERZOFF, PATRICIA HERTZ, AND LAURA MELANO FLANAGAN

It is difficult to write about personality disorders as objective diagnostic entities, as they are so often defined by the prevailing social and political norms in which they are developed. More so than with perhaps any of the other diagnostic categories we have covered in this book, the personality disorders reflect the prevailing culture's norms about adaptive and acceptable behaviors. They are constructions of the "truths" about "appropriate" levels of functioning that are subjective in nature. Concepts of *dependency* and *emotionality*, for example, are not quantifiable in the same way hallucinations or heart palpitations may be. Who decides what represents excessive emotionality? Who judges when behavior becomes too dependent? Throughout this book, we suggest that the social, gender, and cultural beliefs of those who diagnose pathology determine if, how, and when traits are deemed maladaptive. We do believe that the rigidity and pervasiveness of certain character traits may lead to impairment of functioning in people's lives. We simply caution that as clinicians we must remain aware of the assumptions and possible biases inherent in these diagnoses.

In this chapter we consider the other personality disorders: paranoid, schizoid, schizotypal, antisocial, dependent, avoidant, and obsessive. The names of these disorders are based on groupings of character traits that are maladaptive, but these traits can in fact represent wonderful strengths and interesting complexities in people. The eccentric woman may write beautiful poetry that derives in part from her idiosyncratic view of the world; the dramatic actor may give heart to his character portrayals despite superficial relationships with others. The traits themselves should not be equated with pathology; it is their prevalence and clustering that can lead to problems in functioning. Let us look, then, at the remaining personality disorders.

PARANOID PERSONALITY DISORDER

An office worker diligently locks up all his belongings and makes secret notations to himself that no one can decipher because he believes that his colleagues are scrutinizing his actions. A student distances herself from her peers at school because she believes that they are talking about her each time she walks through the halls. A woman refuses to eat because she believes that the C.I.A. is poisoning her food. To varying degrees, each of these people suffers from a paranoia that leaves them isolated, scared, and in emotional pain. When the paranoia reflects a *pervasive and inflexible style* of thinking, feeling, and relating to others that is suspicious, secretive, guarded, and mistrustful, we consider someone to have a paranoid personality disorder. People with this disorder tend to interpret actions of others as being intentionally threatening or demeaning, even if there is clear evidence to contradict their fears. Expecting to feel betrayed or harmed by others, they seek hidden meanings in people's comments and behaviors to confirm their worldviews (Shapiro 1965). Imagine, for a moment, the experience of an author who suffers from a paranoid personality disorder. She repeatedly sends her very fine work to editors for publication, but each time the editors suggest revisions, she believes they are part of a conspiracy to discredit her. She notes, "You are all out to destroy me and my work. You want to take my ideas as your own, and ruin me in the process." In her world, others set out to cause her harm, and all actions are interpreted in that context. The tragedy is that this disorder robs her of the opportunity she so desperately seeks—to have her words in print.

People with paranoid personality disorders often lead lonely lives. They tend to have few close relationships because of their hypervigilance, their constant questioning of the trustworthiness of friends and family, their general lack of humor, their rigidly held moralistic stances, and their tendency to misinterpret information in an accusatory fashion. Friendships are difficult to maintain; a (mis)perceived deceitful act by a previously trusted friend can be enough to destroy the whole relationship with the thought, "I knew it. I shouldn't have trusted her; she was always out to get me." Romantic interests may be constricted. Often harboring underlying anxieties about their sexual prowess, people with this disorder may avoid sexual intimacy despite having intense erotic fantasies (Cameron 1963).

The judgment of people with paranoid personality disorders is impaired, although their perceptions may be keen and accurate. Their attention to details that support their personal beliefs clouds their ability to see the "big picture." They may develop elaborate ideas about how authority figures plan to humiliate them, and then contemplate ways to challenge them or seek revenge. This dynamic is apparent in the following illustration of a man who was referred to a counseling center by his supervisor after being fired from his job:

John is a bright but rigid man who, like many people with a paranoid personality disorder, works in a job that requires little human contact and alteration of routine. He constantly feels that his bosses perceive themselves as superior to him. He seeks out every perceived slight to confirm this belief, and hoards information to prove his greater level of competence. John can report the details of every exchange with his boss and the numbers on every invoice; he cannot recognize, however, that his hoarding of information necessary for the running of the company and his refusal to collaborate with colleagues due to his suspiciousness are what led to his dismissal.

When John was fired he initially plotted strategies to "get back" at his superiors, then had a brief psychotic episode from which he recompensated. Years after his dismissal, John continues to harbor paranoid thoughts about how he was wronged that mask his pain from humiliation and disappointment.

Psychodynamic Factors

How might we understand John's problems in psychodynamic terms? Freud (1911) postulated that sexual impulses, particularly the repudiation of latent homosexuality, lay at the root of this disorder, although subsequent drive and object relations theorists have focused more on the role of aggression and disturbed early relationships in its genesis. Melanie Klein (1946) saw paranoia as developmentally normative during an infant's first six months of life, when intolerable inborn aggression threatens to overwhelm the ego. An infant's aggression is managed by being projected onto others, and then defended against with denial, splitting, and primitive ideation. The infant, and later the adult "stuck" in this position, protects himself from the aggression and persecutory anxiety by using these same defensive operations. Hence, aggression in the self is denied; the person experiences himself as "good" while he projects the "bad" onto others and uses primitive idealization to satisfy fantasies of unlimited gratification from others (Akhtar 1992).

A paranoid personality disorder may also develop from disturbances in early object relations. These relational difficulties may take the form of actual cruelty, betrayal, and violation of basic trust by the caregivers (Cameron 1963, Erikson 1950). A child may yearn for emotional supplies from a caregiver who is perceived as powerful yet persecutory, someone able to humiliate, shame, and control the child. Feeling unloved, inferior, and envious of others, he may become rageful and hypervigilant about possible future deceptions. Rather than experience the "bad" (e.g., the envy, inadequacy, and rage) within himself, he splits off and projects these qualities onto others. He also denies his own dependency needs and wish to hurt people by attributing them to others. A thought, for example, such as "I envy you and want to harm you" is experienced as intolerable, so it is transformed into the more acceptable perception— albeit painful—that others are dangerous and potentially harmful to him. He maintains the illusion of control while his inner world is filled with sadistic self and object representations.

Many of the ego functions of people with paranoid personality disorders are impaired. These are people whose judgment and reality testing are poor, as evidenced by their distorted perceptions and problematic decision making based on these perceptions. Their defenses are primitive and inflexible, with a heavy reliance on denial, projection, splitting, and externalization. On the other hand, their memory and intelligence are usually intact, and, in fact, may assist them with rich details that then support their paranoid fantasies. Their cognitive styles are generally rigid and constricted, compromising their ability to understand the context in which facts unfold. Their superego functioning is usually harsh and poorly integrated, leading to the formation of uncompromising and critical standards and judgments.

Given their suspiciousness and distrust, people with paranoid personality disorders rarely seek mental health services voluntarily. Establishing a therapeutic relationship can be complicated, because they are apt to mistrust the therapist's motives and intentions. They may question the therapist's truthfulness, demand to read everything written in their medical records, refuse to sign a release of information that might help coordinate their care, and accuse the therapist of saying things she never said. The common mistake in working with paranoid people is to attempt to change or correct their perceptions rather than to empathize with their pain. Challenging their perceptions initially may only confirm for them that the clinician is out to get them or has something to hide. Over time, once a therapeutic alliance has been established, clinicians may help clients "own" their feelings, thoughts, and impulses, so that they learn to bear—as part of themselves—the anger, envy, and violence that they have projected onto others.

When working with paranoid people, therapists often worry about the client's potential for violence. Several things should be kept in mind. People suffering from paranoia need space—both literally and figuratively—in order to feel in control and not vulnerable to attack. In therapy, these clients may feel humiliated and inferior, and perceive the therapist as a threat to their safety. When a therapist opens a desk drawer to retrieve a pen or stands up precipitously, for example, they may respond violently in order to ward off an *anticipated* attack. Clinicians must therefore be clear and straightforward, explain what they are doing and help the client "save face" in order to avoid a rupture in treatment or the outbreak of violence (Gabbard 1990). While understanding the source of their clients' fear and remaining calm, direct, and respectful, they may be able to forge a meaningful connection with these individuals.

SCHIZOTYPAL PERSONALITY DISORDER

Many clinicians are understandably confused about the diagnosis of a schizotypal personality disorder, as it has characteristics of both a schizoid personality disorder and of schizophrenia. The concept originated from an understanding of these two disorders, and in some ways acts as a bridge between them. British object relations theorists used the term *schizoid* to describe both a normative developmental position and a form of adult psychopathology. The term captured a way to understand traits of withdrawal, an odd style of communication, a vivid internal life, and a shyness coupled with a hunger for affection. With these traits so delineated and their etiology understood psychodynamically, the concept of schizoid personality disorder became less and less related to schizophrenia (Akhtar 1992). On the other hand, the term *schizophrenia* accounted for an illness with outwardly psychotic features, and not for a *style of interacting* with others characterized by odd, eccentric, and unusual perceptions, affects, and behaviors. The schizotypal personality disorder thus evolved as a way to capture aspects of both schizoid personality disorder and of schizophrenia. If we understand the use of this diagnosis along a continuum, we can see that people with this disorder may be considered closer to the schizoid end of the spectrum if they have odd thoughts and behaviors, and may be considered closer to the schizophrenic end of the spectrum if they have brief psychotic episodes.

What, then, gives this diagnosis its own standing among the personality disorders? A unique constellation of traits characterize people with schizotypal personality disorders. These traits include oddities in thought, behavior, speech, and appearance, as well as significant impairment in interpersonal relationships. The oddities manifest themselves in subtle but pervasive ways. A person may express herself with vague language and diffuse ideas that sound perpetually on the fringes of what is comprehensible to others. The listener may initially think that he is following the discussion, only to realize that there is little logic or reason to what was just said.

This disturbance in thought may emerge in ideas of reference and magical beliefs such as "I have the power to read other people's minds" or "I can create masterpieces." Perceptions and affects can appear inappropriate to content. A woman with this disorder, for example, may laugh when she feels that the room is closing in on her. Her appearance and behavior may also seem bizarre; she may wear oddly matched clothing and have unusual mannerisms, and inadvertently draw attention to herself. Although these disturbances are similar to those seen in schizophrenia, they are milder and less pronounced than in this related disorder. Most importantly, the *reality testing* of people with this disorder is relatively more intact than in people with schizophrenia.

Given their preoccupation with unsettling internal thoughts and feelings, and their disquieting relationship to the world around them, we can understand how disconnected and uncomfortable people with schizotypal personality disorder may feel in the presence of others. Like people with schizoid personality disorders, people with this disorder are usually guarded and isolated, with few friends or confidants. They may have rich fantasy lives that are full of grandiose exploits and imagined relationships, but in reality live on the periphery of life. This pattern, along with many of the traits we have discussed, are evident in the following example:

> Doris is an African-American woman admitted to an inpatient psychiatric unit when she had "visions" that her deceased relatives were cheering her on at a dance recital. In these visions, she was the featured ballerina who received the accolades of the vast crowds who came to see her perform. When these visions—which she knew to be unreal—subsided, she presented as an odd, waif-like woman who avoided eye contact and conversation with staff and patients. She walked the unit floor in ill-matched clothing, moving her arms in graceful gestures and at times talking to herself. She spoke in seemingly poetic phrases that were difficult to comprehend; when she became more trusting of staff, she discussed her unusual beliefs about the universe and her significant powers of influence in it. Her mind was full of grandiose ideas about her dance prowess and about the suitors in her life despite her virtually isolated existence. Although she had no full thought disorder, her manner of relating to others was both distancing and odd, a pattern that her family reported was typical of her long-term functioning.

Doris's fantasy life is filled with people and her real life is devoid of significant contact with others. She has some schizophrenic-like symptoms in a personality structure that has schizoid features, combining in what we call a schizotypal personality disorder.

How do we understand the etiology of this disorder? In psychodynamic terms, the roots of this illness are most likely similar to those found in people with schizoid personality disorders (Akhtar 1992). The significant difference, however, is that people with schizotypal personality disorders may have a genetic predisposition to having a thought disorder. Treatment may therefore include individual psychotherapy as well as medication in order to address the symptoms of the thought disorder.

AVOIDANT PERSONALITY DISORDER

Claire stepped into the restaurant as the hostess walked by. When the hostess glanced at her, she left the restaurant before the hostess reappeared.

This avoidance—this staying away from, or shunning of people and situations—is characteristic of the way people with avoidant personality disorder relate to the world. Due to their fears about being rejected or humiliated, they avoid relationships and social and occupational situations that involve significant interpersonal contact. Unlike most people who experience discomfort in new situations, they are *inordinately* sensitive to judgment and feel shattered by the slightest hint of disapproval. Comments and looks are often misinterpreted as critical, so they avoid contact with others unless they can be assured of unconditional acceptance. If Claire responded in most situations as she had in the restaurant, we might assess her as having an avoidant personality disorder.

The pain people with this disorder feel is a quiet one. Attention is rarely drawn to them as they are more observers of, than participants in, the world around them. They often have few friends and shy away from situations in which they will have to speak up in any way. Despite their social withdrawal, however, they actually long for closeness in relationships. They want to be connected to others, but are consumed by self-doubt and fear of being embarrassed. Unlike people with schizotypical personality disorders, they do not appear as odd or eccentric, but as timid, shy, and isolated. Suffering silently, they live on the periphery of situations and relationships in which they yearn to play a part.

How do we understand the dynamics of people with avoidant personality disorder? Before addressing psychodynamic factors, we must first look at biological factors—particularly at the role of inborn temperament. Some people are simply born with a tendency toward shyness that is usually identified at a very young age (Kagan et al. 1988). How often have we heard parents describe one child as seemingly extroverted and confident and another child as shy and reticent from birth? Shyness per se, however, does not lead in a linear fashion to the development of an avoidant personality disorder; psychological and environmental factors contribute to its genesis. In psychodynamic terms, tendencies toward avoidant behaviors may develop out of children's repeated experiences of being shamed and humiliated for efforts at mastery of tasks at different developmental stages. The experience of being raised in an unencouraging home climate, coupled with few demonstrations of love and pride in the child by the parents, have been found in people with this disorder (Arbel and Stravynski 1991). A shy child who is *repeatedly* criticized by parents when she is interacting with others, or is ignored by teachers in class, may withdraw from interpersonal activities. This avoidance may become a way to defend against being seen as an inadequate or incompetent individual. The following cycle may then develop: the child is sensitive to being exposed, she experiences comments by others as embarrassing and shaming, people may respond to her with hesitation and/or disapproval, she then avoids new situations to protect herself. When this pattern continues into adulthood, it results in avoidant personality traits, like in the following case:

> Alisha, 38 years old and living with her sister, has worked at the same unsatisfying job for 12 years because she is afraid to go on a job interview and talk to new people. She describes herself as having been a shy child, who never spoke in class and who hid the notices from school about extracurricular activities so that she would not be made to attend them. As an adult, she lives a structured and routinized existence. Her only social activity is an aerobics class that she has faithfully attended for five years. She avoids talking to class members, however, because she assumes that they are critical of how clumsy, overweight, and weird she seems to be. Although she has

many dreams about what she would like to be doing with her life, she feels paralyzed to act; she fears picking up the phone and asking for an application for school or for a job, certain that the person on the other end of the receiver will confirm her image of herself as incompetent. Alisha often has ideas about how to better her work environment but she does not raise them, feeling that if others have not brought them up they are not worth discussing.

Psychotherapy can be a helpful tool for people with this disorder. It can offer an experience in which clients' fears are explored and gradually understood, and new behaviors are tested out and encouraged. The problem is that, by definition, people who struggle with this disorder tend to avoid relationships. Those who ultimately find the courage to come for treatment usually do so only when the pain from their isolation becomes greater than the pain caused by their fear. Clinicians need to appreciate how vulnerable, exposed, and easily embarrassed these clients may feel. In treatment, these clients will be exquisitely attuned to any hint of disapproval or rejection, in response to which they may flee. Supportive interventions and behavioral approaches, which encourage clients to deal directly with what they most fear and dread, will ideally precede interpretations so that clients will not be overwhelmed with anxiety and fear. In confronting what they most want to avoid, they may have the chance to experience longed-for connections to others and to engage more comfortably in the potential richness of their lives.

DEPENDENT PERSONALITY DISORDER

As noted in the introduction to this section, the concept of a dependent personality disorder is among the most troublesome to define because of the cultural relativity and gender bias of the term *dependency*. Women are frequently labeled "dependent" in an American society that has arbitrarily deemed independence and autonomy preferable traits to hold. In many cultures (e.g., Native American, Asian, Latino), the traits associated with interdependence are valued as most healthy.

In what instance would we consider dependency, a trait shared for better and for worse by all of us, enough of an impairment to be classified as a disorder? People suffer from dependent personality disorders when they are virtually unable to function on their own without the constant reassurance, supportive caregiving, and decision making of others. Their relationships tend to be passive and submissive. Often they look to others to tell them what to think and do, how to spend their time and money, and whom to befriend. They may have inordinate difficulty initiating projects on their own due to a lack of self-confidence and a pervasive feeling of helplessness. They may cling to other people by subordinating their thoughts and needs in relationships and by avoiding confrontation at all costs.

We can see these traits in the following case:

> Daniel was a 56-year-old man who had been in treatment at a community mental health center for many years. As a child Daniel spent most of his time at his mother's side, doing chores around the house and finding reasons not to be left alone. Teachers in class knew him to be a quiet boy who followed the lead of others and who seemed to volunteer for tasks that no one else wanted in order to be considered part of the gang. Daniel went into his father's business but never excelled, and married his sister's friend, a woman who managed all aspects of their lives. Dreading time on his own, he clung to others although he never initiated plans. Friends complained that he tagged along and seemed to expect them to make arrangements for all social and professional activities. Daniel was invariably surprised that people found him burdensome, denying that there was any underlying anger in his neediness. He sought therapy when his wife became ill, and he found himself crying all the time, unable to function.

What leads people like Daniel to develop a pervasive pattern of dependent and needy behavior? Daniel reported receiving subtle and covert messages from his parents that his independence and autonomy were dangerous, and that his close ties to home were the only way to win their affection and love. His parents seemed both overprotective and intrusive, and discouraged his developing competences that would have led him to separate. For example, they did not let him play sports lest he get hurt; they rarely invited a child to play with him lest he get tired. His anger about these "messages" was not expressed directly; rather it was channeled into a pattern of neediness and incessant demands on other people's time. These kinds of messages alone do not lead to a dependent personality disorder. With few studies available to explain its etiology, we would hypothesize that constitutional vulnerabilities, dynamic issues, and familial and societal expectations and pressures lead to the problematic functioning associated with this disorder.

Like Daniel, clients who are needy and dependent will often look to the therapist to offer advice and to fix the problem, thereby replicating the very problematic dynamic that brought them to treatment. The therapist must stay focused on clear goals, address the impact of the clients' passivity on their life dreams, explore whatever underlying anger and fears of abandonment there may be, and help clients establish a sense of trust in their own competence and self-worth. If clear goals are not set, these clients may remain in treatment, often at community clinics, indefinitely.

SCHIZOID PERSONALITY DISORDER

Sally comes into the therapist's office and sits in a corner of the couch, as far away from the therapist as the furniture arrangement will allow. She faces away, toward the wall, and usually speaks very little and very quietly. When she does talk, most of the content is about work and her plans for more education. What she says is very factual, concrete, and seemingly devoid of emotion. Sally has been doing this for years, yet she considers her therapy to be a success. If asked she would say that the therapist is the one person in the world she is close to, and it would be true.

Sally suffers with a schizoid personality disorder. Like most people with this disorder she is socially withdrawn and unrelated and has a restricted range of emotional experience and expression. Showing little longing for connection with others, people who are schizoid may appear detached, asexual, and indifferent. They tend to become involved in solitary activities in both their professional and leisure pursuits, and seek jobs in which they can avoid human contact. The night watchman, the librarian who only wants to be involved with books, and the mathematician whose life is exclusively absorbed with numbers may all have schizoid traits. The sole interpersonal relationships they may have are with one or two close relatives or friends with whom they feel safe, and who can lovingly perceive them as loners.

In manifestations of the illness, people who appear to be quite social, active, and even outgoing may have internal lives characterized by detachment, coolness, and distance. Winnicott (1956) spoke of this problem as that of the "false self" and Deutsch (1965b) described it as the "as-if personality."

Like people with the other personality disorders, it is important to remember that traits result in an actual personality disorder only when they are *so* intense and pervasive that they lead to identifiable dysfunction. There are schizoid traits and moments in all of us. The full-blown personality disorder can only be diagnosed when the schizoid way of being is so rigid and fixed that it permeates the entire structure of the person suffering from this condition.

Sally rarely spoke about matters of the heart, but when she did it was with a deep longing to have a husband and a family of her own someday. She expressed grave doubts that she would ever be able to achieve this goal because she "probably would never feel safe enough with anyone." How do we understand her dynamics?

Psychodynamic Factors

Dynamically, a person with a schizoid personality disorder may seem aloof, self-sufficient, isolated, even cold. But this is not the arrogant aloofness of a narcissistic person who needs to feel superior in order to combat feelings of inferiority. Rather, the coldness is based on too great a hunger for internal and external objects—a hunger so great that paradoxically the very possibility of closeness itself becomes overwhelming. In the schizoid condition, love is desperately yearned for, yet if it is there, it is unbearable. Therefore, someone like Sally must maintain distance and detachment.

Just as it is difficult to accept the Kleinian notion about the depressive position—that there is sadness and loss in seeing the self and others as whole—so too it is hard to understand that people can be so frightened and needy that they cannot bear love when it *is* there. It is much easier to think of a needy person suffering because care and love are *not* available to them. Terror when love is present confronts us with a much thornier and more complex human dilemma.

In *Tell Me How Long The Train's Been Gone*, James Baldwin (1968) describes Leo, a man who, despite being in a long-term relationship, has kept the schizoid part of himself hidden all his life. When he becomes so ill that death is near, he makes a huge effort to confront being loved, and opens the door to his fear-filled internal world a crack.

> We had known each other for many years; starved together, worked together, loved each other, suffered each other, made love; and yet the most tremendous consummation of our love was occurring now, as she patiently, in love and in terror, held my hand. . . .
> "My dearest Leo. Please be still."
> And she's right, I thought. There is nothing more to be said. All we can do now is just hold on. That was why she held my hand. I recognized this as love—recognized it very quietly and, for the first time, without fear. My life, that desperately treacherous labyrinth, seemed for a moment to be opening out behind me; a light seemed to fall where there had been no light before. . . . Everyone wishes to be loved, but, in the event, nearly no one can bear it. Everyone desires love but also finds impossible to believe that he deserves it. However great the private disasters to which love may lead, love itself is strikingly and mysteriously impersonal; it is a reality which is not altered by anything one does. Therefore, one does many things, turns the key in the lock over and over again, hoping to be locked out. Once locked out, one will never again be forced to encounter in the eyes of a stranger, oneself, who is loved. And yet—one would prefer, after all, not to be locked out. One would prefer, merely, that the key unlocked a less stunningly unusual door. [p. 8]

The British object relations theorist Harry Guntrip (1968) was especially interested in schizoid phenomena. He speculated that when too much loss or pain are experienced in the course of a given life, a regressed, young, frightened part of the self must be hidden from the world and kept secret to the self. He called this the "lost heart of the self." He described, how when neediness remains disavowed and unknown, some people become needier and more desperate while at the same time feeling completely frozen inside.

As a therapist, Guntrip worked with many patients who had completed courses of therapy dealing with conflicts over their sexual, aggressive, and oedipal issues. Their lives often appeared successful yet they did not feel well. Often they presented dreams of tiny, almost petrified babies found in filing cabinets or buried in the woods. They evoked great empathy and yet, in a seeming contradiction, these were the very same patients who insisted on the most distance and caution in their treatments. Guntrip began to understand that he was being asked to deal with one of the most tragic consequences of childhood deprivation and pain—the person who needs too much. This is often the same person who must reject help and closeness when it is forthcoming. Guntrip termed the phenomenon "love made hungry." It is actually a love so hungry that love itself must be pushed away when it is there because the person feels as though any shreds of selfhood and autonomy that have been achieved would be swept away in surrender.

Other British object relations theorists have written about the schizoid condition. Their dynamic understanding of the problem is also based on a deficit model of psychopathology rather than on the conflict model. A deficit model posits that problems arise in psychological development when there are inadequacies in early caregiving. It is an intensely relational paradigm that pays attention to hurt, deprivation, and yearning that occur early in relationships. Klein (1946) wrote about the paranoid-schizoid position as an early infantile time characterized by splitting. In those moments in which the infant (and later the adult) cannot integrate the loving and hating aspects of the self or of others, the internal world is experienced as fragmented and frightening. Fairbairn (1944) described what occurs when optimal contact with the caregiver is overly frustrated. One part of the self remains needy and starving and can feel like a bottomless pit. The other part of the self may identify with the depriving caregiver and hate the self for being so vulnerable and greedy. The schizoid person who may appear withdrawn and uninterested may hide a deep wish for symbiotic union. Balint (1979) coined the term *basic fault* to describe the same state of deadness and emptiness that can ensue when an infant cannot take in enough love and care from the environment, or when the environment does not offer it.

Treatment of people with schizoid personality requires a delicate balance between closeness and distance. Whereas other patients may soak up attention, support, and mirroring, and grow strong, schizoid people cannot tolerate more than tiny doses of closeness. Silence, distance, and a certain respectful formality often need to be part of the treatment so that clients can begin to believe that affection and caring can be safe and will not necessarily sweep away their autonomy and separateness.

Sally, whom we described at the beginning of this chapter, eventually found the courage to join a singles activity and support group at the local Y. When several members were extolling the virtues of warmth and closeness and criticizing Sally for her aloofness, she was able to hold her own and speak about how closeness was difficult for her. She compared her psychic landscape to planet Earth and said, "Just as there is beauty in lush forests and fertile valleys, so too there can be incredible beauty in the vast, seemingly dead and barren deserts where in fact all kinds of tiny animals and flowers grow." By the end of her speech several group members were in tears. Sally had taught them a powerful lesson about the schizoid condition.

OBSESSIVE-COMPULSIVE PERSONALITY DISORDER

People with an obsessive-compulsive personality disorder have difficulty with feeling. Often their attention is on what they think; often they are wedded to their ideas and their achievements, and to the rules, laws, and rituals that bind their feelings. We all know people with obsessive traits: attention to detail, intense concentration, and an ability to isolate feelings. In fact, these traits contribute to our own work successes and achievements. Accountants, technicians, and computer programmers all rely on their obsessive styles to work effectively. But while these traits can be highly adaptive, especially in a culture that values individual achievement, people with obsessive-compulsive *personality disorders* suffer from *enduring* character problems that tend to be difficult for others to work or live with. Others experience them as rigid, as overly attentive to details, as losing the forest for the trees, as bogged down in indecision, as controlling, and as lacking in spontaneity. Interpersonally, people with obsessive-compulsive personality disorders don't always "get it"; they seem unable to experience the feeling tones in their relationships and instead become derailed by trying to find the logic in any interpersonal situation. In their work, as in their relationships, they often rely on facts to anchor them. People with obsessive personality disorders have difficulty making decisions and taking risks; they may seem inflexible because they avoid situations that are undefined.

People with this personality disorder are guided by "shoulds" rather than by their desires. They tend to be inflexible and, given free time, will engage in detailed projects, impose harsh programs, and/or exercise or diet compulsively. These are people who may be unyielding in their expectations of themselves and are equally so in their expectations of others. Because they often try to be perfect, they expect the same from those around them.

> Donald, a 46-year-old psychiatrist, complains, "I feel as if I'm dying inside." He runs an inpatient unit, is married, and is the father of two children. He is in the office at six A.M. daily, completing his paperwork and seeing patients. He works, without evident pleasure, twelve hours a day, seven days a week. When holidays or vacations come, he undertakes reroofing his house, putting on an addition, or driving long distances to work on his mother-in-law's house. He is joyless in his job, and continually strives to "get my numbers up" by seeing more and more patients. He is chronically concerned that his boss doesn't think he is doing enough; at the same time, he is fairly oblivious to the fact that other people who work with him resent his workaholic ways. He expects his staff to behave as he does; when they do not comply, he feels that they are defying him, and becomes punitive, invoking rules and rewards in elaborate systems to require that they work up to his high standards. He expresses the same kind of disappointment in his children and experiences their less than perfect achievements as indifference toward him. With them too, he resolves to toughen up with new rules and regulations.

Freud wrote that the pleasure principle governs psychic life. But for Donald, as for most people with this personality disorder, it is almost as if they are governed by the opposite: by principles of unpleasure. What makes for this evident lack of pleasure?

Psychodynamic Formulations

Drive theorists would understand Donald as fixated at the anal stage of development. Accordingly, he might still have unresolved concerns about controlling himself or being overly controlled by others. He might experience considerable shame but mask it by maintaining control. Struggling with a fear of insufficient internal controls, people with obsessive personalities often harbor unexpressed angry wishes: to mess, to smear, to defecate, and so on. But these angry feelings conflict with their harsh and often primitive consciences. The effect is that they may use the defense of reaction formation to deal with their unacceptable impulses. They may try to be perfect, precise, neat, organized, and overly controlled as reaction formation against their wishes to be messy, angry, and dirty. They may also isolate their feelings because they fear that feeling them will make them feel helpless or overwhelmed. They may "do" and "undo" as a way to discharge in action their own anal ambivalence.

> When Max makes a date with his colleagues or friends, for example, he needs to reschedule the time and place a number of times as a way of mastering his anxiety about closeness. Doing one thing, on the one hand, and then its opposite on the other, helps him manage feeling his feelings of exposure and of humiliation. The outcome is that other people around Max often feel manipulated by him.

Because people with obsessive-compulsive personality disorder tend to be concerned about being dominated or controlled, in practice they may struggle with the therapist over power and control. They may debate when to meet or how much a session should cost, or may do and undo scheduled times. They may struggle over committing themselves to the treatment relationship, overcome by ambivalence about intimacy in relationships. These are people who are conscious of feeling easily taken advantage of, and who may even appear paranoid in treatment because they are so anxious that others will exploit or control them.

From a self psychological perspective, people with obsessive-compulsive personality disorder may suffer from difficulties in self-esteem regulation. Underlying their needs to be perfect, omnipotent, or omniscient are difficulties in their early experiences of grandiosity.

Often others have not helped them create realistic self-expectations. Often they feel weak, frail, depleted. They may choose a partner as a selfobject whose warmth, spontaneity, effervescence, and charm will make up for missing parts of themselves. But given their difficulties with self-esteem regulation, they can become disappointed, angry, devaluing, and critical of the partner upon whom they depend.

Sitting with these clients can be trying. Often therapists want to interrupt the client because they feel so dominated and controlled by the client's exacting precision. Usually therapists need to tolerate their ambivalence and even anger toward the client, and find some way to experience warmth, humor, and connection (Berzoff 1981) if the client is ever to do the same.

The diagnosis of an obsessive-compulsive personality disorder also captures stereotypical male gender roles in Western culture. Men more than women, for example, are expected to be achieving and exacting; men are socially sanctioned to dominate and control others. Men more than women are expected to keep tight control over their emotional lives.

ANTISOCIAL PERSONALITY DISORDER

Enrico is a 35-year-old Italian "hit man" for a local gang who comes referred to his community mental health center because his wife has threatened to leave him. He has been having an affair with another woman, and presents his dilemma in a smooth, charming style; this, however, is not what he defines as the problem. What *is* problematic is that his wife has found out about the affair, and that is unacceptable in his culture and among his peers. Men are expected to have affairs, but to shield their wives from the knowledge of them. He says he wants advice from the therapist on how to better cover up this one (of many) liaisons. Within four sessions, as he describes his illegal activities (including murder), he comes up with a cover-up plan that will restore equilibrium to his home life. Enrico then sends illegal firecrackers to his therapist as a thank you present.

Enrico has an antisocial personality disorder. He has committed a number of criminal offenses including murder, about which he feels little guilt, remorse, or anxiety. He relies on others in the environment to control his behaviors, and seems to have little internal motivation to govern himself. His attachments to others are shallow, and he engages in indiscriminate sexual liaisons. In his brief treatment, he brags of his antisocial acts. If he has hurt others, it is not remorse he experiences, but the need to act differently so that he will not be caught again. It is others who suffer from his actions, not he.

> Sherrie is a vivacious, bright, appealing, and talkative 23-year-old who comes to treatment because her employers have threatened to fire her if she does not seek help. Currently, she works as a nanny for a family with two children.
>
> In her current relationships and in her work, she borrows money and does not return it. She shoplifts and gives as gifts what she has taken. She lies to her employers about where she is with their children, and has been caught taking the children shoplifting, and driving them while she is drinking. She has written bad checks and tells her therapist that she recently stole a thousand dollars from the family for whom she works. As she talks about her antisocial acts, she has complicated and elaborate rationalizations for why her actions are justifiable. These make her therapist feel angry, although Sherrie does not feel angry herself.
>
> Sherrie's family of origin includes her father, a prison guard, who was physically and verbally abusive. Sherrie remembers many incidents of family violence, including being thrown down two flights of stairs. There was financial insecurity as well because her father would drink away his salary. Often the family scraped by without sufficient food, electricity, or telephone. In her early adolescence, Sherrie stopped attending school, ran away from home on several occasions, engaged in fights with peers, and was caught shoplifting.
>
> Her therapist has little conviction that they will accomplish much therapeutic work together, since Sherrie began the treatment saying that she "uses people." In fact, the therapist recently noticed that after three months of treatment, Sherrie has paid nothing toward her clinic bill. When confronted, Sherrie looks hurt and replies that she had handed her therapist a check a few weeks ago. She suggests that the therapist should look for it again.

The therapist now worries that she perhaps has accused Sherrie unfairly.

What antisocial behaviors do we see in Sherrie's personality that are similar to Enrico's? First, Sherrie breaks rules and laws while experiencing only superficial remorse. She tends to manipulate others and is irresponsible and unreliable at her work. She acts deceitfully and impulsively, and disregards the safety of the children she cares for. In fact, she has difficulty taking care of anyone, including herself. When caught in a lie, she denies and rationalizes her behaviors. She evokes anger and anxiety in the therapist, while she appears to feel neither of those feelings herself. She also has a substance abuse problem, as do many people with antisocial personality disorder. In fact, many people with this disorder will often report committing a crime because they drank when, in fact, both the addiction and the antisocial personality disorder are primary diagnoses.

Psychodynamic Factors

What are the dynamic issues that exist within the inner lives of people with antisocial personalities? People with this disorder have often identified with their abusive and neglectful parental figures. They may have developed senses of self based on the internalization of others who have been both aggressive and powerful. Their caregivers may have been sociopathic adults, and so they may have needed to deny, project, and act out their aggression without help to modify it. Often they identify with other models who wield power through antisocial activity or violence. Without taking in the moral authority or prohibitions of valued others, people with antisocial personalities may be left with primitive, harsh, and immature consciences. Often, because they cannot manage their intrapsychic conflicts internally, they unconsciously create conflicts between themselves and their environments. From this perspective, people with antisocial personality disorder may commit crimes to ensure that punishments (and controls) will be imposed on them by the outside world.

Many of their ego functions are also impaired. Acting out, denial, projection, and splitting are defenses used to help protect against their fears of feeling too much—too needy, too helpless, or too sad. Vaillant (1975) suggests that people with antisocial personality disorder have learned to defend against their longings for love from others by becoming angry rather than depressed. These are people who have difficulty experiencing depression, and are like bereaved children who, in the face of irreparable loss, may try to relieve their emptiness, helplessness, or experiences of deprivation by acting out and gaining power over others. They may try to dominate and even hurt others to try to restore their damaged self-esteem (Person 1986).

> Angie is a very bright middle-class 14-year-old girl who came to treatment because she is chronically truant, steals from other children, and seems to experience no guilt about it. She comes from a rigid and disturbed family. Her father is alcoholic and her mother is alternately excessively needy and rejecting. When she talks back to her mother, she is punished by being locked in her room until she has filled a hundred page book with promises never to talk back again. She is often called a whore by her father, dating back to when she became interested in boys. Once, after a fight with her mother, she ran away by jumping from her second-floor window. While walking aimlessly through her neighborhood, she came across a child playing on a large rock. She casually knocked the child over, and despite his obvious hurt, walked away. In treatment, she makes no conscious connection between her own sense of bereftness, her anger, and hurting a child weaker than she.

People who develop this personality disorder are often raised in homes in which the caregivers have had difficulty tolerating anxiety and tension themselves. Anxiety is projected onto others rather than experienced as residing within the self. Often these are people who feel little remorse because they do not experience anxiety, nor do they perceive others as separate individuals who have their own feelings, needs, and desires.

Winnicott (1956) offers a somewhat more positive way of conceptualizing antisocial behaviors by seeing these hurtful and malevolent actions as expressions of hope. In his view, the person with an antisocial personality disorder, like the infant, tries again and again to get his environment to respond to him in ways that it has not in the past. As long as a person with an antisocial personality disorder acts out, Winnicott suggests, he still maintains some connection and hope that his environment will respond.

Biological Influences

There is increasing evidence that biological and genetic factors play a role in the development of this disorder. Many adults with antisocial behaviors have, as children, had attention deficit disorders with hyperactivity that have gone undiagnosed. When they could not conform to limits at home and in their schools, their "soft" neurological signs were not detected nor properly treated.

Genetic factors may also be relevant. In a study of 524 children in a child guidance clinic, for example, Robins (1966) found that having had a sociopathic or alcoholic father was a powerful predictor for developing an antisocial personality disorder in adult life, whether or not the sociopathic child was actually raised by that parent.

Sociocultural Influences

Over the years, people who show patterns of irresponsible and antisocial behaviors have had different labels assigned to them. The terms *psychopath* and *sociopath* have been used inconsistently and interchangeably. It is estimated that 75 percent of people incarcerated in prisons have the diagnosis of antisocial personality disorder although only 50 percent of people with antisocial personality disorder actually commit violent crimes. There are also gender differences in people diagnosed with antisocial personalities: 3 percent of American men and 1 percent of American women carry this diagnosis (Vaillant and Perry 1985). Why should this be so? Perhaps one explanation is that men in American society have been socialized to act out their aggression, while women have been socialized to internalize their aggressive feelings and become depressed. Perhaps the uneven ratio is a result of constitutional differences between the sexes. Perhaps it reflects a bias in diagnosis where women with similar problems are diagnosed as histrionic or borderline.

As with many of the personality disorders, the antisocial personality disorder is as much a *social* diagnosis as a *psychological* one. Antisocial people often experience themselves as helpless in relation to their social environments. They often come from backgrounds of severe poverty, physical and emotional deprivation, abuse, and neglect. Their caregivers are frequently alcohol or drug dependent, unable to provide consistent care, and may be people who also have antisocial tendencies. Their lack of healthy attachments is compounded by experiences of neglect, deprivation, and aggression outside the family.

Our culture itself is saturated with images of violence—on the news, at the movies, on the streets. A recent Carnegie report (Chira 1994) gives us some chilling statistics about the environment in which many of our children are growing up.

> Reports of child abuse are rising with one in every three abused children being a baby less than a year old. Many children spend most of each week in such poor child care that it threatens to harm their development. American children are among the least likely in the world to be immunized. And an increasing number of very young children grow up witnessing stabbings, shootings and beatings as everyday events.
>
> The United States ranks near the bottom of the industrialized nations in offering such services as universal health care, subsidized child care, and leaves for families with children under age three.
>
> . . . Policies and practices around raising children contradict what we also now know: that the early years are critical in the development of the human brain. Hence, millions of infants and toddlers are so deprived of medical care, loving supervision and intellectual stimulation that their growth into healthy and responsible adults is threatened. [pp. A1, 3]

While social conditions alone do not produce people with antisocial personality disorder, it is worth wondering whether antisocial behaviors might be adaptive responses to abnormal and pathological social environments (Kernberg 1989). These behaviors are often associated with gangs, the formation of which often serves to create a sense of belonging and family for many children who feel abandoned and defenseless in the world. Challenging societal rules or engaging in antisocietal actions may be an adaptive reaction to the oppressive, discriminatory norms with which they grew up. While not condoning the behaviors of people who violate the rights of others, we suggest that the context in which these behaviors unfold must be understood. Unfortunately, many of our society's responses to the tragically undermining social conditions are to *punish* and not *treat* people with antisocial traits by warehousing them in ever increasing numbers in the juvenile justice system or, when they become adolescents and adults, the penal system.

Therapeutic Issues

When we work with people with antisocial personality disorders, we need to recognize not only the client's anger but also his or her emptiness. Just as we do not punish a bereaved child, we should not *only* punish the bereaved, but acting-out, adult. These clients challenge us to find ways to be empathic, to be consistent, to be confrontative but supportive. A part of the therapeutic work must be in helping the client become conscious of his or her feelings, anger, and anxiety that have heretofore been unbearable. It is important, then, to help the client distinguish between angry thoughts and angry actions. If feelings can be thought about, rather than acted on, more control can be exerted over them. It is also important that the therapist set clear limits, and be prepared to confront the antisocial person when the therapist is being manipulated. Sherrie's therapist, for example, let three months pass before confronting her, probably because Sherrie evoked such anger in her therapist that she simply avoided dealing with her. Taking the path of least resistance, however, usually just leads to reenactments of neglect (Gabbard 1990) and to repetitions of acting out. Given that the most important therapeutic task is to help the client experience feelings without acting them out, both the therapist and client need to create an environment that will be stable and that cannot be corrupted (Vaillant 1975).

As noted earlier, people with antisocial personality disorders rarely seek treatment voluntarily, and are more often referred by the courts, schools, or youth service programs. Inpatient settings can be constructive environments for these clients, as the structure of the institution may decrease the acting-out behavior and make it harder for patients to run from their feelings. On the other hand, these clients often disrupt the milieu, by breaking rules, devaluing treatment, or manipulating other staff and patients, reaffirming the need for consistent, nonnegotiable limits and rules. Antisocial clients often benefit by working in groups. Self-help groups can be especially effective, because peers who have struggled with the same issues will not be as easily manipulated as therapists who have not. Groups members in recovery can also provide different kinds of models and different kinds of ego ideals. Being accepted by "recovering peers" can be very important in restoring a damaged sense of self.

CONCLUSION

Many of the people with personality disorders we have described in this chapter are challenging to treat. Often their problems are not experienced by the clients as their problems but as someone else's problem. Often the anxiety associated with the problem is too difficult to bear and is instead acted out. Often the clients' behaviors are fixed and rigid, with little flexibility or insight for change. Often therapists experience many of the clients' feelings of helplessness, anger, coldness, longing, dependency, neediness, hunger, or rage while the clients do not experience the same feelings within themselves. Often these are difficult-to-reach clients whose emotional and social environments have been so impoverished that their character pathology may be their most adaptive way of dealing with overwhelming losses and assaults.

The clients' core conflicts and patterns of interacting will almost inevitably be reenacted in the therapy. Unless therapists can tolerate, understand, empathize, and interpret the clients' underlying fears of closeness and loss of control, hunger for relatedness, depression, and helplessness, the clients may continue to act out rather than internally bear their pain.

References

Akhtar, S. (1992). *Broken Structures: Severe Personality Disorders and Their Treatment*. Northvale, NJ: Jason Aronson.
American Psychiatric Association. (1994). *Diagnostic and Statistical Manual of Mental Disorders*, 4th ed. Washington, DC: American Psychiatric Association.
Arbel, N., and Stravynski, A. (1991). A retrospective study of separation in the development of adult avoidant personality disorder. *Acta Psychiatrica Scandinavica* 83(3):174–178.

Baldwin, J. (1968). *Tell Me How Long the Train's Been Gone.* New York: Dial.

Balint, M. (1979). *The Basic Fault: Therapeutic Aspects of Regression.* New York: Brunner/Mazel.

Berzoff, J. (1981). Treatment of the obsessive personality. (Book review.) *Smith College Studies in Social Work* 51:2.

Cadoret, R. J. (1986). Epidemiology of antisocial personality disorder. In *Unmasking the Psychopath: Antisocial and Related Syndromes*, ed. W. H. Reid, D. Dorr, J. I. Walker, et al., pp. 28–44. New York: Norton.

Cameron, N. (1963). *Personality Development and Psychopathology.* Boston: Houghton Mifflin.

Chira, S. (1994). Study confirms some fears on U.S. children. *The New York Times*, April 12, pp. A1, 3.

Chodoff, P., and Lyons, M. (1958). Hysteria, the hysterical personality and "hysterical conversion." *American Journal of Psychiatry* 114:734–740.

Cloniger, C., Sigvardson, S., von Knorring, A. L., et al. (1984). An adoption study of somatoform disorders, II: identification of two discrete somatoform disorders. *Archives of General Psychiatry* 41:863–871.

Deutsch, H. (1965a). *Neuroses and Character Types.* New York: International Universities Press.

——— (1965b). *Some Forms of Emotional Disturbances and Their Relationship to Schizophrenia.* New York: International Universities Press.

Easser, B. R., and Lesser, S. R. (1965). Hysterical personality: a reevaluation. *Psychoanalytic Quarterly* 34:389–405.

Erikson, E. H. (1950). Growth and crises of the healthy personality. In *Identity and the Life Cycle*, pp. 50–100. New York: International Universities Press, 1959.

Fairbairn, W. R. D. (1944). Endopsychic structures considered in terms of object relationships. *International Journal of Psycho-Analysis* 25(1/2).

Freud, S. (1911). Psychoanalytic notes on an autobiographical account of a case of paranoia. *Standard Edition* 12:1–82.

Gabbard, G. (1990). *Psychodynamic Psychiatry in Clinical Practice.* Washington, DC: American Psychiatric Press.

Gabbard, G. O., and Coyne, L. (1987). Predictors of response of antisocial patients to hospital treatment. *Hospital and Community Psychiatry* 38:1118–1185.

Guntrip, H. (1968). *Schizoid Phenomena, Object Relations and the Self.* London: Hogarth.

Horowitz, M. J. (1991). Core traits of hysterical or histrionic personality disorders. In *Hysterical Personality Style and the Histrionic Personality Disorder*, pp. 3–17. Northvale, NJ: Jason Aronson.

Joffee, R. T., Swinson, R. P., and Regan, J. J. (1988). Personality features of obsessive compulsive personality disorder. *American Psychiatric Press* 145:1127–1129.

Kagan, J., Reznick, J. S., and Snidman, N. (1988). Biological bases of childhood shyness. *Science* 240:167–171.

Kernberg, O. (1989). The narcissistic personality disorder and the differential diagnosis of antisocial behavior. *Psychiatric Clinics of North America* 12:553–570.

Klein, M. (1946). Notes on some schizoid mechanisms. In *Envy and Gratitude and Other Works, 1946–1963*, pp. 1–24. New York: Free Press.

Kline, D. F., and Davis, J. M. (1969). *Diagnosis and Drug Treatment of Psychiatric Disorder.* Baltimore: Waverly.

Lilienfeld, S., Van Valkenburg, C., Larntz, D., et al. (1986). The relationship of histrionic personality disorder to antisocial personality somatization disorders. *American Journal of Psychiatry* 143:718–722.

Person, E. (1986). Manipulativeness in entrepreneurs and psychopaths. In *Unmasking the Psychopath: Antisocial and Related Syndromes*, pp. 256–273. New York: Norton.

Reid, W. H., Dorr, D., Walker, J., et al., eds. (1986). *Unmasking the Psychopath: Antisocial Personality and Related Syndromes*, pp. 256–273. New York: Norton.

Robins, L. N. (1966). *Deviant Children Grow Up. A Sociological and Psychoanalytic Study of Sociopathic Personality.* Baltimore, MD: Williams & Wilkins.

Salzman, L. (1968). *The Obsessive Personality: Origins, Dynamics and Therapy.* New York: Science House.

——— (1980). *Treatment of the Obsessive Personality.* New York: Jason Aronson.

Shapiro, D. (1965). *Neurotic Styles.* New York: Basic Books.

Vaillant, G. (1975). Sociopathy as a human process: a viewpoint. *Archives of General Psychiatry* 32:178–183.

Vaillant, G., and Perry, C. (1985). Personality disorders. In *A Comprehensive Textbook of Psychiatry*, ed. H. Kaplan and B. Sadock. Baltimore: Williams & Wilkins.

Winnicott, D. W. (1956). The antisocial tendency. In *Collected Papers: Through Paediatrics to Psychoanalysis*, pp. 306–315. London: Tavistock.

——— (1960). *Ego Distortion In Terms of True and False Self.* London: Hogarth.

——— (1965). *The Maturational Processes and Facilitating Environment.* London: Hogarth.

Zetzel, E. (1970). Therapeutic alliance in the analysis of hysteria. In *Incapacity for Emotional Growth*, pp. 182–197. London: Hogarth.

14

Biopsychosocial Aspects of Depression

JOAN BERZOFF AND MICHAEL HAYES

Depression is probably the first diagnostic category we have encountered about which it is safe to say that every one of us knows what it is. Depression refers not just to a syndrome, with all of its technical definitions, but also to an affective state we have each experienced: a state of sadness, depletion, deflation, emptiness, hopelessness, boredom. And yet because we often start from the position that everyone knows what depression is, we can too easily minimize its potentially debilitating impact and its complexity.

Affective disorders are disorders of mood. When we speak of moods we are speaking of a range of everyday feelings from sadness to joy, anger to acceptance, despair to elation. Moods refer to prolonged emotions that color our psychic lives. Affect, on the other hand, refers to the feeling tone or emotional state at a given moment, and to its outward manifestations. A person's mood, for example, may be sad while her affect is blunted. We may fail an examination and experience a mood of utter hopelessness as if we are stupid and uneducable; or we may get an A on that exam and experience ourselves as exceptional, brilliant, and promising. These states and tempers are not simply transient but can become psychologically, socially, and biologically fixed as psychological disorders. As with several of the other disorders we have studied, mood disorders are complicated precisely because they clearly derive from an interaction between psychological, social, and biological sources. Two major troublesome affects that people experience are anxiety and depression. This chapter focuses on the depressive mood disorders.

In all of its forms, depression is considered the most widespread emotional disorder in the world, afflicting 2 to 3 percent of the world's population, or 100 million people; 10 to 15 percent of Americans are estimated to have moderate to severe depression, with perhaps half of the reported 30,000 suicides a year in this country attributable to those with major depressive disorders.

Mood disorders occur in people of all ages, and from all social classes. No one is immune from them. Some mood disorders are reactive in origin, that is, they are precipitated by an external event such as the actual loss of a person, of work, or of an object of significance. Likewise, an individual may react to a normally positive event—childbirth, promotion, graduation—with depression, because any of these joyous occasions may present a loss to that person.

Loss, however, is not the precipitating factor in all cases of depression. Mood disorders may be endogenous in origin, that is, there may be no obvious external event precipitating the shift in mood. There are some biological causes for these disorders that are genetic, hormonal, and/or biochemical in origin. Intrapsychic factors and life cycle issues play a role in mood disorders. A life-cycle issue that may precipitate depression for some women is having three young children below the age of 6 in the home (Brown 1991, Brown et al. 1989). Another life-cycle predictor is found in older single, widowed men, living alone, who have a physical illness. Such men are most at risk for depression and suicide. Among the elderly, depression occurs equally in both men and women.

Gender plays a role in affective disorders. Women are two to three times more likely to be diagnosed as suffering from depression than men. Social class also plays a significant part in affective disorders. Poor and working class women are most at risk for depression. In fact, people in the lowest socioeconomic classes have a two-times greater risk of being diagnosed with a major depression than those in the middle and upper-middle classes. The risks for depression among the poor may actually be even greater than reported, since poor and working-class people are often overly diagnosed as schizophrenic without adequate clinical justification (Weissman and Klerman 1977).

In this chapter, we first discuss the experience of depression. Next we draw upon psychodynamic theories to help us understand some of the internal psychological dynamics of these disorders. From biology, we consider the influence of genetic, biochemical, and endocrine factors. Social factors that contribute to depression are also explored. The order of these factors in no way represents a hierarchy of any one cause over another. We also examine the experience and manifestations of depression at three different developmental levels. Finally we describe ways in which the mood disorders affect not only the client, but also the therapist.

THE EXPERIENCE OF DEPRESSION

How do we draw the line between ordinary human suffering with all of its sadness, ennui, and pessimism, and clinical depression? The term *depression* is used in many ways. In its wider usage, it often refers to a "lowering," for example, of an economy or of barometric pressure. In a person, it often refers to lowered self-esteem and decreased functioning in a variety of manifestations. To help us understand the symptoms of depression, it is instructive to turn to people who have themselves been clinically depressed. In their own voices, they provide access to what are perhaps universal experiences of depression.

William Styron (1990), for example, who has written many novels and an autobiography, found himself at a loss for words to describe his own severe depression at age 60. He writes:

> Depression is a disorder of mood, so mysteriously painful and elusive in the way it becomes known to the self as to being very close to being beyond description.
>
> For myself, the pain is most closely connected to drowning or suffocation, but even these images are off the mark. . . . [It is] as if my brain has to endure its familiar siege: panic and dislocation, and a sense that my thought processes [are] being engulfed by a toxic and

impassable tide that obliterate[s] any enjoyable response to the larger world. . . . Instead of pleasure, [it is] a sensation close to indescribably different pain. Rational thought [is] absent. [Instead it is replaced by] helpless stupor in which cognition [is] replaced by positive and active anguish.

One of the most unendurable aspects [is] the inability to sleep. The ferocious inwardness of the pain produce[s] an immense distraction that prevent[s] my articulating words beyond a hoarse murmur. I sense myself turning wall eyed, monosyllabic.

The pain of severe depression is quite unimaginable to those who have not suffered it and it kills in many instances because its anguish can no longer be borne. [p. 7]

In this passage, Styron describes depressive symptoms. He feels inward, flat, monochromatic. He feels panicked, anguished, and suffers from a sleep disorder that slows him down and leaves him feeling fatigued. He feels helpless and lacks the capacity for pleasure. He considers suicide and is aware that not only his feeling but also his thinking are disordered by his mood. His despair envelops his world in what he later describes as a "visible darkness."

Poet and novelist Sylvia Plath (1971) similarly describes the depression she experienced at age 18. She had left home for the first time and had begun a glamorous job on a women's magazine. While she imagined herself to be the envy of adolescent girls everywhere, it felt to her as if

I wasn't steering anything, not even myself. I bumped from work to parties and parties to my hotel like a numb trolley bus. . . . I should have been excited . . . but I couldn't get myself to react. I felt very still and very empty the way the eye of a tornado must feel moving dully along in the middle of the surrounding hullabaloo. [p. 3]

Like Styron, she was flat and dulled as she moved within what should have been an exciting world. Later in her life she would elaborate on the dullness she felt when confronted with pleasure, including the metaphoric brightness of poppies (Plath 1962):

Little poppies, little hell flames
Do you do no harm
You flicker. I cannot touch you.

I put my hands among the flames. Nothing burns.
And it exhausts me to watch you
Flickering like that, wrinkly and
clear red, like the skin of a mouth.
A mouth just bloodied
Like bloody skirts
There are fumes I cannot touch
Where are your opiates, your nauseous capsules
If I could bleed or sleep!
If my mouth could marry a hurt like that!
Or your liquors seep to mine this glass capsule
Dulling and stilling
but colorless. Colorless [p. 203]

Here again we encounter the torpor of depression. As with many depressed people, Plath is irritable and angry at feeling so removed from her feelings and experience. Plath is enveloped by a darkness that is colorless but black. Later she writes:

I shall move into a long blackness.
I see myself as a shadow, neither man nor woman.
Neither a woman, happy to be like a man, nor a man
Blunt and flat enough to feel no lack. I feel a lack.
I hold my fingers up, ten white pickets.
See, the darkness is leaking from the cracks.
I cannot contain it. I cannot contain my life. [p. 182]

Like Styron, she is also unable to "contain" her inner life. It is as if the visible darkness, once outside of her, now inhabits her inner world.

Shakespeare's Hamlet also experiences the losses of pleasure and meaning that characterize depression. Hamlet cries out:

I have of late . . . lost all my mirth, foregone all custom of exercises, and indeed it goes so heavily with my disposition that this goodly frame, the earth seems to me a sterile promontory. This most excellent canopy the air, look you, this brave o'erhanging firmament . . . why, it appears no other thing to me than a foul and pestilent congregation of vapors. What a piece of work is a man! How noble in reason! How infinite in faculty! In form and moving how express and admirable! In action how like an angel! In apprehension how like a god! The beauty of the world! The paragon of animals! And yet, to me, what is this quintessence of dust? Man delights not me—no, nor woman neither . . .

In Hamlet we once again encounter the flatness, loss of humor, futility, and pessimism that are signs of a depressed mood. Hamlet is angry—both at himself and at his world, which now seems foul and pestilent. His external world seems depopulated and sterile, and devoid of appeal. People are not only absent but are no longer experienced as valuable. Indeed, what is interesting here is not only that people and events *outside* of Hamlet are devalued, but also that Hamlet includes *himself* among those most devalued. It is not surprising when he says to Polonius "You cannot, sir, take from me anything that I will more willingly part withal—except my life, except my life." Like Plath and Styron, Hamlet experiences his life as a burden to be willingly surrendered. Like Styron and Plath, he is suicidal.

What all three authors have described are the very markers of depression. Each reader, no doubt, has felt these feelings to varying degrees at some time or other and each of us has struggled to override them and regain our zest for life.

SYMPTOMS OF DEPRESSION

What then are the symptoms of depression? Each of these authors has noticed what we refer to as vegetative symptoms: changes in sleep, appetite, weight, libido. Each has vividly described fatigue or even pain. Styron and Plath experienced a slowing down, or what we call psychomotor retardation. Often in agitated depressions or in mania we see the opposite: a state of speeding up or of agitation. Hamlet spoke of his poverty of ideas, and accompanying this, of his own lowered sense of worth. Each author described a prolonged sad mood. Each had difficulty with concentration and indecisiveness.

In fact there can be so many symptoms and combinations of symptoms associated with depression that they become bewildering to the clinician, threatening to make the concept too inclusive. To achieve some useful clarity about depression, we usually focus on three altered mood states described by the aforementioned authors. In Styron, we find a loss of interest (apathy); in Plath, a loss of energy (asthenia); in Shakespeare's Hamlet, a loss of pleasure (anhedonia). None of these states alone, however, constitutes clinical depression. To make the diagnosis of depression at least two of these states must always be present (Sadock and Kaplan 1985).

What is happening psychologically when people experience such symptoms? Our knowledge of drive, ego, object relations, and self psychological theories helps us understand the internal world and workings of the depressive experience.

DRIVE THEORY

Let us begin with drive theory, one of the most important paradigms because it provides a framework for conceptualizing the dynamics of depression. Freud, in his famous "Mourning and Melancholia" (1916), proposes that we understand depression by first looking at normal grief. He describes grief as a normal reaction to the loss of a loved person. When someone we love dies, we feel sad, empty, bereft. All we have left of the person are the images and memories we retain of that person (as we described in Chapter 6). We "hypercathect" their memories: we remember a favorite song, how the person laughed, the ways it felt to be with him or her, the places that were shared. Eventually the energies that are tied up in thoughts of the lost person become freed up to help us form new attachments. When a relationship with a loved person is disrupted forever, memories of that person are cathected as if they were the person him or herself. We turn away from the world to do this work of mourning, and every culture has its customs to honor the process and to make the reality of death or loss official.

Where does this process lead? Freud suggests that when we mourn we do two things: we gradually withdraw feelings from the lost person, and we ultimately reinvest in a world of new people. The process of bringing memories to consciousness and of reexperiencing anew the pain of the loss leads to coming to terms with reality. We are now, to quote Loewald (1980), "sadder but wiser," and with that, become open to new relationships. But Freud also suggests that we never fully give up the lost loved one. We "hold on" to that lost person by becoming like that person in some of the ways that we function. For example, some attitude, behavior, or characteristic of that person (or that which we experienced in our relationship with the person) becomes part of our internal repertoire. Hence Freud presents the view that mourning is a developmental step, not an end point.

Melancholia or abnormal depression share many of the same characteristics as mourning. One feels dejection, loss of interest, and inhibition of activity; but one also feels a new state: a disturbance in self-regard. Often this is expressed in angry, reproachful, self-blaming statements. Melancholia may occur not only in the instance of an actual death of a loved one, but also, Freud adds, when one feels slighted, disappointed, or abandoned by another. When a person is emotionally injured, the object relationship may become shattered. The depressed person, without energy to form new attachments, withdraws into him- or herself and becomes self-blaming.

Freud noticed that the clinically depressed person's self-reproaches almost always turn out to "fit someone else the patient loves" and has "lost." He hypothesized that the person's self-criticism is actually anger at the lost loved one turned against the self. Recall that the bereaved person relates to a part of the self (namely, the memories and representations of the loved one), as she did to the loved one. Freud suggests two things: (1) that the depressed person is more negative or hateful (as well as loving) toward the lost object than she knows, and (2) that the loved one is too essential to the maintenance of the self to be given up through grieving. So the relationship with the deceased is continued internally by experiencing the loss of the loved one as self-depletion, while hate toward the loved one is experienced as self-hate and criticism. Whereas in mourning, it is the external world that has become impoverished and empty, in depression it is the internal world that becomes poor and empty. Freud (1917) writes, "And so the shadow of the object falls upon the ego" (p. 249).

Barbara, a 20-year-old Latina undergraduate, referred herself to a loss group at her college counseling center, having lost her father through death. Her father had died three years before of a long and protracted leukemia. Barbara was beset by crying fits, lack of appetite, lack of interest in school, social withdrawal, weight loss, and self-hatred.

"I'm a jerk," she said at intake. "I ought to be over this thing by now. But I feel so miserable. I just can't relate to anyone or anything. I'm so angry at myself. I don't like who I am and in fact my boyfriend doesn't either. He's broken up with me. I feel worthless and stupid. No one is taking care of me."

Barbara's parents had divorced when she was 3, and she had been raised alone by her mother. Her father had remarried and made a significant amount of money. He lived in the same town, and in his second marriage had three new children to whom he seemed devoted. He offered neither financial nor emotional support to Barbara or her mother, nor did he even recognize their existence. When Barbara was 8 she made an appointment to see him at his office. When he discovered it was she, he denied being her biological father. She saw him rarely after that, but still felt connected to him, especially after he became a successful public political figure. She was not aware of feeling angry at him or particularly humiliated by his rejection of her. However, in the course of treatment it became apparent that his death made his loss final and irreconcilable.

What Barbara had lost was not really a father but rather her hopes and expectations of having a father. Her fantasied object relationship was shattered, and so she had difficulty mourning the father she never really had, a more complicated process than simple mourning. Her current solution, to live life by not needing anyone, does not work either. She has said, "I need to learn to need nothing. I'm trying to stay separate from people; that way I won't be hurt or disappointed. But I'm stupid to feel this way." Barbara's anger and disappointment at the loss of a fantasied father, never mourned, has now been turned against herself in recriminations about her own dependency on others.

EGO PSYCHOLOGY

Ego psychology offers a different but complementary theory for understanding depression. We learned in Chapter 4 how anxiety may serve as a signal to take action to protect oneself from danger. So, too, depression can also serve as a signal—to do the work of mourning that we have seen is a necessary part of growth. In this sense, depression is not necessarily pathological. This is why psychodynamic theorists so stoutly resist the idea that all depressive affects—sadness, bereftness, helplessness—are useless afflictions to be removed or avoided in whatever way possible. In fact, the capacity to bear depression—to live with grief, sadness, and hurt—is one of the greatest and most useful ego strengths (Zetzel 1965a).

Edward Bibring (1968), an ego psychologist, proposed an alternative explanation for depression that extended and modified Freud's original views. He noticed that in everyday life, the death or loss of a loved one is not the most frequent trigger for depression. Rather, depression is precipitated most frequently by a state of felt helplessness. This state results from "a conflict within the ego" between the universal aspirations to be worthy, loved, and strong, and the ego's experience (judgment) that it cannot achieve those aspirations. Bibring reconceptualized depression as a state, not deriving from aggressive drives, but rather from a conflict between one's ideals and one's perceived inability to achieve them. The loss of self esteem that is central to depression is not only the consequence of depression but in fact is often the cause.

> Daniel is a 54-year-old, successful, well-published scholar and professor of Native American studies. Each time he begins a new writing project, however, he reports feeling overwhelmed at the prospect of condensing so much material into something coherent. He finds himself at a loss for words; he berates himself for how inarticulate he is. He feels deeply and with utter conviction that he doesn't know, and never did know, his content area. He reports feeling low, depleted, lacking energy. He feels helpless, and imagines reproaches from colleagues as he harangues himself for his perceived inadequacy.

Daniel suffers from the kind of low self-esteem that most of us have experienced. Although his depressive symptoms are mild and transient, his sense of helplessness is central to his depressive experience.

An ego psychologist, then, would formulate Daniel's difficulty in terms of his felt helplessness. Helplessness involves some negative judgment or negative assessment of one's ability to effect needed change. With helplessness comes self-reproach, and an expectation of similar reproaches from others. These are the essential elements that Bibring identified in the experience of depression. One can easily see how these elements can trigger a repetitive, self-reinforcing downward spiral of felt helplessness, inaction, loss of self-esteem, and self-reproach. If the ego cannot reestablish a reasonable sense of self-esteem, the experiences of unhappiness and self-reproach increase and lead to a greater senses of helplessness. Often clinical depression results. How do we escape such spirals in everyday life? Daniel reports that factors such as the pressure of deadlines (external interpersonal connections), the memory of his past competencies, and the use of some of the energy from self-reproach to "get angry" and "cut the task down to size" and thus to rebut internal criticism, help mobilize him to get on with his work.

An interesting footnote is provided by Saari (1989), who notes that Bibring uses himself as a core example of his theory. Bibring developed his theory of depression when faced with his own helplessness over the diagnosis of terminal cancer. He was able to make his (presumably painful) experience the subject of observation and thereby gain mastery over his depression by contributing intellectually to the field. Bibring wrote that depression in the form of lowered self-esteem is relieved by anything that reverses these conditions of helplessness.

At this point, we have presented two complementary theories of depression. From drive theory, we have suggested that depression results from an identification with the lost object who cannot be mourned. Because the ambivalence toward the lost other is unconscious, an identification is made with the ambivalently held other, and angry feelings toward the other are introjected into and turned against the self. This results in a depressed state. From ego psychology comes the idea that depression involves a discrepancy between one's ideals and aspirations and one's perception of one's capabilities and worthiness. The result is helplessness, lowered self-esteem, and self-reproach.

OBJECT RELATIONS THEORY

An object relations view of depression had already been anticipated by Freud's emphasis on the centrality of object loss to depression. In object relations terms, a melancholic person cannot mourn successfully because she cannot sustain an emotionally useful, enduring object representation in the absence of the lost loved one. Perhaps the key contribution of object relations theory is its elaboration of the development of such internal object representations and of the relationship of that development to depression. Object relations theories address two important aspects of this relationship: one focuses on the developmental level of representations at the time loss occurs, and the other considers the effect of losses at different stages of development.

Recall that object relations theorists depict relationships with others as the organizers of internal experience and functioning from the very first moments of life. Relationships form the structure of psychic functioning. We have seen that central to many object relations theories (Jacobson 1964, Kernberg 1966, Klein 1940, Mahler and McDevitt 1980) is the idea that representations of others (literally, the mental re-representation of the absent person) undergo a developmental progression from the infant's fleeting, poorly differentiated (between self and other) images to the adult's enduring, well-differentiated, multifaceted representations. Obviously, the actual loss of a needed loved one, whether due to death, physical absence, or emotional unavailability, might produce very different depressive reactions depending on the developmental stages of the representation of that loved one in the person experiencing the loss.

Early object relations theorists Spitz and Wolf (1946) and Bowlby (1958) studied the reactions of infants and toddlers to prolonged separation from their mothers to whom they had become attached. Both noted that in the absence of another dependable caregiver with whom to become involved, these infants became distressed, disorganized, profoundly sad, and finally detached, apathetic, and retarded—almost a prototype of the symptoms we have seen in depressed adults. Some infants even died. Spitz and Wolf called such depression "anaclitic." Such depression occurs at the stage when the representations of the lost loved one can only be sustained by the almost constant actual visual and physical presence of that person. Loss of the actual person at this stage of object representations functioning produces intense feelings of emptiness, painful aloneness, helplessness, and equally intense cravings for immediate contact with and love for the lost person. Spitz and Wolf and later theorists (Blatt 1974) note that such depressive experiences are not unique to infants but are seen in persons of any age whose internal world of object representations has not gained a measure of constancy. Such depressions will be marked by intense feelings of helplessness, abandonment, and emptiness, with less guilt and lower self-esteem than in other forms of depression. Indeed, it often seems to the person suffering depression at this level that there is no "self" without the lost other.

Marc was a 28-year-old married man of Italian-American descent with a history of substance abuse (alcohol and marijuana) and of psychiatric hospitalization for "nervous breakdowns," in which he experienced himself as unable to function at all. He referred himself for individual therapy, despite a stated "hate [for] all shrinks," about a year after the death of his father. Suddenly, about 11 months after his father's death, Marc began having symptoms including sudden uncontrollable weeping ("For no reason, I just feel so empty and alone") and intense fear of going to work alone. Marc reported that if his wife or mother accompanied him to his place of business "I can work just fine." Marc had been in business with his father whom he described as "the most unhappy, bitter, critical guy anyone who met him ever knew—not just me." He described working with his father as "me doing all the work while my father stood around criticizing [me]." Marc was mystified that now, so many months after his father's death, he could not do the work he had always done "unless someone [a loved one] is there so I know it's all right." When he was alone, Marc felt "like I forget everything, I don't know anything—I'm not sure I can even remember my name."

An object relations approach to understanding Marc's depression would focus on his difficulty maintaining an object representation of his father that could sustain him in his father's absence. He feels not the presence of the angry, critical father he has known but no presence at all. He feels empty, depleted of all energy and content, almost as though (in his words) "I don't really exist." Marc is experiencing depression with clear anaclitic features. An object relations theorist would note that he seeks relief from this depression by trying to establish a new relationship with a physically and emotionally available, but "hated" person, the therapist. This was exactly the description Marc gave of his relationship to his father before the latter's death. It is as though Marc is trying to reconstitute a relationship without which he feels he cannot survive.

As a child develops beyond infancy, his or her object representations become more enduring than and better differentiated from representations of self. We have seen that object relations theorists picture these newly independent and more stable object representations as first being organized (or "split") along the emotional lines of how the person feels toward the object. Thus representations associated with pleasurable interactions with the object ("good object" representations) may be kept separate from representations of frustrating interactions ("bad object" representations). Later, the child is able to integrate these representations into a more realistic image of the object in which the same loved one both pleases and frustrates. This consolidation, as we have seen, is called object constancy by object relations theorists, or is referred to as the achievement of the "depressive position" by Klein (1940). Both theorists consider it to be a major developmental advance. It is an advance that involves in itself some depression, as Klein's term suggests. Forever after this developmental step, the individual lives in a more complicated, sadder but wiser representational world in which the object, and also the self, are both good and bad, loving and hating, pleasurable and painful. The capacity to bear this developmental step has impact on the individual's lifetime "capacity to bear depression" (Zetzel 1965a) and makes possible the uncomplicated but painful mourning Freud described as normal.

Object relations theorists suggest that when a person whose self representations are unintegrated suffers object loss, she may feel depletion, object hunger, guilt, self-reproach, and lowered self-esteem (Blatt 1974, Jacobson 1964). Here Freud's observations about turning hatred of the lost person against the self remain pertinent. From an object relations point of view, object representations are less stable and sustaining in the absence of the "good" (rewarding) object when there are unstable internal representations. An "anaclitic depression" may follow. In an anaclitic depression, the loss of the actual loved one results in the frustrating object becoming internalized as part of the self. Now it is the self that is "bad." This leads to the harsh self-criticism and guilt noted by Freud.

Object relations theorists have concerned themselves not only with a developmental understanding of depression at the time it becomes a problem, but also with the study of how losses affect representational development. They note that the kinds of losses that occur—*when* they occur, and *how often* they occur—play crucial roles in development. Infant and child studies are beginning to document specific relationships between object experiences and later representational development, and depressive symptoms.

Bowlby (1958) has suggested that different kinds of losses predispose people to different kinds of depression. Bowlby was among the first to note that when faced with prolonged separations, children seem to go through three phases: protest, despair, and detachment. His studies of children separated from their mothers revealed that when a caregiver is emotionally or physically absent for significant periods of time, a child will first try to bring back the lost object. If the child cannot mobilize the caregiver's attention or bring her back, the child may become more disorganized. The child may protest, and ultimately may despair. Finally, if over time the child has been unable to reengage the caregiver or a substitute, she may detach entirely, leading to a kind of hopelessness and turning away from the object world.

Tronick and Granino (1988) have captured this phenomenon in detail on videotape with healthy mothers and their children under experimental conditions. Well-functioning mother–infant dyads were filmed in the process of mutually cueing one another. In one scene, a mother is expressively engaging her child through smiling, laughing, and so forth. In the next scene, her face becomes blank. In response, the child first tries to reinitiate the "dialogue." The mother's face remains blank. When that fails, the infant cries and fusses. When there is still no response, the child's protest becomes louder and the child's behavior becomes more disorganized. Finally, we see the infant look away, no longer interested in bringing or attempting to bring her mother back.

For children with severely depressed mothers, or children who have suffered profound early losses, the experience of withdrawal is not simply an isolated event. When this pattern recurs again and again, depression emerges as a reaction to the accretion of millions of these tiny events. For children who are separated from their mothers for prolonged periods of time, or children who have chronically unresponsive caregivers, a depressive hopelessness and disengagement is frequently the outcome.

Studies of older abused toddlers and preschoolers reveal that extremes of maltreatment interfere with the development of a representational internal world that can represent emotional states of self and other, pleasurable interactions between self and other, and a stable, positive sense of the other in fact or in her absence (Cicchetti 1989). Follow-up studies suggest, as object relations theory would predict, that such children are at greatly heightened risk of depressive symptoms by adolescence (Cicchetti 1989). Such extreme cases provide powerful evidence of the object relations view that later relationships are constructed by earlier relational experiences.

SELF PSYCHOLOGY

Self psychologists conceptualize affective disorders as a result of empathic failures. Recall that every individual needs to have someone strong to mirror and with whom to merge for the achievement of her vigor, grandiosity, and healthy self-esteem. Parents, teachers, coaches, extended kin, and siblings in a child's interpersonal world can serve these selfobject functions. They can affirm the child and respond to the child's needs with empathy, acceptance, and admiration. When this occurs, the child has the building blocks for mature self-esteem, and for the pursuit of realistic ambitions and goals. But when mirroring fails, the child may treat herself poorly—establishing unrealistic ideals, treating herself recklessly, attending neither to danger nor to limits, or being unable to mobilize self-care. How early and how radically these selfobject experiences are missing affects how intact and cohesive the self will be and how vulnerable it will be to depressive reactions to loss.

> Liza, the oldest of six children in an Italian-American family that was both emotionally impoverished and financially drained, described herself as always exhausted as a child and as underachieving in school. She grew up in a family in which she felt that there was "no one home." She felt neither noticed, nor special, nor talented in any way. She spent much of her childhood on the couch, simply too tired to move. It seemed to her that no one noticed her existence nor had any sense of who she was. As a consequence, neither did she.
> Now, as a 40-year-old adult, she lies on the couch much of every day, unable to mobilize, watching TV, and waiting for her husband to come home and make her dinner. She describes feeling like an irritable baby who simply cannot soothe herself. Noth-

ing seems to engage her interest; she looks around her house and is overwhelmed by all the half-finished projects that require her energy. She lacks the sense that she can accomplish anything.

A self psychologist would posit that Liza grew up without sufficient selfobjects to mirror her and help her develop healthy goals and ambitions. Her lack of affirmation from others and the absence of strong adults with whom to merge contributed to her sense of herself as depleted, empty, and like a big baby.

Unlike the drive theorist who might see her depression as her anger at her unmet needs now turned against herself, a self psychologist would understand her anger as an appropriate by-product of unmet selfbject needs. Her inability to soothe or activate herself might be seen to stem from a developmental failure to attain the capacity for activity, given a lack of transmuting internalizations of available and empathic selfobjects.

The differences in the four theoretical perspectives are not simply academic. They lead to different kinds of clinical interventions and choices. A drive theorist for example might help a depressed client get in touch with her anger. An ego psychologist might attend to the client's superego ideals and to the client's helplessness that results from their being excessive or unrealistic. An object relations theorist might attend to early losses and the consequent lack of integration of self and others. A self psychologist might become a new selfobject to the client, offering strength, affirmation, mirroring. There is no one formulation for depression, nor is there one treatment. Instead there are multiple dynamics and multiple approaches for treating depression from a dynamic perspective. As with all of these disorders, choices are made based upon the uniqueness of each individual client.

BIOLOGICAL FACTORS

There are many biological factors to be considered in the etiology and treatment of depression. Genetics, hormones, biochemistry, and temperament may play significant roles in a person's predisposition to the triggering and prolonging of depressive states. Let us consider each of these factors separately.

Genetics

Next to stressful life events, genetics is the second largest risk factor predicting depression. In particular, bipolar illness (formerly called manic depression) clearly has a genetic basis. In one study, 31 percent of the children whose biological parents had bipolar disorders were also diagnosed as having a bipolar disorder, as opposed to only 2 percent of the children whose biological parents were normal. In another study, if one parent had a mood disorder, the lifetime risk to the offspring of having a mood disorder (N = 614) was found to be 27 percent. If two parents had mood disorders, the offspring (N = 28) faced an enormous risk (75 percent) of developing the disorder (Gershon et al. 1982).

The mode of transmission of depression remains uncertain, but it does not follow classic patterns. Several studies have cited similarities between blood types in families that manifest these disorders. Researchers are also seeking to isolate other genetic transmitted traits, such as light sensitivity, which may characterize families with mood disorders. While many research groups actively continue to try to find and isolate the gene predominately responsible for depression, none has currently achieved this. It is important in taking a family history that we ask not only about the history of mood disorders, but also about the history of alcoholism and gambling in the family. These two addictions often mask bipolar illness, and may be genetically transmitted, or cluster with depression. Clinicians clearly should always take a family history of affective illness.

Hormonal Theories

Hormonal theories also contribute to our understanding of depression. Female hormones may play a role in the finding that depression is two to three times more likely to be diagnosed in women than in men. Women's menstrual cycles and menopause may have subclinical effects on their moods, and may result in irritability, sadness, or hopelessness. Likewise, postpartum depressions (which often signal an underlying bipolar affective disorder) and ordinary postpartum blues appear to be related to hormonal changes. No single hormone, like progesterone, has been identified as the causative agent for depression. Rather it seems that multiple hormones may work in concert in predisposition to depression. Also, it is clear that we should not limit our thinking to sex hormones, as many of the hypothalamic and pituitary hormones are also likely to affect emotions. Agents like prednisone and adrenocortico-tropic hormone (ACTH) (administered for cancer, inflammatory reactions, etc.), are commonly found to cause mood disturbances. Naturally occurring opioid-like substances, called endorphins, may be increased by exercise, and are postulated to play a role both in decreasing depression and in contributing to more subtle changes in mood.

Biochemistry

Biochemical theories maintain that in depression there are chemical transmitters that are depleted along specific tracts of the brain. Antidepressant medications block the metabolism of the neurotransmitters and make them more available. The newest class of antidepressant medications, called serotonin reuptake inhibitors, selectively acts on one neurotransmitter, serotonin, lifting mood and lessening anxiety, presumably by making this chemical more available for brain cells to use and reuse.

Interestingly, there is also research in the area of traumatic life events, especially losses in early life, which suggests that such occurrences may actually change brain chemistry (Van der Kolk 1987). Kindling is a concept used in epilepsy to describe the observation that once someone has a seizure the brain becomes altered, sensitized, and more vulnerable to subsequent seizures. This theory provides a biological paradigm to explain why some adults who were severely abused or depressed in childhood may have repeated episodes of depression later in their lives.

Temperament

Yet another biological basis for affective disorders can be found in temperament (Kagan et al. 1988). This theory holds that we are each born with a unique neural chemistry. Children who are sensitive or shy may be more vulnerable to early loss and separation (Kramer 1993). Children who grow up timid and vulnerable to stress or change may be more predisposed to adult depression. The "fit" between a child's and parents' temperaments is also important (Sadock and Kaplan 1985). In fact, one avenue of research into temperament links congenital neurotransmitter balances with behavioral predispositions, thereby providing a hypothetical connection between temperament and brain chemistry known to be involved in depression (Cloninger 1987).

All of these biological explanations offer us complex windows into some of the multiple causes of depression. It is virtually impossible to consider biological factors, intrapsychic factors, or social factors as being entirely distinct or separate causes of depression. Perhaps more than any others, mood disorders require that we take a fully informed biopsychosocial view of psychopathology.

SOCIAL FACTORS

We have observed throughout this book that there are many deprivations in the social world: unemployment; social isolation; discrimination based on race, gender, age, and class; lack of access to housing, health care, and education; poverty; and disability. All of these factors may contribute to an individual's feelings of helplessness, hopelessness, unworthiness, and lowered self-esteem. Since, as we noted at the beginning of this chapter, the lifetime risk of a major depressive episode is two to three times greater for women than for men, it is interesting to look more closely at depression in women.

One explanation for the gender difference may be found in self-in-relation theory. We said in Chapter 10 that many women in Western culture have been socialized to forge identities through their relationships. If women are socialized to be in relationships, then the loss of a relationship or relationships for women may lead to depression (Jack 1987). Often men tend to explain their affective disorders in terms of the loss of a job or a failure to be promoted, whereas women are more likely to attribute their depression to difficulties in relationships.

In a study by Deborah Belle (1982) of 400 women, the presence of a confiding intimate relationship with a partner, even in the face of stressful conditions such as poverty, inadequate housing, young children in the home, and young children with illnesses, was the most important factor that women identified in *not* becoming depressed. Blau (1973) found that among elderly women, having a confiding and intimate female friend was more predictive of women's emotional health than any other factor. In a study of 50 midlife women, Shydlowsky (1982) also found that, except for good health, female friends were cited more than husbands, work, or children as sources that prevented depression. In another study of midlife women, Berzoff (1985) found that female friends were consistently cited as enhancing adult self-esteem. All of these studies bear out the self-in-relation premise that in intimate and confiding relationships, women are less vulnerable to depression.

But dependency on others, in a patriarchal culture that rewards separateness and autonomy, is also contradictory. Women often struggle with conflicting expectations: to be dependent and independent, intimate and autonomous. Many women fear that if they are really independent, they may lose their relationships. Furthermore if we think that depression may be anger turned against the self, what then happens to women, who are consistently socialized to internalize their anger? We might suspect that this dynamic, for women, may contribute to their depression.

When considering the epidemiology of depression in women, we also need to be aware of many of the other social factors that promote dependency and helplessness. Women are physically vulnerable to violence, particularly domestic violence. Such vulnerability undermines self-esteem. In divorce, women who care for dependent children become economically disadvantaged, often resulting in their downward social mobility toward poverty. In a society that pays men more than women, women's worth in the workplace is materially devalued. In a culture in which the norms are that women work full time and still maintain responsibility for the household maintenance, women often feel depleted and empty. In a social structural arrangement in which child care is actually shared, it is often still seen as a husband helping out his wife.

> Judy is a member of a women's therapy group. She came to the group feeling depressed. She is a professor, mother, and wife currently writing two books. She works full time. Her income is close to that of her spouse's. In the group she complains, however, that when any of her children are ill, it is assumed that she will cancel her work. She arranges the social life of the family, remembers and handles all medical appointments, attends parent–teacher conferences, is responsible for providing transportation to school and extramural events and maintains responsibility for the household: shopping, cooking, and so on. She participates in all school and athletic events for her children. Her spouse and children, however, tease and deride her "easy" life. When Judy isn't angry, she feels depressed.

For her, a group that has helped her examine not only her own individual dynamics but also the social structural causes of her depression has allowed her to make systemic changes in her family life that make her feel more effective.

Gender, however, is not the only risk factor in depression. As noted earlier, families in poverty and women in poverty are at serious risk for depression. Consider the effects on low income people of early loss, exposure to pathogenic parenting, lack of social supports, inadequate financial resources, limited education, unemployment, sole responsibility for care of dependent children, and lack of access to safe and affordable housing. In fact, psychosocial stressors have been found to be transduced into the neurobiology of recurrent affective disorders (Post 1984).

As Bibring (1968) noted, depression is likely to occur when there is a gap between aspirations and accomplishments. Consider then the experiences of low-income people who must daily reconcile average expectable environments, as portrayed in the popular culture and on television, with their own less than ideal realities. As we have described in many of these chapters, families living in urban poverty who experience repeated traumatic losses from violence, gangs, and homicide are at risk for depression. It is also important to remember that for many disadvantaged families, the anomie that underlies depression often goes undiagnosed and untreated, given a diagnostic tendency to emphasize acting out, substance abuse, and suicide.

Yet another social factor in the epidemiology of depression is the inherent bias in diagnosis. African-Americans are diagnosed as schizophrenic at twice the rate of white Americans. This means that depression in the African-American community often goes undiagnosed and untreated.

In addition, as with every diagnostic category we have studied, we need also to consider the different cultural meanings of depression. Cultures have different kinds of attributions for depression. For example, clients from developing countries may complain of somatic equivalents of depression (e.g., constipation, insomnia, sexual dysfunction, weight loss). In countries with a strong Judeo-Christian perspective guilt is a predominant feature. It is interesting to note that among the Amish in the United States, there are no gender differences in depression. It may be that as many men as women are depressed but in the culture at large men mask their depression through alcoholism and sociopathy, neither of which are permitted in this culture. In Native-American cultures, for example, it is considered a mark of maturity, not of pathology, to feel profound grief over losses, sorrow for the pain of causing suffering to others, and sorrow for those less fortunate. In that culture, depression is seen as a positive sign of interdependence, of connection to the community, and of moral virtue.

We have now looked at how psychological, biological, and sociocultural factors affect the diagnosis of affective disorders. Now let us consider how depression is experienced and manifested at different developmental levels.

DEPRESSION AT DIFFERENT DEVELOPMENTAL LEVELS

Depression is the first diagnostic category we have considered that is defined in terms of an affect or mood rather than in terms of functioning. We have up until now studied two different developmental levels: psychotic and borderline. In this section we see that depression can be experienced at either of these developmental levels. As clinicians, we encounter depression daily in our clients. A developmental approach offers a way to understand how depression is experienced and how the internal world of that client is "constructed." Only by entering into that world can we join with our client empathically and introduce some discordant and, one hopes, helpful experiences that will be tolerable to the client.

Here we consider three prototypic cases of depression at the psychotic, borderline, and neurotic levels of functioning.

Depression at a Psychotic Level of Functioning

Recall that psychosis is characterized by the loss of reality testing and the concomitant loss of a sense of self and object relationships. These characteristics are also seen in psychotic depression, in which the depressive affects and symptoms we have been studying reach psychotic proportions.

Mrs. Stewart is a 34-year-old married woman of second-genera-
tion Scottish-Irish descent. Prior to the onset of her depression,
she was considered a cheerful, outgoing "perfect" wife, mother, and
part-time dental hygienist who was also active in her church.
Gradually she became more somber at work. At home she spent
more and more time alone in her room. Sexual relations with her
husband stopped. She became extremely apologetic about minor
paperwork errors, worrying aloud that she would be fired by her
boss (whom she knew to be benevolent). She became obsessed with
worries that by lack of proper hygiene or through a neglectful pro-
cedure she would hurt her patients. She began to accuse herself,
giving voice (in mutters) that she should be fired, that her skills
were the worst in the world. Now she was retreating to her room
at home and berating herself for her failing "to feel better." Eventually she could "no longer go through the motions." Life became
meaningless. She did not leave her room and barely spoke, and only
in a raspy low voice. Her husband brought her to the hospital
because he was afraid that her having "nothing to live for" might
indicate that she was suicidal.

In the hospital, she heard a mocking voice telling her that she
was not real, and that she should "die" for an "affair" she had had
six months previously with a fellow church member. The affair had
never been sexually consummated and there had been little actual
time spent with this person. In one early session, Mrs. Stewart
confused her therapist (a male) with her mother, who commanded
her to "go to your room until you get yourself under control" (a clue
to her early object experience). At another time, she thought her
therapist was her minister to whom she was confessing.

At the psychotic level of functioning, the person's greatest fear is
that death or annihilation to the self has occurred. Mrs. Stewart felt at
a level of stark terror and disorganization, as if she were already dead or
disintegrated. Nothing made sense to her—*she* no longer made sense to
herself. With a collapse of selfobject differentiation, Mrs. Stewart was
no longer able to tell whether the mocking, reproachful voice she heard
came from inside (from memories or internal "dialogue") or from outside herself. At such a primitive level of ego functioning, her reality testing was difficult. Thinking was organized along the lines of primary

processes: primitive feelings rather than logic or empirical fact predominated. Thus Mrs. Stewart experienced a psychotic transference to therapist as mother or minister without being able to test the reality of who was actually in the room with her.

Some other aspects of Mrs. Stewart's experience were also typical of a psychotic depression. There were early hints that some of her self-reproaches about being "not real" or psychically dead were criticisms of an "emotionally dead" parent (or one that was experienced that way) who was being treated as part of her (criticized) self. Indeed, Mrs. Stewart had experienced *both* parents as extremely reserved and disapproving of any affective display, happy or sad, on her part. At times (not necessarily times of otherwise overt psychotic functioning), she would experience her dead mother as inside or part of her body. Such experience reflected her fantasied "eating" or incorporation of the loved (and hated) one, a primitive operation that is sometimes the best the ego can do to retain a needed object relationship.

Also typical of psychotic levels of depression is a grossly distorted superego. This client believed herself to be dangerous to others—accusing herself at times of killing her mother and at other times of hurting her family—and sentencing herself to a kind of living "death" or nonexistence in which she felt she could do no more harm. These harsh superego injunctions were at the psychotic level.

What was the usefulness for the clinician of understanding Mrs. Stewart in developmental terms? First, it helped the therapist tolerate Mrs. Stewart's overwhelming feelings of panic, emptiness, and rage, and made these feelings understandable in terms of her internal world. That, in turn, allowed the patient to sense dimly that "someone was with me who seemed to know where we were but was not afraid." Later, as Mrs. Stewart's ego functioning improved, she still suffered intense depressive affects but was able to use her therapist's recognition of her experiences to differentiate herself from her feelings. In her words, "Now I feel there is an *I*, who 'had' those experiences."

Depression at a Borderline Level of Functioning

We previously characterized borderline level functioning as difficulty integrating, as "split" self and object representations, and as primitive ego defenses and intense unneutralized drives. Depression at this level of functioning does not reach the psychotic state of Mrs. Stewart's but has an "all or nothing" totalistic quality to it.

Ms. Ramirez, a 23-year-old Puerto Rican mother of a 6-year-old son, Raphael, was admitted to the hospital in a diabetic coma because of failure to comply with her medical regimen. As she recovered, she complained of many specific physical pains and symptoms, centered in her abdomen, chest, and head, whose location frequently shifted and that could not be successfully diagnosed. Ms. R. gradually became friendly with a nurse who became alarmed at what she heard in conversation and asked for psychotherapeutic services.

Ms. R. told her therapist that she and Raphael had moved to the mainland from rural Puerto Rico about a year before for "no special reason." Ms. R. held a clerical job but was socially isolated except for Raphael who had become "very hostile" over the past year. He had in fact been dismissed from several day care centers for violent behavior. Ms. R. clearly described a cycle at home in which she experienced Raphael's abundant (but perhaps normal) curiosity and activity as maliciously aimed at "getting on my nerves," and she retaliated by getting very angry and raging at him. She would become frightened of her wish to hurt him physically, and angrily withdraw all contact, sometimes for many hours. It was during these times that Ms. R. would withhold medication from herself and self-destructively eat dangerous foods. Death, she thought, was the only escape. She had in fact "taken pills" on several occasions before her son's birth in attempts to die.

Initially, Ms. R. described a "happy childhood." Only after some months of outpatient work did she "remember" her father's desertion of the family when she was 7 (remember that her son was 6) and her mother's alcoholism and physical abuse of her. She had in fact left her home town at age 22 to follow an unfaithful lover with whom she reunited for a time. Her hospitalization was immediately preceded by news that this man had left her for another woman who had just moved to their city. That woman turned out to be her father's stepdaughter for whom "he left me when I was 7"!

Ms. Ramirez, while never manifesting overt loss of reality testing, experienced her depressed moods as timeless and cut off from any hope of improvement. Memories of feeling better held little meaning when she was depressed. She would mainly remember those times when she had been depressed, and then sadness, helplessness, and badness would seem to exist forever in an eternal "now."

Ms. Ramirez's anxiety fluctuated between poles of terror of aloneness, which she experienced when abandoned by her lover or cut off from her son, and a fear of being invaded, which she experienced when she felt her son was abusing her and when she abused him. She tended to experience her son (and her therapist) as "all good" or "all bad," and was more likely to experience herself in a "split" fashion. She was prone to savage attacks upon herself, including physical pounding and even suicide attempts, as primitive superego retribution for her badness. It will be seen how in punching herself, Ms. Ramirez could be both punishing the (poorly differentiated) abusing mother with whom she was identifying and also reexperiencing herself as the abused child.

Work with Ms. Ramirez was also aided by a developmental approach to her depression. Her therapist was able to empathize accurately with her utter hopelessness and the extreme urgency of her need for relief when she and all around her felt "bad" and lonely. Only later, after they had experienced together several cycles of good and bad times, would her therapist begin to bridge these states, which Ms. Ramirez experienced as timeless and "forever" when she was in them, reminding her they had "been here before" and survived. Such bridge building with a reliably available, nurturing other begins to address ego and self and object relations issues underlying depression at this developmental level.

Depression at a Neurotic Level of Functioning

We now consider a developmental approach to understanding depression in people whose depressions are at the neurotic level (as we will discuss more fully in the next chapter). A person who has achieved more integrated self and object representations and whose ego functions are more intact may experience depression as a result of conflicts at the superego level of development.

> Mr. Jones, a school principal, comes to treatment feeling bad about himself. He says he often cannot live up to the expectations of the parents of children with whom he works. He tends to feel overburdened and then becomes enraged at home when demands are

put on him. He feels terrible for being so parsimonious with his children in terms of having time or energy for them, and he feels that he consistently disappoints his wife.

Mr. Jones may be seen as an example of depression primarily at the neurotic level of functioning. His depression is at the superego level, where he feels identified with his father as an irascible spouse and parent and feels bad (guilty) about that. His reality testing is intact. He is able to control his angry impulses, but feels bad for having them. Mr. Jones's low self-esteem and his chronic mild hopelessness about himself may stem from experiences of always feeling "in the wrong" with his parents, which further contribute to his current feelings at his workplace and in his family.

We have now examined clinical cases of depression at three developmental levels. Let us finally turn to how the client's experience of depression can affect the clinician.

WORKING WITH DEPRESSED CLIENTS

When faced with a client's hopelessness, despair, or self-criticism, it is not uncommon for the beginning clinician to feel hopeless or anxious also. Depressive affects often feel to the client like dead ends. We, the clinicians, presumably less depressed, may too begin to wonder how to help the client move on from a seemingly interminable bleak state. Because depressive affects seem to lead nowhere, it becomes difficult for the clinician to hold on to the conviction that, in the telling of a client's story, there can in fact be any relief.

Initially in sitting with depressed clients, clinicians often find that they are experienced as medicine. The client may begin to feel better. But gradually, the clinician may seem to become less helpful, and begin to feel him- or herself lacking in a variety of ways. Finally the clinician often experiences herself as inadequate, heir to many of the same criticisms once directed by the client against herself. This can induce in the clinician some of the same feelings of unworthiness, ineffectiveness, and helplessness that the client feels. Some clients feel so hopeless that, in sitting with them, we clinicians can feel paralyzed. Sometimes suicidal clients can lead us, the clinicians, to feel tormented. There may be times when, sitting with suicidal clients, we may begin to hate them, or even worse than hate, feel aversion toward them and turn away (Buie and Maltsberger 1983). This aversion can be lethal to the clients. But if we can acknowledge our hopelessness and helplessness to ourselves and to our supervisors, then we clinicians may not need to disavow these feelings. When we can be aware of our depression, our hate, or our aversion, we will not be unconsciously asking our clients to bear our own aggression as well as their own.

There are other pitfalls for beginning clinicians who work with depressed clients. One very common error is to try to cheer up or talk a depressed client out of being depressed. To do so may repeat other failures in empathy and lead to the experience of a loss of self cohesion for the client. In psychodynamically oriented work, we need to empathize with a person's depression while enlisting her help to find its causes. Sometimes, a client's depression may make us want to mobilize to action. We want to give advice or do something that will relieve the suffering. This too can lead away from what the client needs—someone who can tolerate painful affects, which up until now may have seemed unbearable. If, as we have said, one of the greatest ego strengths is the capacity to bear depression, then we must be able to do this ourselves if we want to help our clients do the same.

CONCLUSION

Beginning clinicians need to hold a biopsychosocial lens when they work with people who are depressed. Therapists do not treat *depression* but rather the person experiencing it. The therapeutic goal should be to alleviate the symptons and to restore or create the capacity to do the constructive rebuilding work that allows for a more creative and flexible use of the self. Cognitive behavioral therapies and social support therapies can be helpful to depressed clients. In our current practice of managed care, the danger is that we may be moving toward a model of simply medicating mood disorders, without attending to their complex psychosocial causes. In fact, in the worst kinds of managed care, organized only around diminishing symptoms, the cost containment nature may join with the therapist's unexamined countertransference motives to avoid depression altogether. Eighty percent of people with affective disorders improve with the combination of medication and talking therapies. In the move toward intermittent therapies, however, we need to still recognize the value of a treatment relationship in understanding the client's inner world and restoring functions that may have become disturbed.

In Chinese, the word *crisis* is designated with two characters that mean danger and opportunity. Affective disorders pose enormous dangers, not the least of which is the risk of suicide. But these disorders also provide opportunities: to restore lost functions, to heal internal wounds, to gain sufficient mobilization to make social changes, to become able to bear the affects heretofore unbearable, to be able to return to or find community, and to be able to use a helping person to sort out the meaning of the crisis. The felt danger of a crisis is often the loss of meaning or of loved ones. The actual danger is that, without the crisis, we may never discover our own strengths.

References

Belle, D. (1982). *Lives in Stress: Women and Depression.* Beverly Hills, CA: Sage.

Berzoff, J. N. (1985). *Valued female friendships: their functions in promoting female adult development.* Unpublished dissertation. Boston: Boston University.

Bibring, E. (1968). The mechanism of depression. In *The Meaning of Despair,* ed. W. Gaylin, pp. 145–181. New York: Science House.

Blatt, S. (1974). Levels of object representation in anaclitic and introjective depression. *Psychoanalytic Study of the Child* 9:107–158. New York: International Universities Press.

Blau, Z. (1973). *Old Age in a Changing Society.* New York: New Viewpoints.

Bowlby, J. (1958). The nature of a child's tie to his mother. *International Journal of Psychoanalysis* 39:350–373.

———— (1961). Childhood and mourning and its implications for psychiatry. *American Journal of Psychiatry* 118:481–498.

Brown, G. W. (1991). Epidemiological studies of depression: definition and case findings. In *Psychosocial Aspects of Depression,* ed. J. Beicher and A. Kleiman. Hillsdale, NJ: Laurence Erlbaum.

Brown, G. W., Bilfulco, A., and Harris, T. O. (1989). Life events, vulnerability and onset of depression: some refinements. *British Journal of Psychiatry* 150:30–42.

Buie, D. H., and Maltsberger, J. T. (1983). *The Practice and Formulation of Suicide Risk.* Somerville, MA: Firefly.

Chodorow, N. (1989). *Feminism and Psychoanalytic Theory.* New Haven, CT: Yale University Press.

Cicchetti, D. (1989). How research on child maltreatment has informed the study of child development. In *Child Maltreatment,* ed. D. Cicchetti and V. Carlson, pp. 327–431. Cambridge, England: Cambridge University Press.

Cloninger, C. R. (1987). Neurogenetic adaptive mechanisms in alcoholism. *Science* 236:410–416.

Freud, S. (1916). Mourning and melancholia. *Standard Edition* 14:237–259.

Gershon, E. S., Hamorit, J., Dibble, E., et al. (1982). A family study of schizoaffective, bipolar, unipolar, and normal control probands. *Archives of General Psychiatry* 39:1157.

Jack, D. (1987). Self in relation theory. In *Women and Depression: A Lifespan Perspective,* ed. R. Formanek and A. Gurian, pp. 41–46. New York: Springer.

Jacobson, E. (1964). *The Self and the Object World.* New York: International Universities Press.

——— (1971). On the psychoanlytic theory of cyclothymic depression. In *Depression: Comparative Studies of Normal, Neurotic and Psychotic Conditions,* pp. 228–242. New York: International Universities Press.

Kagan, J. Reznick, S., and Snidman, A. (1988). Biological basis for childhood shyness. *Science* 240:167–171.

Kaplan, A. (1984). *The Self-in-Relation: Implications for Depression in Women.* Works in progress, 84–103. Stone Center for Developmental Services. Wellesley, MA: Wellesley College.

Kernberg, O. (1966). Structural deviations of object relations. *International Journal of Psycho-Analysis* 47:236–253.

Klein, M. (1940). Mourning and its relationship to manic-depressive states. In *Contributions to Psychoanalysis 1921–1945.* New York: McGraw-Hill.

Kramer, P. (1993). *Listening to Prozac.* New York: Viking.

Lehman, H. (1985). Affective disorders: clinical features. In *Comprehensive Textbook of Psychiatry,* ed. H. Kaplan and B. Sadock, pp. 786–811. Baltimore, MD: Williams & Wilkins.

Loewald, H. (1980). *Papers on Psychoanalysis.* New Haven: Yale University Press.

Mahler, M., and McDevitt, J. (1980). The separation-individuation process and identity formation. In *The Course of Life,* vol. 1, ed. S. I. Greenspan and H. Pollock, pp. 407–423. DHSPUB No. (ADM) 80-786. Washington, DC: National Institute of Mental Life.

Plath, S. (1962). *The Collected Poems,* ed. Ted Hughes. New York: Harper & Row.

——— (1971). *The Bell Jar.* New York: Harper & Row.

Post, R. M. (1984). *Neurobiology of Mood Disorders*. Baltimore, MD: Williams and Wilkins.

Saari, C. (1989). Personal communication.

Sadock, B., and Kaplan, H., eds. (1985). *Comprehensive Textbook of Psychiatry*, vol. 4. Baltimore, MD: Williams & Wilkins.

Shydlowski, B. (1982). *Friendship among women in midlife*. Unpublished dissertation, Fielding Institute.

Spitz, R., and Wolf, K. (1946). Anaclitic depressions. *Psychoanalytic Study of the Child* 2:313–342. New York: International Universities Press.

Styron, W. (1990). *Darkness Visible: A Memoir of Madness*. New York: Random House.

Thomas, A., Chess, S., and Birch, H. (1968). *Temperament and Behavior Disorders in Children*. New York: New York University Press.

Tronick, E., and Granino, A. (1988). The mutual regulation model: the infant's self and interactive regulation and coping and defensive capacity. In *Stress and Coping*, ed. T. Field, P. McCabe, and N. Schneiderman, pp. 47–68. Hillsdale, NJ: Lawrence Erlbaum.

Van der Kolk, B. (1987). *Psychological Trauma*. Washington, DC: American Psychiatric Press.

Weissman, M. M., and Klerman, G. L. (1977). Sex differences and the epidemiology of depression. *Archives of General Psychiatry* 34:98–111.

Zetzel, E. (1965a). On the incapacity to bear depression. In *The Capacity for Emotional Growth*, ed. E. Zetzel, pp. 82–114. New York: International Universities Press.

———— (1965b). Depression and the incapacity to bear it. In *Drives, Affects, Behavior*, vol. 2, ed. M. Schur, pp. 243–274. New York: International Universities Press.

15

Anxiety and Its Manifestations

JOAN BERZOFF

In the preceding chapter on depression we discussed the *experience* of depression and the possible biopsychosocial causes that contribute to it. This chapter describes the experience of anxiety and reviews various psychodynamic approaches to anxiety. We will consider the biological and social factors that are implicated in the anxiety disorders both as a group and as separate disorders. Whereas depression is felt when loss, hurt, disappointment, and disillusionment have already occurred, anxiety is experienced around what *might be about to happen*. Anxiety is an anticipatory feeling. It is felt about the future, not the past. It is about something dreadful that might happen outside the self or something terrible that might emerge from inside.

THE EXPERIENCE OF ANXIETY

Recently we informally polled some of our colleagues to ask them to describe what they feel when anxious. This is what they said. One reported

difficulty falling asleep and staying asleep as he contemplated a promotion at work. He would awaken with free-floating anxiety and a sense
of impending doom. He began to dread being with his family and being at work. He was short-tempered, preoccupied, and generally restless. The physical illnesses of co-workers, family, and friends loomed
larger than life. He could not put into perspective the newspaper articles
he read documenting wars, ecological disasters, or medical illnesses. He
began to exercise excessively. Another colleague remembered her terror
at having accidentally been locked in a bathroom when she was 5. As
she tried to get out, her head began to pound and her heart raced. She
could not breathe, and was left feeling helpless and alone. To this day,
when in a situation where a bathroom door locks, she feels like that little
girl, anxious and afraid. Another described how the sound of a noon-
time siren makes her heart race and her mouth tingle. Because she was
born at the end of World War II when civil defense drills signaled real
danger, sirens in the present still physiologically revive her anxiety from
her past. Another recalled her annual terror of lecturing to a classroom
of a hundred students. At each first class, she would become nauseated,
clammy, and dizzy, and her ears would ring. Often she experiences examination dreams in which she fails to bring her notes to class, is unprepared, and feels humiliated.

What all of our colleagues described is what every reader has also
experienced. Anxiety is a universal affect. It can make our hearts beat
faster, our tongues tingle, our palms sweat. Anxiety can make us rumi-
nate or obsess. Anxiety can take the form of irrational fears of such things
as planes, bathroom doors, open spaces, or supermarkets. Anxiety can
be experienced as flashbacks or nightmares of horrific events. Unlike
depression, in which the feeling is that something *has* gone wrong, anxiety makes us feel that something *will* go wrong. In fact, anxiety is probably the most common symptom with which clients present. Anxiety
affects 8.3 percent of all Americans, with a 2:1 ratio of females to males
who report anxiety symptoms.

Anxiety can manifest itself in a variety of forms and in varying
degrees of severity. At its most useful, it serves as a signal and motivates
us to act: to prepare lectures, to meet deadlines, to attend to tasks. At its
most disruptive, it paralyzes us, preventing us from leaving home, from
concentrating on work or family, from sleeping, from traveling, from
enjoying pleasures, or from functioning at all.

As in our approach to other psychopathologies, we will use a variety of biopsychosocial lenses when evaluating the symptoms of a person suffering from anxiety. Biological vulnerability, chemical imbalances, drug and alcohol use, and physical illness may biologically predispose an individual to anxiety. Intrapsychic conflicts may also cause anxiety disorders, which in turn create enormous psychological distress as a person's functioning in relationships and work becomes impaired. Social factors—oppression, trauma, powerlessness, abuse, and violence— may increase a person's experience of helplessness and vulnerability and result in the development of anxiety symptoms. An understanding of the interface between these biological, social, and psychological factors allows for the greatest appreciation of the complexity of these disorders.

ANXIETY AND CULTURE

Before exploring the many anxiety disorders on these three levels, it is important to recognize how the *expression* of anxiety differs from culture to culture. For some cultures, anxiety may be an affect that is expressed easily. Jewish, Hispanic, or Italian families, for example, may express their anxieties with emotion that may appear exaggerated to those of different backgrounds.

> Joshua, an 8-year-old Jewish boy from a middle-class family, had been referred to his school's therapist for a psychological evaluation because he repeatedly said, "Oh God, I'm gonna kill myself," whenever he missed the ball at games of kickball or whenever he would forget his homework. While his white Anglo-Saxon Protestant school thought a suicide evaluation might be in order, within his ethnic family norms, "killing oneself" was idiomatic for the expression of any anxiety or frustration and did not reflect pathology.

In Eastern cultures, anxiety is often expressed physically. Often people from Eastern cultures experience anxiety as shame or fear of losing face, and express their fears through blushing, somatic complaints, or obsessive-compulsive rituals. In fact, many cultures present with psychosomatic equivalents of anxiety. Iranians, for example, often express their anxiety as pains in the heart, as weak nerves, as shaking, or as body pain. In Latin America, anxiety is referred to as *susto*. It is often characterized by phobias, tachycardia, irritability, or insomnia (Ho 1987).

Anxiety may also emerge over different kinds of cultural prohibitions. For white Anglo-Saxon Protestants whose culture may value independence and stoicism, anxiety may erupt when autonomy is threatened. By contrast, in Asian cultures where interdependence is the norm, anxiety may arise when there has been some inability to rely on others or too much separateness from others. As a result of differences in attributions for anxiety, individuals from cultures such as Native American, Latin American, Alaskan, or Asian will usually not present to the mental health field with anxiety symptoms per se nor will they seek medication or psychotherapy for symptom relief. Rather than view anxiety as a symptom, they may understand anxiety as a spirit, for example, and seek cures through magic, shamans, monks, or herbs. Thus it is important to remember that cultures encourage anxiety to be expressed in specific idioms, and individuals seek culturally prescribed treatments for this pain and discomfort.

ANXIETY AT DIFFERENT DEVELOPMENTAL LEVELS

Just as we discussed in the previous chapter that depression is experienced at different developmental levels, so too is anxiety experienced differently according to a person's level of psychological structure. When assessing a client's internal experience of anxiety, it is important to assess the developmental level of the anxiety.

> Ginny, a 31-year-old unmarried historian, complained of chronic headaches and anxiety precipitated by her father's recent suicidal ideation. As the oldest of three children, she came from a Jewish family that had initially viewed itself as "golden." Her father was a highly successful and attractive businessman, and her mother worked for a music publishing house. Both parents presented an ideal and enviable life to the community. When Ginny was 5, her youngest brother became ill. Ginny both loved him and felt him to be her rival. In fact, as an adult, she remembered a song she had sung her brother, "Die, die, my little darling pie." As he left for the hospital, she kissed him good-bye. Overnight he developed a pneu-

monia secondary to meningitis and he died. Ginny remembers feeling, as a child, that she herself was the "kiss of death."

To Ginny's delight, when she was 6½, her mother announced another pregnancy. Ginny can remember having previously tried to comfort her mother and father and recalled sitting on her father's lap, reading with him and snuggling. Thus when her mother became pregnant, Ginny felt that she had had something to do with this blessed event. Ginny felt especially thrilled (and a little guilty) to be having a baby in the family, whom she thought of as hers and her father's. When her new sister was born with Down syndrome, however, Ginny again experienced her loving feelings toward her father as dangerous and destructive, given that her new sister was retarded. She grew up associating a sense of danger with both her loving and aggressive wishes.

At age 13, she wrote a birthday song for her retarded sister. Her mother had the song published and it was an overnight success. Ginny was coronated by her classmates for her newfound fame as a children's songwriter. But she renounced the success, not seeing it as her own, and was uncomfortable with her achievement and with the public acclaim it brought her. Her academic successes were henceforth experienced as anxiety provoking and she sought invisibility. Though popular, successful, and intelligent, when angry or frustrated as a child she would literally hide in the back of her closet so as not to be a problem to others. As an adult she experienced anxiety and headaches, often brought on by an event that disappointed or angered her, and that required that she retreat to a darkened room. These often came on after she was happy and excited or angry and frustrated.

We would say that Ginny experienced anxiety at the neurotic level. What do we mean by neurotic? In drive-theory terms, Ginny's anxiety was experienced as guilt over her unconscious sexual and aggressive wishes and fantasies that had occurred at the oedipal stage of development. Freud, as we recall from Chapter 2, described neurotics as suffering from reminiscences. By this he meant that sexual or aggressive memories, fantasies, and feelings are kept out of consciousness through the defense of repression. Symptoms are understood as the return of the repressed. Using structural theory, Ginny's unconscious hostile and loving wishes had been realized by coincidental damage and death. As a result she suffered neurotic guilt and anxiety over conflicts between her superego and her id. In addition, her father's current suicidal ideation had heightened her sense that she was somehow responsible for her damaged sister and lost brother.

In ego-psychological terms, Ginny suffered from neurotic anxiety (as distinguished from psychotic anxiety) because her reality testing remained intact. She used the high-level defenses of sublimation, intellectualization, and reaction formation. She adapted to her family's losses by characterological attempts to be good, quiet, and nonassertive, which were reflective of her characterological style of functioning. She had a critical superego, having identified with her parents' high standards both for themselves and their surviving children. She also had good judgment, humor, and an excellent capacity for insight, which were later invaluable in treatment. Given her strong ego boundaries, closeness was not a threat to the integrity of her self.

In object-relations terms, Ginny's anxiety was at the neurotic level because her early relationships had been secure and she had internalized integrated and coherent representations of herself and others. She could engage in deep and intimate friendships in which affection and mutuality were genuine. She had some difficulties in close relationships with men, feeling that they (like she) could not live up to her parental expectations. But other people were viewed as being whole, and not part, objects.

In self-psychological terms, Ginny's anxiety was neurotic because she had a relatively cohesive sense of self. Because her narcissistically injured parents had needed her as a selfobject to compensate for their many real losses, their own depletion had left them unable to be fully empathic to her. As a result, she sometimes felt that her successes were narcissistic achievements for her parents and not for herself. But as she experienced herself to be understood in the course of treatment, she began to experience greater empathy for herself and for her parents' losses. She could also acknowledge her family's less than ideal lives.

Also indicative of her neurotic-level anxiety was a sufficiently strong observing ego that enabled her to develop a transference to her therapist and to examine it. Initially, she felt that she had to live up to her fantasies of her therapist's expectations, as she had felt she had to live up to her parents' expectations. Often the therapist felt "obligated" to live up to hers. Ginny would bring in volumes of nineteenth century literature and ask if the therapist had read them. She would discuss in great detail the latest avant-garde music, which the therapist had not heard. The therapist often, through projective identification, felt like a disappointment, and not bright, witty, or urbane enough. This paralleled Ginny's own feelings. In the treatment, Ginny dared to become angry and disappointed with the therapist, and later dared to make a career change that required considerable self-assertion and self-differentiation. She chose a career that was different from that of her therapist's, her father's, or her mother's. She ultimately met a man who she felt was good enough for her. Over the course of treatment, her headaches remitted.

Neurotic anxiety is based on Freud's theory of anxiety emerging as a function of intrapsychic conflict. In Freud's tripartite model of the psyche, anxiety erupts when there is conflict between the superego and the id. The feelings and wishes most often disavowed arise during the oedipal drama—anger, envy, competitiveness, sexual desire, and jealously—and often emerge as anxiety symptoms: phobias, obsessive compulsive disorders, generalized anxiety, and anxiety attacks. Yet we know that these anxiety symptoms occur not only in people with neurotic structure, but also in people who have character pathology or are psychotic.

Prior to *DSM-IV*, we would have understood Ginny to be neurotic. Whether looking at her anxiety from a drive, object relations, ego, or self-psychological perspective, we would have pointed to her intact reality testing and her superego conflicts around her sexuality and aggression. We would have assessed the quality of her anxiety as oedipal anxiety. We would have identified her defenses as high level, and would have seen her as relatively successful in work and love, noting her ability to form and maintain triadic relationships. Hence, we would have referred to her anxiety as *superego anxiety*.

Neurosis used to be one of the main diagnostic categories for anxiety disorders until the authors of *DSM-IV* severed the link between psychodynamic theories of etiology and diagnosis. They believed that the standardized diagnostic manual for the country should list only the observable symptoms for each diagnosis and not endorse any particular theory of dynamics or causation. However, the disappearance of neurosis as a diagnostic category does not mean that the neurotic processes cease to exist. An understanding of neurotic anxiety such as that experienced by Ginny is still extremely relevant for the treatment of some anxiety disorders today.

If, on the other hand, Ginny had been psychotic, her anxiety would have looked very different. She would have experienced psychotic anxiety at the level of the annihilation of her self. If she were psychotically anxious, she might have been convinced that she had murdered her brother or had given birth to her father's child. This would have produced anxiety so primitive that it would have been experienced as if her very self were dissolving under the weight of her sexual or aggressive impulses. Were she psychotic, she would have been unable to distinguish wish from deed. Her thoughts would have been distorted by delusions that she was powerful enough to either wreak havoc upon her family or to save them from destruction. She might have had hallucinations that God or the devil had told her to destroy family members. If she had been psychotic, her defenses would have distorted reality. She might have denied her sibling's death, or projected her own badness onto the world outside, making it a dangerous place. Were her anxiety of psychotic proportions, her relationships would have been at the level of selfobject merging with few, if any, boundaries between herself and others. Had her anxiety been psychotic, her capacity for enduring friendships, intimate relationships, or a therapeutic alliance would likely have been compromised. In short, because her anxiety was at the level of superego concerns, she did not experience *annihilation anxiety* as do people who function on a psychotic level.

Ginny also did not suffer from the kind of anxiety that we associate with people who have severe character pathology. She did not express profound *separation anxiety*—the terror of being alone or of feeling that she would be swallowed up or engulfed if separated from those she needed. She did not exclusively use defenses such as splitting, primitive idealization, or projective identification as ways of keeping contradictory feelings separate, each of which would have seriously distorted her perceptions of other people. As we noted earlier, *she* was the one who suffered; she did not cause suffering in those around her. Had Ginny been suffering from anxiety at the level of severe separation anxiety, she might also have had transient breaks with reality.

The hallmark of anxiety at the neurotic level, then, is that it does not impair reality. The function of anxiety at the neurotic level is to signal intrapsychic dangers and mobilize the defenses. The hallmark of anxiety at the character-disordered level is separation anxiety (fear of loss of the other) and its function is to try to restore psychic equilibrium by holding on to needed others. At the psychotic level anxiety is experienced as annihilation anxiety, a fear of the loss of the self.

ASSESSING SYMPTOMS AT DIFFERENT DEVELOPMENTAL LEVELS

To understand and assess the source, the nature, and the developmental level of a person's anxiety it is necessary to go beyond the symptoms to the story. For example, obsessive-compulsive behavior is often an anxiety symptom, a sign that unmanageable anxiety is present. But obsessive-compulsive symptoms (excessive handwashing, checking, counting, or rituals) do not reveal what the anxiety is about, or at what developmental level it is experienced. This point was brought home very forcibly to one of the authors at a time when two of her patients were experiencing severe anxiety that manifested itself in a very similar manner. Yet the cause, the story, of the anxiety could not have been more different.

Both Darla and Patty described themselves as "neat freaks." Everything in their apartments had to be clean and meticulously arranged. Darla spoke of the sense of "relief and safety" that she felt when she would look in her closet at all her clothes "hanging in perfect order and symmetry." Her shirts were all lined up in one section, skirts in another, and so on for all her clothes; each hanger was facing the same way. If anything was out of order she would get very anxious, experiencing a nameless dread. Patty spoke of very similar activities and feelings. Any kind of messiness made her very uncomfortable. She needed to feel that "everything was always under control," that "nothing could go wild."

Both Darla and Patty sought help in therapy because they realized that their anxiety was growing and their ritualistic attempts to control it were beginning to restrict their lives. Darla could no longer go out to eat with friends who might drop crumbs on the table, and Patty was starting to get frightened of driving. As each examined the sources of her fears the following is what emerged:

Darla grew up in a chaotic family. Her father was quite sadistic. In the nature/nurture paradigm, nurture was uneven at best, and Darla's nature was very sensitive, finely tuned, and shy. At the beginning of treatment she presented a line drawing of herself with parts not connected at all, a kind of stick figure in pieces. The figure was a poignant manifestation of her disorganization, fragility, and vulnerability. As the therapist looked at it, she wondered if Darla's love of and need for order arose out of her internal feeling of falling apart and going to pieces, of never feeling whole, solid, and connected. Darla wept as she felt how desperately she needed her closet to look perfect to reassure her momentarily that maybe she could hold herself together a little longer. Developmentally, her level of anxiety had to do with the fear of total disintegration or annihilation. Relating to the consistent presence of the therapist and telling the myriad terrifying experiences of her childhood enabled Darla to heal in such a way that eventually this primitive early anxiety did not recur with any great frequency. She became free to live a much more spontaneous, full, and joyful life.

When Patty talked about *her* life she described a very organized structured family that was quite close, loving, and strictly religious. Patty attended only Catholic schools and had been very influenced by the nuns and priests who taught her. By far the most traumatic event in her life occurred when she was the victim of a rape at age 19. The rapist had held her locked in his apartment at knife point and had forced her to submit to hours of sexual activity. When she tried to resist, he cut her on the throat and ejaculated for the third time as he licked her blood. Arrogantly, he released her, stating that no one would believe he would do such things and he would never be convicted. Patty did report the crime to the police and after years of legal battles, the rapist was hospitalized in a psychiatric facility for six months. Patty, in the meantime, attended a rape victims' group and worked through many of her reactions, but felt that she nevertheless was growing more anxious and compulsive with the passage of time. She was beginning to have short periods of dissociation when she entered treatment. It took many months to get to the trauma because she had total amnesia about it, but what finally emerged was that Patty had, at one point, experienced an orgasm as she was being penetrated by her rapist at knife point. She had not been able to remember it because both her guilt and shame made having an orgasm under such circumstances unacceptable to her superego. Her anxiety was about having to face what she considered a terrible, sinful aspect of herself. Her symptoms of needing excessive orderliness and control were her unconscious attempts at denying the possibility of going out of control as she felt during her orgasm. Eventually Patty made peace with the fact that her body had responded to unwanted sexual stimulation. Her great anxiety then diminished because she had faced what terrified her about herself. In Patty's case the danger (following the rape) did not come from hostile forces *outside* herself but from feared impulses *within*. Whereas Darla manifested annihilation anxiety, Patty experienced superego anxiety. The latter anxiety, like Ginny's, was at the neurotic level.

Freud first referred to two kinds of anxiety. The first kind of anxiety he described was one of intense dread, the second was of overwhelming panic. Freud called the first anxiety *anxiety neurosis* and the second *actual neurosis*. In an anxiety neurosis, he thought the anxiety arose out of an intrapsychic conflict. An actual neurosis, he thought, was more biological, an eruption of anxiety as a physiological state. Today we see these two anxiety states defined in the *DSM-IV* as having both intrapsychic and biological etiologies.

Let us now consider some of the anxiety disorders separately, recognizing that often there are multiple causes of anxiety disorders that may be intrapsychic, biological, and/or social.

GENERALIZED ANXIETY DISORDERS

Imagine the anxiety you feel before taking an examination. You have difficulty sleeping the night before. You feel agitated, distracted, your heart begins to race faster and faster. Now imagine being in that state for days, for weeks, even for years. With generalized anxiety disorders, people are worried and fearful that something will happen to harm themselves or their loved ones. They may experience anxiety dreams and sleep disorders. Their form of anxiety is usually chronic, and people may see themselves as "high strung." Because of how pervasive and diffuse generalized anxiety disorders are, and because of the intrapsychic conflicts that often underlie them, they are more responsive to psychodynamic treatment and the least responsive to behavioral interventions. More often, although by no means exclusively, generalized anxiety disorders are experienced by women.

Rita, a 36-year-old Hispanic medical resident in obstetrics, presented with anxiety symptoms. She was graduating from her training, and came in feeling "like a wreck." She described herself as constantly worried and able to think only of the worst outcome of any event. For example, when her elder son stayed out late, she was sure he had been killed in an accident. When driving with friends, she would implore them to drive safely, despite their safe driving records.

The eldest child of low-income parents from the Dominican Republic, Rita had left her native island at age 24 with two small children after an abusive marriage. Without help from relatives or friends, she had settled in New York, and initially supported her family on welfare grants. She began college part time, completed her premedical training there, and was accepted to medical school with a full scholarship. From her own strengths, she managed to raise her children and negotiate a demanding residency. When she was offered her first job, she was chosen by a prestigious medical center from a pool of hundreds of applicants.

The year before, Rita's mother had come to visit from the island. It was clear that her mother's long-standing problem with alcohol was worsening, and Rita had to hospitalize her at an in-patient facility nearby. When Rita came for treatment, she described having been diffusely anxious for almost the whole year. She was thinking of telling the director of residency training that she could not complete her last month, and would not be able to terminate with any of her patients. In short, she was generally so anxious that she had decided to quit medicine altogether.

Work with Rita revealed her unconscious guilt for having surpassed her mother, relatives, and friends. Despite her growing awareness of her intrapsychic conflicts, Rita also needed medication. Within a week of being medicated and with a brief therapeutic intervention, she finished out her residency and began her new job. In the course of her brief, insight-oriented treatment, she was able to examine how anxious she had become over actually having achieved a medical career. Further, she gained insight into her unconscious superego guilt, which was exacerbated by having had to hospitalize her mother. Finally, she needed to address her survivor guilt about getting out of a cycle of poverty and leaving so many other family members behind. Rita's concerns were at the neurotic level.

Generalized anxiety disorders are also found in people with less-organized psychological structures than Rita's. Psychotic and personality disordered clients may also suffer both chronic and diffuse anxiety. This is what makes diagnosing the client's level of psychological structure so important.

Panic Attacks

We recall that early on Freud described a kind of anxiety that was biological. In fact, today panic attacks are understood largely as a biological phenomenon, even if they are triggered by a psychological response to perceived internal or external danger. A professor said of his panic attacks:

> Scary. It feels like you're not even here on earth. I don't feel human when I get one of these attacks. My heart starts racing, my palms get sweaty, and all I want to do is run! When I experience a panic attack, I feel like I can't breathe, my heart beats very fast and then I feel like I'm going to die! Everything just gets very hazy, almost but not that. It's like I'm dizzy and I'm going to faint!

People with panic attacks often feel that they are going crazy. They experience intense psychological symptoms: choking, hyperventilating, or heart palpitations so severe that they may fear they are dying. Very often clients with panic attacks do not recognize that their attacks have a psychological origin and so they first seek medical help. When their medical findings (often cardiac in nature) are normal, however, they are often sent home with no treatment at all.

Panic attacks can be devastating because they can so dramatically constrict life functioning.

Mark, a potter, spoke eloquently about how his panic attacks made his life a prison. Describing his first panic attack, he said:

> I was standing in front of my potter's wheel, when a feeling of absolute terror overtook me. It felt like an explosion, like a reflex, almost like a sneeze. I had no idea what was happening or why. All I can recall is that I next found myself curled in a ball, on the floor, with my heart racing. Tears poured down my cheeks. I was perspiring, and I couldn't breathe. In fact, my fingers had swollen; so had my eyes. My body had become numb. I felt completely out of control.

As Mark's panic attacks worsened, his freedom in the world decreased. Going to exhibits, out for dinner with his wife, or using public transportation became impossible. The boundaries of his increasingly circumscribed world had become his prison. In trying to describe his feelings, he said:

> Some people compare panic to what you feel when you find yourself unprepared and have to go on stage; others say it's like having to fight in a war, but I think it's more like this. Imagine that you are driving along peacefully when suddenly, out the blue, a car lurches at you. Try to imagine the terror, confusion, instantaneous racing of your heart, the split second when the world is utterly out of your control. Remember the out-of-body experience, the way that your nerve endings are almost electrified, and then take that moment and expand it into hours, even days. That's a small scintilla of what a panic attack feels like for me.

As we have said throughout this chapter, people with anxiety disorders such as Mark's may be functioning at a neurotic, character-disordered, or even psychotic level. While Mark's level of functioning was neurotic, often people with severe character pathology experience panic disorders as a result of separation anxiety. Clients with poorly developed object constancy often experience severe panic attacks when they cannot evoke the image of a needed other. For example, Anne was able to ward off her panic attacks when she called her therapist's answering machine and heard her therapist's voice every night. Her temporary "connection" served as a transitional object that soothed her and diminished her anxiety symptoms.

Both panic disorders and panic attacks have some biological basis. Medications including monoamine oxidase (MAO) inhibitors and tricyclics are currently the most effective in regulating the part of the brain that produces norepinephrine and triggers fight or flight (Noyes 1985). Clients with panic disorders, however, may be reluctant to take medications. They may fear side effects such as weight gain, and often the very act of being medicated makes them feel even less in control.

While there may be psychological and biological causes for panic disorders, cognitive behavioral therapies have been found to be especially helpful in their treatment. This kind of therapy helps the client accept the panic, deal with the fears, and become slowly desensitized to the most feared situations, while teaching the client to reinterpret symptoms as other than disastrous. While the *etiology* of panic may be exclusively biological, psychodynamic psychotherapies can still help a client bear the anxiety, understand some intrapsychic conflicts that may underlie it, examine the toll it has taken, and receive the appropriate behavioral and medical help. Mark wrote this about his recovery from his panic disorder:

> My recovery will continue slowly. I may have painful and discourag-
> ing setbacks. . . . I am not cured. I am still living with, and will for a
> long time, an illness I am learning to manage, the way diabetics learn
> to manage their diet and insulin. I have a long way to go, but I have
> come a long way. I have hope again. The more I speak of my panic
> attacks, the more I realize that I am not simply a potter with severe
> or debilitating anxiety. I am a father, a husband, an artist. . . . I am a
> person with a disorder, not the disorder itself. This is the important
> piece of a story.

Phobias

Phobias are also anxiety disorders. Like panic attacks, they do not have one simple cause or one simple treatment. There are biological, psychological, and social reasons for phobias and different approaches to their treatment. In general, people who suffer from phobias feel dread, panic, or terror when faced with the situations that they fear or cannot control. Their anxiety is anticipatory and very intense. As a result, they go to great lengths to avoid what is feared, even if it interferes with daily functioning.

There have been interesting and valuable psychodynamic formulations of phobias. Freud formulated phobias as symptoms that are com-
promises. Like so many of the anxiety disorders, they partly disable the individual but they also make anxiety more manageable. As long as what

is feared can be avoided, they disguise unacceptable instinctual wishes by displacing them onto something else that can be feared (Gabbard 1990).

One of Freud's most classic cases (1907) was of a phobic 4½-year-old boy named Little Hans. This little boy developed terrible phobias of horses and of open spaces. Like many boys his age, Hans both loved his father and feared him. Hans's mother had recently given birth to his little sister, and Hans was quite jealous of her. Hans clung more than ever to his mother. Freud postulated that being an oedipal child, Hans experienced conflicts over his love for his mother and his unconscious and competitive feelings toward his father. Hans as an oedipal child also feared that his father would retaliate for the intense feelings Hans had for his mother. Since Hans wanted to be loved by both parents, Freud hypothesized that he *projected* his own aggression onto his father and then displaced the aggression onto horses. By developing a phobia about horses and not his father, he could keep his father close.

Hans's phobia had a secondary gain; it kept him close to his mother as well. But as his unconscious conflict around wanting his mother and fearing but wanting his father's love continued unresolved, he became more phobic, projecting and displacing his feelings onto boxcars, railways, and open streets. It was not until some of his unconscious conflicts were interpreted and made conscious that Hans began to experience some symptom relief.

In summary, drive theorists would conceptualize phobias as representing unacceptable sexual or aggressive impulses that are defensively displaced onto something outside of the self. But the defense of displacement is not always adaptive because it circumscribes and ultimately limits a person's functioning.

Object relations theorists, on the other hand, formulate phobias differently. In this view, a phobia may encapsulate a wish for or fear of merging with significant others. People who are phobic may wish to move toward independence, as did Hans, but may also fear losing others and thus need to hold on to them. From an object relations point of view, Hans's phobia expressed an unconscious dilemma over separation. Whether from a drive-theory or an object-relations perspective, the client who has a phobia is truly restricted because the objects, locations, or situations that she fears must be actively avoided. Unlike in Little Hans's day, however, medications and behavioral interventions are now considered the most effective interventions to treat the symptoms. Whereas in Freud's day, we thought of all phobias as the same, today we distinguish between three kinds of phobias: agoraphobia, specific phobias, and social phobias.

Agoraphobia

Ruth entered her sixth anxiety group session with much trepidation. Today she was scheduled to embark on her much feared "mission" with one of the group's co-therapists. She was to drive her car across the bridge that connected her town to the clinic. Ruth sat in the driver's seat, her therapist at her side, and took off toward the city. She chatted comfortably with her therapist for the first ten minutes of the trip until they were about a quarter of a mile from the bridge. Then silence descended upon the car. Her therapist looked at Ruth and noted several things: Ruth's chest was rising and descending rapidly as her breath became shorter and shorter. Her hands gripped the steering wheel so tightly that her knuckles turned white. Beads of perspiration appeared on her forehead. As they stopped at a traffic light, Ruth began to shake. She turned to the therapist and said, "We can't drive over the bridge. We're gonna die."

People with agoraphobia may be afraid of standing in line, being on a bridge, traveling in a bus, train, or car, or being in open places, such as supermarkets, malls, shopping centers, and streets. All of these fears are of being in situations where escape is difficult or in which help might not be available.

It is interesting to note that 75 percent of people with agoraphobia are married women. The onset of their phobias usually occurs between the ages of 20 and 30. Agoraphobia may be more common in women because these symptoms express the stresses in marriage and child rearing for women who stay home. Women who are at home full time with small children often experience lowered self-esteem, have limited social supports, and feel powerless. Agoraphobic symptoms may exaggerate their experiences of powerlessness in the larger world, and at the same time keep women close to their homes where they feel most oppressed.

Often people with agoraphobia suffer from severe separation anxiety and must be accompanied by a husband, child, or other relative in order to be able to leave their homes. From an object-relations perspective, agoraphobia may keep others close and so provide a symptom and its solution. For example, a mother who developed agoraphobic symptoms after her children left home had them return daily to run the errands that she could no longer do. Her symptom represented her symbiotic needs for others. The symptom provided a solution by keeping her children close.

Specific Phobias

Specific phobias are persistent, excessive, and unreasonable fears that come from anticipating or experiencing the situations that are feared (e.g., flying, heights, animals, injections, the sight of blood, etc.). Usually people with specific phobias recognize that their fears are unreasonable, but knowing this does not keep them from anxiously anticipating or avoiding what they fear. People with specific phobias feel great distress as their phobias interfere with social relationships, activities, and many other aspects of life functioning.

> Ellen is a 25-year-old secretary who is terrified about becoming trapped in an elevator. Unfortunately, she works in a high-rise building on the thirty-second floor. When she arrives at work each morning, she often thinks she should try riding the elevator. But her ears begin to ring, she becomes dizzy, she cannot breathe, and finally takes the stairs. She is exhausted and out of breath by the time she reaches her office. Because each time she leaves the building she faces climbing or descending sixty-four flights, she does not join colleagues for lunch. She has been passed up for promotions because she seems disinclined to go the extra mile for her company: to attend meetings with her boss in other parts of the city, to travel when necessary, or even to attend parties and social functions for work.

For Ellen, intrapsychic conflicts around her own ascendence and achievement at work have been displaced onto elevators. She cannot "rise" in her work, but has displaced her fears onto the conveyance that would carry her.

Social Phobias

People with social phobias fear being humiliated or embarrassed by a social situation. Often they must avoid social or performance situations and when they can't, they experience great distress.

> Like Ellen, Marcia, a 56-year-old librarian, has also been passed over for jobs that require expressing herself. She experiences this as yet another indictment of her inadequacy. By avoiding others, she hopes to avoid her own self-criticism. She is terribly anxious around other people. She feels she has nothing to say and that being with others will reveal her inadequacy. She is acutely self-conscious and analyzes any interaction she has. She thinks that every shop-keeper, waiter, and service person with whom she comes in contact, scrutinizes her behavior as she does and has come to the same negative conclusions about her.
>
> She always excuses herself from meetings; she either doesn't show up or says she is physically ill because she is so sure she will feel humiliated by what she does not seem to know. She also does not attend parties, workshops, or lunches with colleagues because it feels too painful to think that everyone else views her as she views herself.

Often we do not see people with phobias in our clinical practices at all because they self-medicate, using drugs such as Valium to deal with their fears. The appropriate medications, however, are antidepressants rather than antianxiety agents. Antidepressants tend to motivate change, while the antianxiety agents have a depressant effect and may become addictive.

For people with phobias, behavioral techniques can also be the treatment of choice. Behavior modification groups may help clients support one another, while teaching them techniques such as assertiveness or systematic desensitization. In these groups people can learn to confront what they most fear in small doses. Groups offer particular support because they provide places to share experiences, information, common symptoms, and methods that have worked. Despite the fact that phobias respond to behavioral and biological techniques, individual therapeutic relationships also have value. A client who is phobic feels a great deal of shame. A therapeutic relationship (or relationships) that helps her to express the shame and acknowledge her fears can act as a bridge in helping her make behavioral changes. A therapeutic relationship can help someone understand and resolve some of the psychological sources of the avoidance.

OBSESSIVE-COMPULSIVE DISORDERS

We mentioned earlier that both Darla and Patty had obsessive-compulsive disorders. Like all of the anxiety disorders, obsessive-compulsive disorders occur at different developmental levels. Because of this they are sometimes confusing. Sometimes they can look like depression or even schizophrenia. They are also confusing because they need to be distinguished from obsessive-compulsive character styles and obsessive-compulsive personality disorders (see Chapter 13).

Obsessions are intrusive, recurrent, and persistent stereotypic thoughts, images, and ideas. They cause marked anxiety and distress. The thoughts are not simply excessive worries about real-life situations, because the people who have them recognize that their obsessions are products of their own minds. Common obsessions include having committed harmful acts, being contaminated, and harboring unacceptable thoughts or impulses toward others.

Compulsions are repetitive ritualized behaviors that feel obligatory and that attempt to manage intolerable levels of anxiety. Compulsions are by their nature repetitive acts that a person feels driven to perform. Compulsions include such acts as hand washing, counting, checking, touching, praying, or other acts that are ritualized. (For a discussion of some of the intrapsychic factors in these disorders, see the case of Mr. Johannson in Chapters 2 and 3.)

> Tanya suffered from an obsessive-compulsive disorder. As is common, her disorder had begun in adolescence. A 19-year-old born-again Christian who attended a religious college, she had come for treatment because she was washing her hands forty to fifty times a day. They were chapped, raw, and bleeding. When she tried to stop, she would be flooded by intolerable levels of anxiety. She was ter-

rified of germs, and would tap three times to avoid them. She was isolated at college and was indeed shunned for her odd behaviors. Tanya was disheveled and had difficulty making eye contact.

At age 2, she had suffered a blood disorder and had since been excessively worried about her fragility and her mortality. When she began menstruating at 13, her obsessive-compulsive disorder flourished and she began washing her hands.

She often looked very disturbed, almost schizophrenic. Tanya was, in fact, quite functionally impaired. But her symptoms could be distinguished from schizophrenia in that people with schizophrenia often overvalue their thoughts and lack insight, and their symptoms are not alien to them. For Tanya, as for many people with obsessive-compulsive disorders, the symptoms were dystonic. She felt enormous shame and desperation over her obsessions and compulsions and wanted them to stop.

Although Tanya's disorder had intrapsychic causes, Tanya needed to be medicated first to help her manage her anxiety. While psychotherapy was not of particular benefit in helping to extinguish her compulsive behaviors, it did provide a safe context in which she could examine her isolation from others, her rigid use of her religion's rituals to bind her anxiety, and her fears of being away from home, which had revived her separation anxiety.

For many people with obsessive-compulsive disorders, it is often difficult to make a direct correlation between psychological events and biological responses. A drive theorist working with Tanya might have emphasized her difficulties with her own aggression and concerns about her sexuality as stemming from unresolved anal issues when she first became ill. From this perspective, Tanya's compulsions might serve to control her sexual impulses, which were revived in adolescence. Tanya's harsh superego injunctions, now expressed as rigid rituals, might have had their roots in earlier unresolved preoedipal issues. An object-relations theorist, on the other hand, might focus on Tanya's attempts to gain control over her fears of separation. Perhaps having faced her own mortality as a child and having been separated from primary caregivers when ill, she was left more vulnerable to severe separation anxiety. Perhaps her blood disease left her filled with self representations full of dangerous, bad, destructive forces. The obsessions and compulsions might be a solution and a compromise to help her manage her own internal world and make it less dangerous.

The most recent work on obsessive-compulsive disorders (Jenike 1990) indicates that, as with many of the anxiety disorders, there is also a strong biological component. Serotonergic antidepressants such as chlorimipramine, fluoxetine, and fluvoxamine have antiobsessional effects. But as with patients with phobias, there is a high rate of noncompliance with drug prescriptions among patients with obsessive-compulsive disorders.

Behavioral therapies are also useful for people with obsessive-compulsive disorders. Here, as with panic disorders and phobias, clients can be exposed to anxiety-provoking situations, and be behaviorally trained not to engage in typically compulsive responses.

Few among us have not at some time experienced a fleeting obsessive thought or compulsive act. Did we remember to lock the door, turn off the oven, or suppress an impulse to shout an obscenity at someone who made us angry? But people who chronically suffer from these disorders feel at the mercy of their impulses, which they cannot ignore or suppress. While there is no gender differential in this disorder, it has been found to occur more frequently among upper socioeconomic classes and among the more highly educated.

POSTTRAUMATIC STRESS DISORDERS

People who suffer from posttraumatic stress disorders (PTSD) have been the victims of severe, overwhelming psychic and/or physical trauma. They may be concentration camp survivors, prisoners, incest survivors, or survivors of physical abuse, domestic abuse, rape, disasters, earthquakes, hostage taking, kidnapping, combat, or torture. They may have witnessed or been confronted with actual or threatened death, serious injury, or a threat to their own physical integrity or that of others. Because they have been overwhelmed by trauma, they have had to use defenses such as depersonalization, derealization, and dissociation to try to manage their overwhelming anxiety. This may result in their feeling nothing, feeling unreal, or feeling fragmented. People who have been traumatized often experience an altered sense of consciousness and of time. Their worlds are no longer experienced as safe, nor do their relationships feel reliable. Sometimes their beliefs no longer have meaning because their values and ideals have been shattered.

When trauma occurs it needs to be integrated, or it becomes split off and dissociated. When it becomes split off, a person's capacity to manage anxiety is undermined. This can result in the experience of helplessness and vulnerability, the sense of being out of control, recurrent and intrusive recalling of the trauma in waking thoughts, and nightmares, chronic anxiety, sleeplessness, irritability, excessive vigilance, or suicidal ideation.

Primo Levi, an Italian Jew who survived the Nazi Holocaust, spent most of his adult life bearing witness to and documenting the trauma he had endured in a Nazi concentration camp as a child. Yet, in his seventieth year, he took his own life. Long before his actual suicide, he had written:

> We have learned that our personality is fragile, that it is in much more danger than our life, and the old wise ones, instead of warning us "remember you might die," would have done much better to remind us of this greater danger that threatens us. If from inside the Lager, a message could have seeped out to free men, it would have been this: Take care not to suffer in your own homes what is inflicted on us here. [Levi, as quoted by Herman 1992, p. 95]

People who have been severely traumatized in situations such as persistent incest often suffer precisely what has been inflicted on them. Sometimes they treat themselves and their bodies with the same contempt with which they were treated. Sometimes they victimize themselves or others with explosive outbursts of anger. Often they are fixated on their trauma, and because of it their lives are constricted and devoid of pleasure. Many times they find themselves in dream-like states of consciousness, not fully engaged in or aware of current life around them. Often they experience startle responses, insomnia, hypervigilance. Usually there are physiological changes as a result of the trauma that are revived under other threatening conditions.

PTSD only became a diagnosis in the 1980s. Before that, we understood trauma victims as "shell shocked" victims of war and did not have adequate language to describe the ways in which trauma systematically undermines ego functioning. However, when survivors of concentration camps after World War II began to seek reparations for the war crimes perpetrated against them, they were required to have psychiatric evaluations. They began to describe what are now familiar symptoms of trauma, common also to victims of physical and sexual abuse: psychic numbing, rumination about the trauma, psychosomatic complaints, a lack of pleasure, detachment, a limited range of feelings, nightmares, flashbacks, startle responses, chronic depression, and despair.

We are now familiar with the recorded memories of people who survived Nazi concentration camps. They remember witnessing babies being tossed in the air and then shot or victims having to dig their own graves before being killed; the selections of who would live and who would die; painful medical experiments on children; and the acrid smoke of the crematoria that consumed millions of lives. Some victims were so psychically numbed as to be considered no longer among the living, but were referred to as the walking dead.

Judith Herman (1992) has suggested that the diagnosis of PTSD, in fact, does not capture the full horror of traumatization. She instead advocates the diagnosis of "complex posttraumatic stress disorders," which would include a category for people who have been subjected to totalitarian control, or who have been chronically abused in childhood, or victims of domestic abuse. Perhaps no symptom list can ever capture the terror or degradation that comes with persistent sexual abuse, war, hostage taking, or murder. Often there can be no normal response to the abnormality of a parent abusing a child, or of a concentration camp guard abusing an inmate. There can be no appropriate response to witnessing the violence perpetrated against innocent people. People who live through terrorism, bombings, or ethnic conflicts may witness the capricious murders of their spouses, children, and peers. They often live with privation and starvation, in proximity to piles of corpses, bloated and rotting, as everyday events. Such experiences alter their reality. For example, Cambodian children who recall Pol Pot's regime remember

sloshing through the bloody streets of Phnom Penh, seeing Khmer Rouge soldiers waiting for a woman to give birth by the side of the road before killing both mother and infant, saving a friend from fatal dehydration by suspending a coconut and dripping its fresh milk through bamboo into her veins, being forced in the work camps to decapitate with portable guillotines other young friends whom the Khmer Rouge considered lazy, hearing the dying words of parents as to how they might avenge all this by becoming the best person they could possibly be. And witnessing all of these between the ages of four and eleven. [Golub 1985a, p. 11]

When veterans returned from Vietnam, they returned not only with those same symptoms, but often with explosive, uncontrollable rage, resulting in antisocial behaviors. But not all PTSD occurs as a function of war, torture, or combat. Many people suffer chronic PTSD as a function of recurrent family violence.

As with each of the anxiety disorders, PTSD occurs in people with neurotic, character-disordered, or psychotic levels of personality. But it is also important to note that chronic trauma itself can erode such aspects of personality development as object relations, identity, defenses, and ego functioning. We can see this in the following example of a woman who suffered persistent sexual abuse perpetrated by both her father and her brother:

> Marge was a 21-year-old Catholic incest survivor for whom trauma had begun early on. She came to the clinic complaining of insomnia, hypervigilance, depression, hurting herself, suicidal thoughts, and recurrent nightmares. Her roommates were concerned that she constantly checked that the doors were locked and the windows covered. She reported feeling spacey much of the time. She had recently fallen off of a horse and had injured her neck. She was prone to hurting herself in a variety of accidents such as skiing, skateboarding, or car accidents.
>
> Marge began treatment by presenting her therapist with many years worth of her journals, which documented multiple traumata. Her father was a judge; her mother a physician. She had been adopted by her parents at the age of 3. Prior to that, she had been in a number of foster homes. Despite the patina of normal upper middle class life, her family life was marred by abuse. Her journal contained an earliest childhood memory of her father taking her to the town landfill and as a punishment leaving her there, saying, "This is where I found you. This is where I'm leaving you." He did not return until early nightfall.

In her journal, she wrote about how from age 7 through adolescence, she would awaken to find her father's penis in her mouth. She wrote of her father shooting the family cat after it had chewed on a piece of furniture. She recorded her father beating her repeatedly when she would violate any family rule. When she was 13 she told her mother about the abuse, and her mother bought her a motorcycle. Being underage to drive, she nonetheless took it out, and totaled it, ending up in a body cast with her father continuing to sexually abuse her.

Marge was able to describe how she had succeeded not only scholastically but also athletically. At 17 she earned a full scholarship to a local college and made plans to leave home. Her mother kept a bottle of pills in an open cabinet and Marge would often take them as well as sell them at her local high school. But as Marge made plans to separate, her mother "noticed" the missing pills which she had replenished many times. She accused Marge of being an addict, and put Marge under a kind of house arrest.

During the first five years of treatment, Marge was quite unable, despite her prodigious journals, to talk about the trauma. Many times, she would arrive mute; many times she would be unable to sit still and would pace, or would sit on the floor.

There were times when Marge's therapist would feel as though parts of her own self were literally fragmenting under the weight of Marge's disorganized ego states. Because Marge's sense of self had been so damaged, there were few solid ego boundaries between herself and her therapist. Often her therapist experienced Marge's confusion, helplessness, and dissociated and depersonalized states as if they were her own.

Marge's trauma history had eroded many of her ego functions. Her anxiety was sometimes at the level of separation anxiety and sometimes at the level of annihilation anxiety. Many cruelties that had been perpetrated against her she visited upon herself and her therapist.

Treatment Issues in Working with Clients with PTSD

For clients with PTSD, a therapist needs to be able to bear witness to the abuse and to its consequences: anger, fear, confusion, and guilt. Often the therapist needs to identify the client's resilience, her strength, and her coping in order to help reintegrate what had been previously overwhelming. Clients who have been severely traumatized may use many different strategies to cope. Some may use spirituality to deal with their abuse; for others, drivenness (in work or in relationships) may permeate their lives (Bass and Davis 1988). For some, addictions to food, drugs, or alcohol help to numb psychic pain. Others may self-mutilate or even try suicide. Some clients demonstrate remarkable strengths—capacities to endure and thrive, and abilities to make new meaning from past abuses. In each case, the therapist needs to be able to help the client bear the trauma and develop strategies to deal with some of the losses and betrayal that so often accompany traumatic experiences.

In work with trauma survivors, there is the danger that the patient can be retraumatized by the therapy, and that the therapist can be vicariously traumatized by the client's experiences (Saakvitne 1995). As trauma is remembered and worked through, there is the potential for both the therapist and the client to experience heightened vulnerability, helplessness, anxiety, confusion, numbness, and despair. Herman (1992) has written that trauma "can actually become contagious," and that if the therapist shares the patient's experiences of helplessness *too* much, she can become afraid of the patient and turn away, again retraumatizing the patient. Hence the therapist must attempt to titrate the trauma with the client to arrive at some integration.

For many people suffering from PTSD, group treatment can be extremely helpful. Survivors can learn to name their traumatic experiences and begin to feel less stigmatized and different. In groups, survivors can share, learn of other members' solutions, and learn to deal with anger, both their own and others'. Groups can provide survivors of trauma ego-building experiences, new models for identification, and new kinds of interpersonal experiences.

In working with people who have been traumatized, then, the clinician needs to assess the severity of the trauma, the client's biological vulnerability to trauma, the developmental phase in which it occurred, the degree of social supports prior to the traumatization, the number of previous traumas, and the kinds of resolutions that were possible (Van der Kolk 1987).

There is also a biological component to PTSD that needs to be assessed. When a person is traumatized, he or she experiences physiological change brought on by an upsurge in hormonal secretions. During PTSD reactions, these secretions can actually alter brain chemistry and then leave the victim feeling more vulnerable to anxiety. Trauma survivors are therefore physiologically more reactive to new situations that revive past traumatic experiences (Van der Kolk 1987).

In working with clients who suffer from PTSD, it is crucial that we not simply view the trauma as a diagnosis in and of itself. People who suffer the same trauma will not necessarily become symptomatic in identical ways. Ten people can be in a bomb shelter and have ten different experiences of the trauma. Their experiences will always be mediated by their own resilience, defenses, earlier histories of traumatic experiences, past relationships, and levels of development. Thus, while it is easy to cluster all incest, or rape, or war trauma as part of the same disorder, we must recognize that each trauma produces different symptoms and characterological changes in each individual, depending on one's biological and psychological complexities and environment.

Other Biological Factors

It is also important to note that there may be other biological factors that precipitate anxiety symptoms. People who are hyperthyroid, for example, may experience a racing heart, have startle responses, difficulty managing emotional feelings, insomnia, or increased anger. Their anxiety symptoms are caused by changes in their hormone levels. Someone with an adrenal tumor may present with a full-blown anxiety attack, often not distinguishable from a panic attack. Those anxiety symptoms are primarily caused by the tumor and are not simply a psychological reaction to the tumor. Clinicians who work with anxious clients always need to ask about the client's medical conditions and medications, and should always keep in mind that physical illnesses may produce anxiety symptoms that require medical treatment.

Substance-induced anxiety disorders can also look indistinguishable from other psychogenic anxiety disorders. When someone is intoxicated or in withdrawal from amphetamines, alcohol, caffeine, cocaine, hallucinogens, sedatives, marijuana, or inhalants, her symptoms of hyperventilation, fear, confusion, derealization, depersonalization, numbness, and/or dissociation may look like anxiety symptoms. It is important therefore to know whether the anxiety disorder has been *induced* by substance or whether it *preceded* taking it. We cannot stress enough the importance of attending to organic factors, including substance abuse, illness, and medications, in understanding the sources of anxiety.

CONCLUSION

We have acknowledged in this chapter that anxiety disorders are complex. They derive from many causes and take many forms. They may express themselves as panic attacks, obsessive-compulsive disorders, phobias, PTSD, generalized anxiety disorders, or as resulting from medical conditions or substance abuse. They may occur in people at different psychological developmental levels. At their core, they usually express experiences, internal or external, of extreme helplessness and vulnerability. They are intense and their manifestations may seriously restrict a person's freedom, creativity, joyfulness, and ability to work and love. There are important distinctions among the disorders as well as cross-cultural differences in their expressions and their treatments.

While there is no question that some anxiety disorders have a biological basis, there has been a tendency in managed-care situations to treat anxiety disorders exclusively by medicating the patient. Little attention is then paid to the environmental stressors or psychological conflicts that may underlie the disorders. Perhaps our zealousness to see anxiety disorders as exclusively biological and/or behavioral is related to just how overwhelmed we, the clinicians, can feel in the face of many of the anxiety disorders. In treating clients with PTSD, for example, it is simply hard to bear the experiences of brutality or human cruelty that we hear. Anxious people can be hard to sit with. People who see danger in situations we ourselves don't find dangerous may make us feel impatient and eager to find a "quick fix" to their problems. These clients can evoke a range of negative and helpless feelings in us, the helpers. Anxiety disorders also confront us with our own confusion and our own sense of being overwhelmed.

As we move toward managed-care models of treating symptoms, and not people with symptoms, it may seem easier to just treat the biochemical conditions by giving medication than it is to pay attention to the social condition and/or the intrapsychic conflicts that may underlie the symptoms. As with each of the disorders we have addressed in this book, then, we suggest using a biopsychosocial lens in trying to understand and treat these often painful disorders.

References

Bass, E., and Davis, L. (1988). *The Courage to Heal: A Guide for Women Survivors of Child Sexual Abuse.* New York: Perennial.

Fodor, R. (1992). The agoraphobic syndrome: from anxiety neurosis to panic disorders. In *Personality and Psychopathology: Feminist Reappraisals,* ed. L. S. Brown and M. Ballou, pp. 177–205. New York: Guilford.

Frankl, V. (1959). *From Death Camp to Existentialism.* New York: Beacon.

Freud, S. (1907). The analysis of a phobia in a four-year-old boy. *Standard Edition* 10:5–187.

Gabbard, G. (1990). *Psychodynamic Psychiatry in Clinical Practice.* Washington, DC: American Psychoanalytic Press.

Golub, D. (1985a). Cross cultural dimensions of art psychotherapy: Cambodian survivors of war trauma. In *Advances in Art Therapy,* ed. H. Wadeson, J. Durkin, and D. Perach, pp. 5–42. New York: Wiley.

—— (1985b). Symbolic expression in post traumatic stress disorder: Vietnam combat veterans in art therapy. *The Arts in Psychotherapy* 12:285–296.

Herman, J. (1992). *Trauma and Recovery.* New York: Basic Books.

Ho, R. (1987). *Family Therapy with Ethnic Minorities.* Newbury Park, CA: Sage.

Jenike, M. (1990). Approaches to the patient with treatment refractory obsessive compulsive disorder. *Journal of Clinical Psychiatry* 51(2):15–21.

Kaplan, B. (1984). Anxiety states. In *Adult Psychopathology: A Social Work Perspective,* ed. F. Turner, pp. 260–280. New York: Free Press.

Levi, P. (1958). *Survival in Auschwitz: The Nazi Assault on Humanity,* trans. S. Woolf. New York: Collier, 1961.

Nemiah, J. (1981). A psychoanalytic view of phobias. *American Journal of Psychoanalysis* 41:115–141.

—— (1988). Psychoneurotic disorders. In *The New Harvard Guide to Psychiatry,* ed. A. M. Nicholi, Jr., pp. 234–259. Cambridge, MA: Belknap Press of Harvard University.

Noyes, R. (1985). Maintenance with antidepressants in panic disorders. Beta-adrenergic blocking drugs in anxiety and stress. *Psychiatric Clinics of North America* 8:119–132.

Rapee, R., and Perry, P. (1990). Maintenance with anti-depressants in panic disorder. *Journal of Clinical Psychiatry* 51(12):24–30.

Saakvitne, K. (1995). Vicarious traumatization: countertransference responses to dissociative clients. In *Dissociative Identity Disorders,* ed. L. Cohen, J. Berzoff, and M. Elin, pp. 467–492. Northvale, NJ: Jason Aronson.

Salzman, L. (1980). *Treatment of the Obsessive Personality.* New York: Jason Aronson.

Steketee, G., and Cleese, L. (1990). Obsessive compulsive disorders. In *International Handbook of Behavior Modification and Therapy*, ed. L. Bellak, pp. 307–332. New York: Plenum.

Van der Kolk, B. (1987). The psychological experience of overwhelming life events. In *Psychological Trauma*, pp. 1–30. Washington, DC: American Psychiatric Press.

Van der Kolk, B., and Greenberg, M. (1987). The psychobiology of the trauma response: hyperarousal, constriction and addiction to traumatic exposure. In *Psychological Trauma*, ed. B. Van der Kolk, pp. 63–87. Washington, DC: American Psychiatric Press.

Zetzel, E. (1949). Anxiety and the capacity to bear it. *International Journal of Psycho-Analysis* 30:33–52.

16

Conclusions

JOAN BERZOFF,
LAURA MELANO FLANAGAN,
AND PATRICIA HERTZ

What, then, have we learned in this book? We began our journey with Freud, the "father of psychoanalysis," whose explorations into the unconscious life of individuals helped us enter into an uncharted, inchoate underworld of internal forces governing psychic life. We learned about how passions, when unknown, may lead to human suffering, and we studied the absolute value of self-knowledge for effecting psychological change. We came to see how important the therapeutic relationship can be to both therapist and client, and examined the symbolic and real aspects of that relationship to the people within it. We came to appreciate the complex ways in which drives shape child development, resulting in lifelong symptoms, character structure, and strengths. We learned how Freud and his contemporaries conceptualized most of mental life as a battleground in which unconscious conflicts between the drives, the self, and society were played out within and between the structures of the mind. We came to see how intrapsychic conflicts result in compromises, called symptoms, and how our understanding of unconscious conflicts can set us free.

We studied the increasingly central role of the ego in mediating between the drives and society and its important functions in providing an individual coherence and equilibrium. We studied the ego's capacities and strengths in adapting to and mastering the environment and we learned about the kinds of defenses it employs to ward off danger. We learned about the ego's other autonomous functions: thinking, feeling, and motility. In addition we saw how the ego seeks coherence and continuity over the entire life cycle, as each individual negotiates psychological and social tasks at every stage of life-cycle development. We learned that ego development is mediated by psychological *and* social forces (race, class, gender, culture, age) so that the individual always interacts within the sociocultural context in which she develops.

We studied some of the many ways in which an individual develops an *internal* sense of self, occurring first through earliest relationships with others. Conceptualized by object relations theorists, we examined the central place of early maternal relationships on a child's sense of self and began to see how external relationships come to be uniquely metabolized as internal representations of the self and of others. We looked at the tragic consequences that can accrue when the external world cannot provide the necessary nurturance for achieving internal psychological wholeness.

From an interpersonal perspective, we moved beyond the earliest years of childhood, and came to understand how ongoing relationships (with peers, friends, and others in the adult's environment) contribute to the development of self-knowledge and self-esteem. From this perspective, the therapeutic inquiry began to shift its emphasis from the individual to the ways in which the *relationship* between the therapist and client becomes the unit of study and of change.

From self psychology, we came to see how a person's self-esteem and self-cohesion are based on the attunement and empathy provided by others in the environment, as we continued to move from models that located psychological problems as deriving only from problems in the earliest years of life. Self psychology offered a more hopeful view of the curative power of ongoing relationships (including the therapeutic relationship) for promoting healthy self-esteem.

We studied the consequences of racism on the individual and the particular contributions offered from drive theory, ego psychology, object relations, and self psychology in understanding the dynamics of racism and its pernicious effects on the individual. We again gained another way of conceptualizing how what is *external* and *outside* of the individual comes to be experienced internally. We learned the ways in which individuals develop their ethnic and racial identities and the value of this knowledge for any cross-cultural therapeutic encounters.

As we looked at the relationship between gender and psychodynamic theories, we again encountered the ways in which psychodynamic theories have both oppressed and liberated our understanding of female development. We came to see the complex relationship between women's internal lives and their places in the social structures in which they live. We saw how a cross-fertilization of social and psychological theories helps us more fully understand intrapsychic and social oppression.

In the second half of this book, we learned about the biopsychosocial aspects of psychosis, borderline and narcissistic conditions, other personality disorders, depression, and anxiety. We studied how each diagnosis is rooted in its social times and expresses particular dilemmas of the culture and the society. We learned the ways in which people with these disorders are more than their symptoms, and we stressed, throughout, our own conviction about the power and value of a therapeutic relationship to effect meaningful change.

Throughout this book, we have held to a stance that "We are all much more simply human than otherwise" (Sullivan, 1940, p. 39) expressing our conviction that every fear, symptom, sense of unreality, passion, urgency, longing, need, defense, and desire that our clients express may be similarly experienced by us, the clinicians. Therefore, as we have attended to the internal experiences of the clients we serve, we have encouraged us all to attend to the experiences of the helpers who work with people in psychological pain.

What do we hope that the readers have taken away from this book? Some awe for the complexity of psychological life, and some appreciation for the unique ways every individual has of mediating between psychological, cultural, racial, and biological variables within and outside of the self. We hope that the readers will be able to enter into and understand the inner worlds of the clients with whom they work, approaching each person with a sense of wonder with which all human phenomena must be clinically approached. We hope that all readers will keep alive their own sense of "not knowing," continually learning anew from each individual client with whom they work.

George Bernard Shaw said, "For every complex problem there is a simple solution—and it is wrong!" As we move toward mental health managed-care models that tend to treat the symptoms but not the person-in-the-environment with the symptoms, we hope that each reader will grapple with the complexities of a biopsychosocial perspective, rejecting simplistic solutions that attempt to reduce people to their manifest problems. In short, it is our hope that the practitioners/readers/clinicians will, whenever possible, continue to keep the work as *complicated* as they can!

Reference

Sullivan, H. S. (1940). Conceptions of modern psychiatry. *Psychiatry* 3:35–45.

Credits

Index

Inferiority vs. industry, psychosocial ego development, school age, 113–115

Initiative vs. guilt, psychosocial ego development, play stage, 112–113

Integrity vs. despair, psychosocial ego development, old age, 119–121

Internal object world, object relations theory, 141–149

Interpersonal relationships, object relations theory, 127–171. *See also* Object relations theory

Interpersonal school, 199–219
current relational theories and, 209–217
developmental factors and, 202–206
overview of, 199–202
treatment and, 206–209

Intersubjective approach, interpersonal school and, 214–217

Intimacy vs. isolation, psychosocial ego development, young adulthood, 117

Introjection, object relations theory, 152–154

Isolation vs. intimacy, psychosocial ego development, young adulthood, 117

Jack, D., 384
Jacobson, E., 376, 378
James, P. D., 153
Jenike, M., 418
Jones, E., 24, 247

Jordan, J., 253, 254
Joyce, J., 43
Judaism, drive theory and, 19
Judgment
ego functions, 72–73
paranoid personality disorder, 339

Kagan, J., 345, 383
Kaplan, A., 253, 254
Kaplan, H., 371, 383
Kaplan, L. J., 136
Kaplan, M., 304
Katz, P. A., 235
Kernberg, O., 133, 302, 304, 312, 322, 323, 332, 333, 360, 376
Ketcham, K., 27
Kety, S., 280
King, R., 39
Klein, M., 127, 133, 141, 142, 143, 145, 180, 250, 340, 351, 376, 378
Klerman, G. L., 367
Kohn, M. L., 289
Kohut, H., 70, 174, 175, 176, 177, 178, 179, 180, 181, 182, 184, 186, 187, 188, 189, 190, 191, 192, 209, 211, 212, 238, 332, 333
Kotlowitz, A., 113
Kovel, J., 224, 225
Kraepelin, E., 271
Kramer, P., 383
Kurtz, S. N., 222

LaBruzza, A., 306
Lasch, C., 175, 324
Latency stage, psychosexual development, drive theory, 39–40

Psychoanalysis
culture and, 222–224
feminism
interpersonal psychoanalytic
theory and, 253–254
postmodern, 256–258
Psychodynamic theory. *See also* Drive
theory; Ego psychology;
Interpersonal school; Object
relations theory; Self
psychology; Structural theory
critical perspective, 9–12
culture and, 221–222
literature on, 8–9
overview of, 4–8
schizophrenia, 281–282
structural theory, 49–66
Psychopathology
drive theory and, 26–27
self psychology and, 191–194
Psychopharmacology. *See*
Pharmacology
Psychosexual development, 28–42
anal stage, 32–33
generally, 28–30
genital stage (adolescence), 40–
42
latency stage, 39–40
oral stage, 30–32
phallic stage, 34–39
Psychosis. *See also* Schizophrenia
anxiety and, 404
defined, 267
depression and, 387–389
ego psychology, defense
mechanisms, 86–87
postpartum, 268–270
symptoms of, 267–268

Psychosocial ego development, 103–
125
adolescence (identity vs. role
confusion), 115–116
adulthood (generativity vs.
stagnation), 117–119
critique of, 121–123
early childhood (autonomy vs.
shame and doubt), 110–112
infancy (trust vs. mistrust), 107–
110
old age (integrity vs. despair),
119–121
overview of, 103–107
play stage (initiative vs. guilt),
112–113
school age (industry vs.
inferiority), 113–115
young adulthood (intimacy vs.
isolation), 117

Rabelais, F., 84
Race and ethnicity. *See also* Culture
anxiety and, 399–400
cross-cultural perspective,
therapeutic value of, 237–242
depression and, 386–387
developmental factors and, 234–
236
drive theory and, 224–226
ego psychology and, 226–228
object relations theory and, 229–
232
psychoanalysis and, 222–224
schizophrenia, 289–290
self-esteem and, 236–237
self psychology and, 232–234
women and, 257, 263–264